Angus Roxburgh studied Russ ~~KU-444-437~~ .... of
Aberdeen and Zurich. He was *Sunday Times* Moscow correspondent
(1987–89), BBC Moscow correspondent (1991–97) and BBC Europe
correspondent (1998–2005). From 2006 to 2009 he was media consultant to the Kremlin, and is now a freelance writer and journalist. He is
the author of the acclaimed *The Strongman: Vladimir Putin and the
Struggle for Russia* and was consultant on the award-winning BBC documentaries *The Second Russian Revolution* and *Putin, Russia and the
West*. *Moscow Calling* was *Sotsman* and *Herald* Book of the Year and was
shortlisted for the Saltire Non-fiction Book of the Year award.

Praise for *Moscow Calling*

'Nobody has a better ear for Russia than Angus Roxburgh – a joy to
read, often very funny, often profoundly sad, and in both respects a good
reflection of the Russian experience'

Justin Webb, *Today* programme (BBC)

'An enthralling memoir of the great, raging days of turmoil in Russia and
the USSR, as witnessed and recorded by an honest man'

Peter Hitchens, *Mail on Sunday*

'If you are looking for the Russia beyond the political cliché then this is
the book for you. An intimate and incisive account of a famous journalist's long-term relationship with the country, a relationship as complex
and intense as any Russian novel'

Peter Pomerantsev, author of
Nothing Is True and Everything Is Possible

'Angus Roxburgh has produced a book that illuminates discerningly the
dramatic changes that have occurred in Russia over the past 40 years,
many of which he witnessed at first hand. His account is often amusing,
sometimes grim (when he recalls his experience reporting wars in
Chechnya and Afghanistan), but consistently perceptive'

Archie Brown, Emeritus Professor of Politics
at the University of Oxford, *History Today*

'Roxburgh writes beautifully, with a lyricism and descriptive touch
beyond ordinary reportage that any serious novelist would be proud

of. Those looking for the memoirs of a foreign correspondent will find them in this book. But what they will find too is an elegy to Russia by someone deeply etched by its influence and its continuing presence in his life'

David Pratt, *Herald*

'These memoirs show us the understanding, empathy and the compassion that underpinned the knowledge and authority of Roxburgh's reporting. A gripping story, scintillatingly told. Essential reading for any young person thinking of a career in the media. It will have you laughing out loud in places, move you close to tears in others'

Scotsman

BY THE SAME AUTHOR:

Books
Pravda: Inside the Soviet News Machine
The Second Russian Revolution
Preachers of Hate: The Rise of the Far Right
The Strongman: Vladimir Putin and the Struggle for Russia

Translations
A Prisoner in the Caucasus (Lev Tolstoy)
Taras Bulba (Nikolai Gogol)
The Glade with Life-Giving Water
Dmitri Shostakovich: About Himself and His Times
Fifty Russian Artists
Building a Prison (Vladimir Kornilov)
Girls to the Front (Vladimir Kornilov)

Music
Harmonies for One

MOSCOW CALLING

MEMOIRS OF A FOREIGN CORRESPONDENT

ANGUS ROXBURGH

BIRLINN

This edition first published in 2021 by
Birlinn Ltd
West Newington House
10 Newington Road
Edinburgh
EH9 1QS

www.birlinn.co.uk

ISBN: 978 1 78027 718 9

British Library Cataloguing in Publication Data
A catalogue record for this book is available from the British Library

Typeset by Biblichor Ltd, Edinburgh
Printed and bound by Clays Ltd, Elcograf S.p.A.

Contents

Illustrations

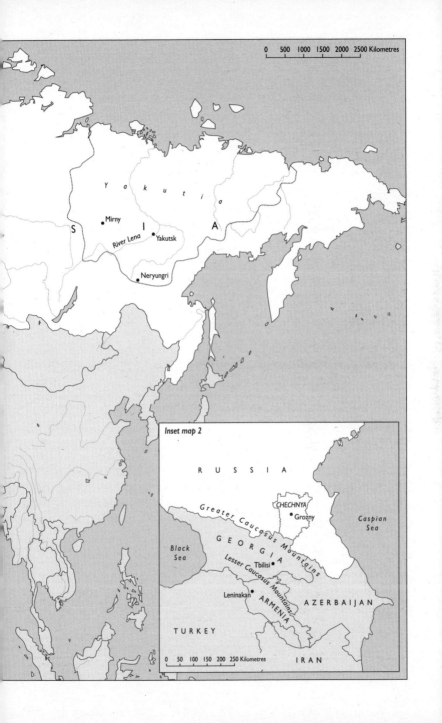

0   500 1000 1500 2000 2500 Kilometres

Y   a   k   u   t   i   a

S   I   A

• Mirny

River Lena   • Yakutsk

• Neryungri

Inset map 2

R U S S I A

Greater Caucasus Mountains

CHECHNYA

• Grozny

Caspian Sea

Black Sea

G E O R G I A

Lesser Caucasus Mountains

Tbilisi •

Leninakan •   A R M E N I A   A Z E R B A I J A N

T U R K E Y

0   50 100 150 200 250 Kilometres   I R A N

Preface to the Paperback Edition

AFTER PUBLICATION OF the hardback edition of *Moscow Calling* in 2017, I travelled the length and breadth of Britain talking to audiences at book festivals about Russia. There was, I realised, huge interest in a country that was rarely out of the headlines – but also, I sensed, a real appetite for deeper, more sophisticated coverage than was available in newspapers and on television.

There was certainly plenty to worry about. Russia had used internet trolls and secret agents to interfere in the 2016 American election that put Donald Trump in the White House. Russian assassins had deployed a deadly nerve agent, Novichok, in the streets of the English city of Salisbury. President Vladimir Putin's most influential opponent, Alexei Navalny, was attacked with the same poison. The Kremlin had annexed Crimea and started a war in Ukraine. It sent troops into Syria and was deploying an array of sophisticated new nuclear missiles. Russia's state media spewed out lies and propaganda, and opposition activists were thrown in jail. Worryingly, Moscow deployed a new secret weapon – using social media to sow confusion and spread fake news in Western democracies. And in 2020 Putin, by now the world's most feared man, already serving his fourth presidential term, changed the Russian constitution to enable him to remain in power, if he wished, until 2036 (when he would be 83). The demonisation of Putin in Western media verged on something much more insidious – Russophobia, the stereotyping of an entire nation as villains. A former British defence minister cited the perfectly ordinary Russian word for 'lying' – *vranyo* – and claimed with a straight face that it denoted a particularly heinous 'Russian' form of mendacity.

The people who came to my talks were keen to know what lay behind the headlines and were wary of the hysteria that seemed to inform so much of the coverage. How could they square what was going on in

Russia today with what they knew about Russian culture, literature, music? It seemed to strike a chord when I lamented that the prevailing portrait of Russia was so one-dimensional and politicised, as though there was nothing more to this great country than Vladimir Putin and his evil machinations.

When I started writing this memoir, I had no greater ambition than simply to retell some of the stories that have emerged from my long association with Russia. But in the telling, the book grew a second skin. I wanted to let readers *feel* what it was like to live in the Soviet Union and through the turmoil that followed it. This background – the history, the culture, the people and traditions – is not just an 'optional extra', but essential if we are to understand what Russia is today.

No country has suffered more than Russia (or the Soviet Union) in the last hundred years. Ever since the communist revolution of 1917, the nation has been hit by wave upon wave of hardship and killing. The revolution itself was followed by a bloody civil war; then came the Stalinist purges and enforced collectivisation of farming, leaving millions dead and millions more incarcerated in Siberian prison camps; then the Second World War that took 25 million Soviet lives and left half the country in ruins; then more purges, and the grinding hopelessness of the Soviet Union's final decades; then the upheaval of change in the 1980s and 1990s, when the communist regime was ousted amid great hopes for the future. Those hopes quickly fizzled out, as democracy was stifled, and the promised market economy produced millions of poor people and a handful of billionaires – many of them Putin's own cronies, propping up and benefitting from his corrupt, mafia-like rule. Millions of Russians emerged reeling from this horror movie. Those who had believed in the great Soviet utopia felt betrayed and duped as their heroes and ideals were ridiculed, while opponents of communism saw their dream of liberty fade to black.

My memoir covers the last forty-five years or so of this tragedy, the years I witnessed personally. It is the story of my own experiences in Russia since the 1970s, when I first visited the USSR as a student. In later years I worked there as a translator, as a correspondent for newspapers and for the BBC, and as a media consultant to the Kremlin. From the darkest days of communism and the Cold War, through the exhilaration of Mikhail Gorbachev's *perestroika* reforms and the chaos of Boris Yeltsin's rebuilding of capitalism, to the recidivist Russia of Vladimir Putin, I have seen four decades of contradictions and surprises.

Russia – as most people who fall in love with it agree – is an exasperating country that inspires and disappoints, attracts and horrifies in equal measure. This book is about the friendships I made, the hardships and the delights, the maddening way Russia makes you want to love it, despite everything! In the end it is simply about the way Russians live and have lived, what they have endured, what has kept them going, over these decades of upheaval.

And the pain goes on . . . In the summer of 2017, I made one of my frequent trips to Russia and once again experienced the paradoxes that seem to mark the country in every age. On the one hand I was welcomed, as always, by my dear Russian friends, who see their way through every dark cloud with a mixture of stoicism, resignation . . . and vodka. Some of them were with me one Saturday afternoon when supporters of Putin's arch-critic, the anti-corruption campaigner Aleksei Navalny, staged a large demonstration on Tverskaya Street in the centre of Moscow. As usual, peaceful defiance was met with violence. Black-helmeted riot police ploughed into the crowds, beating people with sticks and arresting random protestors (including – I had to laugh – one man who was telling a journalist what a fine leader Putin was).

If that wasn't enough to persuade me that Russia had once more become a police state, then a day spent under arrest in the city of Nizhny Novgorod certainly helped. I was there with a group of tourists on a study trip, and we were meeting a local politician (not a critic, but a member of Putin's own party) over breakfast, when a posse of leath-er-jacketed agents dragged us off to a police station. Most of the group were released after about four hours; I was detained for seven. A young plain-clothes officer interrogated me about the 'real reasons' for my visit, demanded to know why anyone should want to go on a 'study trip' to 'Putin's Russia' and released me only after extorting a small 'fine'.

A few days later, back in Moscow, we were invited by Anatoly Kuzichev, the host of a political talk show, to sit in the studio during a live broadcast on state television's Channel One. Nominally the topic under discussion was the anniversary of Hitler's invasion of the USSR on 22 June 1941 – but that turned out to be a pretext for a hate session against Ukraine, Poland and anyone who dared to criticise Russia.

In George Orwell's *Nineteen Eighty-Four*, citizens gather for 'Hate Week', where images of the state's chief enemy are shown and the audi-ence scream their hatred at him. Here, pictures of a man being arrested in Ukraine for carrying a Soviet flag flickered on the screen, and a token

Ukrainian 'expert' was allowed to explain why communist symbols are banned there. But within seconds she was shouted down by the two alpha-male hosts, who sneered at her, denouncing the Ukrainian government as Nazis and Russophobes. Her only role, it seemed, was to act as a punch bag. After the show I asked her why she agreed to put herself up for such humiliation. She turned away and refused to speak.

One of the presenters, Artyom Sheinin, a veteran of the Soviet war in Afghanistan, strutted around like an exploding parcel of boorishness and manufactured anger. He cursed the Polish parliament for voting to remove memorials to the Soviet occupation of their country. 'I won't shy from the word,' he said, 'these people are bitches, animals . . .' His lip curled as he spat the words into the camera.

Sitting next to me was a young floor manager, scarcely in her twenties, whose job was to orchestrate the applause. Whenever the hosts made some particularly venomous comment, she cracked her palms together – giving the signal for the audience to burst into applause – and then after about four seconds gave a circular 'wind down' signal, which the audience also followed. I had seen shows like this on Russian TV and found them distasteful and crude – but seeing it behind the scenes left me speechless. I turned to the hate-leader during a commercial break and asked her if she had read George Orwell. She didn't know who he was.

This, sadly, is Russia today. But how did it come to this? Why has this wonderful country, the home of Tolstoy and Chekhov and Tchaikovsky, ended up, once again, in the international doghouse? And, more importantly for its own people, in the hands of a ruling clique that smothers dissent and enriches itself at the expense of ordinary folk? How do Russians feel about themselves, as they struggle – still – to emerge from decades of totalitarian rule? I can't claim that my memoirs answer all of those questions – far from it. But hopefully they add some perspective and context to today's depressing narrative.

Edinburgh
January 2021

Prologue

THIS IS THE book I have been slowly writing in my head for the past forty-odd years. Little did I suspect, back in 1970, when I first closeted myself in the school library for hours on end to teach myself Russian, that the rest of my life would be shaped by a country of which, at the time, I knew very little. It was communist, had put a man in space, and had athletes with see-see-see-pee on their shirts. That was about it. Oh, and everyone was scared of it.

But it was none of these things that first ignited a Russian spark inside me. No, it was a beautiful tawny wooden box that sat on my bedroom table, a Pye wireless set, with five valves, eight wavebands and four Bakelite knobs, which I twiddled ceaselessly, entranced by the world's languages, voices and music. As a teenager, I lived a double life, half-hippy, half-nerd. I spent much of my time playing guitar in a rock band and glued to the side of a girlfriend through the rain-soaked summers of north-east Scotland, vainly trying to bring some of the Woodstock spirit to my home town. The rest of my time I spent in front of that Pye radio set, mind-travelling around the world and marvelling at all the languages I didn't speak. I wrote to scores of stations asking for QSL cards (proof that I had listened to them and sent a reception report) and pinned them to my wall, next to the posters from The Beatles' *White Album*. The communist stations showered me with cards, magazines and brochures. Prague, Warsaw, Sofia, Bucharest, Peking – I knew the sound of their languages and the odd-looking typefaces they used in their publications long before I understood anything about their politics. And Moscow . . .

The signal from the USSR was the clearest and most powerful on the ether. Inexplicably, the very sound of it made my heart jump. The ten-note call-sign pealed like frozen iron bells being struck on a black winter night. At the start of every broadcast a voice would declaim: '*Govorit Moskva!*' Just two words, but they quivered with emotion:

'Moscow calling!' Then a choir struck up a Russian song that haunted me almost as much as the spine-tingling opening bars of *Good Vibrations*. I didn't know then, but I know now, that the song was a classic piece of Soviet propaganda. Here's a rough translation:

> *Wide is my motherland*
> *Full of rivers, fields and trees.*
> *I know of no other country*
> *Where people breathe so free.*

The station – *Radiostantsiya Rodina*, or Radio Motherland – broadcast in Russian and was mainly targeted at what it called 'our compatriots abroad'. I had no idea what was being said, but I luxuriated in the euphony of the language – its dark, soft, sexy vowels, the clatter of its consonants, the susurrus of its fricatives and sibilants, the music of its intonations. Folk songs spirited me to Siberia. Readings of poetry, even if I understood no word, left me breathless at their beauty. Perhaps my subconscious was telling me: lips that produced such heavenly sounds surely had to be kissed. I sent off for the booklets that accompanied the station's Russian lessons.

Meanwhile, in an Edinburgh bookshop I bought what must surely be the most unsuccessful textbook ever published. Titled *Teach Yourself Russian through Reading*, it aimed to plunge learners straight into the delights of Russian literature – to wit, in the very first chapter, a passage from Tolstoy's *War and Peace*. Thus the first Russian sentence I ever tried to learn was: 'When Prince Andrew entered the study, the old prince in his old-man's spectacles and white dressing gown, in which he received no one but his son, was sitting at the table writing. He looked round.' From such texts one was supposed to 'assimilate' Russian grammar, and by the end of lesson one we'd done reflexive verbs, past tenses, possessive pronouns and several conjugations – and learned interesting phrases such as 'The splutters flew from his creaking pen'.

I struggled on for a few more pages, but was thankful when the Radio Moscow booklets finally arrived, and I was soon practising more useful sentences such as 'Hello, my name is Viktor', 'This is my house', and 'My mum is a crane-operator'.

It was the language itself that attracted me at this stage. The love of literature came later – indeed, at school any hint of it was expertly snuffed out by our English teacher, a gargoyle of a man called Mr Watt, who rejoiced in the nickname 'Killer'. (Had I been English I might have recognised this as a rather amusing pun, but as a Scot, given to pronouncing the 'r' at the end of the word, the joke only dawned on me many years after leaving school. At the time I thought he existed only to beat small boys and kill their interest in books.)

The USSR insinuated itself into my mind in other ways too. When I was seven Yuri Gagarin flew into space. A year later the West was on the brink of nuclear war with Russia during the Cuban missile crisis. The Soviet national anthem kept being played at the Olympic Games. Some of the most colourful postage stamps in my Stanley Gibbons Swiftsure album were marked CCCP, and showed men in welder's goggles, women with sheaves of corn, athletes, sputniks, the hammer-and-sickle motif, and an earnest man with a goatee beard, gripping the lapel of his overcoat – whereas our stamps in those days rarely depicted anything but the Queen's head.

I came from a politically engaged family – my parents were active in the Labour Party – but I knew little about the realities of the Soviet 'workers' state' . . . until 1968. That August two boys from Czechoslovakia were staying with my family for a couple of days before they went off to camp in Perthshire with the Scottish Schoolboys' Club. They were a year or so older than me (I was 14), and when they spotted my shortwave wireless they excitedly tuned in to Radio Prague. To their horror it was broadcasting a stark announcement that the country had been invaded by Soviet and Warsaw Pact troops and that the reforming 'Prague Spring' government (thanks to which the boys were able to travel abroad) had been overthrown. The joy of two lads looking forward to a fortnight in the Scottish Highlands drained from their faces as they heard the announcer call upon the Czechoslovak people – including their parents, back in Prague – to remain calm and not to provoke the occupying forces into causing bloodshed. We heard the announcers' voices falter, and the rattle of gunfire as Soviet tanks began to shell the radio building. Now I had another reason to learn Russian. What *was* communism? Who was Brezhnev? Why did they invade other countries?

A year or so later I had learned enough to persuade my school to assign me 'self-study' hours in the library (there was no Russian teacher) so that I could prepare for an 'O-Grade' exam, and perhaps go on to study Russian at university. After two years of memorising declensions and imbibing Radio Moscow, I found the written examination easy – but when I opened my mouth at the oral test I realised it was the first time I had ever spoken Russian to another human being. Only then did I discover how important it was to emphasise the correct syllables in Russian words: a misplaced stress could change the meaning altogether, or simply make your words unintelligible. An 'o' sounded differently depending on how close it was to the stressed syllable: so *moloko* (milk) was pronounced muh-la-kó . . . how marvellous! I couldn't wait to get to university, and have a proper teacher.

I studied Russian at Aberdeen University, and for a year in Zurich, where I also searched in vain for the exiled writer Alexander Solzhenitsyn, who was said to keep his memories of Russia alive by pacing through the snowy forest on the Zürichberg, near my student dorm. Finally, with my degree in my pocket, I was ready to set off. Something was hauling me away from Scotland like the tugging tide of the North Sea, and it was Russia.

1

On the Devil's Horns

IT WAS OCTOBER 1978, and the coldest Moscow winter in a century was just revving up. Sadly, the district of Moscow in which we were going to spend it was only half-built. Our apartment was so new you could still smell traces of the plumber's last swig of vodka.

Soon there was ice creeping across the double-glazed window. Across the *inside* of the double-glazed window. The bolts holding the frame together had merely been placed loosely in the holes, allowing Siberian gales to whistle through the gaps between glass and wood. Apparently that crucial final step, where you take a spanner and turn the bolts clockwise, was an advanced-level skill not included in the Soviet builder's manual, so the first thing we had to do was buy some tools to finish off the work. Cupboard doors also needed straightening, and flapping electric sockets had to be attached securely to the walls. The drainpipe under the sink in the bathroom was sealed with an old rag, and leaked for months until we learned how to bribe a plumber to fix it. A three-rouble note – a *tryoshka* – seemed to do the trick for most odd jobs, though since this was almost exactly the price of a bottle of vodka there was no point at all in calling a plumber after about eleven o'clock in the morning, by which time he might have drunk his way through several odd jobs already.

The flat was provided, free of charge, by my employer, Progress, the Soviet Union's foreign language publishing house. I had landed the work in April, after doing a translation test while in Moscow with a group of language students. I also fell in love with one of the students in the group: like me, Neilian was Scottish, and equally fascinated by Russia. In September we got married, and set off for a year of adventure in Moscow. We were rare specimens in those days – foreigners who came to the heart of the communist world not as diplomats or businessmen or journalists, but to work for a Soviet organisation, with none of the perks that most Westerners enjoyed – just for the sheer joy of learning Russian and experiencing a forbidden place.

Vadim, the weasel-faced head of Progress's foreign relations department, met us at the airport with a driver. Our route to the apartment seemed to take hours. Vadim tried to scare us with talk about bears and wolves in the forests we travelled through. (Why we even travelled through forests remains a mystery to this day.)

On arrival, Vadim showed us up to our one-roomed apartment. 'Where are we?' I asked.

'On the devil's horns,' said Vadim with a strange cackle.

'What?'

'Yasenevo,' he said.

I was none the wiser. 'Is that in Moscow?'

Vadim hesitated. 'Mmm, yes,' he said. 'More or less.'

The room contained a table, a couple of bottle-green patterned armchairs, and a matching sofa which folded out to become our bed. It was identical to many Russians' flats we would visit, apart from one extra accoutrement – a small metal plate which we discovered later under the wallpaper just above our bed. This appeared to conceal a microphone. Over the next two years snippets of our private conversations would make their way back to us courtesy of the army of perverts with language degrees employed by the KGB to snoop on foreigners' bedrooms.

Vadim left us with 50 roubles to tide us over until I received my first pay – 200 roubles a month, which at the official exchange rate in those days was about £200. Two hundred roubles went quite a long way. (The average Soviet wage was 170 roubles.) Over the next months we would be able to buy curtains and a strip of carpet (both chosen from the tiny selection of unconscionably ugly state-approved styles), a TV, a record-player and eventually a refrigerator. For now, there was no need for that: like many Russians, we hung our butter and cheese outside the window in a carrier bag. But come spring we would need one.

Our priorities on that first evening were a cooking pot, a packet of tea, some bread, and a few vegetables or meat for our first meal. But within seconds we realised we lacked the most essential item for life in these parts – rubber boots. It was not just our apartment windows that had not been finished off: the pavements and roads had not yet been tarmacked, and the 400-metre walk to the *universam* (universal store, or supermarket) was a swamp. By the time we reached the shop our shoes, indeed our ankles, were coated with thick mud. The floor of the supermarket was a sea of sludge, despite the best efforts of a very old woman in a charcoal overall and felt boots who dragged a black rag around with a stick, slopping the mud from place to place.

The shop somewhat resembled a Western supermarket, in that it had rows of shelves, but they contained almost nothing but cans – mainly conserved fish and meat – and identical oatmeal-textured paper bags which could be distinguished only by searching for the word written on them with a Biro: rice, sugar, flour, semolina. In the section marked 'milk', squishy pyramid-shaped plastic bags of milk were leaking onto the floor. The section marked 'meat' was bloodstained but empty. The section marked 'vegetables' sported several cage trolleys containing a few muddy potatoes, carrots and onions. Sparrows were flying about under the ceiling, chirping away as if they hadn't noticed that the woods they used to nest in had been chopped down and replaced with a housing estate.

An assistant appeared from a back room wheeling another trolley, filled to the brim with huge pale-green cabbages, like a mountain of skulls from Pol Pot's Cambodia. The supermarket had appeared to be almost empty, but now a horde of women appeared from nowhere and descended upon the trolley like a plague of locusts. First I saw the headscarves, then the flailing elbows, and suddenly the entire space was heaving with brown coats. As the cabbages vanished I had a cartoonish vision of the trolley stuffed with upside-down women scrabbling for the final one, their legs sticking up in the air like a packet of French fries. Within seconds the trolley was empty, bar a few tattered leaves, and the lucky shoppers were emerging from the dust cloud with smiles on their faces, while fights broke out among the losers. One woman who had a cabbage clinched under each arm was physically assaulted by a member of the losing team, and the supernumerary one was snatched away from her. My wife, who had merely been observing the fray with her jaw ratcheting towards the floor in disbelief, was verbally abused by a woman with an enormous puce face under a fluffy wool hat, who shouted: 'I know you're a foreigner. Why should you get one? Just go to the devil!'

They used to say Russians could always tell foreigners by their footwear. But even with our feet caked in mud, we stood out from the crowd. We would never fool any Russian into thinking we were one of them.

Hundreds of days lay ahead during which we would learn more about the finer arts of Soviet shopping, but now a small disturbance at the fish section caught our eye. A new consignment had just arrived. The blocks of ice in which the fish were frozen were far too big to go in the display counter, so the salesgirl was breaking them up. To do this, she had placed an old-fashioned two-kilogram weight on the floor and was now hurling the refrigerated blocks at it. On impact the ice shattered into tiny fragments and the rigid fish burst out of captivity and slithered across the mud in all directions. One of them, possibly a cod, skimmed over to the wall, slipped up the back of a heating pipe that ran along the skirting board, came to rest on top of it, and eased itself down comfortably in the heat, its glassy eyes goggling at the spectacle. We quickly bought some bread, tea and a pan, and fled from the supermarket.

Yasenevo turned out to be a brand-new neighbourhood in the very south of Moscow, just inside the outer ring road. That's what Vadim meant by 'on the devil's horns' – it means 'very far away'. Our flat was in a housing estate so anonymous the address didn't even merit a street name: it was 'building number 32, block 3, *mikroraion* (or micro-district) number 5', Yasenevo. From our fifth-floor window we could see a forest of apartment blocks, identical to our own, as though someone was holding up a set of gigantic mirrors. They stood at a not-quite-safe distance for getting undressed – nine and sixteen storeys high and as long as ocean liners, all brand-new, all faced with coloured tiles, this one pink, that one mint-green, another one lilac, but in the dark they all looked the same, an endless grid of glowing windows.

Next morning we went out to explore. What we found presumably exemplified what Soviet urban planners envisaged as a perfect creation, since they had built it from scratch, just as they wanted it. They took a blank piece of land on the edge of Moscow and were able to design it exactly as they wished, with no concern for existing structures. (The only old building left standing was the little Peter and Paul church, which survived not to comfort the souls of Soviet workers but because the local state farm deemed it the perfect place to repair tractors.) So Yasenevo represented the acme of Soviet planning, a glimpse of the radiant future, when everyone would live in micro-districts, not streets. It was all completely new, constructed from prefabricated concrete panels over the past two years.

The dozen or so micro-districts were virtually identical. This induced mild panic attacks as we wandered from one to the next, wondering if we would ever find our way back home, or would be arrested for trying to break into a flat precisely the same as ours but in the wrong *mikro-raion*. Each micro-district was approximately half a mile square, and consisted of a semi-circle of elongated 16-storey buildings, plus a few 9-storey ones, surrounding two kindergartens and a school. There were no actual streets, and the numbering of the individual buildings had been devised either by a dyslexic state planner or by a cunning security operative who wanted to baffle foreigners. The houses in our micro-district, for instance, were numbered 13, 17, 30, 32, 4 and 6. Even more confusingly, some of these were subdivided: for example, 32 (block 1) was the enormous 16-storey semicircle, while 32 (block 2) was the kindergarten; 32 (block 3) was actually four separate 9-storey buildings (including ours); and 32 (block 4) was the other kindergarten. Who would want to be a postman here? Each micro-district had a polyclinic, a few small shops hidden in various entrances, a first-aid point, and sundry administrative buildings. Each had a little stall selling bread, and a newspaper kiosk. The main buildings, being perhaps a hundred metres long, had several entrances, each with a porch, and each porch had a bench outside, where old women sat, even in winter, wrapped in shawls, exchanging gossip. Narrow access roads threaded around the buildings, and through arches in them, connecting the neighbourhood to the main six-lane thoroughfare leading north to Moscow. Planners had even thought of planting trees in some of the spaces – but had given less thought to the basics of life. Our micro-district, number 5, shared a single *universam* with four or five other micro-districts, serving some 30,000 people – which would explain why we often spent more than two hours in the line to the check-out.

The next day was Monday. I found my way into the office. Progress occupied a new six-storey block near Gorky Park. Vadim greeted me with his weaselly smirk and asked how we had coped with the wolves. The head of the English section, a matronly lady named Maria Konstantinovna, gave me a contract to sign, and handed me a manuscript to translate (at home, since there was no room in the office for all the translators). An editor called Viktor Schneerson then ran me through the style guide – English spellings such as 'realise', not 'realize'. I asked whether they used single or double quotation marks, and he instantly concocted the most bizarre reason for using singles: 'Actually, it saves ink,' he said, as if this was a brilliant example of the efficiency of Soviet industry.

'How are you settling in?' he asked as I got ready to leave.

'Fine, thanks. Getting a bit cold, isn't it?'

He laughed and shook his head. 'This is nothing. I used to live in Siberia. There it gets so cold birds freeze in mid-flight and just drop straight out of the sky. People there watch each other's faces closely, to spot signs of frostbite before it sets in. Otherwise your nose can fall off . . .'

What was it about these Russians who all wanted to scare me with something?

Not a single colleague at Progress told me about the things I really needed to know. The little food stall that sold good steak, for instance, and the system of *zakazy*. It took me months to discover that once a week you could sign up for a *zakaz* (an 'order'). Three options were usually available. Each consisted of three or four items – two of them scarce and desirable (a jar of gherkins, perhaps, tinned salmon, or even caviar or smoked sausages), and one or two that were padding – a bag of sweets or a pack of sugar lumps, for example. On Monday you signed up for one of the options. A couple of days later you went in to buy it . . . and trotted back home feeling tremendously lucky. By such means Progress's workers (and those in many other institutions and factories) beat the shortages in Soviet shops. It helped to explain that eternal Soviet conundrum – empty shelves in the food stores but full shelves in people's fridges.

As the first snows fell that evening I sat at my desk beside the puny central-heating radiator, pulled my scarf a little tighter, and looked out through the uncurtained windows. It was dark and still outside, as though everything was muffled in cotton wool. All life had retreated indoors. I toyed with the keys on my blue Imperial typewriter and stared blankly at the page of Russian beside it. I couldn't for the life of me think how to make my first translation sound at all English. It was about liberation movements in Asia and Africa. Translating it was part of my little stint in propaganda purgatory: ahead, they told me, lay more interesting works of literature – perhaps some of the classics – and next year, I'd be translating for a special magazine they were bringing out for the 1980 Moscow Olympics. But meanwhile it was this:

The victory of the Great October Socialist Revolution, which brought about a radical change in the correlation of world forces, provided the foundation for the implementation of Lenin's great plan for the struggle against imperialism.

What did that actually *mean*? More importantly, how would I stay awake to translate it? There were about 500 pages like this. How many quotation marks' worth of ink was that, I wondered.

The table I sat at had an oval tin number plate attached to it, because it belonged to the state-owned publishing house. Out there in the darkness, too, everything was provided by the state: the apartments, the shops, the theatres, the newspapers, the lorries, the buses, even the heat. Our central heating came from a white building down there, which pushed scalding water along foot-wide pipes that snaked around the buildings and into basements, to be pumped around all the apartments. The authorities switched it on, for everyone, in early October when the average temperature dropped below eight degrees Celsius for five days running. There were no thermostats: if it got too hot inside, you opened a window. (In the summer we would discover that not just the heating but even the running hot water supply was turned off for three weeks – 'for maintenance' – and we had to boil water in pans to wash.)

Living in Britain, we used to worry about heating our flat for too long. Those were the days of putting shillings in a meter to keep the electricity on. Many people thought twice before switching on a two-bar electric heater. But here, you were relieved of such concerns. The state decided when it was cold, and the state decided how much heat to give you. And it practically paid for it too, since the cost of communal services was so low.

So here we were, living in what the West called a communist country. They didn't actually call it communist here, though, because, well . . . there had been a little glitch in the historical timetable set out by Marx and Lenin. According to them, as every Soviet schoolchild knew, 'communism' (a future classless society without private property, in which individuals would contribute according to their means and receive everything they needed from the state) was supposed to arrive only at the end of a period of 'socialism'. Khrushchev had impetuously predicted in 1961 that the transition from socialism to communism was imminent. But now, it had to be admitted, the advent of the communist nirvana was taking rather longer than planned. So the Communist Party decided to tweak Marxism a little, and came up with a new interim term: according to General Secretary Leonid Brezhnev we were now living in the era of '*developed* socialism', defined as a 'second stage' in the transition from socialism to communism. Getting the jargon right was very important for Soviet ideologues. They couldn't improve the standard of living, but they could work wonders with the terminology.

'Developed socialism' (sometimes known as 'mature' socialism) was a cocoon. Russian babies were, and still are, tightly swaddled from head to toe at birth. In the Soviet Union the swaddling never stopped – schoolchildren were wrapped in layers of Marxism-Leninism, adults were tucked up in blankets of Party propaganda, and at bedtime an avuncular television newscaster told them fairy tales about the ogres and monsters who inhabited the world outside the USSR's secure borders. People lived in low-cost apartments, but they didn't own them; they all had jobs, mostly low-paid but guaranteed for life; the shops provided a very limited, if erratic, supply of goods; there was mediocre but universal health care, and pretty good (though ideologically stultifying) education for all, and so long as you turned out to vote in pretend elections every now and again and trotted along to Party meetings at work without raising any objections, then ... life went on. It was warm, safe, and comfortable. You didn't even need to have views about anything: every flat was provided with a plastic radio receiver tuned to *Mayak* ('Lighthouse'). You could turn it off, but you couldn't choose another station. The state understood things for you.

Of course, some people wanted to be butterflies, not larvae. For them the silence of the cocoon was suffocating. One night as I gazed out at the ranks of glowing windows, turning dark one by one, I heard something odd. An eerie, warbling call-sign. It was so quiet you could easily miss it, but I recognised it from my days as a short-wave radio ham. Somebody was listening to Radio Liberty, the CIA-financed station, broadcasting all the news that Russians couldn't hear on their own channels.

A few weeks into our stay we realised that no one in the world, apart from our families, had the faintest idea that we were in Moscow. Progress had registered us with the local police office, but we had no foreign friends or contacts here. What if there was a war? There was a nuclear bunker under our apartment block, but would the Russians even let us in? We went to the British embassy, a grand former sugar merchant's mansion across the river from the Kremlin, and presented our passports to a Soviet guard who reluctantly agreed to let us through the gate. At the consular section we waited an eternity for anyone to come and deal with us. The nerve of it! As if we were Russians or something!

'Hello. We just wanted to let you know that we're here.'

'What?' said a disdainful face from behind the glass partition.

'We're British. But we're working for Progress publishers. And it occurred to us that you don't know we're here.'

'Should we?'

'Well . . . you know, just in case something happens to us . . .'

'Like what?'

'Well, like if there was a war . . . Maybe it would be good if you knew where we lived?'

The shoulders below the face shrugged, and a hand pushed a piece of paper under the partition. 'Write down your address then. If you like.'

Ah, how marvellous to be British, I thought, as I wrote down our names and address and pushed it back. We stood for a moment, wondering whether the diplomat might say something to reassure us, or even invite us to meet the ambassador, or use the facilities. But he had already disappeared. As we walked away in the slush, we wondered whether that sheet of paper had gone anywhere other than into a wastepaper basket. That was the only contact we would have with any Western official in Moscow in the entire two years of our stay.

Four hundred and ninety pages to go, then, before I would get more rewarding work. The tract I was translating was mind-numbing, impenetrable propaganda. Here is a short example – the last, I promise!

As distinct from the earlier examples of nations that avoided the intervening stage of developed capitalism by completing this process within the framework of the proletarian state of the USSR (during the twenties and thirties) and under the guidance of a Marxist-Leninist party, socialist orientation today in nearly 15 countries of Asia and Africa is carried out under the guidance of revolutionary national-democratic parties, which are variously placed in their approximation to scientific socialism.

The book was written by a man named Rostislav Ulyanovsky. How I cursed him for his pompous, vacuous prose. But as I write this memoir, with the benefit of my notebooks, hindsight and now the internet, I have made an interesting discovery. Ulyanovsky was among the millions of victims of Stalin's Terror. Born into a Polish aristocratic family, he pretended after the 1917 revolution to be the son of a railway worker: his proletarian credentials allowed him to study oriental history, specialising in India. He became a professor at the Institute of Oriental Studies. Then, in the dark night of 1 January 1935, he was hauled from his apartment, accused of belonging to a Trotskyite organisation. His arrest warrant was signed by Nikita Khrushchev, then Moscow Party chief. Khrushchev would rehabilitate him twenty years later, but only after the poor man had wasted the best part of his life being interrogated and tortured and doing forced labour in the notorious stations of the Gulag – the Lubyanka, Butyrka, Vorkuta, Komi. Now, under Brezhnev, he was writing books extolling the inexorable progress across Africa and Asia of the very system that had destroyed his life. This is how the intelligentsia survived. Now when I look at the paragraph above from his book, I wonder whether he was not just amusing himself with the clichés of communist discourse, throwing word-cards up into the air to see how they fell. He had to make a living somehow, after all.

2

A Russian Englishman

OUR FIRST EXCURSION was to see a man whose name was known to almost every English speaker who had ever used a Russian textbook. The words 'Translated by V. Korotky' appeared on the title page of so many grammars and readers, he seemed to be the only translator Russia had. My professor in Aberdeen had given me Volodya's number, so I was able to call in advance and arrange a visit. We set off in a light blizzard for the south-western suburbs of Moscow where he lived, in a dingy, early Brezhnev-era block a couple of stops beyond Moscow University.

He greeted us with a look of childlike wonder and adoration, tilting his head and gazing beatifically into our eyes, as if two representatives of Heaven had rung his doorbell. And indeed, that was practically how he perceived us – for Volodya was a devotee of everything and everyone that Great Britain had ever produced. (That included, for the sake of argument, America.) The corridor of his little flat, which he shared with his foster-son, Seryozha, was lined with glass-fronted bookshelves containing a large selection of English and American literature, plus photographs of the Queen and Prince Charles. Born in 1926, he had started speaking English at an early age with his Scottish nanny, Mrs Gilbertson, who had come to Stalinist Russia with her communist husband. By the age of ten he had read Dickens and Shakespeare, and now, aged 52, he was far more widely read than I, a mere 24-year-old – despite my degree in German and Russian literature (or perhaps because of it).

'Angus,' he asked me, his eyes still full of disbelief that he had real flesh-and-blood Britons in his apartment, 'and . . . what do you think of John Updike? Is he as good as they say he is?' I got the feeling he didn't require an answer: he just wanted to luxuriate in the experience of chatting to two native English speakers. His accent was delightful, with no trace at all of Russian, but also not entirely British. His English conversations in recent years had mainly been with a middle-aged couple from

New Zealand who had settled in Moscow and infected him with some interesting vowels, so that 'say' became 'sigh', and my own name began with an elongated 'e' – Ehngus rather than Angus.

In the kitchen he tapped the shortwave radio on the window-ledge: 'This is our lifeline,' he beamed. 'BBC World Service. We listen to it every die.'

'Every hour, nearly!' Seryozha corrected him. And Volodya launched into a quick rendition of 'Lilliburlero', the World Service's signature tune.

His bedroom, where he worked, was full of dictionaries, including an extraordinary edition of the complete Oxford English Dictionary which crammed the customary twenty tomes into just two volumes of microscopic print, and came with a huge magnifying glass. His writing desk was topped with a protective sheet of glass under which Volodya kept various mementoes – a photo of his mother, some dollar bills, pictures of motor cars, and numerous photographs of bodybuilders with rippling muscles. These contrasted with his own physique, which was frighteningly frail. He looked like an ancient, sickly waif – small, bony, bald, hollow-eyed and pale-skinned, like an escapee from the Gulag.

In the main room, which doubled as Seryozha's bedroom, a table was set with gold-rimmed bone china cups and an array of salads and cakes. Volodya couldn't wipe the grin from his face as he fussed around, offering tea and food, constantly practising his English. 'Please, take beetroot salad. Please, take this one – it's cabbage, a very good source of vitamins in the winter. We grow our own green onions on the window-ledge . . . do you say "green onions" or "spring onions"? You see, in winter it seems strange to call them spring onions . . . And this is black bread. Do you like Russian bread? They sigh we have one of the best selections of bread in the world . . .' Then he would stop suddenly and gaze at us again with that radiant, blissful smile.

Seryozha poured an inch of strong dark tea into our cups and topped it up with hot water. It remained far too strong. I could feel the skin shrivelling off the roof of my mouth. 'Is it Russian tea?' I asked.

Volodya looked as though he could scarcely believe I had made such an accusation. 'No! It is Ceylon tea. Of course it is not to be had in the shops for love or money. Here – take lemon. And jam.' He poured some runny strawberry jam into a little dish and showed us how to sip from it with a spoon while drinking the tea. This helped to soothe the palate a little.

'Jim told us about you – we knew we would like you! Thank you for visiting us!' said Seryozha. Jim Forsyth was my Russian professor in Aberdeen.

'Ah, how I would love to see your country,' said Volodya. 'Buckingham Palace. Stratford-upon-Avon. Baker Street. You see, these are the places I dream of.'

'Is it just impossible?'

'Ha!' Volodya let out a yelp of a laugh and gazed at us again, smiling now with pity at our lack of understanding. Then he gestured with his hands, at possible hidden microphones. 'Well,' he said brightly, for the benefit of unseen listeners, 'we can always dream!'

'In the spring,' said Seryozha, 'we will get our car out of the garage and take you to the countryside. It is beautiful near Moscow . . . and . . . we can . . . *talk*.' He pronounced the final word with emphasis.

In fact, they didn't really suspect their own flat was bugged, and spoke about most things freely (though they tended to avoid direct criticism of the Party or KGB while indoors). Volodya referred to Leonid Brezhnev as 'Mr B.', usually with his highly elastic mouth twisted into a new shape, a downward curl of derision. When I moaned about the awful piece of propaganda I was translating, he remarked: 'Well, think yourself lucky they haven't given you Mr B.'s masterpiece to translate.' Throughout 1978 Brezhnev had published three short 'memoirs', starting with *Malaya Zemlya*, his account of a hitherto unnoticed World War Two battle in which he had played a starring role and which suddenly turned out to have been pivotal in the defeat of the Nazis. Newspapers now wrote about the event every day; television news featured the reminiscences of war veterans who unexpectedly found they could recall Brezhnev's exploits in detail; Politburo members had to quote from the memoir in every speech. The book was obligatory reading at all Soviet schools – even in English classes.

'Can you imagine?' Volodya sneered. 'The world is full of exquisite English literature, but our young people are learning it from a translation of Mr B.'s memoirs!'

Seryozha was a post-grad student at the Institute of Latin American Studies. There, the Communist Party 'organiser' held compulsory seminars for all students and staff to study the significance of the general secretary's outpourings. Jokes were already circulating (not at Party seminars) about the hugely inflated importance of the Malaya Zemlya operation. 'Where were you during the War? Fighting at Malaya Zemlya, or just relaxing in the trenches at Stalingrad?'

Volodya had been too young to fight in the war. As a boy, he had been evacuated from Moscow, and witnessed terrible scenes of famine as his train travelled east. 'We passed through villages where people were collapsing from hunger in front of our eyes. They ran up to the train, like skeletons, begging for a crust of bread.' He had witnessed the Stalin period close-up. His father's side of the family were dyed-in-the-wool Bolsheviks. His father, the editor-in-chief of a major newspaper, was killed at the front, early in the war. His uncle, an associate of Stalin's rival, Bukharin, edited the first edition of Lenin's complete works – before being executed as an enemy of the people in 1937. Volodya's mother, Lyubov Sula-Petrovskaya, by contrast, hailed from the aristocracy. Indeed, she would have been a countess had the Revolution not occurred. Her sister – 'Aunt Sonya' – was educated, clever, beautiful, and happened to be the secretary of the USSR's nominal president, Mikhail Kalinin, one of Stalin's closest henchmen. Kalinin soon found he preferred her to his wife, who went off to live in Siberia rather than share her husband with Aunt Sonya. Sonya became Kalinin's common-law wife, enjoying all the privileges of Kremlin life – even after he died. Volodya showed us a photograph of himself at the age of about four, with his mother and aunt, picnicking with the goatee-bearded president of the Soviet Union.

'Tfu!' Volodya ejaculated, summing up his disgust with the Soviet system in a spitting gesture which showed that under his meek, culti-vated English exterior, he remained a Russian at heart. We would grow very fond of Volodya over the coming years, and learn much from him.

3

My Arbat University

ANOTHER OF OUR Moscow universities was in the basement of a pre-revolutionary tenement building in the Arbat district. The Arbat was one the few areas of the city that retained the spirit of days gone by, and the only one that could in any way be described as 'cool' in communist days. Close to the Kremlin, it was originally inhabited by courtiers, artisans and the nobility – until Napoleon's troops stormed through it in 1812 and it was demolished by fire. Rebuilt by the aristocracy, its stylish apartments later became popular with writers, thinkers and artists. For Bulat Okudzhava, a popular guitar-strumming 'bard' of the Sixties and Seventies, the Arbat embodied the very soul of Russia: he sang of it mystically as his 'religion' and 'fatherland' – a strange river of asphalt clicked by the heels of thousands of ordinary Muscovites going about their business, bound together by their joys and troubles.

We arranged to meet an artist friend, Garif Basyrov (or 'Garik'), on Gogol Boulevard and walked with him down Sivtsev Vrazhek Lane in the heart of the Arbat. To the left he pointed out the house where the poet Marina Tsvetayeva once lived, and to the right a new brick apartment building, with deep balconies and picture windows overlooking the haphazardness of the Arbat. 'Servants of the people,' he explained – the block belonged to the KGB. He popped down some steps to buy Stolichnaya vodka, Armenian cognac and, to ensure a decent hangover, three bottles of Moldavian wine. A woman in a fur coat was walking her poodle in the snow, smoking a long, thin cigarette like an actress who'd blundered out of a Thirties film-set. The sound of a budding Rachmaninoff drifted from a dimly lit window.

To get to Garik's studio we had to negotiate four locked doors. From the street, heavy wooden doors led to a gloomy entranceway and an old-fashioned cage lift. But it was through a padlocked iron door to the right of the lift that Garik led us, then down some dank stone steps into a basement corridor lined with heating pipes, thick with ancient dust. Here was another padlocked door, and immediately beyond it an iron-mesh door, also locked. Finally, we were inside, and Garik turned a knob on the wall to spark the lights into action. He took off his jacket and instinctively reached out to switch on a transistor radio, which was tuned to Radio Warsaw, playing crackly jazz tunes. Soon his wife Inna arrived with bread, cheese and sausage. A demijohn of swamp-coloured pickled cucumbers, which was kept in the little kitchen, completed the victuals for the evening.

Garik and Inna were about 34, ten years older than Neilian and I. They had met as teenagers, both studying at art school in Moscow and then at the art faculty of VGIK, Russia's premier film school. On a wall were some black-and-white photographs from those days. Inna looked like a film-star, pouting cigarette smoke from her lips; Garik, with a thick black beard, resembled a Cuban revolutionary.

Their studio was the best place I ever visited in Moscow. It was full of intriguing artworks, artefacts and art paraphernalia, including a large mechanical press for printing etchings. Basically it provided everything a wide-eyed foreigner – and I was certainly one of those – could hope to find in the Soviet Union: artistic glamour, subversive and free-wheeling conversations, and a touch of Dostoyevskian seediness (the grubby WC had no toilet seat and was lit by a bare light bulb hanging from a twist of wire).

Though they both now worked as artists, Inna freely admitted that her husband was the genius. He had a curious background, being one of those rare human beings who experienced life in a Stalinist labour camp before actually being born. His mother had been sent to a prison camp for 'wives of traitors of the motherland' in Kazakhstan, after her first husband was accused of treason and shot in the back of the head in 1938. She married one of the male workers in the camp (that was allowed), and in 1944 gave birth to Garik. In later life he would remember nothing about life in 'the zone', as it was called, but as a toddler he ate prison rations, attended nursery together with the children of jailors, and sang songs about Stalin. When he played outside, his world was delimited by barbed-wire fences and watchtowers guarded by sentries with dogs and machine-guns. After a start like that, any kind of life was going to be a breeze – though it always seemed to me that behind his habitually smiling eyes lay some vestigial sadness. On their release from the Gulag in 1948 the family moved to live in Ukraine, where Garik quickly revealed his talents as an artist. He won prizes and scholarships, and soon ended up at art school in Moscow – where he met Inna.

All this we learned not from Garik, who was far too self-effacing to speak about his background, far less his successes. He just sat smiling and ironically nodding his head, and constantly tried to interrupt the story by filling up our glasses and proposing toasts so we could get on with the main business on the evening's agenda – the examination of beverages from three Soviet republics.

Like many artists in the days of 'mature socialism', Garik earned a living by doing 'official' work, while also creating hundreds of pieces 'for the desk drawer'. In his case, both were equally brilliant – meticulously and beautifully drawn, and thoughtfully humorous. His official work was as an illustrator for a magazine, *Chemistry and Life*, which was popular in intellectual circles for its literary section and general 'leftish' tone. His illustrations to accompany scientific articles and works of science fiction came right out of left field. Readers loved them because they were often surreal, counter-intuitive and gently subversive. One that sticks in my mind – the galley proofs were pinned up in the studio – showed a man, fully dressed in a crisp gabardine coat, hat and shoes, sitting on a deck-chair reading a newspaper *under the sea*, with fish and crustaceans swimming around him. This was Magritte, in the age of mature social-ism. The magazine's art editor was known for his adventurous spirit, but on one occasion he went too far. In 1981, ahead of the Communist Party's 26th congress, when every Soviet worker, writer, scientist and toilet-attendant was obliged to come up with initiatives for the future, Garik illustrated an article about genetic engineering with a little draw-ing that showed trucks full of fertilisers being driven in convoy by . . . geese and pigs! The art editor placed the drawing above the head-ing, 'Towards the 26th Congress of the Communist Party', heavily implying that the country was led by a bunch of farm animals. When this was discovered, all 438,000 printed copies of the magazine were seized, and hundreds of schoolchildren were employed to tear out the offending page and replace it with a new one featuring the same article, but without Garik's drawing.

I loved those lapses in the censors' concentration. In December 1981, a small Leningrad literary magazine called *Aurora* published a humorous article on page 75. It took the form of a speech to commemorate a writer's birthday, and began: 'It is hard to imagine that this wonderful writer is alive. Hard to believe that he walks among us. It feels as if he must be dead – after all he has written so many books. Many people really think he died long ago ...' It didn't take long before someone pointed out that Leonid Brezhnev – the ancient, half-dead president, who had published his idiotic memoirs to massive acclaim – was 75 that month. The editor of *Aurora* was duly sacked.

There was a knock at the outside door. 'Good God, have they found out already that we're having an illicit meeting with foreigners?' quipped Garik.

It was Grisha Tarasov and his wife Zoya. They were both university teachers: Zoya taught English to physics students, and Grisha taught Russian to foreigners, specialising in slang. He had met Neilian when he was teaching Russian for a year in Scotland, and it was he who introduced us to Garik and Inna. Grisha and Garik had been friends since they were little boys in Ukraine. It was a relief to think that the bottles Garik had bought would be split among six rather than four – but of course Grisha had brought his own supply: Polish vodka and Bulgarian wine.

'Well, that's nice,' said Garik. 'We thought we would only be discussing the merits of Soviet alcohol production, but now we can include the people's republics too.' (The east European communist countries like Poland and Bulgaria were known as 'people's republics'.)

The evening went the way most evenings in the studio went – headlong towards oblivion. Grisha had been reading a new book by Yuri Trifonov, *The House on the Embankment*. Its publication was a small sensation. It was one of those rare works published under 'mature socialism' that managed to be truthful about the Stalinist era yet still scraped past the censors. The novel described life in one of Moscow's most notorious apartment blocks, a sprawling grey building across the river from the Kremlin where top political figures lived – and disappeared, one by one, during the purges of the Thirties. Under Brezhnev no discussion of Stalin was allowed, and Trifonov's novel did not mention politics, far less the word 'purge'. But he got away with painting a portrait of the times by describing a group of school friends who lived in the house – their decisions, compromises and betrayals. The atmosphere of the period, with the ever-present fear of arrest and disappearance, was an unspoken backdrop.

'It's not about the purges,' said Grisha. 'It's about values, it's about the way we lived.'

'And still live,' said Garik.

'So how did it manage to get published?' I asked.

'The same way as Garik gets published,' said Inna. 'By leaving things unsaid.'

'Well, that's what makes great art,' I ventured. 'So maybe the communist system is actually good for art, since it forces artists to find less obvious ways of saying things . . .'

'Garik, may I show them your man in a corner?' said Inna. She went to a drawer in Garik's work desk and took out one of his new drawings. It showed – well, just that – a man in a corner. He was dressed in a belted trench coat, and was standing in the corner of a room, facing the wall, with his hands over his ears. It was devastating: you could hardly sum up the tragedy of Soviet life better, without so much as mentioning it!

Being a literalist, I proffered my little uncalled-for explanation nonetheless. 'So it's a Soviet man, as you can tell from his old-fashioned clothes, and he's been driven into a corner, and he's shutting out the noise of life, or maybe the propaganda . . . yes?'

Garik gave his usual ironic smile, managing not quite to suggest I was an idiot. 'Probably,' he drawled amiably, and proposed a toast to art.

'Garik doesn't like his work being interpreted,' said Inna. 'It's just what it is.'

His old friend Grisha was in a very generous mood. 'Garik is a genius, Angus. He sees things that we don't see. Let's drink to my old friend, Garik . . .'

'Could that drawing be published?' I asked.

'Well . . .,' said Inna, 'he might slip something like that into *Chemistry and Life*, but it's unlikely. The censors know exactly what he's trying to say there!'

'Hey, I know what it is!' Garik laughed. 'It's a censor standing in a corner with his hands on his ears . . .'

At some point I mentioned the singer Okudzhava, the bard of the Arbat, some of whose songs I had learned to play on the guitar.

'We all love Okudzhava,' said Zoya. 'But it's Vysotsky you really need to listen to if you want to know about our life. Even the Politburo listen to him – and cry into their vodka.'

'Forget our newspapers and TV,' Grisha added, 'forget even your BBC, forget all the books written by "experts" on the Soviet Union. If you want to know about what we all feel and what life is like here, listen to Vysotsky!'

Vladimir Vysotsky was an actor at the avant-garde Taganka Theatre, but he was known primarily for his gritty songs, performed in a voice that sounded as if he didn't so much smoke fifty cigarettes a day as stuff the burning tobacco in his throat and douse it with several bottles of vodka. Only a few actual records of his songs were released in the Soviet Union, but hundreds of them were in circulation, recorded at parties and impromptu concerts, or from the few discs released in the West. These performances were tape-recorded, and re-recorded, and passed from hand to hand – the same way banned literature was typed up in barely legible carbon copies and passed around.

'There isn't a single section of society that doesn't adore him,' said Grisha, starting a list on his fingers, 'because he is Russian, he's Soviet, he's proletarian, he's an intellectual . . .' He splashed some vodka in the general direction of our glasses and added: 'Brezhnev loves him, they say, because his songs sum up the entire fucking mess he's created! And everyone else loves him . . .'

'. . . for the same reason,' Garik interjected.

'To Vysotsky!'

The Polish vodka was judged to be slightly better than the Stolichnaya, which, they insisted, was made from sawdust these days.

Garik found a cassette of Vysotsky songs and stuck it in a player, but the quality – of the recording, and certainly of my Russian – was so poor that I couldn't understand a thing. I decided to listen to him properly at a later date, with a clear head and Grisha's dictionary of slang. At this particular moment I was having trouble understanding why the little glass in my hand always seemed to be full of a colourless liquid, no matter how often I emptied it. I was in no state even to repeat my brilliant new thesis about how it may have been precisely the oppressiveness of the Soviet system that led to great art, though I did try.

Inna set a kettle to boil on an electric ring that was barely visible in its corner, behind heads, busts, tins and tubes of paint, and various artistic implements. Then she brought a pot of tea and plonked it on the patterned oilcloth, amid the cigarette ash and remains of bread and cheese. We looked at it, and opened the Bulgarian wine.

There were a number of other pressing issues still to resolve, so it was two or maybe three o'clock before we all finally got to our feet and stumbled up past the four padlocked doors and out into the snow-filled street. Meeting the rush of sub-zero Moscow air after a full eight-hour shift of hard philosophising in a basement is rather exhilarating. For the first couple of seconds you remember that air has oxygen in it, not just tobacco smoke. Then there are a few moments when you try to fathom why the Arbat, which was fairly motionless when you last saw it, is now whirling round you like a high-speed merry-go-round. And then you fall head first into a snowdrift, which feels like a duvet that you never want to emerge from.

In all the years we knew them our hosts would never allow us to walk off alone to find transport home – especially so late at night, when the metro was no longer running. So we all drifted somehow along Sivtsev Vrazhek Lane, the red star on the top of the foreign ministry guiding us towards the Garden Ring Road. Taxis, being state-run, were almost non-existent in Moscow in those days, and if one did appear there wasn't the remotest chance that it would stop for you. The normal practice was to flag down a passing car, and Garik or Grisha would always be there to assess the driver and agree a price for us in advance, before waving us off. On this night, there were few cars of any description around, but a snowplough eventually hove into view, half-heartedly sweeping and gritting the road. Garik decided this would be our taxi.

'But isn't he working? I mean ... he's gritting the roads, isn't he?'

'Pah! He'll rather have 15 roubles,' said Garik and entered into a brief discussion with the driver. Next thing we knew, Neilian and I were in the passenger seat, and the snowplough was racing, as fast as a snowplough can race, along the 25 kilometres from the foreign ministry to Yasenevo.

We could have been riding in a horse-drawn carriage, for all I knew – whirling along on the famous troika that Gogol likened to Russia herself.

The flying road turns into smoke beneath you, bridges thunder and pass, everything falls back and is left behind! Russia, where are you speeding to? Answer me! All things on earth fly by and other peoples and states look askance as they step aside and give her the right of way.
(*Dead Souls*, 1842).

Yes, this was surely why I had spent five years studying Russian! To fly through the streets of Moscow on a snowplough in the dead of night. Gee-up, coach-driver! How could I describe this spell the country had put on me? That intoxicating mixture of politics, literature, language and ideas that I had studied at university was spread out before me now in the flesh. I had longed for Moscow like Chekhov's three sisters. Now

I wanted to be Levin from *Anna Karenina* (but feared I was more likely to bumble around like Pierre from *War and Peace*). I wanted to lose my head at Patriarch's Ponds (though maybe not so literally as Bulgakov's Berlioz in *The Master and Margarita*) and see the house where Zhivago came to life in Pasternak's brain. I wanted to walk the same streets as Sakharov, in the shadow of the Lubyanka, and understand that cycle of history that started with Blok's revolutionary *Twelve* and ended in Solzhenitsyn's *First Circle*. How would I ever get inside that crazy, drunken, impetuous, remorseful, loving, wide-open, tight-shut heart? I wanted to absorb that mystery of Russia, that inexpressible essence that I knew was there but could not define. I wanted to learn to speak Russian flawlessly, though I reckoned I would need a tongue operation before I could get some of the sounds right. And I wanted to write, too, but there was an admonitory passage from my Russian studies that nagged me and nagged me. It came from Isaac Babel's short story, *Awakening*. The young Babel shows one of his first attempts to an old man, a proofreader on the *Odessa News* who becomes his mentor. The man points at a tree with his stick . . .

'What tree is that?'
I did not know.
'What grows on this bush?'
I did not know that either. We were passing through the square on Alexander Avenue. The old man pointed out all the trees with his stick, caught me by the shoulder whenever a bird flew by, and made me listen to the different bird-notes.
'What bird is singing now?'
I could give no reply. The names of trees and birds, the division of them into species, where they were flying, where the sun rises, when the dew falls the heaviest, all these things were hidden from me.
'And yet you dare to write? A man who doesn't live in nature like a stone or an animal lives in it, will never write two lines worth anything. Your landscapes are like descriptions of stage scenery.'

At least Babel had an excuse – he was only fourteen. I did spend the next two years with my Observer's books of birds and trees, pacing through the forest near Yasenevo, trying to come up to the standards of Babel's mentor. But to this day I forget the names of most wild flowers from one summer to the next, and it was only last year that I finally worked out there is a difference between a chaffinch's song and its call.

If I couldn't even memorise something as simple as the names of common flora and fauna, what hope did I have of understanding something as inscrutable as Russia?

4

Who Is Last?

SADLY THE QUEST for Russia's soul usually took second place to the search for food. This became a major preoccupation, worsened for us by the fact that we lacked certain things that almost all Russians had: firstly, *blat*, or connections – a network of friends in the right places; secondly, a granny to stand in line for us; and thirdly, basic knowledge of the system – or rather, of how to deal with the fact that there was no system. The Soviet planned economy turned out to be barely controlled chaos, further muddled by everyday corruption and sheer bloody-mindedness.

In a Western country shopping has a certain rationale to it. You want to buy something, so you go to the shops, normally to one that you expect to stock the product you're interested in. In the Soviet Union there was no point in doing that because the thing you wanted was rarely on sale, or at least not where and when you might expect it to be. So you went out shopping with a totally open mind, no plans or expectations, and enough money to buy huge quantities of whatever goody happened to turn up. It was a game of chance. Indeed, the string shopping bag most Russians kept in their pockets was known as *avoska* – a 'lucky bag'.

The mere existence of a queue snaking along a pavement outside a store was taken as a good sign. Here we soon learned two useful expressions. One was 'What are they giving?' (or sometimes 'What are they throwing out?'). In other words, what is on sale? Often the people in the line didn't know; they'd just joined because if there was a queue it meant that something decent was on sale at the other end of it. The other expression was 'Who's last?' This was to ascertain who you would be standing behind in the line. You could then go away for ten or fifteen minutes and perhaps join another queue as well, and be able to re-join the first one by asking your place-marker to confirm you hadn't just turned up but had already booked your place. Such etiquette was essential to avoid fisticuffs with irate shoppers, or with the self-appointed 'guardians of the queue' who inevitably pitched up to police the ranks.

We once saw dozens of people walking about with piles of boxes of Dixan washing powder, imported from West Germany. If something was *importny* then it was automatically a must-have purchase. And if it was imported from the west, you might be prepared to kill someone to get it. Naturally we asked one happy purchaser of Dixan where they had bought it, and set off with most of the other passers-by to the shop, only to find a half-mile queue outside it. After a few days Moscow's supply of Dixan seemed to run out, and you no longer saw anyone walking about with it. After that it was never seen again.

Russians never bought dainty portions of cheese or cold meats. If they came across their favourite brands of butter or sausage they bought enough to sustain them through a nuclear war. We once chanced upon Ceylon tea and bought four small packets, thinking that would last us a few weeks. Our friends were aghast when we told them: 'What have you done? No one ever buys less than fifty packets – plus another fifty for their friends!' We couldn't help thinking that this kind of attitude helped to create the shortage in the first place.

Certain goods were only on sale in a tiny number of stores, all at opposite ends of the city. There was precisely one frozen-food shop, for instance, selling bags of deep-frozen vegetables from Poland. All the 'people's republics' had big department stores – with names like Leipzig, Belgrade or Bucharest – and were reputed to sell fashionable furniture and clothes. There was even a Kabul, where we would eventually buy a beautiful Afghan carpet very cheaply. But you had to have plenty of time on your hands to brave the hassle of getting to these shops, so far from the beaten track, on the off-chance that they might have something worthwhile. On the other hand, sometimes you came across a nice surprise: you'd just have emerged from a metro station, and a little truck would pull up at the side of the road. Then a trader would set up a table, and start selling cabbages, or chicken legs, or jars of preserved fruit. On those days, people arrived home with bulging 'lucky bags', and eyes full of gratitude and wonder, that some unexpected treat had dropped out of the communist heaven for them.

Shoppers were often baffled by the items that turned up, and were quite unembarrassed to ask about them. One day a man saw me coming out of a wine shop with a roll of aluminium foil in my hand (don't ask me why it was on sale in a wine shop). 'What's that?' he asked me.

'Aluminium foil.'

He shrugged his shoulders and fingered it. 'What do you do with it?'

'Well . . . you can cook things in it, a chicken for instance, or you can wrap food in it – for a picnic, or to keep it in the fridge . . .'

I guess my description was inadequate: I didn't actually explain that the foil was rolled up. The man weighed it in his hand and gave me a very queer look, as if to say, 'How the fuck can you cook a chicken in a *stick*?', and shambled away.

On another occasion our local shop received a load of cans from Czechoslovakia. Even while they were being unpacked from their cardboard boxes a crowd formed. I had never heard of 'Lečo' but I could understand most of the ingredients on the label and worked out that it was a kind of ratatouille with pieces of sausage in it. Most of the Russians were stumped by the Latin letters and resorted to turning the tins round and round in their hands, shaking them and listening to them. Then one man pushed the crowd aside, picked up half a dozen cans and strode off to the cash-desk. This improved morale, and several people followed suit. Others still stood shaking their heads. Then one woman declared with great authority: 'I don't know what it is, but I recommend frying it up with onions and serving it with soured cream.' Within minutes the boxes were all empty.

The actual presence of something that appeared to be on sale didn't necessarily mean you would be able to persuade a shop assistant to sell it to you. My wife and I once ventured into a vegetable shop having seen a customer emerge from it with a bag full of cucumbers. 'We'd like some cucumbers, please,' Neilian said to the girl behind the counter.

'We don't have any.'

'But we just saw someone who'd bought some . . .'

'We don't have any.'

My wife and I had a quick confab about whether to probe further or to accept that the cucumbers were sold out. In the meantime another young woman came in, asked for cucumbers, and was promptly given a bag full of them from under the counter. So we went back.

'We'd like some of those please.'

'Some of what?'

'Cucumbers. Like the ones you just sold to that woman.'

'We don't have any.'

'Yes you do.'

There was no reply. The girl was now very studiously examining her fingernails, which had suddenly assumed enormous importance to her.

She even had a little mirror, and started holding her hand up to it so she could see just how lovely her red nail-varnish was.

As Christmas was approaching, we went to a huge department store called *Detsky Mir*, or Children's World, near the KGB headquarters on Dzerzhinsky Square, to buy something to send back to our nephew and niece in Britain. The store was rather grand inside, with massive wooden doors and high ceilings, like Harrods but without the contents. It felt like most of the population of Moscow had squeezed into it. It was so busy you didn't so much walk around as allow yourself to be borne on a swirling tide of human beings, going wherever the current took you. There were no mobile phones in those days: if you lost your partner in this ocean, you would never see them again, you would just have to report them as drowned. We managed to keep afloat and near each other by holding hands – to the disgust of an enormous woman with her hair in a bun who thrust her belly against my back and ordered me to let go of my wife's hand because we were taking up too much room.

The tide swept us into the 'children's knitwear' section and we found ourselves at a counter behind which a salesgirl was standing with her arms folded, leaning lightly against a pile of boxes and pretending to whistle through her pouted lips. She appeared to be in a huff about something. Perhaps someone had dared to ask her what was in the boxes. A woman with a tornado of peroxide hair balanced above her head was screaming at her, while her husband beat his fist on the counter in solidarity. A petulant lock of fair hair dangled in the salesgirl's eye, and she tried to flick it aside without letting it appear that she was losing control of the situation. Behind me people shoved and argued, and anxiously asked, 'What's on sale, what's on sale?' The peroxide lady was now crimson in the face and bellowing at the salesgirl: 'Have you no conscience? Impudent hussy!'

At that moment a sensible man muscled his way to the counter and asked the girl in a very restrained voice whether she had a size 42. This had an astonishing effect on her, as she now had a chance to demonstrate to the cackling farmyard how she expected to be treated. She pushed herself away from the boxes and ambled with sexy, catwalk elegance over to a pile of black garments in the corner. For just a few seconds the men in the crowd, at least, had something to take their minds off their dreary lives: this was the closest the Soviet Union got to pornography. '*Pozhaluista* [Here you are],' she purred indifferently as she laid a size 42 in front of the polite man. Now we could see that what she was selling was a kind of jogging pants or tracksuit bottoms. The man decided to buy a pair, and the assistant pulled the garment from the snatching hands of at least four other people, and wrapped it in brown paper. For the customer, however, this was only the start of the transaction, for in Soviet shops you had to stand in line not once but twice for every item. First you queued to choose what you wanted to buy; then you queued at a cash-desk (which could be some distance away) to pay for it and receive a little chit; then you battled your way back to the first counter to pick up the item.

This crazy principle applied even in food shops where you might have to queue separately for, say, milk, cheese and eggs, then go to a cash-desk for three separate receipts, and finally return to the three sections to pick up your purchases. A transaction which could theoretically have taken two minutes was thereby transformed into nine different processes totalling half an hour at least. It was at times like this that one seriously pondered whether the Soviet way of life had been devised by raving lunatics.

We didn't need black jogging pants, so turned to fight our way out to the space beyond the crowd where the air was less steamy and garlicky. I glanced back briefly and noticed the salesgirl prepare herself for the rest of this day that had started so badly. For a moment she turned her back to the customers, closed her eyes, drew in a very slow, deep breath that made her a couple of inches taller, then turned around and asked, quite calmly, 'Who's next?'

In the toy department we found little to bring joy to the hearts of our nephew and niece, nothing to compete with the fancy toys people would be buying them back home. But we did see a couple of traditional, old-fashioned toys – some papier-mâché masks and a big inflatable rubber frog. They were in different sections, and each section was served by a different cash-desk, so Neilian and I split up. It was hard to tell who was standing in line and who was just milling around, but eventually I discovered the end of the queue I needed. A hundred people were ahead of me. I took off my fur hat in anticipation of a long, hot wait. Some forty minutes later I reached the cashier, who calculated the price by clicking the beads on an enormous wooden abacus and took my money. Soon I was clutching a little slip to prove I had paid my two roubles and thirty kopecks. Then the real problems began. Not surprisingly, the masks were the least popular item on sale at my counter. The only things anyone was interested in were illuminated plastic red stars for the top of a New Year's tree, and a special appliance containing a hole in the centre for the tree and an electrical socket for the lights; when you plugged it into the mains the whole caboodle – tree, lights and red star – revolved. This was quite an achievement for the Soviet consumer-goods industry. Judging by the crowd, thousands of Moscow apartments would have spinning trees this year. Unfortunately, most of them didn't work, and the two assistants were absorbed with testing all the red stars and tree stands, while assiduously ignoring any queries related to anything else. My plight was desperate. Tottering on tiptoes behind three rings of customers around the counter, I could barely even see the salesgirls. After about fifteen minutes' futile pushing and pleading to be allowed in to pick up my papier-mâché masks, I was still no closer – and then the two assistants decided it was lunchtime and disappeared. It took another ten minutes for a replacement to arrive, and another ten before I managed to get her attention, by frantically waving my sweaty, wilting chitty in the air. 'Please,' I pleaded, 'you only have to pick them up, it'll only take a second.' I must have looked close to tears because the girl actually stopped what she was doing, picked up my masks, and even wrapped them, though I told her not to bother.

Suddenly I found myself expelled from the crowd, like a champagne cork popping from a bottle, and I saw my wife stumbling zombie-like through another throng towards me, clutching her rubber frog. We met wordlessly and headed for the door.

5

Oh! Bananas!

SO WHO WAS this Vladimir Vysotsky chap that everyone raved about? Grisha obtained a cassette for us, and I spent days trying to work out the words, and beyond that, the meaning, of his songs. It wasn't easy. His lyrics were full of prison slang and allusions to Russian experiences that were beyond my ken. For many of his songs he adopted a kind of jailbird persona, and it turned out that some Russians actually believed he had been in prison, though he hadn't. His singing voice was astonishing – you could imagine the tendons standing out on his neck as he strained every sinew to produce an unmistakable, gut-wrenching sound.

The first song that struck me, partly because it was copied from a professional Western recording so I could actually make out the lyrics, was a spine-chilling tale about a man who tattooed his chest 'during the period of the personality cult' with a profile of Stalin. Like so many Soviet citizens the man had believed unthinkingly in communism, but ended up in a Siberian prison camp, breaking rocks in a quarry. It was here that he and a cell-mate decided to get their tattoos done, so that Stalin 'would hear our hearts breaking'. Then came the anti-Stalin thaw – 'it turned out I was branded in vain' – and he sat in a steaming Russian bathhouse screaming to the attendant to make it hotter and hotter, thrashing his skin with birch twigs to try to erase 'the legacy of those dark times'. Ouch! No wonder he was so popular. That was the history of communism in one song: idealism, betrayal of those ideals, oppression and terror, and an irrational lingering belief that somehow Stalin would hear your cry and save you – and then the discovery that what you had believed in was all a sham.

In 1974 the state record company Melodiya released an EP with just four innocuous Vysotsky songs. But millions of illegal recordings circulated in the country, and he is thought to have written about 600 in total. He touched on every aspect of Soviet life – sometimes savaging the communist system and its bureaucracy, but sometimes just poking fun at the everyday tribulations of ordinary Russian people. Most songs had a 'character' – the brilliant neurosurgeon who 'unfortunately was a Jew'; the university lecturers packed off on a bus to pick potatoes on a collective farm; the drunk in the police station who keeps insisting that his mate, who keeps nodding off, is only acting strange because he's 'seen the light'; the inmate of a lunatic asylum who writes to the TV editors because he's nonplussed by the incredible things he sees on a programme about scientific discoveries; the man planning to go on a trip to the West who is frightened out of his wits by the lecture he's given by the KGB about 'what's allowed over there and what isn't' and their dire warnings about the curvaceous spies who will try to seduce him; the ex-convict who gets a taxi-driver to give him a tour of the prisons where he suffered, and dreams of the day when there will be no jails and camps in Russia.

One of his songs – about the privileges enjoyed by foreigners – made us feel guilty. After a few months we discovered a special hard-currency store on Dorogomilovskaya Street known as *Beriozka* (Birch Tree). Even here not everything was available all the time, but with fruit and vegetables in abundance, fresh pork and beef, chickens, imported cheeses and salamis, even frozen suckling pigs, very few Russians would ever have seen such a display in their lives. The customers were mainly diplomats and foreign correspondents. We didn't use it much, partly out of solidarity with our Russian friends and partly because we couldn't afford it. But I remember going there one winter's day to buy some foreign wine to take to friends who had invited us to dinner . . . and also some toilet rolls, which were almost impossible to find in ordinary shops. (When they did appear, people would buy far more than they could stuff into a 'lucky bag', so they would loop them together with string and wear them as a necklace, all the way home.) A Scandinavian couple were leaving the Beriozka shop at the same time as us, and I held the door open for them. Their trolley was stacked with boxes of provisions and two cases of canned beer. In the street a woman in a woolly headscarf was passing. She turned her head abruptly, and I heard her gasp two words as she headed off into the gloomy winter night: '*Oy! Banany!*' Sure enough, in pride of place on top of the diplomats' trolley was a cheery fistful of bananas – an almost unheard-of delicacy.

We could also get into restaurants more easily than Russians. Traditionally, the best Moscow restaurants had a sign saying 'NO TABLES' hanging permanently on the door, but flashing a foreign passport at the uniformed doorman was often a way to persuade him to let you in. You then sat in an almost empty restaurant, while the serving staff glared at you for having disturbed their evening. Russians didn't even have that option, unless they bribed. Vysotsky put it this way:

> The people were complaining and complaining
> The people wanted justice, that was all:
> 'Hey, c'mon now, what the hell, we were standing first in this bleedin'
>   queue!
> And them that came after us are in there scoffing!'
>
> The manager came out to explain:
> 'Please, dear people, just go away.
> The people in there eating are foreigners.
> And you, excuse me, who the hell are you?!'

6

Forty Degrees

MOST PEOPLE WHO have been to Moscow in the winter like to boast about how cold it was. But unless you were there on the last day of 1978, forget it. Whatever you experienced was peanuts. This winter was worse than the ones that defeated Hitler's Wehrmacht and Napoleon's Grande Armée. This was a winter where car keys snapped off in the lock, and men's lips stuck to the frozen metal as they injudiciously tried to defrost them with their breath.

The temperature began to fall steadily from around zero in the middle of December, to minus forty Celsius (which happens to be minus forty Fahrenheit too) at the end of the year. We couldn't stop staring at the thermometer outside our kitchen window, watching the red line slip lower and lower until it seemed it would disappear into the blob at the bottom. Outside we noticed how the sound of walking on snow changed as the temperature dropped. At first it made a light swishing noise. Then it crunched. Then it creaked. And finally, when the air was so cold that breathing became painful, it emitted a high-pitched squeal, as though warning you to get the hell back inside.

Friends brought us rolls of paper, about three inches wide, and showed us how to insulate our windows. First we stuffed all the gaps between windows and frames with cotton wool, then we mixed a paste from flour and water, and finally gummed the paper all round the windows. It didn't look elegant, but every Russian house was the same. It didn't help much either. By the end of December the layer of ice across the inside of the window was a full centimetre thick.

At a certain temperature – it may have been about minus twenty – a strange tableau unfolded outside our windows. Men, women and children gathered in the playground by the kindergarten and started whacking the snow with squash rackets like maniacs. Not for the first time, it seemed as if Russia had gone mad. I wondered if this was some weird

December ritual, like the custom of swimming in frozen ponds at New Year. But after an hour all was revealed. The squash rackets were in fact carpet beaters, and when they swept the snow aside some stunning oriental rugs appeared. Apparently the dry powdery snow was better than carpet-cleaning detergent (even supposing it had been possible to buy such a thing).

Incredibly the building of the communist future went on regardless of the approaching ice age. Yasenevo's horizon bristled with cranes, which continued to operate right through December. If we rubbed a hole in the ice on our window we could see a new polyclinic going up next to our apartment block. A crane lowered huge concrete panels into position, while men and women wearing thick jackets and caps with long flaps to cover their necks steadied them and welded them fast, with a blizzard blowing around them. I hope they were paid well, for this was truly heroic work. Day by day the building grew. Nearby, lorry-drivers kept their engines running constantly, for at minus-thirty they might never be able to restart them. (By the end of the month they weren't just running the engines but lighting fires under them.) I kept expecting the project to be abandoned, but every day at eight o'clock the cranes and diggers would rumble into life and workers would appear, almost immobile in their many layers of clothing. Charcoal braziers flamed up in the morning darkness. Lights went on in the cluster of blue and orange workmen's huts. 'GLORY TO LABOUR' said a red banner strung up on a neighbouring building.

Christmas wasn't officially celebrated in the USSR, either on 25 December or on the Orthodox Christmas Day of 7 January. But New Year was approaching – the biggest family celebration in the Soviet calendar. Despite the weather, there was plenty of warmth and good cheer around. Fir-tree markets sprang up all over the place, so those revolving stands would not go to waste. Progress held its end-of-year *kapustnik*, literally a 'cabbage show' – a kind of revue at which editors and translators performed sketches and silly songs about how over-worked they were. At the very end of the year the shops would make a big effort to stock up with festive food – ducks and turkeys would even appear – but in the days before Christmas they suddenly became cavern-ously empty. Perhaps they were holding things back for the end-of-year splurge. You could have played football in our local *universam*. There were hardly any shoppers, because there was nothing to buy. We searched all over the city but could find not a scrap of meat. The only vegetables were onions, carrots and beetroot. You could buy one variety of tasteless cheese. The only thing in abundance was green mandarins from Georgia, which seemed to be on sale on every street corner, shining like fairy lights in the snow.

So as we imagined our families back home tucking into traditional Christmas dinner, we conjured up what we could from those ingredients – lentil soup, followed by a half-hearted pizza – and ate it at our kitchen table while gazing out at the Stakhanovites still toiling away on that polyclinic. It was, I guess, a good lesson in Christian humility.

In the evening we set off to the central telegraph office on Gorky Street to call home and listen to them choking on their turkey and stuffing and Brussels sprouts and roast potatoes and Christmas pudding and trifle – not that we were envious or anything. The central telegraph office was quite a striking building from the outside – a cross between Art Deco and Soviet constructivism. Inside it was wood-panelled and dingy, but otherwise just the kind of place you would want to spend Christmas evening, and just as amusing as Morecambe and Wise. Two young women were on duty – one was taking telegrams, the other putting through long-distance calls. Both were wearing coats, scarves and hats. One or two customers were standing at high writing desks filling in telegram forms with the nib-pens and ink provided. Those wishing to make a call had to fill in a slip of paper stating the town, number and duration of call required. We ordered five minutes, knowing we would be cut off immediately when the time elapsed, and sat down to wait to be called to one of the telephone booths. There were six of them. In booth number 1 a woman had a bad line to her mother in some god-forsaken village in Tambov region.

'Mam! Mam!' she was crying into the receiver. 'I can't hear you. How are you? Eh? Mam! I said, "How are you?" What? I can't hear you. Mam, mam . . . Eh? No, I said, "How are you?"'

At this point the telephonist told another customer that her call to Leningrad was through, and she should go to booth 3. Meanwhile the husband of the woman in booth 1 complained to the telephonist that his wife couldn't hear anything – as if we didn't all know. 'What am I supposed to do about it?' said the telephonist in a sarcastic voice. 'It's a bad line.'

The line from booth 3 to Leningrad seemed to be good enough, but the caller was having difficulty hearing because of the woman in booth 1, who was still demanding to know, at the top of her voice, how her mother was. 'Mam, I wrote you a letter,' she tried, for variation, but that also seemed to be inaudible, so she reverted to the original question: 'Mam, mam! How are you?'

Then the woman from booth 3 came and hammered on the door of booth 1: 'Be quiet, will you? I can't hear anything!'

The woman in booth 1 tried a few more questions, added for good measure that she herself was fine, and concluded: 'Mam! Mam! I'll call for another chat next week.' Then she and her husband marched straight out of the office without paying, informing the telephonist as they passed that they hadn't been able to hear a word. Good for them, I thought. Nice to see customers standing up for their rights. But I thought too soon. As soon as the couple had gone, the telephonist called the central exchange and told them not to accept any more calls in future to a certain number in the village of Krasivka, Tambov region, because the customers had refused to pay. Poor people! Little did they know that a mere telephonist had such power, and that the next time they tried to phone dear old mam, they would be told it was impossible.

It was our turn. We were ushered in to the blighted booth 1, and after much whirring and clicking, a reasonably clear connection was made to Scotland. After precisely five minutes of festive banter the line was cut. Christmas Day was over.

A few days later we ventured out of doors again to call Volodya and Seryozha from a phone booth near the *universam*. It was like standing inside a deep freezer. Half an inch of hoar frost covered all the metal surfaces, and icicles hung from the ceiling. I was terrified my mouth might touch the frozen receiver and stick to it. Eventually we got through and arranged to visit them on New Year's Eve. Calls from phone boxes were unlimited, in theory, but within half a minute several yeti in the queue outside were tapping their two-kopeck pieces on the window to hurry us up.

At forty degrees of frost, the 31st was the coldest day in Moscow since 1940, and before that 1892. In the suburbs, like Yasenevo, it was even colder. The plastic radio receiver in our kitchen broadcast emergency appeals to citizens – not to allow small children to go outside on their own, and not to drink alcohol to keep out the cold. (At New Year? Some hope!) We waited twenty minutes for a bus. Five more and we'd have needed a hearse. Every inhalation froze the nostrils. The fluid on the eyeballs became viscous. Escaping breath turned white on our eyelashes and hats. My coat turned to cardboard. If I had tried to speak my jaw might have snapped off.

At Volodya's and Seryozha's it was cosy and warm, and – as if to confound every story you ever heard about Soviet food shortages – they had prepared a delicious meal. We had *zakuski* – Russian starters of various salads, meat in aspic, pickled herring, cabbage pie, tinned sprats (a rare delicacy these days) and bread, followed by chicken cooked in Georgian herbs and boiled potatoes served with soured cream and chopped dill and parsley. Then came tea and cakes, sweets, jam, and at midnight we drank Soviet champagne. We listened to the chimes of Big Ben on the BBC rather than the Kremlin chimes. Our friends proposed the kind of long, sincere toasts that make you blush with embarrassment.

After three months I was beginning to learn something new about Russia, and maybe about myself. However awful things were on the surface – the shortages, the queues, the day-to-day aggravation and humiliation, the political suppression and the freezing cold – Russians didn't seem less happy than British people. For one thing, they had developed mechanisms to help them cope with the shortages – hence the ability to serve up a lovely meal despite the bleak emptiness in the food stores. They also had seemingly endless endurance, that allowed them to withstand such bleak, bitter winters. But above all, it seemed to me – perhaps naïvely – that they were less dependent than Westerners on *things* for happiness. Of course they all dreamed of well-stocked shops, but you didn't actually *need* stores bursting to the seams with fancy foods and consumer goods in order to be happy, because there was also joy in the small, simple pleasures of life. When you stopped expecting something, anything you received felt great. Over sixty years Russians' expectations had been lowered, and now happiness existed at a lower level of prosperity: instead of looking for it in the acquisition of wealth or consumer goods (though you naturally welcomed whatever came your way), you found it instead in friendship, sharing, nature, laughter.

7

Here Comes the Sun

SOMEHOW WE MANAGED to survive the winter without losing any body parts to frostbite or being forced to retreat to Paris or Berlin. This was fortunate, for in March we were able to witness a great political event, as the country's leaders bravely submitted themselves to re-election. The Supreme Soviet was what the communists pretended was a parliament, and to make it seem really important they made it huge – with 1,500 members. Their only duty was to turn up in the Kremlin for a couple of days each year, buy nice things in the special shops, and vote unanimously for laws already decided by the Communist Party, which wasn't elected by anybody.

Now, the Russian word for 'election' is *vybory*, which is just the plural of 'choice', but in this case they were using a fairly loose definition of the word, in that there wasn't actually a choice on the ballot paper. There were 1,500 seats available, and precisely 1,500 candidates, all of whom were definitely going to be 'elected'. Voters could, it's true, strike out the name of the candidate and write in a name of their own choice, thereby also electing to spend some time with the local KGB. According to one of those lame Soviet jokes that we heard around this time, God created Adam, then created Eve from one of Adam's ribs, and said to him: 'Now, please, choose yourself a wife.'

Despite the lack of competition, every night TV news showed candidates at election meetings in factories, and the candidates spoke of their party's achievements while in power, and plans for the future – just like in a real election. Pictures of our local candidate were pasted up all over Yasenevo. On voting day triumphant marches blared from loudspeakers on every building, and big red arrows marked the way to the polling station.

I went along to see Soviet democracy in action. An official showed me round. It looked just like a polling station in any country – but better, really, because stalls had been set up where you could buy some scarce food products after casting your ballot. I told the official I thought that was a very nice touch – we didn't do that in Britain. He showed me a ballot paper, and emphatically explained how secret the voting was: in the curtained booth nobody could possibly spy on you to see how you voted. He asked me what ballot papers were like in Britain, and I said they looked similar, except they had lots of candidates on them. 'Ah,' he said, 'so basically the same system.'

I noticed that voters were just picking up their papers and walking straight to the ballot box and dropping them in.

'So, does an unmarked paper count as a vote for the candidate?' I asked.

'Oh, yes,' he said.

I was about to suggest that the vote wasn't really very secret then, because the only reason to use the booth at all was if one wanted to score out the name of the candidate, or perhaps draw a Mickey Mouse face on the ballot paper, but he interrupted with a question of his own: 'Do you have secret voting booths like these?'

'Yes,' I said. He looked extremely doubtful, and immediately ushered me out with a cheery 'All the best then, goodbye.'

A few days later *Pravda* revealed that 99.99 per cent of the electorate had taken part, and all candidates had been returned. Here's the interesting thing, though: 74 ballot papers (out of nearly 200 million) had been spoiled, and – wait for it – 185,000 people had actually voted against the candidates by scoring their names out! I wonder what happened to them.

Springtime in Moscow was over in a flash. It took little over a week in April to go from snowy, or rather, grubby winter to glorious summer. You could almost watch the buds unfolding on the trees as the temperature soared. Very conveniently Vladimir Lenin had been born on 22 April – perfect timing for the authorities to mark his birthday every year by forcing all the workers into the streets to clean them up after the winter, for no pay. This 'voluntary' work was known as a *subbotnik*, from the Russian for Saturday.

The clean-up was certainly needed. For six or seven months every public area had been permanently covered with snow. Only the pathways had been cleared, and snow was piled up on the grassy areas. No cigarette ends, rubbish or dog shit had been cleared away for more than half a year. It all suddenly appeared in April when the snow melted, and Moscow looked as if Jackson Pollock had been let loose on the lawns with a particularly foul-smelling box of paints.

The weather for this year's *subbotnik* was superb. Muscovites took to the streets as though emerging from hibernation. With that indomitable ability Russians have to make the best of a bad lot, they turned this day of compulsory work into a day of fun in the sunshine. By nine o'clock the city was teeming with people, armed with rakes and brushes, scouring the ground like beachcombers. At last they were out in their summer clothes. The men were in shirt sleeves, and most of the women had abandoned their winter mohair hats in favour of white cotton headscarves. Jackets and handbags hung on the branches of nearby trees. Friends and neighbours leaned on their rakes, chatting and sunning themselves. Little groups of women even burst into song – performing *chastushki*, funny rhyming peasant songs, with bawdy lyrics made up on the spot, while an audience gathered and clapped them on. It felt more like an ancient celebration of spring than a communist tribute to Lenin. I suddenly realised that throughout the long Moscow winter you see no bright colours outdoors. Everything is monochrome – grey sky, white snow, black roads, and colourless buildings barely visible in the winter gloom. The *subbotnik* was the day when the grainy black-and-white film finally burst into Technicolor.

Throughout the day piles of dirt were heaped along the sides of the roads, to be picked up later by trucks. By evening almost the whole of suburban Moscow was looking dry and freshly swept. Even the tired, yellow grass, brushed into life and crew-cut, seemed to be growing greener. Moscow was ready for the summer.

In the days after the *subbotnik*, as the warm weather held, the good citizens of Yasenevo continued to beautify the place. An old proverb (actually an observation by French travellers) says, 'Scratch a Russian and you'll find a Tatar'. But you could also say, 'Scratch a Muscovite and you'll find a peasant', for throughout the spring and summer the people of Yasenevo contrived to turn our ugly socialist housing scheme into something resembling a Russian village. Trees that had been black skeletons all winter turned out to be luscious poplars, limes, larches and birches – the foliage so thick that the housing blocks were almost hidden. People planted bushes along the sides of the pathways that crisscrossed the micro-district, and regularly watered all the verges, not distinguishing between flowers and weeds, but encouraging everything green to grow rank and high. There was no such thing as landscaping, but rather a wild, untidy proliferation of long grasses, ferns, nettles, white and purple clover, dandelions and buttercups – like portions of virgin steppeland transplanted to the city. As a result, however ugly and monotonous the buildings themselves might be, in among them it was shady, fragrant and quiet. Bees droned around the flowers, and birds added their commentary from the bushes. The ramshackle telephone boxes stood half-hidden under leafy trees. *Babushki* sat on their benches by the porches, rested their chins on walking sticks, and exchanged gossip. It was wonderful! Micro-district number five had become a village, and the busy main road and city were somewhere far, far away. Once again the Russians proved that their greatest asset was adaptability: they took what they were given by the state and made it their own.

As I strolled back from the *universam* one afternoon with my string bag full of bread and onions, two men standing in the shade of a tree called to me: 'Wanna be the third?' I was thrilled. Not only did I understand it (they were looking for the traditional third person to share a bottle of vodka they'd bought), but they had taken me for someone who might be willing to partake. I didn't – but it felt good. Accepted, at last!

Not so accepted, though, when it came to joining the workers' parade in Red Square on May Day. We were invited by friends from the Pushkin language institute, who had red armbands and special papers, with official stamps, to show they had the right to represent their institute at the parade. They thought it would be no bother for my wife and me to join them. It was another scorching day. We met up at the Belorussky station, about three and a half kilometres north of Red Square and joined the tens of thousands of marchers. It was all good fun – balloons, banners, and music blaring from loudspeakers. Down on Red Square Leonid Brezhnev and the Politburo – that's not the name of a pop group but the Soviet leadership – were lined up on top of the Lenin mausoleum, waving their hands like wooden levers at what they called 'demonstrators', this being the only part of the world where people went out to demonstrate *for* their government. Some even marched with portraits of the Politburo. Others carried pictures of Marx, Engels or Lenin, or just red placards saying Work, or Peace, or Long Live the Communist Party. As we progressed down Gorky Street our friends' papers were checked at every intersection by stewards and they managed to persuade them to allow us to continue. I held one leg of a *Miru Mir* (Peace to the World) banner, but it wasn't much of a disguise. As we got closer to Red Square the checks became stricter, and we were finally told that was it: sorry comrades, but without an armband and a stamped document you're just not proletarian enough. So much for spontaneity. We ended up, as I remember, in a snack bar just off Gorky Street, drinking vodka with two young policemen (in uniform). Much better fun.

It was the Yasenevo summer, the riot of colours and fragrances, that persuaded us to stay for a second year in Russia. The warmth made communism bearable. For just four months or so, you could almost imagine it was a normal country. Actually, for us, this was better than a normal country. Normal countries were boring. This was exotic.

There were cherries – red ones and yellow ones. Romanian tomatoes were sold by two women in kerchiefs from boxes just next to the kindergarten. Well, where else would you expect to find them? We bought mosquito nets for our windows. Short, sharp thunderstorms left the air scented like the steppe. It was fun to watch cars screech to a stop whenever the rain started: the drivers would all jump out and fit their windscreen wipers, which they kept in the glove compartment so they wouldn't get stolen. Street vendors popped up with big yellow tanks on carts, selling kvass – that tangy, yeasty Russian drink made from dark rye bread.

I even had a Damascene experience with the lady at the newspaper kiosk where I regularly went to buy *Pravda, Izvestiya* and the *Morning Star* (the British communist paper, the only foreign one available). One morning she handed me my papers and said, 'Well, that should be nineteen kopecks, but yesterday I overcharged you by two kopecks, so that will only be seventeen today.'

I was more delighted to be recognised than to be saving two kopecks. '*Spasibo* [Thank you],' I gasped, as if she had just awarded me the Order of Friendship of Peoples.

'You were away before I noticed!' she added in an apologetic tone.

What the hell! Where were all the nasty, bored, insulting, mendacious, officious, corrupt, supercilious and downright devious shop assistants? The sun seemed to have melted them into a big warm pool of decency.

Volodya and Seryozha took us in their beloved Zhiguli (or Lada) for our first glimpse of the countryside in half a year. All through the winter the car had been laid up in a garage some fifty miles from Moscow.

Volodya was a member of a 'cooperative' which was building a huge communal garage, but it wouldn't be ready for another year (and even when it was it would be a half-hour bus journey from their flat). Volodya stroked the orange paintwork as though it was a baby's head. They had been on a waiting list for years before being able to buy it. We drove around the Moscow ring road – today a multi-lane highway, but in those days a pot-holed, bumpy, two-lane country road – and then headed out westwards into the loveliest part of *Podmoskovye*, as the area around Moscow is known.

Being the loveliest part, it had of course been commandeered by the Soviet elite. Mr B.'s dacha was hidden somewhere in these pine and birch woods, and there were also high-class sanatoria and 'rest homes' for prominent composers, writers, scientists and artists. Along the roadside itself stood quaint wooden houses with carved window frames, water pumps and clucking hens: these, Volodya explained, were ordinary country folk's homes. But almost all the sideroads were marked with no-entry signs (the Russians called them 'bricks'), and some were guarded by policemen. Near the village of Zhukovka we pulled into a car park beside a food shop. Among the cars were a few foreign makes – Mercedes, Volvo, BMW – which drew murmurs of admiration from our friends. Volodya patted the gleaming bonnet of his Zhiguli defensively and strode off towards the shop. We waited outside. A man was roasting skewers of meat over a charcoal grill; beside him a woman in a white overall sold beer from a table under a pine tree. Volodya returned from the shop with only a couple of jars of fruit. He was disappointed: 'Last year we bought tinned salmon there, and also new potatoes from a peasant woman outside.' We were too early for potatoes, but several old women in gumboots and headscarves were standing near the entrance to the car park selling little bundles of parsley, dill and radishes. Another had some tiny new carrots. That was the extent of private enterprise in the Soviet Union: fresh vegetables grown on collective farm workers' personal plots and sold at the roadside, or at the official farmers' markets in town. The statistics were phenomenal: private plots accounted for just three per cent of the cultivated land, but produced a quarter of the nation's food. You would think Mr B. might have twigged there was something amiss there.

Back on the road, a low, black Zil limousine darted past us, whirring like a shell, and almost pushing our little Zhiguli into the verge. Cars belonging to the Party's central committee had MOC plates.

This one was so grand it had no plates at all. A policeman saluted as it flashed by.

In an hour or so we left the road and parked on the grass by a delightful bend in the Moskva river, near a village called Nikolina Gora. We weren't the only ones. The bank was covered with sunbathing bodies and parked cars, most of them (the cars, I mean) neatly shrouded from the sun under fitted tarpaulins – as indeed was Volodya's Zhiguli, as soon as we had taken what we needed from it. We picnicked on hard-boiled eggs, tomatoes and little warty cucumbers, then went for a swim in the river. A police launch purred by – 'checking we don't swim down to the official dachas further along the river,' said Seryozha.

In the afternoon we walked down the river bank towards a 'diplomatic beach'. 'Strictly speaking,' said Volodya, 'it's out of bounds for us. But they have a wonderful kiosk at which we once found bananas.'

Bananas again! And 'we once found'. That's what Soviet life was made of, not five-year plans and socialist achievements!

The diplomatic beach was much the same as the one where we had had our picnic, except that here the spread-eagled bodies lay beside cars with tell-tale number plates beginning with D or K, showing they belonged to diplomats and foreign correspondents. Volodya's eyes darted from car to car and settled on a Chevrolet.

'A Chevy,' he gushed.

A short distance upstream from the foreign cars, groups of young people were drinking beer and champagne, barbecuing meat, and playing loud Western music on cassette recorders. These were not diplomats, or even foreigners (who by contrast were quiet and reserved), but the Soviet *jeunesse dorée*, people who had access to hard-currency stores and were happy to flaunt it. They were tanned, flabby and voluble. Volodya's smile faded to a sneer as his eyes tracked from the Chevy, by way of a topless blonde lying prone on the grass, to a man with a heavy gold necklace, an expansive, deeply-tanned stomach, a can of Carlsberg in one hand and a dried, salted fish in the other.

'Well,' Volodya explained in his sardonic way: 'We come here for the kiosk, not the company.'

The kiosk had no bananas today. But it did have Pepsi Cola and Czech beer. The long walk was not in vain.

As we walked back along the riverbank Volodya recalled an incident he had observed earlier in the week. 'There was a crowd of people outside a shop selling carpets, and they were so uncultured they had to have a policeman there with a loudhailer, to keep order and stop them from mauling each other to pieces.' He clicked his tongue. 'That's what it's come to, you see!'

'People didn't use to be like that,' Seryozha added. 'Russians used to be as polite and civil as any other nation, but gradually they are changing.' I noted the word 'they', as though our friends considered themselves somewhat apart.

'Why do you think that is?' I asked.

'Because they've forgotten God,' said Volodya. 'That's the root of the problem. They used to believe in something "higher", but now they only believe in themselves. You know the Russian expression? "Your own shirt is closest to your body." Religion at least taught people to have a conscience.'

'Also,' said Seryozha, 'Stalin destroyed our intelligentsia. Can you imagine Akhmatova or Pasternak fighting over a carpet? The intelligentsia were the guardians of our morals . . .'

'Even Estonia has changed,' said Volodya. 'We were there recently, for the first time in about ten years, and were shocked. You know our history? Stalin occupied Estonia after the War – they've had more than thirty years of communism now, and every year they become coarser, more aggressive. More like us!'

He told us about a street brawl he had observed in Moscow. Two men were wrestling on the pavement, and Volodya got drawn into a ring of spectators. Horrified, he watched for a moment, then cried out: 'Why doesn't someone do something about it? Pull them apart, someone!' I could just picture the scene: little, frail Volodya with his briefcase and refined voice, wagging his finger at the ruffians. Some of the spectators turned to see who this upstart was. 'Who asked you?' sneered one woman. She then added derisively: '*A yeshcho shlyapu nadel!* He's even wearing a hat!'

'You see,' Volodya explained, 'this was her way of saying I was just some high-minded intellectual! Only sissies wear hats and object to street brawls, you see!' He chuckled merrily and flapped the air dismissively with his hand.

As we drove back to Moscow, along the same government road as in the morning, a policeman in shirtsleeves waved us down and indicated with his white baton that we should turn right into a side road. Seryozha, who was driving, rolled down his window and protested: 'But we want to go to Moscow.'

'That road will get you to Moscow too,' said the policeman.

'Yes,' Seryozha muttered as he wound up his window, 'but it'll take us an extra half-hour.'

Not wishing to risk an argument, since he had foreigners in the car, he turned off into the forest as indicated. Volodya shook his head, perplexed but not surprised. 'The big cheeses must be throwing a party. They need their privacy.' Irony was his only weapon.

8

To Red Lighthouse

GIVING A BRIBE, if you are not used to it, is a most difficult thing.

In the early summer we decided to make our first trip out of Moscow – to Tallinn, capital of the Baltic republic of Estonia. One of the perks of working for Progress Publishers, and having a Moscow residence permit, was that this gave us the right to pay for flights and hotels all over the USSR in roubles, at Soviet prices, which were a fraction of the dollar rates charged to foreigners. 'Having the right', of course, was not the same thing as 'being able to'. I tried to book a room in Tallinn's main Intourist hotel, the Viru, but my telephone conversation with them seemed to confirm Volodya's impression that in terms of rudeness the Estonians were now fully-fledged Soviet citizens. They were clearly only interested in customers arriving from abroad, paying in hard currency.

Never mind, our Russian friends said. Just turn up at the hotel. Of course they will let you in – you're foreigners! And if all else failed, they said, ask to speak to the manager personally, and you hand her your passport with a five-dollar bill tucked inside it. She'll just quietly take the dollars and give you a room. It seemed there was nothing to it.

So off we went on an overnight train and arrived in the beautiful Hanseatic town of Tallinn. Just walking from the station to the hotel felt like stepping into another world. After Moscow it felt cosy and old-fashioned, built on a human scale. Cobbled streets, the smell of coal or wood burning in chimneys. Gabled houses and gothic spires. A medieval castle perched on a steep hill.

The Viru hotel, on the other hand, was a 23-storey hulk built in true Soviet style. The foyer was full of very drunk Finns and beautiful young women. Practising our lines, we approached reception.

'We'd like a room for three nights.'

'We don't have any rooms.' The voice came from the top of a head that didn't bother to look up.

'We wrote you a letter to say we were coming.'

'We don't have any rooms.'

I kept smiling. 'We're from Great Britain. We'd like to stay in your beautiful city for a few days.'

The head slowly tilted up, and revealed a young woman in a smart black suit and white blouse. She said: 'What is it you don't understand? We don't have any rooms available.'

Our hearts were thumping, and the blood rising in our cheeks. I swallowed hard and prepared to speak, while realising in a panic that I hadn't yet put the five-dollar bill inside my passport, which I had already placed on the counter in full view of everyone. How was I going to take it back in order to insert the money? Anyway, there was no going back, so I said: 'I'd like to speak to the manager please.'

Then we discovered the flaw in our friends' plan. They hadn't thought things through at all. For the young woman said: 'I am the manager.'

My mouth fell open. What was I to do now? Take my passport, shove dollars in it, hand it back to her with a big wink and say: 'Well? Do you *still* have no rooms?' Of course I couldn't! She wasn't going to accept a bribe in full view of her staff and the other guests who were milling around. I had completely messed up!

Neilian and I looked at each other and withdrew, blushing like criminals, to some chairs on the other side of the foyer. Except I don't suppose criminals do blush. It's only failed criminals that blush.

We had no Plan B. We didn't know the names of any other hotels, and had no idea what to do next. We decided to go for a little walk and ended up in a bar. After a beer or two it turned out that Estonians weren't by any means all Soviet bureaucrats. We got talking to a man called Kalju, who was an actor at the Nukuteater – the puppet theatre.

'Where are you staying? The Viru?' he asked after twenty minutes.

'Well . . .' we said, 'that was the plan, but . . .'

He immediately invited us to stay with him, and we trundled our suitcase through the cobbled streets to his flat, where he rang the doorbell and called through the door to his partner to make sure she was not naked as he had guests with him. Kalju and Annely became wonderful friends – and Tallinn one of my favourite places. Volodya was wrong: Estonia had not lost its dignity and culture, and ten years later I would go back as a reporter to watch in celebration as they threw off their Soviet chains and became free again.

*   *   *

We returned to Moscow refreshed and settled in our decision to renew my contract with Progress for another year when it ended in October. It was now June. Moscow was full – and I mean full – of *pukh* – the fluffy seeds given off by female poplar trees, which had been planted prodigiously to give shade all over the city. The fluff filled the air like snow, and gathered along the edges of pavements where little boys set fire to it with matches, to watch it flare up and sizzle along the road like an explosives fuse. Our urban village of Yasenevo was wonderful now, scented with lilac and lime blossom. Whenever we mentioned to any Russian that this was where we lived, the reaction was always the same: 'Ah – Yasenevo? The air is good there!' There must have been a TV programme about it. But they were right: compared to central Moscow, the air was good, especially in the huge Bitsa forest which was right on our doorstep. We spent hours here, strolling in the shade, ignoring the tedious manuscripts waiting to be translated at home.

Wonderful it was, but nonetheless we had been promised from the outset a two-roomed flat, and I decided to insist on this before agreeing to stay another year. That required a little cooperation from the KGB, in the shape of Vadim, the head of the foreign relations department. I found him in his office one morning, scarcely able to open his watery, red-rimmed eyes, far less his mouth. It didn't look like an auspicious moment. I had already broached the subject with him four or five times, and every time he would either fob me off with some excuse, saying there were no two-roomed flats available, or he would say 'yes, of course', but then do nothing about it. He donned a bored expression as soon as I entered his office, and lit a cigarette.

'Hello,' I said, taking a seat. 'I wanted to ask about the two-roomed flat again . . .'

'Please do,' he slurred.

'Are we any closer to getting one?'

'Of course, every day brings it a little closer . . .' He dragged on his cigarette and looked as if it would make him vomit.

'But you said you would sign an order for me, so it would happen.'

'Did I?'

'Yes, last month.'

He nodded his head repetitively and looked out from his hooded eyelids.

'So did you sign it?'

'No.'

'No? Why not?'

'Because.'

'What do you mean, because? Why didn't you sign it?'

'I don't know. I forgot.'

My blood was boiling, but I tried to stay calm. 'You forgot . . . ?'

'Forgot . . . or something. I don't remember.'

'So may I ask you to do it this week?' I asked, remaining so polite I even surprised myself.

'Yeah. Probably.'

I realised there was no point in even discussing it with him. Of course, I knew exactly what the problem was. Other foreign translators – whom I tended to meet only briefly, as we all worked at home – had told me all about Vadim. I had a coffee with one Englishwoman who assured me that Vadim was the nicest person in the world 'if you got on the right side of him'. She had lived in Moscow for eleven years, and to judge from her comments found the Soviet system right up her street. She claimed to have no difficulties whatsoever obtaining all the meat and groceries she required: she just 'rang up the shop and ordered them'. She was also planning to go back to England soon to 'shock the whole country' by putting a group of schoolchildren through their O-level maths in four months using Soviet methods. It would be splashed all over the front pages, she said. I assumed she worked for the same organisation as Vadim. Other translators didn't, but also managed to get Vadim on their side. One English translator regularly brought him electric shavers, cassette recorders and other valuable gifts every time she returned from a holiday in Britain. She had been moved to a larger flat as soon as she asked for one. There was no way I was ever going to do that.

In August we went back to the UK for a couple of weeks. Before we left we decided to do something finally to exterminate the cockroaches that plagued us, despite the fact that our building was new. Since all the *kanalizatsiya* – the plumbing – was shared with dozens of other flats, the beasts recognised no borders. They swarmed up and down the pipes as if they owned the place. In Russian they're called *tarakany* – which even sounds like the drumbeat of an invading army. It didn't matter that we kept our own kitchen and bathroom spotless, and removed every crumb as soon as it hit the floor – the Nazi hordes still kept coming. They were under the skirting boards, behind built-in cupboards, and seemed to crawl out of the tiniest cracks. We put down borax, but it was only partially effective, and only for a short time. The *tarakany* didn't normally stray as far as our living-room-cum-bedroom, but to be on the safe side we started standing the legs of our bed-settee in little bowls of water at night, in the hope that if there was at least one thing the little brown bastards couldn't do, it was swim. Once I swatted a cockroach in the middle of the kitchen floor with a newspaper, and walked away in disgust. It must have been pregnant: when I returned to clear it away two minutes later, *thousands* of minuscule dots were spreading out like a slow-motion supernova from the dead body. Baby fucking cockroaches! Another fresh-born battalion. Enough was enough. We bought 'the best' anti-cockroach spray, emptied our shelves, threw out all remaining foodstuffs, and sprayed every inch of the kitchen, all the skirting boards, and all the accessible parts of the communal water pipes, before going on holiday.

When we returned, the kitchen floor was gratifyingly strewn with dead roaches. But we noticed something else too: among them lay a squashed cigarette butt. There had been an intruder. This was the KGB's none-too-subtle way of letting us know they had been in to rifle through our belongings and papers.

We swept up the cigarette and the dead cockroaches from the surfaces and floor, and then opened the wall cupboard – the one place we had not sprayed, since it was where we kept food and we didn't want to put poison there. The scene that greeted us was so horrific it was hard to decide whether to scream first or take a moment to vomit. The entire cupboard was a heaving brown mass of cockroaches. It was as if every roach in the building had gone there – the only place to escape from our poison. They say the cockroach is the only creature guaranteed to survive a nuclear war. I believe it.

This was the final straw. I stormed in to Progress to demand the two-roomed flat we had long been promised. I went first to see Maria Konstantinovna, the head of the English section, who gave me some really interesting new work – a biography of the composer Dmitry Shostakovich – and also made it clear they wanted me to stay on for another year. The book was a high-level assignment, more important to my bosses than the propaganda they had given me earlier. With this ace up my sleeve I went in to see Vadim. He sneered at me as usual and said, 'But I understand you've signed a contract for another year.' His meaning was clear: to his mind there was now no need to do me any kind of favour. But he was wrong. I had not yet signed a contract, and I was able to go straight back to Maria Konstantinovna, and told her that unless we were moved to a bigger place I would leave, and the Shostakovich book would have to go to someone else. Miraculously, within a week, we had a new apartment – without bribing a soul.

The new flat was on the other side of the Bitsa forest – almost as remote from the centre of Moscow, but in a more established district. We loaded our Progress furniture plus our personal acquisitions – the curtains, rug and fridge – onto an open military-style truck and sat beside them in the back as the driver hurtled round the ring road to our new neighbourhood, Chertanovo. This time we were on the fourteenth floor, and celebrated the tiny upgrade in our situation. Now we had a balcony (three cheers!), a view of the forest and the sunsets (three more cheers!), and a parquet floor instead of linoleum (we were real toffs now).

Our new street even rejoiced in a name, not just a micro-district number. It was called Krasny Mayak (Red Lighthouse) – although if we had moved in a few years earlier we would have been lumbered with 'Thoroughfare Number 5168'.

I could write an entire chapter about the naming of things in the USSR, but will restrict myself to a paragraph or two. Like everything in the Soviet universe, names had an ideological purpose. Calling a chocolate bar 'Snickers' or a café 'Pret' would have been a dereliction of duty – a missed chance to remind citizens, just in case they hadn't noticed, that they lived in a communist dictatorship.

Soviet planners appeared to have a repertoire of only a dozen or so approved words from which they had to choose when naming new streets, factories, shops and products. The most common names were: Rodina (Motherland), Moskva (Moscow), Sputnik (Russian for satellite), Pobeda (Victory), Chaika (Seagull), Mir (Peace), Progress, Yunost (Youth), Zarya (Dawn) and Oktyabr (October) – plus anything else you liked so long as it was prefaced with the word Red. So you got Chaika automobiles, cinemas, hotels and candies. There were plenty of Pobeda cinemas, and a Pobeda car. Red Moscow was (among other things) a perfume, and Sputnik was used for any number of things in the travel business. Our street name was an agitprop double whammy: not only did Mayak (lighthouse) suggest a beacon, the shining light of communism, but it was Red! All of these names were supposed to be uplifting reminders of the glorious march to the communist future ... although one brand of cigarettes – Belomorkanal – bucked the trend: it was named after the White Sea Canal, a notorious Stalinist construction project, on which thousands of convicts were worked to death. Once upon a time that had also been considered a glorious achievement.

I could never understand why the publishing house I worked for – Progress – dealt with literature and propaganda, while its sister, Mir (Peace), published scientific books. Surely it should have been the other way round – 'Progress' for science, and 'Peace' for humanities and books extolling the USSR's peaceful foreign policies. Both were given their names in 1963, and I suspected it may have been a mistake – the result of a careless functionary presenting a Party leader with wrongly worded decrees for signature and then being too terrified to point out his error. Something similar allegedly happened with the design of the Moskva hotel, just off Red Square, whose front-facing façade sported two wings of quite different designs. The story goes that in 1931 the architect Shchusev submitted to Stalin a plan for the hotel showing two *alternative* designs – one constructivist, the other somewhat more ornate – divided by a vertical line down the middle. Stalin didn't notice, and put his signature right in the middle, across both versions. Since no one dared to tell the Great Leader and Teacher he was an idiot, the builders had no option but to use the blueprint he had apparently approved. Nowadays they say that this is an apocryphal tale ... but I think it is a legend worth perpetuating.

9

The Unpredictable Past

LIVING IN THE USSR was always going to be a political education. What I didn't expect was that I would also undergo a musical re-education. As a student I had been immersed like everyone else in pop music – though by the time I went to Moscow in 1978 the eclipse of gentle Californian singer-songwriters by punks with ironmongery in their noses was doing my head in. In Russia I lost track entirely of what was going on in Western popular culture. The Soviet media played mainly patriotic music and Russian romances, plus a few approved Western artists like the French singer Joe Dassin, whose '*Et si tu n'existais pas*' seemed to get more airtime than any other single piece of music. It then seemed to become the template for a million schmaltzy Russian pop songs. Western rock music circulated on bootleg tapes, but they didn't come in my direction, and in any case mainly featured bands like Deep Purple and Black Sabbath whom I had enjoyed as a lad but could happily do without now.

Instead I started listening to classical music. I allowed myself to be guided by Neilian, who played cello and had more sophisticated musical tastes than I did. We bought dozens of LPs at Melodiya, the state music store on Kalinin Avenue, and a Soviet-made record player which was so shoddy that Saint-Saëns came out of the speakers sounding a bit like the Clash – but with the advantage of at least having started out as music. The Conservatoire on Herzen Street became a haven from the madness of Soviet life. All the frustrations and tensions dissolved in a sea of strings and oboes. The portraits of Russia's great composers on the walls of the Great Hall reminded us that this was not just a country of bribe-takers and communist party creeps, but was also home to some of the most sublime art and music ever produced. The people sitting in the audience – and promenading in the foyer during the interval – might well have jostled you in a queue for potatoes, but here they were elegant and refined. The whole world seemed better. Of course, buying tickets for concerts was as problematic as anything else, but by regularly checking the theatre kiosks dotted around town, one sometimes came across a gem – and like everything else tickets were incredibly cheap.

But nothing changed me more than the book I was given to translate about Dmitry Shostakovich, the great Soviet composer who had died in 1975. He was acclaimed as a genius but there was much controversy about the extent to which he had kowtowed to the communist system. Twice he had angered Stalin with his works, and come close to being jailed or even executed, and on each occasion he responded by doing exactly what he was told by the authorities – denouncing his own work and that of his friends, or writing works dedicated to Lenin and the Revolution.

The book was a biography, written by Dmitry Sollertinsky, the son of Shostakovich's closest friend, Ivan Sollertinsky. The biography itself avoided controversy, as was inevitable in those days: it barely touched upon the composer's fateful clashes with Stalin, and depicted him as a patriotic communist who had occasionally made 'mistakes', but always repented and rediscovered his devotion to socialist art. In order to make sense of the book, and especially of its descriptions of Shostakovich's works, I bought as many records as I could find in Melodiya, and became obsessed with him. As a student of Russia I was fascinated by his conflicts with the Kremlin; as an amateur musician I was in awe of his sheer genius. Shostakovich had perfect pitch: not only could he identify any note he heard, but if you pressed a dozen discordant keys on the piano and then released just one of them, he could identify which note had disappeared. Once, in Leningrad, he arrived at a party at which another composer was due to perform a new piano work for the first time. Shostakovich was let in quietly and sat in a neighbouring room listening to this unique performance. He then pretended to have just arrived, and announced that he himself had just composed a new work: would people like to hear it? He sat down at the piano and to the amazement of everyone, not least the poor composer, repeated note-perfect the piece he had just heard through the wall.

I came to realise his works described a whole era. The second piano trio, written in 1944, symbolised for me the tragedy of communism. With its Klezmer motifs and electrifying, agonising dance of death in the final movement, it may have referred to the plight of Jews in Hitler's Germany, and even to the atrocities committed by the Nazis during the occupation of Russia, but for me it also evoked the agonies of the Purges and the Gulag.

After *Pravda*, on Stalin's direct orders, denounced him in 1936 for his opera, *Lady Macbeth of Mtsensk*, Shostakovich responded by writing his magnificent Fifth Symphony, and meekly accepted a description of it in a newspaper article as 'a Soviet artist's creative response to just criticism'. But when I listened to the symphony, all I could hear was a repressed Soviet artist crying out in pain. I couldn't believe that anyone could perceive that work as an obedient response to Stalin's diatribe: it was so clearly a scream of anguish against injustice! But that is the beauty of music: it is the perfect art form, in which the artist can bare his soul while also hiding it. I became convinced that Shostakovich was a true liberal, an avowed opponent of the communist system, and that his speeches and articles were simply the price he paid in order to be left in peace to create – or, indeed, to avoid being led to a firing squad. Articles written or signed under duress did not represent him in the slightest; only the music that flowed from his fingers did.

I met an old lady who had known Shostakovich personally. Mitya, as she called him, didn't even write those articles, she said. 'He loathed the system as much as the rest of us, but he compromised himself occasionally – partly for his own sake, but mainly out of fear for his children. He was compromising himself when he went to America with a Soviet peace delegation, and when he eventually joined the Communist Party. What else could he do? He couldn't refuse.' She told me about music he wrote to words by Dolmatovsky, a eulogist of Stalin: 'His friends laughed out loud when they heard it. They didn't take it seriously for a moment. They knew Mitya was just playing a joke on them . . .'

I had just finished translating Sollertinsky's biography (which despite all the ideological constraints was pretty interesting) when something extraordinary happened. The book was quietly withdrawn from Progress's publishing schedule (I later discovered they had sold the rights to an American publisher), and I received an urgent summons to see my editor-in-chief.

I sat in the metro as it clattered towards Gorky Park station, with my heart in my mouth. What had I done wrong? They had generally been pleased with my work, I thought, but I knew I had pissed off Vadim by refusing to bring him presents. Maybe they just wanted me to do some 'lightning' translation, or finish off the last chapter of someone else's book to make sure the section's quarterly plan was fulfilled. I knocked on Maria Konstantinovna's door and went in. She was dressed in a British-looking light-green twin-set, and her hair, as always, was drawn back in a severe bun. But she was smiling: it didn't look as if I was in trouble.

In fact, she wanted me to translate a new Shostakovich book. This one, she said, was a kind of 'master's diary' – a collection of the composer's speeches and articles, arranged in chronological order. The work was urgent. Maria Konstantinovna gave it to me on condition that I worked on it together with my wife and completed it within two months.

That was all I was told. But I discovered later that this new, top-priority publication was part of the ideological struggle with the West. What had happened was that a man called Solomon Volkov, a Russian journalist and musicologist, who had emigrated to America, had just published a book called *Testimony*, which he claimed was the composer's memoir, as related to Volkov in a series of interviews. The book was hugely controversial. Many experts denounced it as a fake, and refused to believe that Shostakovich had dictated his memoirs to anyone. The composer came across as strongly anti-Soviet. He suggested that several of his works had been intended as veiled attacks on the system – confounding those who had sought to portray him as a spineless stooge.

The Kremlin branded *Testimony* as a fraud, and the new 'master's diary' was to be their response. It was, needless to say, a totally cack-handed response – not to say an insult to the average reader's intelligence. How could anyone, even in the Kremlin's sclerotic propaganda department, possibly imagine that the way to counter a tell-all *autobiography* was to republish articles and official speeches written for him by Party hacks, mostly at the height of Stalinism?

By translating this book, I was of course participating in the fabrication of a 300-page lie – a fact made only slightly less uncomfortable by the fact it was so crude that no one in the West would be taken in anyway. The fascinating thing was: everybody knew this was the case. Maria Konstantinovna knew it, my editors knew it. They did it not because they wittingly wanted to hoodwink the West, but because lying for the Party was part of their job and came naturally to them. For the editors at Progress, correcting an ideological slip was as natural as inserting a missing comma. References to the likes of Mstislav Rostropovich, for whom Shostakovich composed his first cello concerto, had already been filleted from the text before I was given it to translate. Rostropovich had been stripped of his Soviet citizenship in 1978 and was now a non-person. But I was surprised when my 'control editor' on the book – a lovely woman, quite frank in conversation about life here – scored her pen through the name of the conductor Kirill Kondrashin, which had been mentioned in the Russian version I had translated.

I asked her why she had scored it out. It seemed fairly important to mention who had conducted the premieres of the fourth and thirteenth symphonies. 'Oh,' she looked round, a little surprised. 'Didn't you hear? He defected last week.'

Working on these two Shostakovich books became a vital part of my Soviet education. It was exactly as Orwell had foretold. Traitors (and inappropriate manuscripts) disappeared into the memory hole. And editors had to be extra vigilant, for the past – as the Soviet joke had it – was unpredictable.

10

Strange Encounters

SOVIET NEWSPAPERS DIDN'T publish classified ads, but lampposts served the same purpose. If you had something to sell, or gave private lessons, you typed your offer on a piece of paper and pasted it to a lamppost, or bus-shelter, or a wall near public telephones. Usually the notice was cut into fingers at the bottom, with the seller's telephone number written on each, so that you could just tear one off rather than searching for a pen and paper.

The most common notices were posted by people wishing to exchange apartments. Soviet citizens did not own their flats but rented them from the state, which allocated living space strictly according to 'requirements', based on the number of occupants. So unless you had good connections or were expert at bribing (or willing to go in for a fictitious marriage), exchanging flats was the only way to improve your living conditions. If you had a small flat in the centre of Moscow and wanted to exchange it for a bigger one of similar value in the outskirts then the lampposts were the place to advertise. You might see a 'headline' that read 3=2+1, which meant someone with a three-roomed flat was looking to exchange it for a two-bedroomed one plus a one-bedroomed one. This business was a major Soviet preoccupation, which often involved illegal payments of cash (to offset differences in value) and dodgy ethical conundrums. In Yuri Trifonov's novel, *The Exchange*, the hero's mother is terminally ill, and his wife urges him to quickly exchange their own room in a communal flat plus the mother-in-law's room in a different apartment for a two-roomed flat, so that the old woman's housing allocation won't 'go to waste' when she dies.

We were scouring the lampposts not for a flat but for a second-hand bookcase. The number we dialled led us to a smart block of flats at the southern end of Leninsky Prospekt, and a strange new acquaintance. A young man, about 35, greeted us and introduced himself as Sasha. He had very short hair and a clean-shaven, angular face. He nervously smoked a cigarette, jabbing it in and out of his mouth. A jumble of boxes, books, papers and chairs spilled out of the front door into the corridor. He explained that he had not been living there long and was doing a big clear-out. There was something distinctly odd about him. He insisted that we should name our price for the bookcase, since he hadn't the faintest idea what it was worth. Then he noticed we were foreign and began babbling away in English which contained many mistakes (and made him even more nervous) but was full of colloquialisms, as though he had lived abroad. The flat was in the same disorder as the corridor. He invited us into the little kitchen, which was littered with yet more books and magazines, and piles of dirty dishes. He wondered for a moment what to offer us, then produced a half-full bottle of Martell cognac – quite a rarity in the USSR. He cleared a couple of stools for us, poured large glassfuls of cognac, drained his at once and filled it up again. Meanwhile he found a kettle somewhere and promised some English tea – 'Lipton's, do you like it?' This was also something you couldn't buy in your local *universam*.

Sasha fumbled with a pair of bendy wire-rimmed spectacles as the conversation wandered spider-like from books to languages (he was fluent in French) to music. 'The reason I am selling off all this furniture and the books,' he said, 'is because I want to buy a grand piano!' It turned out he had studied international relations, and served briefly abroad as a diplomat, but his first love was music. It was ten in the morning. We finished the cognac, and Sasha produced a bottle of champagne from an otherwise empty fridge. I spotted an old icon hanging on a wall, and a little framed photograph of the Polish Pope on the table beside his bed (which was in the kitchen).

Little by little, some facts about this strange man emerged. He gave French lessons, lectured somewhere or other, and had written articles about English stately homes. Natalia Gutman, one of the country's greatest cellists, was his close friend. 'I'll take you to see her at the Conservatoire, you must meet her!' The phone rang several times and he explained to the callers (sometimes in French) that he was enjoying a nice chat and a drink with 'some friends'. His mother called, and he even spoke to her partly in French. Then she turned up in person, and was not happy.

'What the hell are you drinking cognac and champagne for? At eleven in the morning!'

'Well . . . I just met these nice people . . .'

'Nice people? They're foreigners, you idiot!'

'*Maman* . . .'

'What do you want?' she turned to us.

'We saw Sasha's notice, selling furniture, and came to see the bookshelf.'

At this, *maman* exploded. It turned out the books and furniture Sasha was selling off in order to buy a grand piano belonged to her, not him. As Sasha and his mother argued, Neilian and I made a discreet getaway.

A few weeks later Sasha called us and invited us to lunch with him at the Havana restaurant. He had booked a table and was waiting for us, dressed in a dark suit with a bow tie. On this occasion he was even more nervous and spoke very loudly, in stuttering English, about Soviet politics and other sensitive subjects, while we ate. Was he trying to compromise us, by encouraging us to voice our opinions about the Soviet Union? Or were these really his views?

We met him a few more times. He took us to the Conservatoire to hear Natalia Gutman play Shostakovich's cello concerto, and introduced us to her at the end. We met his girlfriend, Natasha, who was a doctor – and also an 'energy healer'. When she placed the palm of her hand near your skin it burned with an intense heat. One day she told us that Sasha had been admitted to a psychiatric hospital. She wasn't allowed to visit him. When he was released, several weeks later, he was much calmer than he had been, and parried all questions about touchy political subjects. He had always been keen to mouth off about how awful the system was. Not now.

Only now did we tell our best friends about him. We had gathered as usual in Garik's basement studio in the Arbat, with Inna, Grisha and Zoya. Their reaction to our eccentric friend came as no surprise.

'*Rebyata* – guys – be very, very careful,' said Inna, drawing earnestly on a cigarette. 'It's not easy for you here. You can't assess people the way we can.'

'*Da, da*,' said Garik. 'When we Russians meet someone new, we think very carefully about them before we would dream of opening up to them. Who are they, what is their background, why are they acting like this?'

Zoya shook her head gravely: 'Every foreign country is difficult . . . but Russia . . . !'

Grisha had lived for a year in Scotland. 'It was like that for me too,' he said. 'These people come up to you in the pub and say all sorts of

shit to you, and you've no idea who they are . . . But in Britain people
are civilised. Here, there are too many reasons for strangers to want to
make friends with foreigners . . . either they want to buy something from
you, or they want to spy on you, or recruit you . . . *rebyata*, just steer
clear of them!'

My wife objected that it was we who had approached him, just to buy
a bookcase, not the other way around.

Inna puffed a long stream of smoke out. 'That doesn't matter.
That's how the KGB works. They look for chances, they take any
opportunity.'

'He could be very dangerous,' said Garik. 'Guys, why do you need
him?'

We shrugged, having no answer. I suppose we had just enjoyed the
edginess of the situation – the very fact that Sasha was an eccentric, an
enigma, was quite thrilling.

Inna said we should avoid him: 'There are plenty of normal Russians
to make friends with, you know! Who is this guy who makes such a big
deal out of criticising the system while apparently enjoying all the perks
of it himself, with his Martell cognac and his "short" stay abroad as a
diplomat.'

'Diplomat!' scoffed Grisha.

Zoya rocked her matryoshka-like body. 'Of course he's KGB, *rebyata*.'

Inna leaned forward, very serious: 'For Heaven's sake, don't ever
mention us to him. You understand this, yes?'

But for some reason we did not stop seeing Sasha and his girlfriend. At
Easter time we went to see Natasha at her flat. She met us at the metro
station with her three-year-old son, Alyosha. He had a little painted egg
with him. We took a tram, which squeaked and rumbled along the centre
of a wide street. I looked out at the endless, depressing blocks of flats
with their corrugated balconies and blank windows, and at the dull, dead
shops, and the chiselled banks of snow. Sleet splashed quietly on the
windows. People picked their way carefully around puddles and through
mud. As we were leaving the tram, Alyosha dropped his egg and it got
trapped behind the door.

Natasha pointed to her apartment block, a couple of hundred yards
away, across a sea of snow patched with brown where the spring was
trying to make an impression. The Russians have a word to describe this
time of year: *bezdorozhye*, or 'roadlessness'. Normally it is applied to the

countryside, where the spring floods turn dirt tracks into impassable quagmires, cutting whole villages off from civilisation.

'This is nothing,' said Natasha. 'You should have seen it a few years ago. Friends of mine live in that block over there . . . When they moved in they had to carry all their furniture half a kilometre from the removal van to the house, because no roads had been built. There were no shops either, for a year. And when they finally got round to building one, it was a pet shop!'

We scraped as much mud as possible off our shoes and climbed the stairs to the second floor. It was only now, on entering Natasha's flat, that we realised she lived in a *kommunalka* – a communal flat. In fact, we had thought there were very few communal apartments left, most families having been moved into new self-contained flats in the outskirts. But Natasha, a doctor, lived with her son and her grandmother in a single room of a flat which they shared with two other families.

The front door was opened by a woman, one of Natasha's neighbours, with a tired smile that suggested they saw more of each other than they cared to. We took off our shoes and put on slippers provided for guests. From the hall, the flat looked like any other, with doors off to the toilet, bathroom and kitchen; but the other three doors had locks on them. The lack of privacy struck us as soon as Natasha opened the door to her room. Her grandmother, who had not heard us coming, was sitting on her bed reading Natasha's diary.

The room was small: there couldn't possibly have been nine square metres of floor space per person – the minimum laid down by law. Along one wall stood the grandmother's bed and Alyosha's little bed, end to end, and a small cupboard. Along the other long wall were Natasha's narrow bed, which served as a couch for guests, a wardrobe, and the door. At the shorter wall stood a sideboard, with boxes and books piled on top of it and stowed beneath it. At the other end of the room, in front of the window, was a small desk, and a little round table from which Natasha served us with tea and *kulich*, Easter cake. It was the first time I had seen a communal flat, and I confess I was struck dumb. I could not believe that three people could live in such a tiny area, sharing a kitchen, toilet and bathroom with two other families.

As we drank tea and ate *kulich* and *paskha* (a delicious paste of sweetened curds and raisins), Natasha related how she had tried to attend an Easter service the night before. The service started at midnight, and she had gone in good time to her nearest church. But both sides of the road leading to it were cordoned off by police and civilian helpers with red armbands, who were allowing only old people to pass through. Natasha, along with scores of other young people, were simply turned away.

'Usually,' she said, 'they arrange pop concerts and discotheques to coincide with Easter night, to attract youngsters away from the churches.' Last year it was advertised that the film *Jaws* was to be shown at the university, late on the night before the Easter service. 'The hall was packed with students, looking forward to this rare treat. But at the last minute the organisers came out and announced that they had been unable to get hold of the film after all. What a surprise, eh?'

The last time we saw Sasha he was throwing a small party in his flat. Few of the guests seemed to know one another. Some appeared to have known Sasha for only a short time. In the kitchen I again noticed things that made it clear he had access to special stores or other privileges – bottles of French cognac and Scotch whisky, tins of Earl Grey tea, foreign magazines. His bathroom contained an impressive array of foreign razor blades and aftershaves. On the bookshelves was a six-volume set of Winston Churchill's *History of the Second World War*, printed on quality paper and smartly bound, but embossed on the back not with the price but with the words *Not For Sale* (in other words, intended only for the trusted few at the top of Soviet society). There was, however, no food. Natasha was supposed to be bringing a takeaway meal from the Praga restaurant.

In the meantime Sasha kept our glasses full of cognac or whisky and consumed enormous quantities of both himself. As he got drunker he began swearing about Jews and Africans (not in itself unusual in Russia), and roared with contempt at a little cleaning lady who appeared at the door and wanted to sweep the corridor, where most of the guests were standing, or sitting on the floor, in order to keep the rest of the flat free of cigarette smoke.

Suddenly, everything changed. Among the odd collection of guests were two men wearing raincoats, to whom Sasha suddenly addressed himself at the top of his voice. 'I declare,' he slurred. 'I declare, in the presence of these KGB agents here . . . that I loathe this fucking country.' He spat out the words with such venom and mockery, and so unexpectedly, that everyone fell silent. The two men smiled amiably. Sasha continued: 'Do you have your [KGB] cards with you? Eh? 'Cos if you do, maybe you could be kind enough as to show them at the Praga and expedite the delivery of our food. Eh? Could you?'

I could feel the sweat breaking out on my arms and face as he continued to denounce the two agents and the system they represented. They merely looked at him insolently and allowed him to carry on incriminating himself. Evidently Sasha had no fear. Remembering the tell-tale signs in his apartment of his privileged position, I understood why. Garik and Inna had been right to warn us off.

It was too intriguing to leave, though. A new guest swaggered in from a neighbouring flat with his paunch wobbling in the cradle of his tailored Western shirt. I could hear him reciting poetry as he made the rounds of the women, trying to pick them up. When he approached Neilian, she quickly brought me into the conversation, and we learnt that he was a diplomat, home on leave from the Soviet embassy in Berlin. (It appeared that Sasha's block was owned by the foreign ministry.) He didn't like Berlin much, he said, and always dreamed of his motherland.

'You can't understand what a Russian feels for his motherland. You're British – you don't understand the breadth of the Slavic soul. Nothing, nothing in the entire universe, can compare with it. Do you know what a Russian feels when he is travelling back to Russia and sees those trembling silver birches – first a single tree, then a little grove, then forests upon forests of them? Of course you don't! You – you have nothing like that.'

'Do you think we never feel homesick?' Neilian asked him.

'Pah! Homesick! This is not homesickness, what I feel when I am not here. It is love. No, it is not even love . . . Ah, what's the point? You cannot understand, for it is a purely Russian emotion.' He paused, then decided he could be even more ridiculous. 'Do you not think,' he said, 'that the Russian nation is the greatest nation?'

My British hackles were up. 'That's claptrap, if you ask me.'

He made a gesture of condescending despair.

Later, when he was holding forth about the 'greatest literature in the world', I ventured the irrefutable comment that, though it is indeed fine, none of the Russian classics was freely available in any bookstore in Moscow.

'What?' he protested. 'My dear, how long have you lived here? You just don't know our life.'

'So where can you buy them?'

'I have *all* the classics at home. I can show you them if you don't believe me.'

'I dare say.'

'There you are then.'

A girl whom he had looped around the shoulder and brought into the conversation tried to help us out of our impasse. 'I know there aren't *many* in the shops, but you can buy them second-hand.'

'Not in the second-hand bookshops, you can't,' I retorted, unwilling to give up, and knowing I was right.

'But people sell them, er, privately,' said the diplomat.

'You mean on the black market,' I said. 'Yes, that's true – now and again, and at ten times the normal price.'

'Not *ten* times,' mocked the diplomat.

'Near enough.'

'Well, there you are then, so you *can* buy books here.' And with that he turned to speak to someone else.

The food from the restaurant had still not arrived, and Sasha was evidently ravenous as well as drunk. He was ranting in the next room about the fucking Soviet system and 'the bastards in the Kremlin who stuff their faces but can't even provide food for people.' Then he was throwing over chairs and falling against the walls.

We left. A week later Natasha told us Sasha was back in a mental hospital, being treated for his illness. In the Soviet Union that meant: being treated for his views.

11

Cold War Walls

SEPTEMBER 1979 BROUGHT a superb *bab'ye leto* – an Indian, or 'woman's', summer. Golden leaves dangled in the birch trees like little coins. We had picnics by a pond in the forest and watched old men playing dominoes on benches in the slanting afternoon sun. Red Lighthouse Street, with its long, functional buildings, was far from beautiful, but it was lined with fiery trees and full of little pleasures. I enjoyed the half-mile walk from the forest end where we lived down to the few shops around the *klumba*, or 'flower-bed', as the roundabout was known. The local wine shop was selling a rare Algerian red, Médéa. Our friends warned that it was bulk-transported to the Soviet Union in oil tankers and could be dangerous – but it was delicious, and who was ever harmed by a spot of petroleum in their claret? I discovered a shop that sold Arabica coffee beans from Ethiopia, which they would grind for you on the spot, transporting you – if you closed your eyes – to a little café somewhere near the Boulevard Saint Germain. A little stall sold fresh *ponchiki* – doughnuts. A flower shop was always full of blooms.

There was no escaping ideology, though, even on a stroll to the shops. At the *klumba* a huge portrait of Brezhnev covered an entire side of an apartment block. Fresh newspapers were pinned up every day on stands by the roadside. The wine shop had a portrait of Lenin on the wall behind the counter. And a huge metal hoarding near the vegetable shop proclaimed that the Soviet Constitution was the most just in the world – until it collapsed in a ferocious thunderstorm. One day, passing near a building site, I chanced upon a team of housepainters – all women – who were sitting in the sunshine, some on crates, others on the grass, in a semicircle. A middle-aged woman in paint-splashed overalls was addressing them – I caught the words 'work discipline' and 'our plan' as I passed. Some of the painters were very young. A girl who couldn't have been long out of school untied the kerchief from her blond hair and produced a hairbrush from the pocket of her baggy dungarees. A burly colleague, her smock splashed from head to toe with whitewash, was perched on a creaking crate with her legs apart and her elbows on her knees, enjoying lunch along with her political education. In one hand she held a baton of bread, in the other a stick of pink garlic sausage half the length of her forearm. Gender equality – guaranteed by the Constitution that fell down in the storm – ensured that some of the toughest physical jobs in the Soviet Union – housepainting, building, street-sweeping – were done by women. They also did most of the jobs in schools and hospitals. And of course *all* the work at home. It was worthwhile, though, because once a year, on International Women's Day, men made long, beautiful toasts and told them how wonderful they were.

Listening to the BBC World Service in our kitchen and watching Soviet TV news in our living room, I was becoming more and more aware of the reality of the Cold War, which seemed to be far more about thought control than about the dangerous build-up of nuclear arsenals. The Soviet people – through their media and political education sessions – obtained a weird view of the world which for the majority (who did not bother to listen to foreign broadcasts) went entirely unchallenged. The 9 pm news programme, *Vremya* (Time), began with a fanfare to stir the heart, and always followed the same running order. First there were reports of whatever General Secretary Brezhnev had said or done that day. The wording was *precisely* the same as you would read in the papers next day, for even the slightest change of emphasis would send out unnecessary signals. Similarly the line-up of leaders on a stage was thought through precisely, and any change was noted. If a junior Politburo member edged one place closer than usual towards the general secretary, for example, this was a significant signal of his advancement. The second part of *Vremya* consisted of reports of economic successes (there were no failures in the Soviet economy), recitations of vertiginous grain-production statistics, profiles of 'heroes of socialist labour' and 'shock brigades', and details of how this or that work collective was preparing some great exploit to mark the upcoming congress of the Communist Party. Then came the foreign section, which had only two themes – the West's arms build-up and preparations for war against the Soviet Union, and the struggle of Western workers to better their conditions. The only beacon of hope for ordinary folk in the West was the example of the USSR.

Russians were not stupid, and could see for themselves that their own lives did not quite match up to the paradise depicted on *Vremya*. In a Soviet joke, a man goes to hospital and asks for the Ear and Eye Department. 'Don't you mean the Ear, Nose and Throat Department?' says the woman at reception. 'No, no,' says the man, 'I need the Ear and Eye Department – I keep hearing one thing, but see something completely different.'

But they were less able to judge how distorted the picture of the West was, since they could not travel there to see for themselves. A friend from student days called Lena, who lived in Volgograd, came to visit us. She breezed into our flat and took it over completely for four days. It was wonderful: like every Russian woman she insisted the kitchen was a woman's domain and that a man should eat more and not interfere with the cooking of it. Even my wife didn't get a look in. Our flat no longer smelt of British stews and toast but of Russian cigarettes and fried cabbage and onions. We drank lots of vodka and sang Ukrainian songs. We played 'who's got the worst shortage?' She told us there wasn't a scrap of butter in Volgograd at present, and we told her there wasn't a single carrot in Moscow. She laughed: 'You know, I never used to believe you when you said life was better in the West. The Soviet brain is an amazing thing: it can simultaneously see that the West produces jeans and make-up and all the other things we want to get hold of, and at the same time we believe that everything over there is a nightmare.'

She admitted that as a student she had never pondered why it was that the Soviet Union couldn't produce decent jeans and make-up. She had dutifully memorised scraps of 'Diamat' (Dialectical Materialism) the day before the exams each year, without understanding or caring about a word of it. From the obligatory study of the history of the Communist Party she knew that Stalin was a great leader under whose guidance the Soviet Union had collectivised agriculture and developed its industrial base, but who had unfortunately made a cult of his own personality – a regrettable aberration from Leninist norms which the Party had now put entirely right. Of his murderous reign of terror she learned nothing. She had other concerns. She emerged from the cocooned life of a student, where 40 roubles a month, a subsidised canteen and a bed in a shared student dorm were all she needed, into the real world where having connections and knowing how to grease palms was more important than what was written on your diploma. She had married less out of love than from the need to have a husband and thus the guarantee of a small flat. 'I'd love to live in

Moscow,' she said, 'but you need a *propiska* (special registration) and to
get that you have to have a job here, or a husband who's registered
here . . .' The vodka fuelled an escapist dream: 'Maybe my husband will
get sent to Egypt, or Pakistan . . .' But it was only a dream. Like Chekhov's
three sisters, Lena would remain stuck in the provinces.

The ability of a state like the USSR to control its citizens' minds –
literally to limit the scope of their thinking – was awesome. On one of
my first trips to Moscow on a language course I caused a small diplomatic incident by revealing things to an auditorium full of Soviet students
that they weren't supposed to know about. I was one of half a dozen
British students who were invited on to the stage to answer questions
about British life. I was asked what Russian literature I studied as part
of my university course, and I had the nerve to answer truthfully. I
named, for example, Pasternak's anti-Soviet novel *Doctor Zhivago*, and
works by Yevgeny Zamyatin, Andrei Sinyavsky and Alexander
Solzhenitsyn. There was a frisson in the hall: so complete was the Soviet
rewriting of history that most of the students had never even heard of
Sinyavsky or Zamyatin, knew Pasternak's poetry but not his famous
novel, and of Solzhenitsyn knew only that he was a traitor. I had quite
unwittingly revealed a wider world of Russian culture that existed beyond
the walls of the Soviet prison. It reminded me, in fact, of Zamyatin's
prescient 1924 novel *We*, which depicts a state where mass surveillance
and control is total, and the known world is separated from a hostile
outside world by a Green Wall: I had opened a door in the USSR's green
wall. The Institute lodged an official complaint with the British embassy,
as though I had carried out a deliberate act of sabotage.

With such ignorance of the West, indeed of anything outside the
restricted world of knowledge permitted by the Communist Party, it was
hardly surprising that suspicions and fears flourished. They were
mirrored in the West. In the autumn of 1979 the Cold War was about to
enter one of its most dangerous phases, despite the signing of a major
arms control agreement in the summer. People on both sides of the Iron
Curtain prepared for nuclear war. In Britain the government issued
Protect and Survive, a booklet of instructions on 'how to make your home
and your family as safe as possible under nuclear attack'. Diagrams
showed fathers building a 'fall-out room', blocking windows with ward-
robes, and stocking up on food and batteries to survive a nuclear winter.
It gave the impression that a nuclear holocaust might be survived by
hiding under tables and 'lean-to' doors covered with suitcases and

sandbags. In the USSR preparations were much more serious. At school children had formal civil defence lessons and learned how to use gas masks and Geiger counters. Buildings had proper shelters, and the Moscow metro had stations so deep you might really be able to survive a nuclear war in them.

Without the invention of radio, the Soviet authorities could have kept their citizens in complete darkness. Shortwave radio signals, not nuclear missiles, were the weapons that would eventually kill communism. Western broadcasts suffered terrible indignities as they bounced around the ionosphere to find radio antennas bristling across the Soviet Union: the voices crackled and warbled and faded . . . and just when you thought you had found a decent signal the Russians would switch their jammers on, obliterating the sound with unbearable crashing and grinding. It really sounded as though they had sent in bulldozers to demolish the transmitters. It cost the Kremlin millions of dollars, just to broadcast a wall of noise. Some Russians went to their dachas to listen, as jamming was less severe in the countryside. Others tried to find clear frequencies at home. Most didn't bother.

Jamming wasn't entirely effective, and in Red Lighthouse Street we often tuned in at night to Radio Liberty (financed by the CIA), or the US government-run station, Voice of America. ('Voices' was the generic term used by the Soviets to refer to foreign broadcasts beamed into the USSR.) The very act of listening to a shortwave broadcast was exciting: the sound quality was awful; sometimes you had to move the tuning needle just to the left or right of the correct frequency to make it audible. The 'voices' changed their frequencies at different times of the year, and also to try to evade the jammers, so finding them was a game of cat and mouse. Suddenly, out of the whistling and wheezing, a signal would come through – maybe the 'anthem of free Russia' with which Radio Liberty began its programmes, or VoA's *Programme for Nightbirds*, and you felt you were part of a conspiracy, listening in the darkness with a silent community of Russians who hungered for the truth. On the BBC Russian Service (call sign – Purcell's *Trumpet Voluntary*) we listened to the *Chronicle of Current Events* (news about human rights abuses in the USSR, compiled by dissidents), and broadcasts of Solzhenitsyn reading from his own works.

But most of our news came from the BBC World Service. English-language broadcasts were not jammed. Nowadays, when one is bombarded from every side with information from TV, radio and websites, it is hard to recall what it was like having just one English-language source of information – for everything! The newsreaders became personal friends. We loved the presenters with their cut-glass accents. One used to announce a magazine programme called 'Outlook' as though it rhymed with 'might look'. We called it 'Ightlook'.

On Christmas Day 1979, we had a decent dinner, having learned from the previous year that we must stock up in advance, and then heard on the BBC that the Soviet Union had invaded Afghanistan and overthrown the government. On *Vremya* we heard that a limited contingent of Soviet troops had entered Afghanistan at the request of the government in Kabul. The phrase 'limited contingent' became a bitter joke, as thousands and thousands of troops were sent – and got killed. Every Russian family with boys in their late teens was terrified they would be sent to Afghanistan. Now the temperature of the Cold War was plummeting. President Carter announced funding and weapons for the mujahideen in Afghanistan who were fighting against the Soviets. He also announced a boycott of the Olympic Games, which were to be staged in Moscow in the summer. Meanwhile American diplomats were being held hostage in their embassy in Tehran.

Neilian gave English lessons to a nine-year-old girl, Dasha, the daughter of a prominent scientist. Dasha's schoolteacher had explained the world situation to the class. The Chinese (sic!) had invaded Iran because it was a good country that had had a popular revolution. President Jimmy Carter didn't want American sportsmen to come to the Olympics in Moscow because he had been telling people that Russians lived in hovels and that bears roamed the streets. He didn't want them to come and see 'our beautiful buildings'. Dasha was only nine, but I suspected most Russians had a similarly topsy-turvy view of the world.

On 22 January 1980 we were listening to the BBC as usual, around teatime. I'll never forget the rather breathless report – one of the first that made me want to become a journalist – by the BBC's Moscow Correspondent, Kevin Ruane. He said one of the country's most respected dissidents, Andrei Sakharov, and his wife Yelena Bonner, had been seized by KGB officers as they were walking in the street. He could confirm that they had been driven to one of Moscow's airports, and police had told him 'they have probably already flown out'. Sakharov had recently given an interview to American television in which he had criticised the invasion of Afghanistan and supported Carter's proposed boycott of the Olympics.

I was astounded. Could they really have done this? Was he going to join Solzhenitsyn in exile abroad? Would they dare? He was a national institution – an academician, awarded the Stalin and Lenin prizes for his part in developing the Soviet Union's hydrogen bomb, then shunned because of his human rights activities, which earned him the Nobel Peace Prize in 1975.

I wanted to check whether there was any mention of it in the papers. I almost ran down the icy pavement of Red Lighthouse Street to the newspaper stand near the *klumba*. I bought the two evening papers, *Vechernyaya Moskva* and *Izvestiya*, and scanned every inch. There it was, hidden away, almost invisible. The tiny report didn't say anything about deporting Sakharov, or even arresting him, but it did say he had been 'stripped of his state awards and prizes'. The rest was obvious.

I folded up the papers and trudged slowly back home. People hurried back and forward to the shops, stood in bus queues, sat in steamy buses looking out through the tiny portholes they rubbed in the frosty panes. I could see people standing at the lit windows in a long wall of flats. I felt utterly powerless. I had knowledge – about something momentous that had just happened in this very city, and these people knew nothing about it. The ground in front of the long wall of flats was covered with deep snow – a huge white expanse, like writing paper. I stopped for a moment and imagined writing on it, in giant letters: САХАРОВ АРЕСТОВАН – Sakharov has been arrested. I could have informed a thousand people. I tentatively drew a shape in the even snow with my boot. Then I sighed, and continued on my way. I was no hero.

'Who is Sakharov? Whom does he serve?' asked the newsreader halfway through *Vremya* that evening. 'Sakharov has chosen the road of direct betrayal of the interests of our Motherland, of the Soviet people. He has turned into a shameless enemy of the socialist system, and has gone over to the camp of militant anti-communists and ardent champions of the Cold War.' The character assassination developed into a litany of lies. Sakharov had chosen politics because he had reached a 'creative crisis' as a physicist; he had supported Pinochet's bloody clique in Chile, and defended the murderers who had spilt the blood of innocent women and children by exploding bombs in the Moscow metro; he had encouraged the USA to raise their armed forces to two or three times the size of the Soviet Union's and to deploy neutron bombs in Western Europe – to be used against the Soviet Union, the country in which he had grown up . . . Finally, viewers were told that the physicist had been expelled from Moscow.

Sakharov and Bonner were sent not abroad but to the city of Gorky (now Nizhny Novogorod), where they lived in isolation and under close KGB surveillance for almost seven years. The city was chosen because it was closed to foreigners, effectively ending their human rights activities. This was another of the walls the communists built. Physical ones like the Berlin Wall and the sealed borders of the Soviet Union kept citizens from travelling. Closed cities like Gorky kept 'dangerous' people isolated. Radio jammers were virtual walls that kept the imprisoned population in ignorance.

Three days later a delegation of Scottish trade unionists arrived in Moscow to celebrate the birthday of their national poet, Robert Burns. Burns was glorified in the Soviet Union, where schoolbooks claimed that 'when socialism and communism are finally victorious all over the globe, the most beautiful dreams and hopes of all people will come true – hopes and dreams about which Robert Burns wrote with such inspired faith.' *Vremya* showed a giant haggis flown in from Scotland for the Burns Supper. The Scots were treated to sightseeing, copious food and drink in the best hotel, and meetings with Kremlin propagandists. In the eighteenth century Prince Potemkin built decorative villages along the route to be taken by his empress, Catherine the Great. In the twentieth the Kremlin ensured foreign visitors also only saw a prettified facade. Another wall, another world of make-believe.

12

Not Any Other Country

IT WASN'T JUST the authorities who built walls. One group of Russians built them for themselves, as insulation from the brutal reality of communist society. It was called *vnutrennyaya emigratsia* – internal emigration – and it described the way of life of that group of people we call the intelligentsia. Most of my friends in those days were like that: they 'emigrated' to an inner world of poetry or science, philosophy and longing, and animated discussions at their kitchen tables. The outside world existed, of course – Party committees and decrees, the five-year plans, the lies and bombast of *Vremya* and *Pravda* – but they observed it from a distance, like a masquerade, a dance of demons round a fire, while they created for themselves a better world of integrity and honesty, far from the dark century's horrors.

In Solzhenitsyn's novel *The First Circle*, a prisoner tells his interrogator: 'When you've taken away everything from a person he becomes free again.' That's what the intelligentsia felt like – inside, they were free, probably freer than people in the West, who took their liberty for granted.

A member of the intelligentsia is known as an *intelligent* (with a hard *g*) – a very Russian concept, not exactly the same as 'intellectual'. Years later, when I became a journalist, I met the great Russian poet and songwriter, Bulat Okudzhava, and asked him how he defined the intelligentsia. The Soviet definition, he said, was just someone with higher education, while in the eyes of ordinary people, 'if you have a diploma, glasses and a hat, you're an *intelligent*.' But in fact it was a question of values.

'If you've got an education,' said Okudzhava, 'you're an intellectual, but you might not be an *intelligent*. Being an *intelligent* is a state of the soul. Roughly speaking, the qualities of an *intelligent* are: respect for the individual, revulsion against violence, thirst for knowledge (and the desire to pass that knowledge on to others), doubt in one's own rightness, and the ability to be ironic about oneself, to laugh at oneself. I knew

intelligenty among working people, and I knew bastards who were acad-
emicians. And when they say Lenin was an *intelligent* I say, how could
he be when he was inclined to violence? He was merely an *obrazovanets*
[educated person], as Solzhenitsyn put it.'

Once, standing with my friend Volodya on an escalator in the metro,
where a strident voice on the public address system was exhorting
'comrade passengers' to be polite to one another, Volodya whispered to
me: 'You see! They don't even trust people to behave like normal human
beings! That's the kind of people who rule us – they're rude and uncultured themselves, so they assume everyone else must be. If the country
were run by *intelligenty* they wouldn't do such a thing.'

In February Neilian and I walked down Lenin Avenue from Gagarin
Square, past the House of Porcelain (a crockery shop) and the Sputnik
Hotel, to a long, eight-storey apartment block made of honey-coloured
bricks. This was the nearest Moscow had to a 'posh' part of town – not
because it looked particularly affluent but because it was close to
Moscow University and a host of lesser institutes, and was populated
by internal migrants wearing metaphorical hats. Our friends here
included the daughter-in-law of a Nobel Prize winner, and the family
of Nikolai Nikolayevich Vorontsov, an eminent professor of genetics.
His wife, Yelena Lyapunova, was a professor of biology, and one of their
daughters was the little girl whose teacher told her the Chinese had
invaded Iran.

We had tea and cake in the Vorontsovs' sitting room, which like every
other room in their big flat was crammed full of books and artefacts
gathered on their travels around the Soviet Union. One wall was hung
with dozens of framed black-and-white photographs. Most of them
were portraits or group photos of very distinguished, brainy-looking
people, including Yelena's father, a renowned mathematician, complete
with Dostoyevskian beard and furrowed brow. One showed a little
curly-haired Mozart lookalike with a violin – this was Nikolai at the age
of five. It turned out he had been a wunderkind: before going on to
study biology at Moscow University and beginning an illustrious career
in science, he graduated as a violinist from the prestigious Gnesin
Institute, sang as a soloist in the university choir, was accepted into the
Leningrad Philharmonia, and even starred as a boy actor in several
movies. 'Oh,' he said, 'I just wanted to try out a few possibilities before
deciding on a career.'

Now he sat smiling through his thick spectacles and puffing on a cigarette, which he always placed in a long holder. Nikolai made a name for himself in the 1950s by opposing the madcap theories of Trofim Lysenko, Stalin's favourite (and utterly misguided) agricultural 'expert'. Soviet leaders were always susceptible to scientists who claimed they could do extraordinary things to bend the forces of nature to man's will. Brezhnev spent millions on a plan – thankfully later dropped – to reverse the direction of the great north-flowing Siberian rivers so that instead of draining into the Arctic Ocean they would irrigate the arid cotton-growing republics of central Asia. (The small flaw in this cunning scheme was that it would have wrecked the global climate and possibly brought on a new ice age.) Stalin's particular obsession (due to the fact that he had liquidated all the most productive farmers in the 1930s) was with increasing yields of Soviet crops, so he fell for Lysenko's pseudo-scientific claims that just as Soviet artists could 'engineer' the human soul, so Soviet farmers would be able to train plants to grow in regions unsuited to them, transform rye into wheat, and fertilise fields without any kind of fertiliser. Since he had Stalin's support, scientists who openly disagreed with this quackery would generally end up dead or in a labour camp. After Stalin's death Vorontsov became one of the first scientists to openly denounce Lysenkoism and begin the restoration of classical genetics.

In 1964, when Khrushchev was deposed and the post-Stalin Thaw came to an end, the Vorontsovs chose not only internal emigration but a kind of self-imposed exile – and intellectual freedom – in the scientists' city of Novosibirsk. Akademgorodok ('Science City') was founded as a special centre of excellence and became an oasis of liberal thought, far from the Kremlin. The Vorontsovs remembered exhibitions of banned artists, and a festival of underground songs in March 1968. It was there that the dissident Alexander Galich, who ranked along with Okudzhava and Vysotsky as the greatest 'bards' of the Soviet period, gave his only public concert in the USSR, and played a song that condemned the authorities for their persecution of Boris Pasternak, the author of *Doctor Zhivago*. Three years later Galich was expelled from the Writers' Union, and then forced to emigrate.

Nikolai and Yelena conjured up a world I would love to have been part of. In the West it was the time of Dylan, Baez, Seeger, the first music festivals, flower power, Vietnam, and student protests. The Soviet Union's free spirits were cut off from all of that, but they also found ways to reject authority. Some of the photos on the Vorontsovs' wall showed them on expeditions in the remotest regions of Soviet central Asia, where they collected specimens of rare rodents to study their chromosomes, and revelled in the freedom and space of pine-clad mountains or scorching deserts. In August 1968, when Soviet tanks rolled into Czechoslovakia to crush the Prague Spring, they were camping in khaki tents somewhere in the Tian Shan mountains or on the Cherny Irtysh river, singing quietly rebellious songs around a camp fire, their backs firmly turned against the anti-Western hysteria coming out of the Kremlin.

Over vodka and salads – we had moved through to the kitchen, and this might have been on another day, I can't remember – Vorontsov reminisced about a friend from his schooldays, and told me one of those stories that would always bring home to me that Russia is not any other country. In 1939 when Nikolai – or Kolya – was five, and acting in a film titled 'Puppetland', he became friends with the son of the female lead, an actress called Galina Kravchenko. Her son, Vitalik, was two or three years older than Kolya. His father was a pilot called Kamenev, who happened to be the son of Lev Kamenev, one of the original Bolshevik leaders, who was executed by Stalin in 1936. All of Lev Kamenev's closest family, including Vitalik's father, were also shot. Galina reverted to her maiden name. Little Kolya and Vitalik became best friends, and stayed close as Vitalik went off to study law and Nikolai zoology. Was that the end of the story? No. In 1951 Nikolai returned from an expedition to discover that his friend had been arrested, tried, found guilty and sent to the Gulag. For what? For being the grandson of a man who had crossed swords with Stalin two decades earlier.

One night in March we were rudely awakened from our sleep by a thumping on the door. We sat up in bed, wondering what was going on. I looked at the clock. It was after three o'clock. The noise stopped and we lay down, but it suddenly started up again, louder than ever. Someone was hammering on our front door with his fists. The knock on the door in the middle of the night! This was no joke in the Soviet Union.

With my heart in my mouth I put the light on in the hall and called: 'Who's there?'

'Open up!' said a hoarse voice.

Slowly I turned the handle and opened the door a little. I was greeted by a strong smell of cow-dung, and when the dishevelled figure leaning against the doorpost spoke, there was also a strong smell of alcohol. His hair was tousled and his fur hat askew, he was wearing an old misshapen jacket with a bag over his shoulder, and his trousers were all muddy up one side.

'Telegram!' he just about managed to say, and held towards me a crumpled piece of paper. Then he held out a little notebook and a pencil and indicated that I was to sign it. He smelt like a sewer, and I was glad to get the door shut again.

No summons to the Lubyanka, then. Just a telegram from our friend Lena, saying she hadn't been able to get through on the phone and was thinking of visiting us again. The telegram had been sent the previous morning, and was stamped at our local post office at 4 pm. The man had taken eleven hours to deliver it, apparently via the ditches of some collective farm.

At the end of Gogol's story, *The Overcoat*, a watchman is described as being so feeble that 'once, an ordinary, full-grown pig running out of a private house knocked him clean off his feet'. No reason for this extraordinary event is given, and it has no relevance to the rest of the story. Why would a full-grown pig – an 'ordinary' one, even – come running out of a private house at all, far less knock over someone who plays no part in the story whatsoever and whose 'feebleness' is thus irrelevant? Critics have tried for more than a century to analyse the passage. But there's nothing to understand. It's just the madness of Russia! Things happen. Postmen get lost.

We invited our artist friends, Garik and Inna, and Grisha and Zoya, to dinner, and spent a week buying food – most of it at the Moskvoretsky market where the private farmers always managed to fill their counters with top-quality pork and beef, and beautifully presented fruit and vegetables. Here, the market functioned just as in any capitalist economy: almost every kind of fresh food was available, but at a high price that controlled demand, and sold by dodgy characters who you knew were trying to get one over on you but did it with great charm.

'Let's not speak about politics tonight,' we decided early on. 'There are thousands of other things in our lives – let's speak about them instead.' It wasn't just a desire for a change of subject. Speaking about politics in a foreigner's flat, where all manner of 'devices' might be secreted, was not a great idea. We drank a toast 'to an apolitical conversation' to strengthen our resolve. But we also closed the door to the hall, where the telephone was. (Yes, we now had a telephone!)

It was hard to stop the conversation from being sucked towards politics, though. We were all heavily affected by something that had been shown on television just the previous evening, 20 June. Garik and Inna didn't have a TV, so we described the scene to them. Halfway through *Vremya*, a dissident priest, Father Dmitry Dudko, had appeared in a horribly staged 'interview' in which he recanted his 'sins'. Dudko was well known for his articles and outspoken sermons at his little church near Moscow, many of which reached a wider audience via Western radio 'voices'. He had been arrested six months earlier, yet he looked remarkably fit during this strange television appearance, as he calmly and readily confessed to his 'anti-Soviet crimes' and denounced his own writings as a 'stream of lies and slander'.

'Fuh,' snorted Garik when he heard the story. 'Of course he was coerced into doing it! They must have drugged him.'

'*O Bozhe,*' sighed Inna. 'Oh God! First Sakharov, now this. Things are getting worse and worse. It's a Stalin show trial all over again.'

'*Rebyata, ne budem o politike,*' Zoya begged us with a glance at the door. 'Guys, let's not do politics tonight.'

But what else were Russians supposed to talk about? Other grumbles soon started, running around the rim of politics. There were no decent films at the moment, no food in the shops, and no decent clothes either. Grisha and Zoya were hoping for permission to visit Czechoslovakia on holiday, but would have to undergo all sorts of political checks and interviews. For Garik and Inna even visiting a communist country was out of the question. Grisha wanted to buy a new typewriter, but would have to wait a year. The vodka was grim. You couldn't even buy a box of chocolates in Moscow these days . . . So the grievances went on. But it wasn't, I noticed, really 'complaining'; rather, they seemed resigned to the raw deal that was their unfortunate birthright. Once again I found myself thinking that, taking everything together – the hardships, the good times, and the comfort brought by acceptance of one's lot – the Russians were probably no unhappier than Americans or Britons or any other people in the affluent and free West. Worrying about mortgages, muggings, high prices, and finding a job, was not necessarily less of a burden than the particular cares that marked the Soviet way of life.

The difference, perhaps, was that in the West a rosier future was at least conceivable. 'Do you think things will improve here eventually?' I asked.

'Not so long as they spend all their money on tanks instead of people,' said Zoya.

'Not so long as *they* are sitting in the Kremlin,' said Garik.

Inna was even more pessimistic. 'The only way things could change here would be as the result of a world war. So it's better to leave them as they are.'

Only Grisha wagged his head a little and twisted his moustache in dissent. 'Who knows? Perhaps, somehow, it will get better . . . Not everyone in the Party is bad . . . Let's wait and see what it will be like in twenty years' time . . .'

'In a hundred years' time!' Garik scoffed.

'Two hundred . . .'

We fell silent for a few moments. 'They say a quiet angel just flew by,' said Inna.

I pointed out that just because we were able to elect a new government every five years, it didn't mean life in Britain was always as rosy at it seemed to them. People had just elected Mrs Thatcher, for God's sake! Of their own free will! There were millions of poor people, and many had no jobs or were even homeless. Prices were soaring. I had been attacked, just walking down the street, whereas I didn't ever feel unsafe in Moscow. That only made things worse for our friends. They didn't really want to hear this. Western life was an ideal for them, and it was hard to accept the cracks in it. Was unemployment really as bad as it sounded – or was that just Soviet propaganda? Why was there violence in the streets? Was pornography widespread? Surely Mrs Thatcher couldn't be so bad, if so many people voted for her?

After the main course, Grisha went out to the balcony with his cigarette, though the room was already full of smoke. I joined him, leaning with our arms folded on the balustrade fourteen storeys up, looking out at the swooning sun over the forest. Men and women in shirt-sleeves and summer dresses were returning from their evening strolls in the woods. The pendulous branches of the silver birches shimmered like cool, streaming water over the hard dirt pathways.

'*Nichevo, druzhok, posmotri, kak prekrasen gorod v eto vremya!*' said Grisha, slapping my back. Never mind, my old chum, just look at how lovely the place looks!

13

Oh! Oh! Oh! Oh! Oh!

SUMMERS IN MOSCOW were always quiet, because most of the children went away to holiday camps – another little perk for parents provided almost free by the state, for the mere price of abandoning little Vanya or Tanechka to 24/7 indoctrination. Other children vanished with their families to their dachas. But the summer of 1980 was extra-quiet, because preparations were in full swing for the Olympic Games. As the opening ceremony in mid-July drew nearer, unsightly vagabonds were expelled from the city, and the country folk who used to descend on Moscow every day to stock up on supplies – the 'paratroopers' whom Garik caricatured with gigantic rucksacks on their backs – were kept out. The suburban trains were almost empty, and patrolled by volunteers authorised to kick off anyone who didn't look wholesome enough to be glimpsed by Western visitors.

Armies of women were sent out to scythe down long grass at roadsides and roundabouts. Some streets in the centre were re-tarmacked, and buildings given a splash of fresh paint. New sleek brushed-aluminium telephone booths appeared, to replace the ancient, lopsided, rusting ones whose doors never closed properly. The Americans – and dozens of other spiteful nations – might not be coming, but those who did were going to be damned impressed by mature socialism.

The Soviet people also had to be impressed, so the authorities conjured up all sorts of unheard-of delights for them too. Pepsi Cola stands appeared. So did stalls offering coffee and cakes, and salami or sturgeon sandwiches – making it possible for the first time ever to pause in the middle of your busy day and enjoy a snack at a street corner. The fact that this seemed utterly wondrous spoke volumes about how miserable public catering normally was. (And how miserable it became again when the Olympics were over.)

The food shops seemed a little fuller, but that was mainly because there were fewer shoppers around to scoop up the still meagre supply of products on offer. A few new delights from Finland – cellophane-packed sliced salami and little tubs of spreading cheese – gained celebrity status, if only because of their fancy packaging.

A dozen new hotels were built, and one of them – the huge Kosmos, in the north of the city – was opened by none other than Russia's favourite French crooner, Joe Dassin, whose trendy white suit was the biggest sensation of the entire Olympics, causing thousands of young men to stand over their wives and girlfriends while they sewed them outfits exactly like Joe's. Every young person in the capital received warnings about the dangers of 'getting too close' to a capitalist, and underwent special training on how to deal with awkward questions about food shortages, human rights and Afghanistan. Suggested answers included: 'Russians like to shop very early in the morning, so you probably came too late to see the food . . .' 'Sakharov prefers to live in Gorky because of the good weather there.' And 'The Afghans asked us to send some specialists to help them, and it would have been churlish to refuse . . . Also, they love Pushkin.'

Finally the great day arrived, and the Central Lenin Stadium was crowded for the opening ceremony, at which General Secretary Leonid Brezhnev, who astonished everyone by still being alive, was propped up for long enough to read the official welcome. 'Oh! Oh! Oh!' he began, 'Oh . . .', until an aide whispered in his ear: 'Comrade Brezhnev, you don't need to read the Olympic logo.'

We managed to get tickets for one of the athletics days, but our seats were so high and far from the action that, while I enjoyed the glorious blue sky and scorching sun (to which I seemed to be very close), and certainly remember seeing the huge mascot, Misha the bear, waddling about the arena, sadly the athletes remain in my memory as rather colourful specks teeming round the track like baby cockroaches. Despite the partial boycott, the Games were a tremendous publicity coup for the Kremlin, proving that the Soviet Union could match any capitalist country. The authorities devoted hours of television programming and acres of newsprint to coverage of the sport, the 'cultural programme', and the West's boundless admiration.

But for many Russians the Olympics were entirely overshadowed, one week in, by an event that merited just a tiny paragraph on the back page of *Vechernyaya Moskva*. Vladimir Vysotsky, their beloved actor and singer, the great satirist and minstrel of their lives, died, aged just 42. On the morning of 25 July, long before the announcement in the evening paper, word of his death spread across the country. Thousands of people came spontaneously to lay flowers on the pavement at the Taganka Theatre, where just a week earlier Vysotsky had played Hamlet for the last time – before going on a mighty binge on drugs and alcohol. On the day of his funeral, with the Olympics still in progress and the city in lockdown, hundreds of thousands of mourners turned out for Moscow's biggest-ever unauthorised gathering. Police, including officers on horseback, were diverted from the Olympic venues to control the crowd, but they weren't needed. Vysotsky's followers were too shocked and saddened to cause trouble. As the coffin was carried from the theatre and placed in a funeral bus, the throng began to chant, very quietly, 'Farewell, Volodya. Farewell, Volodya . . .' Then the bus slowly wound its way through Moscow, while bystanders threw flowers and Vysotsky's songs resounded from tape-recorders at open windows along the eight-kilometre route to the cemetery.

This was the real Russia revealed. Most of the Olympic visitors, shepherded around the official venues, would have been unaware of it. Soviet television ignored it. But for the majority of Russians, it was Vysotsky's death, not the Olympic Games, that was the main event of that hot summer of 1980. The funeral was an unprecedented display of civil disobedience. And there was nothing the authorities could do about it. In the Politburo they may have wondered how much longer they could suppress the pent-up frustrations of ordinary people, which Vysotsky had expressed so brilliantly. Luckily for them, Vysotsky had always poked fun, but never called for rebellion. Otherwise there might have been a revolution that day.

After the funeral, life returned to normal. The people continued to seek solace in Vysotsky's songs – this was the masses' form of internal emigration – while the authorities continued to pretend he had scarcely existed.

There was an even bigger display of civil disobedience going on just a thousand miles west – in Poland. Two weeks of strikes at the Lenin shipyards in Gdansk led to the creation of the eastern bloc's first free trade union, Solidarity. On the BBC we heard all about the growing anti-communist movement and its charismatic leader, Lech Wałęsa. *Vremya* couldn't just ignore what was going on, but it couldn't bring itself to use the word 'strike' in a people's republic. Workers in a workers' state couldn't possibly strike against themselves. The announcer said the fraternal Polish people were trying to 'overcome difficulties' and 'restore the normal rhythm of work and social life'. He warned that anti-socialist elements were at work in Poland, and – clearly aware that Soviet TV was not the only source of news available – he warned of the bias of Western reporting. The Kremlin wasn't taking any chances, though. A few days later jamming of Western broadcasts was stepped up, obliterating every hostile 'voice'. Even the British communist newspaper, *Morning Star*, disappeared from the news stands.

At work one day I found myself discussing the situation with Viktor Mikhailovich, the man who had urged me to save ink by using single quotation marks. It would be very dangerous, I said, if the Kremlin intervened to put a stop to Solidarity, as it had done to the Prague Spring in 1968. For a man who was a brilliant translator, and probably even an *'intelligent'*, he gave me the straight Party line.

'The invasion of Czechoslovakia was necessary to prevent the outbreak of war in Europe.'

'I don't follow. I would have thought it brought Europe a lot closer to war.'

'No. If we hadn't gone in when we did, Czechoslovakia would have left the Warsaw Pact, the Americans would have swooped in, and the whole balance in Europe would have been upset.'

'That still doesn't justify an invasion, if change was what the people wanted.'

'But it wasn't what they wanted,' said Viktor Mikhailovich.

I must have adopted one of my 'are you completely crazy?' looks, which only encouraged him to dig in deeper. 'I happened to be living in Prague at that time,' he said. 'The people were afraid of Dubček's experiments with capitalism. I remember speaking to my barber about it. He preferred the protection he enjoyed under socialism – his job was secure, he had no worries, whereas as a private entrepreneur he would have to fight for his living. The Czechs didn't want a return to the rat race of capitalism.'

Maybe he wasn't such an *intelligent*, after all, I thought. I felt free to argue with him in a way that would have earned me the sack if I was Russian. 'Viktor Mikhailovich, of course your barber would have more security under the state system, but that's not necessarily a good thing! Look at what it does to the economy – when there is absolute job security, employees can do as little as they like and be as corrupt and dishonest as they like. That's exactly what's happened in the Soviet Union.'

'But that is the way most people want to live. Go out into the street here and ask people whether they would rather live under capitalism. Ninety-five per cent of them will say they prefer socialism.'

'But that's because none of them knows what capitalism is actually like!' I sputtered.

Viktor Mikhailovich tried to interrupt: 'Oh, they do . . . !'

But I was not going to be knocked off my high horse. 'Also . . . it may be nice and easy to live without having to make decisions all the time, but it means people don't feel any sense of responsibility for anything. Russians hardly ever take decisions because they hardly ever have a choice. Whether they're in the polling booth or in a grocer's shop, they take what they are given. Your Prague barber wanted to sit back and know that everything was "taken care of" by the authorities – but that's the perfect recipe for totalitarian rule. Human beings deserve better than that.'

I suddenly realised I'd better back off a little. 'I'm sorry to criticise your country, Viktor Mikhailovich. I know it's painful to hear a foreigner criticise. I feel the same when you criticise Britain – but by the way, I agree with most of your criticisms!'

He smiled, and I swallowed hard.

I realised that the reason for my anger, perhaps, was that my own fragile illusions, the faint hopes I had come here with, had not lasted long. After almost two years living in the USSR, the balance sheet on the Soviet system was overwhelmingly negative, even if people seemed basically happy. It wasn't just the political oppression. The system just didn't work! Yes, there were positives, but there was a downside to all of them. It was certainly the case that a larger proportion of the population had warm, dry, cheap housing than in the UK, and it was certainly a more equal society. But the general standard of living – even if more equally shared out – was far, far lower than it should have been in a country like Russia, with all its talent and resources. Healthcare was free and tolerably good, and education was brilliant at teaching the basics and produced well-adjusted young adults and a society that seemed less divided and less aggressive than in Britain. But in hospital you had to pay the nurse to bring a bedpan, and you might pay huge bribes to get the best treatment from good specialists. Parents paid bribes or pulled strings to get their children into better schools and universities. Giving 'presents' to those on whom you depended was normal, in fact essential. My friends hated the whole thing, but millions of others just put up with it, and knew no better – or believed that the West was worse.

As I pondered whether to prolong my contract for a third year, Progress tempted me to stay by giving me real literature to translate – stories by Lev Tolstoy, for instance, and Nikolai Gogol's novella, *Taras Bulba*. It was then that my youthful arrogance and ignorance got the better of me. I argued to myself – and managed to persuade myself – that since Gogol wrote his novella (the action of which was set two centuries earlier) at roughly the same time as Sir Walter Scott was writing his historical novels, I would render Gogol's Russian into 'the kind of English Gogol might have used if he'd been Scott'. Not that I told my editors I intended to write faux-archaic English, with thees and thous and maybe even the odd prithee; I just got on with it, determined that this was the right thing to do. I studied Scott's writing, decided I knew how to do it, and produced a quite ridiculous translation of *Taras Bulba*, every copy of which I sincerely hope has since been pulped. When I submitted my manuscript, my editor was shocked and tried to persuade me to turn it into contemporary English, but I stuck to my youthful guns.

I also translated a collection of beautiful short stories by Baltic writers – not, of course, from the original Lithuanian, Latvian and Estonian, but via Russian translations. I hope I did them justice, but a double translation is far from ideal. It was good, of course, that some of the best Baltic writers would have their stories published in English, but the process was a little microcosm of the Russification and subjugation of the Baltic peoples. Instead of the translations being done in Tallinn or Riga or Vilnius, from the original languages, they were done in Moscow via Russian, for a book brought out by the Soviet foreign language publishing house. All that really remains with me now from those stories is a vague vision of a magical island called Saaremaa, and the repeated use of the word for 'juniper' – *mozhzhevelnik* – which became and remains my favourite Russian word.

In the autumn we went out to the suburb of Matveyevskoye to visit Garik and Inna at their apartment. We took an *elektrichka* – a local stopping train with hard wooden benches – from the Kiev Station. The ticket cost just 20 kopecks, but nobody ever checked anyway. The train was full of commuters, some travelling to the suburbs, others to villages and towns beyond Moscow, places like Peredelkino, where Pasternak had lived. We alighted at what looked like a country platform, though it was well within the city limits, and strolled along a wide road that could have been anywhere in suburban Moscow. Farms and peasant cottages had been demolished in the Sixties and Seventies, replaced by the usual tall apartment blocks, most of them thankfully well-hidden by mature trees and bushes. At the foot of one building was a little beer bar, an achingly soulless place with the décor and ambience of a public toilet. This was no place for socialising, just a watering point on the way back from work. Here, you filled your glass with 435 millilitres of weak beer from a slot machine (20 kopecks again), downed it while standing at a chest-high aluminium table, then handed the glass to the next man to wash on a little plunger, and shuffled on homewards.

Soviet housing blocks were all much the same from the outside. Inside too, the little bathrooms and WCs were identical, and at best functional – not places where you wanted to spend a great deal of time; only long enough to put little squares of *Pravda* to their proper use. But otherwise, people personalised their apartments. The Vorontsovs' was full of books and trophies from their expeditions. Garik and Inna tastefully filled theirs with antique furniture and oil paintings hung from picture-rails, like a little orphaned room from the Hermitage.

We sat around the polished oval table in their tiny living room and Inna brought out dish after dish to accompany the vodka and conversation – which in the way of Russian conversations seemed to become ever more profound – or nonsensical – the more we drank. Eventually we reached the inevitable stage at which I felt there was no harm in demonstrating my excruciating naïvety just one more time, and I suggested that the real problem with the Soviet Union was that the 'idea' was not properly implemented – the concept itself was good, but it had got corrupted, being in the hands of idiots and bureaucrats. I didn't actually believe this, though perhaps I wished I did, and said it mainly to make Garik laugh – and he duly obliged.

'What idea are you talking about?' he guffawed. 'Dialectical materialism?'

It sounded so preposterous we all burst out laughing, but I persisted. It was as if some obscure purpose drove me to air ideas I had already left behind: I had no illusions about the Soviet Union, but I wanted to relive the process of disenchantment that the actual country had gone through in the years following the Revolution, by processing it in my own head. I wanted to believe, and find myself disillusioned – just as so many Russians had been.

'Well,' I said, 'Marx did a pretty good job explaining history – thesis, antithesis, synthesis, you know . . . that's the way mankind has progressed, isn't it? Maybe his predictions weren't so good, but his analysis was good, wasn't it?'

'Well, maybe. Maybe!' said Garik. 'But you can't manipulate history. You can't take a book, some "Communist manifesto", and then twist life to fit it. You can't build an entire society based on some German's analysis of history! People are not guinea pigs!'

Inna butted in: 'That's what they turned us into. Lenin and Stalin and all of them . . . they turned the Russian people into guinea pigs for a huge experiment . . .'

'Just to see if Marx's ideas were right!' added Garik, shrugging his shoulders.

This was about the most specific I'd ever heard him being. I enjoyed his way of thinking precisely because, unlike most of our other friends, he didn't even try to explain or interpret everything. He simply *knew* what was what – or to be more precise, he knew that he didn't know. That was what his art was about – the mystery of existence. It floated on a plane high above the muddle and depravity of Soviet politics. His latest series of paintings was wonderful. 'Cosmos' was the title. The characters were drawn in his typical style – Soviet people, mostly men dressed in bulky overcoats. In one picture a man stands alone in a boundless landscape staring up at the stars in the cosmos. In another, a man in a suit is lying asleep, not on a bed but in space, hovering above the city. He would hate me to interpret them, but the meaning was clear: these works were about the smallness of man, the ignorance of man, the uncomprehending powerlessness of man, in the universe. The theme was universal; but in the Soviet Union it had even greater piquancy. Garik might even have said his work was about God – but Garik's God was just the essence, a distillation, of all the forces that make up life and nature and art. God was in everything, giving it sense and structure.

I felt more at home in the company of my Russian friends than anywhere else in the world. One part of me wanted to stay here for ever. But even our friends urged us to leave: two years of experiencing developed socialism, they said, was quite enough: we should go and have a real life back home. It seemed that this would be our last autumn here.

Volodya and Seryozha drove us out into the countryside to pick mushrooms in the forest. To my untrained eye there was little difference between a *podberyozovik* (which grew under silver birch trees) and a *podosinovik* (which grew under aspens), and I certainly wouldn't have trusted myself to eat either of them. But like all Russians, our friends rejected one type of fungus and gloried over others that had a slightly different configuration of spots or gills. They started salivating over the prospect of cooking them before we even left the forest.

We wandered through the trees, their eyes on the ground, mine – having succeeded only in finding a couple of bright-red toadstools – content to marvel at the colours of the leaves.

Volodya said there was a great scandal at his publishing house. They had just issued a new Russian-English dictionary, in which the word *bulka* had been translated as 'bum' instead of 'bun'. Neilian and I roared with laughter, but Volodya looked horrified. 'But it is serious,' he said, his face seeming whiter than usual, even though he had had nothing to do with the dictionary. 'It's considered an act of sabotage!'

He wanted to check: 'Is it a *very* rude word?'

'No,' we assured him. 'It's just a child's word, or a playful word, for bottom.'

Volodya winced at the word 'bottom'. 'And in American it means a tramp or a hobo, yes?'

'That's right. There's nothing to worry about. It's just a typo.'

'Oh! They're more than worried. They'll have to replace the page in every single copy. The proofreader will lose his bonus.'

We thought it was all hilarious. 'Well,' said Volodya, seeing the funny side, 'I suppose it's less serious than the things that used to happen. You know that when they compiled the *Great Soviet Encyclopaedia*, the letter B had just been published, when Beria was arrested and shot, so they sent subscribers a fresh page with a huge article about the Bering Strait, together with a note asking them to replace the Beria entry with the new page!'

I later found the note that had been sent to the encyclopaedia's subscribers. It was even more Orwellian than Volodya had described – for it basically asked readers to be their own censors and help the Communist Party to consign Beria, Stalin's odious chief of the secret police, to non-history. Comically, they wanted readers to do the job very neatly:

The Great Soviet Encyclopaedia publishing house recommends removing from volume 5 of the GSE pages 21, 22, 23 and 24, and also the portrait page between pages 22 and 23, in exchange for which pages with a new text are being sent to you. The indicated pages should be cut with scissors or a razor blade, leaving a margin next to the binding, to which the new pages may be glued.

Somehow, among the boleti and the fly agarics, we got on to nuclear weapons. Volodya was furious with Britain's campaigners for nuclear disarmament (it pained him to see his beloved British people being naïve). 'They're mad,' he said. 'Don't think that just because you give up your nuclear arms, ours will do the same. They won't.'

Having been on a CND march myself, I objected. 'But Britain's so-called deterrent is useless. It just makes us a target. And anyway, they're immoral – if they were ever used they would destroy human civilisation . . .'

'Well,' said Volodya, 'I'm sure Maggie [he meant Mrs Thatcher] wouldn't use them . . . but don't trust our lot not to use them. Don't forget our country states that the spread of communism all over the world is historically inevitable – and of course they are willing to "help" that happen!' And he spat again in that Russian way, over his left shoulder, and hissed: '*Svolochi*! [Bastards!]'

We brooded a while. The evening air filled with silky, soft colours.

'But still,' I insisted. 'Somebody has to make a start. If nobody takes the first step, the arms race will just go on and on.'

'Tfu! Get rid of them if you want! But don't expect us to follow suit!'

The path back to the car was getting darker, as though someone was dropping dark veils over the trees. We were all hungry, and looked forward to having the mushrooms for supper.

'Ehngus,' Volodya suddenly asked me. 'What do you think of my English? Honestly?'

I was taken aback, and complimented him. 'It's wonderful,' I said. 'Your vocabulary is fantastic, and you rarely make even the tiniest of mistakes in grammar. You speak it more correctly than most English people.'

'You see,' he went on, 'Pyotr Mikhailovich [a colleague at Volodya's publishing house] said the other day that he "had heard" that my English was a bit old-fashioned.'

I looked at Volodya, not sure what to say.

'Of course, I don't trust Pyotr Mikhailovich one bit,' he said, and patted his own shoulder. That was Russian sign language to refer to a KGB stooge – someone 'with epaulettes'. 'But, well, maybe he is right . . .' Volodya looked peeved, and needed reassurance.

'That's nonsense,' I said. 'What would he know about it?'

My wife and I had been so carefree at home, so careless, never think-ing about who might be listening to our private conversations. It was only a couple of weeks earlier that we had been discussing Volodya's English, and agreed that though it was brilliant it was a bit bookish and old-fashioned.

'How will you prepare the mushrooms?' I asked. 'Fry them? Or ...'

14

Goodbye to Moscow

WAS IT COMMUNISM (sorry, developed socialism) or something in the Russian diet – perhaps a surfeit of dill, which turned up in every salad and sauce – that turned perfectly nice people into insufferable idiots when they were given even a tiny modicum of authority? The iron rule of Soviet life was: if there isn't a rule, invent one.

We had heard about a brand-new dry-cleaners not far from our flat, which had *German* equipment. Finally, somewhere we could surely trust not to leak engine oil onto our clothes. Off we went with my wife's autumn coat. The machines in the back of the shop were gleaming and new, and the place even smelt like a proper dry-cleaners, not a chemical weapons factory. We were very impressed. We laid Neilian's coat on the counter. The assistant, wearing a white lab coat, examined it closely, but seemed more interested in its style than in finding marks to clean. Finally she spoke.

'The buttons have to be removed.'

'What?'

She rolled her eyes, as if very tired of having to talk to fools.

'You have to remove the buttons,' she repeated.

'Why?'

'In case they harm the machines.'

My wife and I gave each other one of those oh-bloody-hell-here-we-go-again looks. 'These are Western machines, yes?' I said. 'You never have to remove buttons from your clothes in a Western dry-cleaners.'

'That's our rule.'

So we sighed, deeply, and asked for some scissors. Obeying even the most dunderheaded commands was the Soviet way of life.

'We don't provide scissors! Why should we? You should know the rules.'

So we walked home, had a stiff drink, cut off the buttons, and went back to the dry-cleaners with the coat.

*   *   *

I also have a good-news coat story, though. Before coming to Moscow Neilian had bought an old second-hand fur coat at Glasgow's famous flea market, the Barras. It wasn't the height of elegance, but it was very thick and long and it kept her warm even through the winter of 1978–79. And it cost just five pounds. Now, at the end of our two-year stay, we decided to sell it. A friend of a friend was delighted with it, and knew enough about seamstressing to turn it into something more elegant. I can't remember how much she paid for it, but it was enough to finance a two-week holiday . . . in Georgia, Armenia, and travelling around central Asia from Khiva to Bukhara to Samarkand. We even stayed in the best hotels – without bribing anyone. Maybe the fact that we were paying for the trip with the proceeds of a black-market deal was sufficient proof that we were now true Soviet citizens.

You would have thought that leaving Moscow to return home would be easy. We had, after all, chosen to come here in the first place. But no. After two years we were treated almost as though we had become Soviet citizens. They saved up all the best red tape for the end – so much that it took us two extra months just to get permission to go.

Why did I imagine that when my contract was coming to an end, we could just apply for exit visas, pack our bags and leave? Had I learned nothing? In order to obtain visas, I had to apply for permission from the director of Progress. Before I could do that I had to have a separate application signed by my head of section. I also had to prove I was not in possession of any state property (typewriter, sports equipment, bed linen, books from the Marxism-Leninism library – none of which I had ever had). To prove this I had to get a sort of 'circulating' form signed in ten different departments. We also needed tickets, and I was still due my last month's pay. Before I could be given that, I had to hand in the 'circulating' form so that any money I was due them could be deducted. But before I could do that the form had to be signed by the personnel department – and they wouldn't sign it until I handed in my pass-book (which made it impossible for me to get in and out of the building any more).

On leaving the country I was permitted to exchange the princely sum of 130 roubles into foreign currency. But first I had to wait several weeks for an official letter from the finance ministry allowing me to export hard currency reserves, which would have to be presented to the bank when I went to change the cash.

We also had a great deal of luggage to get out. Many items could only be exported with official permission, but no one, in any institution, was able to give us a complete list of such items. It was up to us to think of things that might be forbidden and ask around to confirm our suspicions. They were always confirmed. The restricted items included books, works of art, wooden folk artefacts, crystal, amber and carpets. Books published before 1976 were subject to 100 per cent tax, plus 30 kopecks per book (valuation fee). We had hundreds of books. A complete list of them, stating title, author, date and place of publication, had to be taken to the Lenin Library. Several days later we were able to collect the permit – but only after paying the fee (in a different building, naturally).

Works of art were evaluated at the Novodevichy convent, on Tuesday mornings only. We had been given a nineteenth-century religious painting as a present, and took it for inspection one frosty Tuesday in mid-November. The paintings expert, a young man with a beard, admitted he felt sorry for us having to go round gathering permits for everything. He kept apologising for what he had to do, and emphasised that he only did this one morning a week: his real job was restoring old paintings. One glance at our picture, however, was enough for him to tell us – again with endless apologies – that there was no way we could take it out of the Soviet Union. 'No work of art dating from before 1940 can be exported.'

We also had with us some drawings done by Garik and Inna – portraits of my wife and myself that they had dashed off one afternoon. These would have to be taken to a different office of the Ministry of Culture, which was open on a different day. Moreover, we would need three photographs of each drawing plus a letter from the artists affirming that they did not object to the export of their works from the USSR. The letters would have to be signed, and their signatures authenticated by an official at their local housing office.

All of this took so long that we twice had to postpone our date of departure. Finally, by the end of November we had collected all the documentation and were ready to 'emigrate'. But we could not take hundreds of books on the plane with us, and the cheapest way to send them home was by post. Now . . .

No parcels in the Soviet Union, whether international or inland, could be taken along to the post office already wrapped by the sender. A post office clerk had to inspect every item, wrap it, tie it with string, seal it with wax, weigh it, fill in forms and stamp both them and the parcel, and finally affix stamps – with a little pot of glue – to the package. In the case of international parcels – which could only be sent from the International Post Office on Warsaw Chaussee – the sender also had to fill in four detailed customs declarations and one accompanying form for every package. Your parcel was inspected and wrapped for you at a different desk from the weighing – and there was a long queue at each.

It took us four days to accomplish our modest aim. Every day we arrived at the post office only minutes after it opened, and on three occasions we ended up queuing behind a group of Armenians who were sending enormous crates of household articles to their relatives in the USA. Heaven knows what concept these people had of life in the West, but their offerings for their emigrant brothers included towels, pots, plates, pressure cookers, quilts, toothpaste and even dozens of bars of foul-smelling Soviet laundry soap. Every item was unhurriedly examined by an officious potato-faced clerk.

When our turn came the official insisted on searching in every single book for the publication date, in case we were trying to smuggle out precious folios from the 'pre-1976 period'. Most of the books were Penguins and other British paperbacks that we had brought into the Soviet Union in the first place.

'Look,' I said, 'I've already been to the Lenin Library and I've got permission for all the older books. Why should I try to slip them in with this lot?'

'It doesn't matter,' she said through the little dent in her physiognomy, 'I have to check them all. If they discover an old book at the customs office they'll send back the whole parcel.'

That stunned me into silence. I realised with horror that her beautifully wrapped parcels (each not a milligram over the allowed five kilos) were going to be opened up again at the customs office. What state would they be in by the time they reached Britain?

She wrapped five parcels of five kilos each, and then announced that this was our daily limit. So we lugged all the other books home again, and went back next day with just 25 kilos worth – only to discover that a different clerk was on duty, in whose opinion we could send as many parcels per day as we wished. But we only had five parcels' worth with us. So we had to go back the following day ... when of course the first shift was back.

On the third day I nearly came to blows with the stroppy administrator on duty. We wanted to send two blankets to Britain. No, said the administrator, it was permitted to send only one blanket per month.

'*Per month*!!!!' I screamed. It was definitely time to give her an ideological spanking. I had been holding myself back. 'Do you realise that in

Britain you can post any damned thing you like, and no one even looks at it. The whole business can be over in one minute flat. I've been here for two and a half hours every day this week!'

She had an answer to that. 'I am well aware that in Britain you may be able to send certain things which are restricted here. Do you realise the problems we have in our customs department, sending back articles which may not be imported under Soviet law?'

Her logic was impeccable, for a Russian. But not for me. 'I'm sorry,' I said, 'but I think your "problems" are caused by your ludicrous Soviet laws, not by the freedom we enjoy to post whatever we wish.'

'Every country has its own rules. We have to protect our national treasures. Otherwise all the wealth would flow out of the country.'

'Oh yes? And I suppose these blankets, these miserable little Vietnamese-produced blankets, are "national treasures", are they?'

'In a certain sense, yes.'

'Oh, forget it. We'll leave them with our friends.'

She replaced her black-rimmed glasses and went on with her paperwork. Probably she was learning the commas in the rule-book by heart.

Back at the wrapping-desk, the clerk was insisting that my wife remove a bookmark that had been left inside one of the paperbacks: 'You're not allowed to send *notes* inside books.'

When we weren't procuring official stamps, discussing the world's postal systems and trying to second-guess the next made-up rule, we spent our last weeks in Moscow wandering around our favourite places. I was – I admit it – incurably in love with Moscow.

Although I had come to enjoy living in those much-maligned 'communist suburbs', I loved the centre of Moscow even more. The old names of streets betrayed their original functions. Marx Prospekt used to be Mokhovaya – Moss Street, where they sold moss that was used to fill the cracks in timber houses. Okhotny Ryad – Hunters' Row – was an old marketplace. The present-day GUM – the horribly named State Universal Store – didn't always have empty shelves; it used to be the Gostiny Dvor, inadequately translatable as Guests' Court, a huge, swanky covered market. There were oddities in the toponymy: Kitaigorod translates as Chinatown, but there were never Chinese living there; rather, it was named (probably) for the materials used in wicker fencing. The area just south of the Moskva River, known as Zamoskvorechye, was always a favourite, because its lovely houses had withstood most of the ravages of

Soviet improvement. One of the main streets here was called Bolshaya Ordynka, along which during the Tatar-Mongol occupation, which lasted for two centuries, until 1480, the Mongol Horde (Orda) transported tribute collected by the Kremlin princes out of Moscow. In the seventeenth century foreigners were forced to live a couple of miles from the Kremlin in a suburb known as Nemetskaya Sloboda, or German Quarter. The Russian word for German is *Nemets*, which comes from the word *nemoi*, meaning 'dumb', and was used to describe any foreigner who couldn't speak Russian. Peter the Great, who was obsessed with Westernising Russia, spent much time in the German Quarter, admiring the foreigners' manners and customs and learning from them.

Our favourite shop on Gorky Street (formerly Tverskaya, the road leading to the city formerly known as Tver) was Gastronom number 1. It still looked almost as splendid, with its chandeliers and stucco, as it must have done before the Revolution, when it was a private grocery store. Its founder, Grigory Yeliseyev, was so proud of his shop, and so anxious to please his posh customers, that when a lady came to complain about a cockroach she had found in his bread, he plucked it from the loaf, popped it into his mouth and exclaimed unctuously: 'Good Heavens, madam, a raisin! How on earth did that get into the bread?' Those were the days! Nowadays, if you could persuade a manager to speak to you at all, he would shrug and say: 'Yeah? And what's wrong with that?' or 'Take a different one then, if you don't like it.' Or even: 'Well, you've *handled* it! I can't sell that now!' They were all in the Soviet Managers' Customer Service Handbook.

We also liked GUM's sister, a seven-storey department store called TsUM (Central Universal Store) near the Bolshoi Theatre – not because it was better stocked than any other shop, but because it was founded before the Revolution by Andrew Muir and Archibald Mirrielees, two Scotsmen who had made their fortune in St Petersburg. Muir & Mirrielees had been the Harrods of Moscow, the classiest store in all the Russias, with 43 departments, unheard-of elevators, a restaurant, and the finest range of clothes, fabrics, foodstuffs, jewellery and perfumes. It would dispatch orders to aristocratic homes in every corner of the empire. In 1917 the communists nationalised it, opened it up to the working classes, and employed the sulkiest, sullenest salesgirls they could find to alienate all customers.

Stumbling down the little lanes on either side of Gorky Street, piled up with snow in winter, fragrant with lilac in summer, it was easy to imagine scenes from Tolstoy: horse-drawn carriages, silk gowns, soirées. There used to be little tea-shops here where merchants would meet to discuss business and order 'tea with a towel' – the towel being thrown over their necks to soak up the sweat produced by the strong infusion.

Gorky Park never appealed to me, with its sad, rickety attractions and constant patriotic music or propaganda blaring from loudspeakers. But just next to it was the beautifully named *Neskuchny sad* – the 'not boring garden' – the city's oldest park, a quiet, leafy haven on the bank of the Moskva river. On one of our last days we strolled from here to the nearby Gagarin Square, dominated by a soaring steel column, topped with a massive statue of the first man to fly in space. The apartment blocks surrounding the square were built after the War by convicts, including Alexander Solzhenitsyn. In one of them was a big shop called *Tysyacha melochei*, which Volodya insisted on translating as 'A Thousand Trifles'. It was not a cake shop, however, but a kind of haberdashery or ironmonger's. The display windows sported a sad array of little plastic gadgets that looked like hangovers from the Fifties. Even Soviet plastic was strange: it seemed to come in only three or four anaemic shades of pink, green and blue. How did they manage to put the first man in space, and yet struggled to fill a hardware shop with anything worth buying? Maybe that was part of the unsolvable conundrum that lay at the heart of my love for the place.

Russia pulsed with a silent inner music, beyond explanation. Beneath the dissonance, I was beginning to hear the deep-lying harmonies. They were there in the melody of the language, the intonations of speech, in the quotidian sounds and smells of the street. There was more to this symphony than the sum of all the individuals, places, conversations, thrills and experiences I had had. Here I had found new pleasures, in simple things – the friendships, the togetherness, a willingness to help out one's friends that was already rare in the West. What looked at first sight like a downtrodden nation was in fact a people practising passive, sullen, unspoken resistance to evil, helping each other to survive the idiocies imposed on them by the system. Sugar and hope were equally scarce commodities, and friends shared them generously. Part of the trick was to submit to things that would incense one in the West. I had accepted that shopping was a game of chance, and found that there was greater joy to be had in the unexpected discovery of a rare item on sale than in standing in a Western shop bewildered by the array and choice. I had accepted that a shop could be unexpectedly shut on any old whim – 'Sanitary day', the sign on the door might say, or 'Repairs', or 'Stock-taking', or 'Closed for a Party meeting'.

I had learned to find the freezing cold exhilarating, not uncomfortable, discovered that 'micro-district' landscapes could be as starkly beautiful as the ice cracking on the Moskva river, that a snatched illicit radio signal meant more than all the celebrity gossip spread over miles of Western tabloid pages.

I loved the daft oddities of Soviet life – customs that you would never imagine existed if you had not lived here. Now I pushed my way like any Russian onto an overcrowded bus and handed my five-kopeck piece to whoever I was squashed up against, with a curt '*Peredaite pozhaluista!*' ('Pass it along please!'); the coin would travel down the bus from person to person until it reached the passenger standing next to the ticket machine, who would drop it in the box and tear off a ticket, which then made its way back to you, hand to hand, passenger to passenger, until it reached you. It was a perfect system, like a colony of ants working silently together. Then when the bus was approaching the stop you needed, and you were separated from the exit by a solid mass of human bodies, you would ask the person beside you, 'Are you getting out at the next stop?' and they would either nod, having asked the same question of their neighbour, or perform a little shuffle to swap places with you . . . and you would repeat this little routine, all the way down the line, until you reached the door.

What I hadn't acquired yet was the extreme patience, the apparent ability to put up with any adversity. Maybe for that you had to have lived here for a lifetime, maybe you had to be a Russian. Maybe it was something a foreigner could never acquire – a strand of DNA inherited from stoical forebears, shaped by the climate, by history, by a collective memory of suffering and surviving.

On our last morning we took a tram up to the Chertanovo market, this time with a camera, not a shopping bag, for a few last mementoes. I was still adjusting the shutter speed for a shot of Neilian in conversation with a peasant farmer when a middle-aged man rudely grabbed my elbow.

'Young man, what do you think you're doing?'

'I'm taking a picture of my wife.'

'Well, I think it's prohibited to take photographs at the market.'

'Do you really? Well, I am sure it's not.' I tried to put the camera to my eye.

He pushed it away, saying, 'Give me your camera. I'm going to expose your film.'

'Oh no you're not,' I said. 'Who do you think you are? A policeman?'

'Never mind that. Give me your camera. And show me your documents.'

The man was drunk and unshaven, so I felt pretty sure he was just a meddler. 'Look,' I said, 'I'll show you my documents if you can prove you've got any right to demand them.' The man stormed away, threatening to call the militia.

Finally I was able to take my picture. The farmer was delighted to be photographed with his display of fine vegetables – and a foreign lady. Just as the shutter snapped, an army officer walked in front of the lens. I gulped and held my breath: what if it really was prohibited?

In the afternoon Volodya came to see us off. In the Russian tradition we sat on our suitcases for a moment before leaving. As we closed the door on our empty flat it felt as if some invisible spirit was pushing with all its might to keep it open. Why were we doing this? What was the hurry to get back to Britain? There was so much still to learn. My wife and I looked at each other through tears and wondered whether we would ever have such an amazing two years again.

We put our four big suitcases into a taxi and set off through Moscow to Sheremetyevo airport. Here, the authorities decided to repay our two years of work, our good will, our affection for Russia, by . . . humiliating us. At the customs desk they made us open each suitcase one after the other, and went through every single item of clothing, every piece of paper, all our toiletries and souvenirs – slowly, meticulously, mockingly. The female officer, in her ill-fitting uniform, went through my wife's underwear, and called over a colleague to discuss different items as she held them up for examination. Then they moved on to the skirts, the trousers, the shoes. They held jumpers against themselves as if sizing them up in a shop. They pretended to read my notebooks. They emptied each suitcase and shook it to see if anything else might fall out, then ordered us to repack it and watched us doing so, with folded arms and a derisive smirk on their mouths. They interrogated us about who we were and why we had been in the Soviet Union. Time was passing quickly, and we begged them to hurry; otherwise we would miss our flight. They didn't even respond to this, but just kept on slowly sifting through our belongings, making sarcastic comments. They even took breaks and strolled over to chat and have a cigarette with colleagues, leaving us standing helpless over our opened suitcases. Neilian and I were in panic, pouring with sweat, nerves jangling. But these customs officials were like glaciers.

The airport tannoy announced the departure of our plane, and we gesticulated furiously at our tormentors. 'There'll be another one,' they said, continuing to finger every item of clothing. I couldn't understand it. I could well imagine them doing this to the few Russians or Jews who were allowed to emigrate. But we were *foreigners*! And we'd been working for *them*! It was as if we were now Soviet citizens, and they were punishing us for betraying the motherland by leaving. Or else they had been ordered to treat us as potential spies, smuggling out secrets in our luggage.

I can't even remember exactly how it ended now – I think my brain has wiped the indignity from my memory. But after many hours they finally stopped the torture, and let us proceed. Somehow or other we ended up on the next available flight to London. We didn't change our tickets. The KGB had caused the problem, and now somehow they fixed it. I didn't give a damn. My love for Russia had vanished.

15

Back in the UK

THE TELEPHONE STOPPED working. Just like that. We'd called Moscow a couple of times, once to tell our friends we'd arrived back safely and were settled into a rented flat in Glasgow, and again to wish them a Happy New Year. And then one day it went dead – there was no sound at all when we picked up the receiver. I went to the Post Office to report the fault, and a few days later a van turned up and an engineer came in to fix the line. After that the phone worked fine, but whenever we called Moscow our voices echoed as if we were calling through a metal tube. There were clicks and buzzes. Once I called Seryozha and instead of getting through to his number I was connected to a recording of a previous conversation we'd had.

This procedure was repeated several times over the next five or six years, every time we changed address and had a new telephone number: it worked, then it didn't work, then it got 'fixed'. I'll say this for MI5: they're much more polite than the KGB. They didn't leave a cigarette butt on our floor while installing their bugs.

Neilian found a job as a Russian teacher and for the next few years she was the main breadwinner, while my career as a journalist got off to the kind of flying start that a headless chicken might achieve. My complete lack of experience did not strike me as a significant drawback. I was mustard-keen, and appeared to believe that this was the only qualification required. I had, after all, translated Gogol into archaic English and faced down all attempts to make me see sense! What more could an editor want? If overconfidence, pigheadedness and total unawareness of one's own weaknesses were assets, I was your man. Moreover, it was 1981, Poland was in turmoil and I fancied I knew a thing or two about it – having lived for two years a mere thousand or so miles away, in a quite different country, where there was an almost total blackout on news from Poland.

As chance would have it, a new weekly newspaper was about to be founded in Scotland – the *Sunday Standard* – so I haunted their offices during the weeks before it launched, hoping they might mistake me for a member of staff, and eventually marched into the deputy editor's office and informed him I would be writing the Poland story for their first issue. He was remarkably forbearing, at this point, and probably muttered something like 'well, we'll take a look at it', which I took to mean, 'we'll clear the front page for you.' I spent a few days listening to Radio Warsaw, composed a stunning piece of analysis, delivered it by hand to the newspaper office, and waited for Sunday. In the place where their new Eastern Europe correspondent's article was supposed to be was a report from Warsaw which didn't even have a byline, just '– Reuters' at the end. An agency report! I kept looking, but mine was nowhere to be seen, not even in the sports or entertainment sections.

On Monday I strode into the newspaper office, and was told that was their day off.

On Tuesday I strode into the newspaper office and sat down, facing the deputy editor across his desk. 'You didn't use my piece!' I blustered.

'What piece?'

'The piece you agreed to take from me about Poland.'

'Oh . . . Oh, yes . . .' The deputy editor reached behind him to a metal spike and lifted a sheaf of papers that were impaled upon it, including my masterpiece. He cast his eyes down it, and said: 'Yeah. Wasn't what we were looking for.'

'What do you mean?' I gasped. 'You printed a Reuters piece – an agency report – in a *Sunday* paper! Surely people are looking for in-depth analysis on Sunday, not just a report of yesterday's news.'

The deputy editor twitched a little, and then I made a fatal mistake. I criticised his baby. 'I mean . . . There's no proper analysis in the paper at all. The *Sunday Times* has a whole separate section of analysis and comment. But you've just got one section for everything. It looks like a daily paper!'

'Well, I'm sorry if we're too "thin" for you . . .'

At this point the editor, Charlie Wilson, a man famed for his silver tongue, popped his head around the door and said, 'Hello, Jack, this young man seems to spend a lot of fucking time in your office.'

'Yes,' said Jack, 'I'm just about to throw him out. Into the street.'

'Look,' I said, raising my palms. 'Sorry. I didn't mean to be critical. I was just really keen to get published, so I was a bit disappointed.'

Jack seemed to take pity for a moment and cast his eyes down my article. Then he spoke words that burned themselves into my soul – and I vowed to prove him wrong. 'I just don't think you've got it,' he said. 'What's this – "Jaruzelski *reiterated*." We don't use words like "reiterated", mate. I can't really see you as a journalist. Not unless it's for the *Times Literary Supplement*.' He spoke the last words with particular disdain.

I left with my tail not just between my legs but wound around them, tripping me up all the way to the nearest double whisky.

In October I enrolled with Glasgow University as a graduate student, to work on a doctorate – about *Pravda* and the Soviet mass media. For the next three years I would research *Pravda*'s history, methods, personalities, censorship, and how the propaganda machine worked. It was fascinating, but I still longed to get into journalism. A whole year passed after my humiliation by Jack before I plucked up the courage to approach an editor again – this time at the *Glasgow Herald*. They took four articles from me – about corruption, the arms race, *Pravda*, and an up-and-coming Party boss, Yuri Andropov. They even used a special logo – Russia Today, with a hammer and sickle. I thought my dream had come true. But the next time I offered a piece the features editor informed me that the National Union of Journalists had forbidden them to take any more articles by me, because I was not a member. I wrote at once to the trade union's local freelance branch, and after about a month received a reply – a badly typed sheet that purported to be the NUJ's standard membership rules, but was in fact clearly written specially for me. It explained that I must join the union in order to work as a journalist, and that in order to join the union I had to prove that journalism was my prime source of income. (That, since I was now receiving a university grant, was impossible.) The letter was signed by the membership secretary – whose name I recognised. He was at the time almost the only Scottish journalist who published articles about the Soviet Union and communist bloc. He was clearly letting me know that Scotland was not big enough for both of us. Thus ended my second attempt to enter journalism. Clearly, getting into newspapers was not going to be, as the Russians say about life, just 'crossing a field'.

In the summer of 1982 Neilian and I went back to Russia for a couple of weeks, as interpreters to the Glasgow Youth Band, who made a highly successful tour of Moscow and Leningrad, bringing Souza marches and

Glenn Miller-style swing to Soviet audiences reared on sing-along tunes about five-year plans and blast furnaces.

The tour began with a little embarrassment that gave me grave doubts about Soviet medical standards. One of the trumpet-players developed a mouth ulcer which became septic and started a fever. The hotel doctor prescribed the usual Russian remedy: wipe down the entire body with vodka every two hours. This we did, but while his temperature went down the ulcer remained, so I took him to a *stomatologiya* clinic – an 'oral medicine' or dental practice. The poor lad almost passed out when he entered the cavernous surgery, where ten patients were lined up on reclining chairs like cars at a quick tyre-change station, with muscular lady mechanics wielding slow-grinding drills in the patients' mouths and passing unsterilised implements from one to the other. When his turn came, a cursory glance at the ulcer produced a swift and incontestable diagnosis: syphilis!

Highly unlikely though this was, and despite our protests, we were dispatched to a VD clinic for a thorough examination (not, unfortunately, of the boy's mouth) during which I had to do some of the most uncomfortable interpreting work of my life, calling up vocabulary I never expected to use in public, as the female doctor demanded to inspect the boy's most intimate parts in great detail. My embarrassment, it goes without saying, was nothing compared to the boy's. His was so great, indeed, that his mouth ulcer made an almost instant recovery, without any further 'treatment'. By the time he got to Leningrad I believe there was no sign of venereal disease left at all. All in all, a great triumph for Soviet medical science.

We were hosted in Leningrad by a Soviet song-and-dance troupe whom we had met a few months earlier in Glasgow, where they had come – as guests of the wind band – to perform acrobatic Cossack dances and balalaika music. We had treated them to the usual Scottish fare – fish and chips, mutton pies, and pints of beer, in a number of Glasgow pubs. The hospitality they offered us in exchange was far more lavish. I remember a fabulous afternoon at a lakeside somewhere in the country outside Leningrad, where the ensemble's choreographer Leonid and musical director Yuri treated my wife and me, plus the wind band's director and his wife, to the most amazing impromptu alfresco feast. There were none of your fancy Western barbecue sets in the Soviet Union in those days: Leonid came armed with a clear plastic bag full of meat he'd been marinating overnight and proceeded to strip long thin birch branches with a pen-knife to produce perfect two-feet-long skewers. Yuri meanwhile chopped down branches from the forest and built a huge bonfire – on the embers of which we cooked the most delicious *shashlyk* kebabs. Several bottles of vodka were kept chilled in the waters of the lake, and rapidly consumed.

And so it was that we passed a few merry hours in the Soviet countryside, far – it seemed, though perhaps not – from the prying ears of the KGB. Not that it made much difference to the conversation. Leonid, in particular, was a staunch believer in the communist cause and his namesake, Leonid Brezhnev, the senile Soviet leader who was by then only a few months away from death.

On our last day in Leningrad, Leonid drove us in his beautifully polished Lada (his pride and joy, acquired after only a few years on the state waiting list thanks to his exalted position as choreographer) to Yuri's flat for a farewell meal. It was another sumptuous banquet, *de rigueur* for foreigners entertained by official or semi-official Russian hosts, accompanied by dozens of toasts. To friendship! Gulp. To peace! Gulp. To peace and friendship! Gulp. To peace in the world! Gulp. To feace and prenship! Groan.

Then I provoked an incident. Only a small one at this stage. I said: 'Isn't it marvellous how Russians and British people at our level can get on so well. What a shame our leaders can't do the same. I propose a toast to Mrs Thatcher and Leonid Brezhnev – let them forget their ideologies and get on as well as we do!'

Leonid wasn't at all happy with this. '*Nyet, nyet, nyet*,' he said, wagging his finger. '*Nash Leonid* – our Leonid – is a fine chap. He only wants peace. It's you, it's Mrs Thatcher and Reagan who want war.'

I had to argue back, of course. And though things were eventually smoothed over with the help of a few more fleeces and wenships, the atmosphere was spoiled.

Leonid, by now scarcely capable of standing up, offered to drive us back to our hotel. In his car. In his shining Lada, which was parked in the courtyard of the apartment block, separated from the street by a long narrow lane between two buildings. 'No, no,' we said, 'we'll find our own way home.'

But Leonid insisted. It was beneath the dignity of a leading Soviet choreographer not to. We got into his car and he reversed through the narrow lane . . . or rather, along the side of the narrow lane. Instead of stopping and going forward to correct the mistake, Leonid put his foot down and reversed all the way to the street along the wall, sparks flying in the darkness, and reducing one side of his lovely Lada to a horrible mangled, scarred chunk of metal.

No matter. He got us to the hotel, where we continued our discussions in, I think, the youth band director's room. There were about eight of us, half Scottish, half Russian. At about two in the morning the door suddenly burst open, and three KGB agents wearing leather jackets and stinking of drink stormed in and demanded that I go with them. Clearly the bugs in Yuri's house, or in the hotel, had been working. One of the thugs tried to drag me away, but Neilian sat on my knees to prevent the arrest. This was unquestionably more Laurel and Hardy than James Bond, but somehow my wife's tactic worked. The agents shuffled off. They returned a few times more, always a little more sloshed, but our Russian friends, flashing red ID cards to prove their status, persuaded them to leave me alone. Leonid and company stayed with us till dawn. When we emerged, to leave for the airport, our KGB friends were slumped on chairs at the end of the hotel corridor, a sorry sight, a disgrace to the service.

It's only now, on reflection many years later, that I realise the greasy goon who tried to arrest me bore a close resemblance to the current Russian president, Vladimir Putin. Same fishy lips, fair hair and cold eyes. Putin was, of course, a KGB spook in Leningrad at that time. His job: counterintelligence, that is, snooping on western visitors like me and the Glasgow Youth Band. I wonder . . . Surely not?

In November 1982 Mr B. passed away – mourned only by Moscow wits who were suddenly deprived of their richest source of jokes. His successor, Yuri Andropov, didn't seem like much to laugh about. He had been Brezhnev's KGB chief, who had helped crush the Hungarian revolution and the Prague Spring, demanded the invasion of Afghanistan, and made incarceration in a *psikhushka*, or mental hospital, the commonest way to deal with political dissidents. Less than a year into his leadership, in September 1983, the Soviets shot down a civilian Korean airliner, and Andropov refused to apologise or accept responsibility. When I visited Moscow in November my friends were worried, but they also hoped he would not die soon: they wanted stability more than the chaos of a power struggle – and the younger men who might take over were either unknown quantities or known to be hardliners. Andropov, who was 69, had just missed the traditional Red Square parade to mark the October

Revolution, so Kremlinologists and Russians alike were trying both to guess his illness and to work out what clues the line-up on the Lenin mausoleum might give as to his prospective successor. It wasn't an encouraging sight: all three of the Politburo wraiths who hogged centre stage were even more doddering than Andropov. And there was another reason to wish him a longer life: a new, cheap vodka was on sale. They called it 'Andropovka'.

Ostensibly, the reason for my month-long trip was to spend time at the Lenin Library doing research for my thesis about *Pravda*. I loved working at the dark wooden desks with their green-shaded lamps, pretending to be an academic, but the books I could call up from the stacks were limited. Anything at all sensitive, or containing references to historical 'non-persons', was held in what was known as the *spetskhran* – the 'special storage' section, which was out of bounds to foreigners and all but the most privileged Russians. It was so secret that the librarians wouldn't even admit to me that it existed.

One and a half words summed up the Soviet world of privilege. One was *nomenklatura* – the communist party elite who held all the leading positions in every sphere of society. The half-word was *spets* – a prefix added to all the things to which the *nomenklatura* had exclusive access. There was the *spetsmagazin* – the special store on Granovsky Street where officials and officials' wives or servants would drive up in their black Chaikas or Volgas to buy all the foodstuffs that their useless planned economy failed to provide for ordinary shops. There was the *spetspayok* – literally 'special rations' – the exclusive food parcels delivered to the elite. They drove around in *spets* automobiles, using the *spets* lane down the centre of the road, and got special treatment at *spets* hospitals and spas. And if you were a member of the tiny academic elite, approved by the Party, then you could read books from the *spetskhran*. Some years later a man called Boris Yeltsin, himself a member of the *nomenklatura*, would endear himself to the entire Soviet population by demanding at a televised Party conference that the word *spets* should be expunged from the language, because, he said, 'we don't have "special" communists'. But that was in the future, not in Andropov's 1983, when no one inside or outside the Party elite could even imagine such heresy.

My main mission during this trip was to approach some foreign correspondents. I needed tips on how to batter down the door that still barred my way into the world of journalism – and used my *Pravda* research as an excuse for approaching them. Top of my list was my hero,

Mark Frankland, the great Moscow correspondent of the *Observer*. He was a lovely, gentle man, who exuded experience and knowledge of Russia. He encouraged me to haunt the doors of editors and gave me some useful names on various papers. My ears pricked up when he revealed that the *Guardian* were thinking of appointing a Moscow correspondent and were mainly deterred by the cost. He didn't think it would be presumptuous of me to write to the foreign editor and ask about it.

Frankland lived alone in a small and rather spartan flat in a 'diplomatic block', a guarded compound for foreigners. He almost apologised for the fact that his furniture was imported from the West. This left me somewhat underprepared for the next hack I visited – the maharaja of the *Daily Telegraph*. Nigel Wade lived in an enormous, sumptuous apartment in an older foreigners' block where many of the main papers and agencies were based. I rang the bell, and was let in by an elderly maid, who assumed I had come to see Nigel's wife. She showed me into the luxuriously furnished parlour, bowing and scraping like a Chekhovian servant, and announced: 'Madame, madame, please, somebody . . .' Madame was reclining on a chaise-longue, wearing a silk dressing gown, her hair perfectly styled, a thriller clasped in her manicured fingers. She looked surprised to see me, rather as the Queen might be surprised to stumble across a tramp in Buckingham Palace, and indicated, when I explained my purpose, with a limp wave of her hand the direction in which I might find her husband. The maid bowed her body almost double, backed out of the room ahead of me, and led me cringingly down a long corridor to Nigel's study. The master was writing Christmas cards. He offered me coffee but little in the way of insight into *Pravda*, which he appeared never to read. Nelly, his translator, did that, so he referred my questions to her.

Apart from Mark Frankland, most of the correspondents I met spoke only in clichés about *Pravda*. Some doubted the point of my studies, since 'it hasn't changed in sixty years' and 'there has never been anything interesting in it'. One suggested the paper was prepared 'three days' in advance, which I knew was nonsense: ideological control didn't require that. I had studied the small print of *Pravda* in such detail that I knew not only the codenames of its censors but even the shift patterns they worked. I was beginning to feel ever so slightly superior – and more than slightly annoyed that I wasn't yet a Moscow correspondent.

The Reuters junior reporter, a man named Martin Nesirky, who was about my age, did more to encourage me in my quest than anyone else.

He invited me one evening to his small but beautifully appointed flat, where he took two huge frozen steaks from his freezer, defrosted them in a microwave oven, cooked them up and served them with a French-style salad and French wine – all astonishing things I had never witnessed before in the Soviet Union. All at once, I knew this was the life for me! He earned about £13,000 tax-free – a fortune to me in those days. Plus car loan and free flights home three times a year, because Moscow was considered a hardship post. If this was hardship, what had I just endured for two years while working for Progress?

Martin explained some basics of journalism to me – the Reuters 'inverted pyramid' rules of writing a news story (start with the essential facts, then gradually expand) – and advised me to apply for their trainee scheme. I did, as soon as I got back to Britain. I was told I was 'too old'! I also discovered I was too late for the *Guardian*, who had already appointed their new correspondent.

In February 1984 Andropov died after just fifteen months in power, and the next phantom to be helped into the general secretary's chair was Konstantin Chernenko, a white-haired man who seemed to have difficulty with some of the basic skills required to run a great country, such as breathing, walking, staying awake and thinking. On my next trip to Moscow, jokes were back, all on a common theme.

A newsreader announces: 'A plenum of the central committee of the Communist Party has decided: 1. to elect Konstantin Chernenko as general secretary; and 2. to bury him on Red Square.'

TASS announces: 'Today, at 9 a.m., following a grave and prolonged illness, without regaining consciousness, Comrade Konstantin Chernenko assumed his duties as general secretary of the Communist Party of the Soviet Union.'

On my return, I set up meetings with the foreign editors of the *Economist* and the *Sunday Times*, and both took a couple of articles from me. But things didn't really begin to look up until I got a job at the BBC's Monitoring Service – work that wasn't journalism in the strict sense of the word, but which gave me the right to a coveted NUJ card.

The Monitoring Service was based in a beautiful country house in Caversham, just north of Reading, an hour from London. The mansion was set in a gorgeous park, with ponds full of carp, glorious views of the

Berkshire Downs and little thickets of satellite dishes. I was a Russian Monitor – essentially a translator, since the work entailed few journalistic skills. On my eight-hour shifts I would be assigned a number of radio broadcasts to monitor, and sit in front of an ancient receiver, listening to Soviet news bulletins through hard Bakelite headphones. It was like being back in my bedroom as a boy. When each programme started I pressed a button on a cassette recorder, made notes as I listened, and then took my cassette to a little booth where I would transcribe the bulletin – either in full if it merited it, or just the headlines if not. If there was a major event, I flashed it to the newsroom, and then did a verbatim translation in triplicate carbon copies (known as 'flimsies'), which were popped into pneumatic tubes to swish their way, like cash in an old department store, to different editorial sections. It was all very old-fashioned – but exciting when a major news event occurred. Everything we monitored was publicly available (unlike the secret signals monitored at the Government Communications Headquarters in Cheltenham), so it was odd that we all had to sign the Official Secrets Act. Perhaps it was in case of war, when I guess we would have been taken under government control. The only spying that I was aware of was carried out not by the BBC's monitors but by our American colleagues who shared part of the building – and even then it was just a case of using technology to get their hands on public information early, rather than access secrets. What made this possible was the fact that the main Soviet newspapers were all printed in several cities across the USSR's eleven time zones: the pages were transmitted from Moscow by satellite to printing plants in Vladivostok many hours before the papers appeared in the capital. The Americans at Caversham had receivers which intercepted those signals and printed out full copies of *Pravda* and *Izvestiya* long before they hit the streets anywhere in the Soviet Union. This little wheeze gave our governments a few hours' advance notice on certain announcements.

After a few months of monitoring radio news – sometimes from barely audible shortwave broadcasts – I was entrusted with watching television news as well, which was brought in via the enormous satellite dishes in the park. Our instructions were the same – flash urgent news, transcribe interesting commentaries and economic data. I think the Caversham monitors were the only people in the world who actually paid attention to the mind-numbing grain and pig-iron statistics that opened almost every bulletin. Obviously there was great interest in reports about the 'limited contingent' of Soviet soldiers helping the good people of

Afghanistan. And, curiously, we were instructed to report in detail any items about tractor production – because, the chief monitor confided in me, tractor factories doubled as tank factories.

I continued to write occasional pieces for the *Economist*. I could do this in secret because the magazine didn't use bylines, but on one occasion I almost landed in trouble. In those days of serial deaths in the Politburo, Kremlinologists were quick to spot the tell-tale advance signs – sombre music on the radio, presenters in dark suits on TV. So when, on 10 November 1984, a newsreader appeared on screen in a lacy black frock, Western diplomats and journalists went into orgasm – confidently declaring that a senior member of the Politburo, almost certainly the defence minister, Marshal Ustinov, who had missed the Revolution parade in Red Square a few days earlier, was dead. The West's papers were full of it. Glued all day to Soviet television, I was pretty sure this was nonsense, and wrote a gentle piss-take for the *Economist*:

> Next day there was an even more startling development. A different announcer wore a sweater divided diagonally across the front, with one side black, the other white. Had Marshal Ustinov unexpectedly rallied? On Monday, Moscow television left no doubt that he had indeed had a spectacular recovery. The announcer wore a brilliant jumper in rainbow hues, running from red on her right sleeve to dark blue on the left.

When I came into work the next day colleagues were gathered around a cutting of the article which was pinned up on the Monitoring Service notice-board, with a grim demand, in red ink: 'Who wrote this?' Nobody owned up, of course. I just clamped my headphones tighter and immersed myself in a report about maize yields in Kazakhstan. Up 5 per cent. Huh! Fancy that.

It was during these months that the Cold War became very scary. The Americans were deploying Pershing II missiles in West Germany, and in late 1983 a NATO exercise was so realistic that the Politburo became convinced the West was about to launch a nuclear attack. The propaganda furnace on Soviet TV was red-hot. One programme in particular has stuck in my memory ever since I watched it at Caversham – an hour-long documentary titled *Conspiracy against the Land of the Soviets*. It was a brilliantly produced piece of propaganda, designed to chill Soviet spines with evidence of the imperialists' plot to destroy the USSR. The message was conveyed with rare archive pictures and incriminating documents and 'confessions'. The film was narrated in an icy Big Brother voice that mixed menace with sarcasm. Dissidents were portrayed as stooges of the CIA. The bit that struck me – so strongly that I recorded it onto a cassette – was a song that was used to illustrate the treachery of Russian anti-communists who were plotting the downfall of their motherland from émigré drawing-rooms in Paris and New York. Over jerky, Chaplin-style, black-and-white images of 'white guard' Russians dancing the gopak, drinking champagne and dusting off portraits of the Tsar, they played a haunting Thirties-style Russian romance. The lyrics evoked the longing and sadness that filled the émigrés' lives, and the futility of their cause.

> Don't be sad, gentlemen-officers,
> We cannot regain what we have lost . . .
> We have no fatherland, and no faith,
> And our thorny path is soaked in blood.
>
> For four days now the farmsteads are burning,
> And rains pour down on the land of the Don.
> Don't lose heart, Lieutenant Golitsyn,
> Cornet Obolensky, pour out the wine!

I loved the song, and spent years trying to track it down. It turned out not to be a genuine émigré song at all, but was written in the 1970s in the Soviet Union. I wasn't the only viewer to be enchanted by it. The romance became hugely popular in Russia, and, ironically, was practically the only thing that most viewers remembered from that propaganda film.

On 10 March 1985, after thirteen months of near-invisible rule, it was Chernenko's time to fill the space waiting for him at the Kremlin wall. Within hours of his death, Mikhail Gorbachev – a mere stripling at 54 – was appointed in his place.

As it happened, the previous week I had offered the *Sunday Times* a profile of the ailing Chernenko. Now they called me and asked me to write instead their main profile of Gorbachev for the following Sunday. I was astonished. The *Sunday Times* was by far the biggest Sunday newspaper and one of the most influential in the world – and they were asking me, a complete rookie, to write their profile of the new Soviet leader! For a moment I thought I should talk them out of it. Then I slapped myself and realised it was the chance that could transform my career.

The timing was perfect. Chernenko died on Sunday evening, but his funeral was not until the Wednesday. By good luck, my four-day shift at the Monitoring Service ended on Tuesday and I was not due back at work until Saturday, so I would have three days at home in Glasgow to write the article. On my eight-hour drive from Caversham to Glasgow on Tuesday evening I was in a state of dangerous over-excitement. I discovered the long-wave band of my car radio could pick up Moscow radio, so I became a mobile monitoring service – listening to every word being broadcast as I sped up the motorway, recording the news bulletins on a Dictaphone, and stopping at service stations to scribble down notes. The next day I watched and recorded Chernenko's funeral, which was broadcast in full on the BBC. I noticed that as soon as the old man's body was in the ground, the band struck up the Soviet national anthem at a brisk marching pace, much faster than normal (I even compared the timing with a record of the anthem). This discovery gave me my opening line: 'Mikhail Gorbachev looks like a man in a hurry.'

I telephoned my article in to a 'copytaker' (a new word to me), and drove back down to Caversham for the start of my week. On Sunday the commentary appeared on the main editorial page, next to a cartoon by Gerald Scarfe. It was the most thrilling moment of my life. At work, the atmosphere struck me as odd. None of my colleagues had a clue that I did any newspaper writing, and though they all read the piece, only a few mentioned it to me. I sensed a degree of frostiness, which could have denoted envy, or contempt for my getting above myself. Then I was summoned to the boss's office. Frosty would have been an understatement. He could barely control his fury. He accused me of stealing material from the Monitoring Service (which was entirely untrue as I had done all the research at home or while careering up the motorway at 80 miles an hour) and bawled me out for writing for the press without his permission. I must never, ever, do that again. That half-open door had swung shut again: once more I was condemned to peer at the world of journalism through the keyhole.

When I got over my fury, I realised something rather more important was going on in the world. The USSR had a bright new leader. The Soviet population, I wrote in my *Sunday Times* piece, was 'longing for a leader with a vigorous image to match the country's boastful ideas'. Things were going to change, I was sure of it.

16

Lemonade Joe

MY FRIENDS IN Moscow were markedly less enthusiastic about their new general secretary than I was. Whatever Gorbachev's skills were, his first move – an attempt to prise Russian lips away from the vodka bottle – was hardly designed to win friends and influence people. He was promptly nicknamed Mineral Secretary, or Lemonade Joe, and some even resorted to impolite words to indicate what they thought of the sudden flooding of vodka shops with fruit juice and mineral water.

On a visit to Moscow in November 1985, eight months into the anti-alcohol campaign, I walked past the seedy beer bar near Garik and Inna's flat in Matveyevskoye. It was shuttered and derelict. Even that dismal pleasure had been taken away from the toiling man returning home from work.

Russians had responded with their usual resilience, inventiveness and defiance. Garik told me that getting drunk was now seen as an obligation rather than a pleasure. Anyone who could get hold of alcohol was regarded as a hero. One of the new jokes played on the widespread humorous phrase, 'Do you respect me?', which is the tipsy Russian's slightly aggressive way of insisting that you have a drink with him: if you show any sign of not wanting to share his bottle, he takes it as a sign of disrespect. 'An intellectual meets a drunk,' said Garik, 'and the drunk asks him: "Do you respect me?" And the intellectual says: "Respect you? I *worship* you!"'

In real life, Garik said he witnessed a drunk man, who was standing quietly at a bus stop, being given a hard time by a policeman. A crowd gathered, and even the women, who might otherwise have disapproved of drunkenness, defended the poor man. A bus drew up, and the drunk jumped on at the last minute, just before the doors closed, escaping from the policeman's clutches. The crowd broke into applause.

Gradually, my friends said, the Kremlin was realising the alcohol crackdown was futile. 'Now everyone is learning how to distil moonshine at home,' said Garik. 'Neighbours are being encouraged to report if they smell it . . . but now there's a new recipe for a rice brew that makes no smell!'

'You see how resourceful our people are?' said Inna, ironically.

When a Politburo member visited a factory in Gorky, the manager complained about the new highly restricted licensing hours which meant that many of the men on the production line, who worked shifts, could never find an off-licence open. He would have a rebellion on his hands soon. The next morning a truck turned up at the factory gates selling booze for the workers coming off night shift. It seemed Gorbachev's fine idea was slowly turning to dust.

At this point, less than a year into Gorbachev's rule, his signature policies of *perestroika* (reform of the economy) and *glasnost* (openness in the media and arts) had not yet been announced – or even, probably, formulated. The only watchword so far was *uskorenie* (acceleration), which provoked wails of laughter through tears among my friends. 'You know our Soviet cars?' said Inna. 'The marvellous Lada, that nobody in the world wants to buy! The Lada, that breaks down on every corner! And he wants to make it go faster!'

Gorbachev was nothing but hot air. It was a novelty, it was true, to have a leader who didn't just deliver wooden speeches at Party plenums, but went out into the streets and engaged directly with ordinary people. But he had that wife of his, Raisa Maksimovna, with her chipmunk face and fancy clothes, with him all the time. And he just talked too much, blah, blah, rambling on in that terrible southern accent, like a country bumpkin.

It was even worse than that. Garik and Inna reported a new wave of denunciations at workplaces. The *anonimka*, the anonymous letter, had long been a feature of Soviet life, deployed by disgruntled or jealous workers hoping to get a colleague sacked (and take their job), or by neighbours hoping to get their hands on your apartment . . . but now a whole new field of opportunity had opened up. You could denounce your rivals for drinking, or home-brewing; it didn't have to be true – you were showing you were a true Party stalwart. Garik's application to travel to India had been stopped because of an *anonimka* (he even knew who had written it). Someone else had denounced his magazine, *Chemistry and Life*, as ideologically unsound, and the Central Committee set up a whole commission to investigate. No, Gorbachev was nothing but blather and trouble.

He was a great source of jokes, though. This one still makes me chortle. In 1940 the Soviet leadership – Stalin, Molotov and Bulganin – are standing on the mausoleum reviewing the parade on Red Square. It's cold and they fancy a drink. Molotov has a bottle of vodka and some glasses with him, but they feel embarrassed to drink in front of the crowd. Bulganin suggests they wait until some children come up to present them with huge bunches of flowers, so they can hide behind them. When a nine-year-old boy comes up with an enormous bouquet Molotov says to him: 'Here, hold this bottle while I get the glasses out.' The nervous boy takes the bottle but drops it, and it smashes. 'You little fool!' shouts Stalin. 'What's your name?' The boy cringes and says, in a little voice: 'Mishka Gorbachev.'

In April 1986 I moved from the Monitoring Service in Caversham to the BBC's Russian Service on the fifth floor of Bush House in London. My job was to write daily commentaries on Soviet affairs, which were translated into Russian and beamed into the Soviet Union. For those Russians who – to this day – believe Western broadcasts were pure propaganda, every topic and message dictated by the CIA or MI6, I can reveal that not once did I receive a single word of guidance about what I should say in my commentaries, and not a single word was ever changed. I was trusted entirely – all on the basis of the few articles I had published and the (apparently convincing) answers I gave during the job interview. The only training I received was in how to use a tape-recorder, and how to cut and splice magnetic tape with a razor blade (helpfully known as a 'sharp') without covering the machine in blood.

Frankly, I could have done with more guidance – especially as within days of starting I faced a truly historic and sensitive story – the explosion of Reactor Four at the Chernobyl nuclear power station. This was the kind of occasion when Russians tuned in to foreign 'voices' in their millions, to hear what their own media were covering up. Each day, as the truth unfolded, and an invisible radioactive plume billowed north across Belarus and Scandinavia, I had to sift through acres of reports from agencies and correspondents, and compose calm, trustworthy analyses of what was going on – knowing that many listeners could be taking life-and-death decisions based on what they heard. It was a baptism by fire. Luckily, this being radio, listeners could not see the panic behind the scenes, as I struggled, less with the story, than with the technology and the basic skills of journalism! I can vividly remember calling up some professor at a British university to interview him about isotopes and half-lives. I had to go into a big cupboard, where there was a tape-recorder and headphones, and a sheet of instructions about how to switch the line from telephone to recorder when you wanted to start the interview. The professor must have wondered who the gibbering idiot was that he could hear dropping headphones, aimlessly shouting 'one-two-one-two', and stabbing at buttons, while miles of quarter-inch tape whizzed out of the reels and spewed onto the floor. I can tell him now that the plopping noise that accompanied my breathless, amateurish questions was the sound of sweat dripping from my brow onto the microphone. The recording was unbroadcastable, but luckily I only needed to find a few decent quotes from it, which I covertly transcribed before stuffing the mound of mangled tape into my bag so I could take it out of the building at the end of the day and deposit it nonchalantly in a rubbish bin.

Broadcasting did not come easily to me. My other memory is of being interviewed for *Outlook* by a young World Service producer called Bridget Kendall. It was about the dissident, Andrei Sakharov, whom Gorbachev had allowed to return to Moscow from his exile in Gorky. I was so nervous about being in a studio in front of a microphone for the first time that I had no idea what noises my mouth was bringing forth. Bridget was very kind and spent at least an hour with me, recording thousands of the random words I emitted, from which she was able to piece together, using sharps and sticky tape, some actual sentences that could be put on air. To think that this was the programme we had listened to in Moscow with such faith in the BBC's professionalism.

In the spring of 1987 I travelled to Moscow as a 'fixer' for the BBC's *Newsnight* programme with the venerable correspondent, Charles Wheeler, to do a series of reports on Gorbachev's early reforms, ahead of a visit by the British prime minister, Mrs Thatcher. 'Private' enterprise was still unmentionable in the Soviet Union, but by calling it 'cooperative' Gorbachev got away with his first step in economic reform. (In the same way, he had to use the word '*perestroika*', restructuring, as a euphemism for 'reform', which remained taboo.) We filmed a sequence in the very first cooperative restaurant – Kropotkinskaya 36. Until the cooperative revolution, the Soviet Union had only two types of eating place – the swanky restaurants that wouldn't let you in, and Orwellian self-service canteens serving grey knots of gristle or little patties of botulism, which you ate with a buckled aluminium fork (no knives were ever provided).

The only impressive thing about these places was the menu (neatly typed up, with two signatures and an official ink stamp), which told you precisely how many grams of each dish you could expect the server to slop onto your plate. Kropotkinskaya 36 was another world – with romantic lighting, white tablecloths, tasty food and exemplary service. At least, that's what it was like until we barged in and erected football-stadium lights in every corner and shoved an enormous television camera under the noses of the diners. The owner was frantic, and as fixer I had to mediate between him and our impossibly brainy producer, who insisted that without the lights the camera wouldn't pick up anything at all. 'Tell him it will look beautiful – just the way it is in real life,' he said to me. But the proprietor didn't care what it would look like on TV; he knew that right now, in real life, it looked like a KGB interrogation cell, and he could see his customers, who had come for some expensive candlelit romance, threatening to storm out if we didn't switch our lights off.

I shall not name the impossibly brainy producer because I witnessed him doing something very odd and it would be unfair on him – especially as he went on to become a senior BBC controller and then the head of an Oxbridge college. On an overnight train to Tallinn, when Charles, the cameraman, the soundman and I suggested popping down to the restaurant car, the producer declared he was too busy and would eat what he had brought with him – a packet of Knorr soup, which he proceeded to consume straight from the packet with a spoon. 'You're supposed to mix it with boiling water,' we explained. But he insisted that eating the dry mixture was quicker: 'I'm making the soup in my mouth,' he glubbed, his cheeks full of wallpaper paste.

With radio so terrifying, and TV full of nutcases, I suspected I would feel more comfortable working on a newspaper, and wrote to the *Guardian*'s foreign editor, Martin Woollacott. He interviewed me in the Coach and Horses over a couple of pints of beer, which I apparently drank with sufficient skill for him to call me up a few weeks later and offer me a job as a sub-editor. He knew my aim was to become the paper's Moscow correspondent, and this, though he wasn't promising, was the first step.

I started on the foreign subs' desk in April 1987, processing correspondents' stories – editing them, combining them, checking facts, writing headlines. Predictably, I was useless at first, prompting a colleague to bring in a copy of the *Simple Subs Book* for me. In those days, newspaper copy was marked up by hand, with pencil and paper, but over the next months I witnessed momentous changes in the industry, as the *Guardian* moved from old-fashioned 'hot metal' printing to computerised on-screen editing and page design. I was in my element, but to my great embarrassment, just three months into the job, I was offered something I couldn't refuse – the post of Moscow correspondent for the *Sunday Times*. My heart had been set on the *Guardian* – but even more so on Moscow. I apologised profusely to the editor, worked out three months' notice, and in the autumn finally set off on the career I had longed for.

17

Into a Whirlwind

THERE WERE THREE of us now: our son Ewan was sixteen months old when we moved to Moscow on 25 October 1987. And we had moved up in the world: no longer were we sub-Soviet citizens, living on the devil's horns. I inherited from my *Sunday Times* predecessor a two-bedroomed flat in a 'diplomatic' block on October Square, right next to Moscow's biggest and most ornate monument to Lenin. As the first snows of winter fell Ewan clambered around on the red granite pedestal, exclaiming 'hot, hot!' as he touched the unfamiliar freezing stone. We were worried that the next word to enter his vocabulary might be 'Lenin'.

'Diplomatic' apartment blocks all belonged to a government department known as UPDK, which in those days had a monopoly on providing accommodation to foreigners. They also provided staff, such as translators, maids and drivers, in an uneasy bargain that most diplomats and journalists (including the *Sunday Times* correspondent) struck with the Kremlin: on the one hand, you knew that your maid and driver were reporting every conversation or domestic tiff to the KGB; on the other they provided services without which it would be hard to get a full day's work done in Moscow. The driver, for example, circumvented the drunk-man-rolling-in-dung postal service by hand-delivering letters and reams of application forms and requests to various Soviet ministries. He also fitted the car with studded winter tyres every October, and knew who to bribe to make sure it passed its technical inspection. The maid, who cleaned, baby-sat, and occasionally cooked excellent *borshch*, was, admittedly, an embarrassing luxury – but everyone else had one!

The *Sunday Times* office was in a yellow-brick building ten minutes' walk from the Kiev railway station. It came with a rather glamorous translator called Tanya, whose first task was to teach me how to drive around Moscow in the *Sunday Times* Lada. This was more terrifying than some war zones I would later report from. You had the feeling that most Russian drivers had probably paid for their licences rather than bothering to learn any rules. Lack of skill was compensated for by sheer daring, plus lightning-fast reactions, and cars darted from lane to lane as though the object of the game was to shave a few molecules of paint off every vehicle you passed without actually crashing into them. Swerving violently to avoid unexpected pot-holes added to the hilarity. And obviously there was no point in using your indicator when you had a perfectly good horn. Tanya introduced me to Moscow's eccentric system of road junctions, which often involved some kind of slip road, underpass or flyover; if you missed the right moment to turn off it could involve a half-hour journey to correct the mistake. Most bizarre of all, turning left from a main road in Moscow (where vehicles travel on the right) was well-nigh impossible. Instead of having traffic lights at the actual junction, you had to drive straight on for perhaps half a mile, then move into a lane on the left, queue there to perform a U-turn (if you could spot a gap in the oncoming traffic), and then travel the half-mile back to where you wanted to turn off in the first place, where you could now exit to the right. This manoeuvre, I would discover, was known in expat Runglish as 'doing a raz' (from *razvorot*, the Russian for U-turn), as in this sentence, often roared by some inebriated diplomat at a blank-faced traffic cop: 'Excuse me, *pozhaluista*, can you tell me where one can do a ruddy raz in this God-forsaken town? I want to be over *there*, not over bloody *here*.'

I estimated that at any given moment perhaps ten per cent of Moscow's cars were actually travelling in the wrong direction, just to get back to where they wanted to turn left. There may have been some logic to this when the system was devised (I can think of no other explanation than the general absurdity of communist planning), but it survives to this day, and causes even worse congestion now, since there are ten times as many cars on the roads.

When working for Progress Publishers, we had had no contact with Westerners. Our new expat life was very different: cocktail parties, diplomatic dinners, foreign currency to spend. Tanya explained how most diplomats and foreign correspondents ordered food every week from Stockmann's, a shop in Helsinki. Yes, Helsinki, in Finland – 1,200 kilometres away. Every Saturday morning I would send them a grocery list from the telex machine in the office. The order included everything from milk and butter to fruit and veg, from toilet paper to disposable nappies – perhaps some smoked salmon and capers if we were hosting a dinner ourselves that week. On the Tuesday some fair-haired Finn in an embroidered costume (well, that's how I always imagined it, as if the stuff came from Santa's Grotto) would cram all these goodies into boxes, packed with ice and tissue paper, and dispatch them on an overnight train to Moscow. The following afternoon Valery, my driver, would go to the railway station to pick up the boxes, get them through customs, paying any duty required, and deliver them to our flat. For that alone, he was worth his salary. Did we feel guilty? Of course. But we also felt very glad not to have to queue for hours and hours in the Russian shops. At least I never availed myself of the Hong Kong tailor who turned up periodically in Moscow to measure diplomats and a few sartorially fastidious journalists for new suits.

The office was a standard, dingy, two-roomed apartment, which I shared with the correspondent of the London *Times*. In the kitchen stood a stately old telex machine, which in those days, long before email and internet, was the only means to transmit text around the world. A bulky cream and yellow affair, like something from a government war bunker, the machine had a central teleprinter section that was a bit like a typewriter, but with clunky buttons rather than keys; on the left side was a ticker tape, on the other a telephone dial by which I could connect to a similar telex machine in the London office. My *Times* colleague, Chris Walker, used to file his stories either by dictating them over the phone or by standing at the telex machine laboriously punching in the text, letter by letter. It was a strange operation: once you were connected, each button you pressed, standing in our Moscow kitchen, clacked out a single letter in the newsroom in London. (Needless to say, it was also clacking out letters in a KGB office somewhere.) It was incredibly slow – you could do about one letter per second, two at the most. I wrote my stories for the *Sunday Times* on a recently acquired Amstrad word processor, one of the earliest home computers. But since the articles were often two or three thousand words long, it could take at least half an hour just to re-type the entire copy into the telex machine.

But there was an alternative! It amazes me to this day that the whizziest computer whizz-kid I knew back then was a Russian – in a land where computers were nowhere to be seen. Sergei Petrov, a young dissident photographer, who had been refused permission to emigrate, was well known in Moscow's foreign circles as the go-to man for all computer problems. He reprogrammed my Amstrad and connected it to a little punch-machine that encoded text as thousands of dots on paper tape. Now, when I finished an article, a single mouse-click turned it into yards of ticker-tape, which I would carefully carry through to the kitchen and feed into the telex machine, sending it to London in just a couple of minutes. I wonder what happened to Sergei. I hope he's a millionaire now, enjoying a luxurious retirement in Silicon Valley.

So there I was: telex, Lada, food parcels and maid all in place. All that was left was to start reporting. Luckily, Gorbachev's Russia was chucking stories at me.

A few days after arriving, with Tanya navigating, I nervously wove through the rush-hour dodgem traffic to Dom Kino – the cinematographers' club – for an evening of political discussion organised by a radical weekly newspaper, *Moscow News*. It was clear at first glance that this was not the Soviet Union I once knew. At least 800 people were crammed inside the hall (with another 200 outside, begging for tickets) for what was essentially a massive, and perfectly legal, gathering of dissidents. A couple of years earlier they would all have been arrested and sent to a *psikhushka*.

Moscow News used to be a Soviet propaganda rag, published in English and other foreign languages. It lay around in hotel lobbies trying, like the hard-currency prostitutes, to catch the eye of naïve foreigners. But since the summer of 1986 it had been edited by a man called Yegor Yakovlev, and its Russian-language edition had become the flagship of Gorbachev's policy of *glasnost*. The 'news' it printed was mainly old. And that was the point. Yakovlev was obsessed with telling the truth about the Soviet Union's terrible past. And Russians – or at least the Russian intelligentsia – were obsessed with reading about it. Long queues formed every week to snap up the latest edition, with its revelations of Soviet crimes and cover-ups. The very mention of a forbidden name, the exhumation of heroes (and scoundrels) from the silent grave of Soviet history, was sensational. Millions of Soviet citizens had never heard of Nikolai Bukharin; now they discovered he had been Lenin's right-hand man. Lenin's death-bed 'testament', in which he warned the Party against Stalin, was unearthed and printed. The history of the Soviet Union, as formulated under Brezhnev, was now exposed as a lie. Readers were intoxicated. Some found in the revelations hope that socialism could be resurrected, in a purer, humane form; others found confirmation of their belief that the entire communist experiment was a disaster. Either way, *glasnost* cleared the rubble, so that a new future could be contemplated.

First up on the podium was Yakovlev himself, introducing some of his best writers. They were all of a certain generation, approximately Gorbachev's age. They were born during the years of Stalin's Terror, before the War; many had lost family members in the Purges; then they had lived through the horrors of the War itself; as young men they had experienced the brief lifting of oppression during Nikita Khrushchev's Thaw – only to see it re-imposed by Brezhnev in the 1960s, when they had retreated into various forms of internal emigration. They were known as the *shestidesyatniki*, or Men of the Sixties. It was they who became the motor of *perestroika*, championing the cause of freedom, even as the Old Guard of hardliners tried to cling to the past. The next two years, as I would witness, would be a tug-of-war between the two groups: the Men of the Sixties always pressing Gorbachev to be bolder, the Brezhnevites constantly forcing little retreats.

My notebook from that night is an excited, barely legible scrawl. A historian, Yuri Afanasiev, said: 'Until we fully understand that we are still living under a Stalinist perversion of socialism, we will never progress.' Len Karpinsky, a journalist expelled from the Party in 1975, said a 'mythological fog' was slowly lifting: 'I want to prove that the Soviet scheme of development was anti-scientific and un-Leninist, and led to the discrediting of the very idea of socialism.' The columnist Yevgeny Ambartsumov said he had just visited West Germany and assured the audience that 'we shouldn't think of the West as something alien to us.' Lev Voznesensky, an economist, asked the audience whether they wanted the price of meat to rise. There were loud shouts of 'No! No way!' 'Read my article in next week's *Moscow News*,' he replied. 'It's about a private farmer in Arkhangelsk who produces meat more cheaply than the state. That's the way to avoid price hikes – not by keeping subsidies but by giving people the land and making them feel like they own it again.' There was a stunned silence, slowly resolving into cheers. Then came Arkady Vaksberg, a delightful man who would become a friend of mine. He was a journalist with *Literary Gazette* who even under Brezhnev managed to publish exposés of corruption. It was the authorities at the lowest levels, he said, who were holding back *perestroika*, by covering up every violation to make themselves look good. Ales Adamovich, a Belorussian writer, said the problem was even wider: *perestroika* hadn't yet penetrated into the provinces – that's where all the ideas were dying.

It was as if whispered conversations at a hundred Soviet kitchen tables had suddenly been blown together on a public stage and whipped into a hurricane. 'What about Solzhenitsyn?' came a voice from the auditorium. Solzhenitsyn – a name only heard until recently on those shortwave 'voices' in the dead of night. 'He deserves our gratitude,' said Afanasiev, 'for being the first to raise the topic of Stalinism so boldly.' The audience applauded warmly, as though a spell had been broken. I could feel the hairs on my arms standing on end. Then, another question that might once have earned its asker a short course of electric-shock treatment: What did Afanasiev think of Mikhail Suslov, for years the grey guardian of Marxist-Leninist ideology under Brezhnev. 'Suslov?' A pause, and a rueful shake of the head. 'He did immense harm to our society. The only difference between the Brezhnev era and the Stalinist was that there were no mass murders. Otherwise it was the same.'

The questions – and the astonishing answers – kept coming and coming. One speaker, a theatre critic, told the audience that Yegor Yakovlev had joked to his staff: 'Every article you write should be one that I could get sacked for!' Eight hundred people seemed to concur: the age of censorship was over – there had to be a complete re-telling of Soviet history, the rehabilitation of Stalin's victims, an end to all bans on creativity, publishing and religion. At the end, Yakovlev himself took the stage again, with the impish smile of a man who has not only let the genie out but smashed the bottle. The first stage of democratisation was over, he proclaimed – meaning the freedom to speak the truth; the next would be to enshrine it all in law and make the changes permanent.

But that very week, in the last days of October, rumours were swirling around Moscow of a furious row in the Politburo that showed how hard it would be to make the changes permanent. The protagonists were the angel and the devil that sat on Gorbachev's shoulders – Boris Yeltsin, the firebrand chief of the Moscow Party organisation, and Yegor Ligachev, the hardline heir to Suslov in the Politburo, whose job it was to ensure the Party never acquired a human face.

The first I heard of their spat was when I went to my maiden cocktail party at some foreign diplomat's apartment. My *Times* colleague, Chris, took me there, but quickly disappeared, possibly with the host's wife or a dainty waitress, leaving me to contemplate the little scrums of journalists and diplomats, of whom I could see only the backs of their jackets, and hear only a vague hum of conversation. I think I know how my son felt the first day I left him at kindergarten. Suddenly I recognised someone I knew, the *Guardian*'s correspondent. I sidled up to the group and eavesdropped for five minutes but couldn't understand a thing that was being said, so I turned to him with a bold 'Hi, Martin', and asked him what they were talking about. 'Pick it up as you go along,' he replied, with barely a glance in my direction.

In fact there wasn't, as yet, a great deal to pick up. The word was (though none of it could be confirmed) that Yeltsin had made an unprecedented speech at the 300-strong central committee meeting (or 'plenum') on 21 October, in which he had criticised the slow pace of reform, complained about a 'cult of the personality' being fostered around Gorbachev, derided the prominence of Raisa Gorbachev as 'First Lady', and disparaged Ligachev for sabotaging his work in Moscow. Ironically, it was Ligachev who had recommended Yeltsin for the job of Moscow party boss, never imagining that he would become the darling of the city, riding the buses and popping into shops to chat with ordinary folk. The rumoured speech – exaggerated and embellished with everybody's personal fantasy – was rapidly turning Yeltsin into the hero of *perestroika*, eclipsing Gorbachev.

On 31 October four central committee members gave a press conference (another novelty!) at which one of them confirmed that Yeltsin had made some 'incorrect assessments' at the plenum, and had offered his resignation. This was sensational – the first time the inner sanctum of the Party had washed so much as a dirty sock in public. There were limits to *glasnost*, however. While foreign correspondents rushed from the news conference to report the first official acknowledgement of ructions at the top of the Party, TASS, the state news agency, issued what it termed a 'categorical recommendation' to all Soviet media not to mention a single word about the Yeltsin affair.

In fact we had been told the barest minimum, and the Kremlin did its damnedest to control the news for the next two weeks, for the truth was, Yeltsin had chosen the most inappropriate moment to challenge the leadership – the seventieth anniversary of the Revolution itself. For weeks the media had been building up to the great celebration on 7 November. Seven decades of communist achievements were being lauded to the skies – and the last thing they wanted was some party-pooper nit-picking about mass murder or empty shops.

For a week or so the leadership mounted a pretence of unity. At the Red Square parade on Revolution Day, Yeltsin stood glumly on top of the Lenin mausoleum together with his Politburo colleagues – and also a scattering of foreign dictators, from Castro to Ceaucescu – while Gorbachev, with Ligachev standing smugly at his shoulder, waved at the marching crowds.

Then all hell broke loose. On 9 November, Yeltsin tried to kill himself in his office by stabbing his chest with blunt scissors – not the most convincing suicide ever attempted, but enough to have him rushed to hospital with a suspected heart attack. The next day the Politburo met without him and agreed to sack him immediately. And the day after that Yeltsin was hauled from his hospital bed and forced to face a hall full of braying hyenas who comprised the Moscow Party Committee, at a meeting specially chaired by Gorbachev himself.

I should say that few of these details – the scissors, the hospital, the Politburo meeting – became known until memoirs were written a few years later. But the hyena attack was emblazoned all over the papers; it was absolutely intended for public consumption. It bore a strong resemblance to the kind of public humiliations to which Stalin's foes were once subjected. 'Comrade Yeltsin' had 'delivered a calculated, treacherous stab in the back of the Party'. He was described as vain, bombastic, over-ambitious, showy, sloganizing, destructive, afflicted by 'big-boss syndrome' and given to 'pseudo-revolutionary phrases' – you name it, they had two-and-a-half pages of venom to describe it. Yeltsin himself abjectly confessed his 'guilt' – and was then formally stripped of his duties and rushed back to hospital to continue his heart attack.

I went to see my friend, Volodya, who was white-faced. It was like a Stalinist show trial, he whispered, shielding his mouth with his hand, as though it went without saying that the KGB had already reinstalled bugs in everyone's flats. 'You see – this is what the Party does when its privileges are attacked . . . they turn on the traitor like wild animals. Tfu!'

One of Yeltsin's 'mistakes' (which had particularly infuriated Ligachev) was to have authorised political demonstrations in the capital. Now, after his ritual slaughter, people took to the streets without even asking for permission. The knuckleheads in the Politburo, thinking they had consigned Yeltsin to history, had in fact turned him into a martyr, the hero of all those who were disenchanted with the system, with the aloof and pampered Party elite, with the seventy years of lying. One demonstrator brandished a copy of *Pravda* at me, with its two pages of denunciation: 'Do they really think we'll all now start thinking he's an enemy of the people? Boris Nikolayevich is one of us!'

18

More Light

FOR ALL THE hullabaloo surrounding Yeltsin and his enemies, this was really the age not of politicians but of the intelligentsia. Finally, all those internal émigrés emerged from the Gulag of their kitchens – as writers, publishers and consumers of the ideas that would revolutionise the Soviet Union. And like Russia's nineteenth-century thinkers, the heroes of *glasnost* held their debates mainly in the pages of the so-called 'thick journals' – 200 or 300-page monthly literary magazines with no real equivalent in Western countries.

Now when I visited my old friends all they talked about was the latest sensation published in *Novy Mir* (*New World*), *Znamya* (*Banner*) or *Yunost* (*Youth*). They devoured everything – poetry, plays, novels; new polemics; old works of literature banned by Comrade Plod, the state censor. There was a lot of catching up to do – decades of writing that had never been published, or at any rate not in the Soviet Union.

'I can hardly find time to work,' said Garik, picking up a pile of journals from a chair. 'Look at this – *Children of the Arbat*! Fantastic! And look, *Znamya* published this story by Okudzhava, and Akhmatova's *Requiem* is in *Oktyabr*, and – oh, by the way, look, we've bought a TV, it's incredible what they're showing, have you seen that new programme, *Vzglyad*? And Platonov – have you read him yet?'

'Woah, slow down,' I said. I'd never seen Garik so excited.

Inna, as ever, sat placidly at the head of her oval table, presiding over the salads and the conversation like a wise owl. 'Whatever we once said about Mikhail Sergeyevich [Gorbachev], he's done a fantastic thing.'

There were fresh opportunities for Garik himself now. In the past few years he had branched out in new directions. A flamboyant British collector and publisher, Edward Booth-Clibborn (described by *Vogue* as the sharpest mind in art publishing), had bought some of his works and included them in a beautifully produced annual called *European*

Illustration, bringing Garik to the attention of a worldwide audience for the first time. I became a go-between, ferrying Garik's works out of the country, and enjoying lunches with Booth-Clibborn in fine Mayfair restaurants.

Garik had also started a new line of work – humorous cartoons, which were already winning gold medals in competitions all over the world, from Tokyo to Knokke-Heist. These were simple line drawings, less complex than his etchings or magazine illustrations, but with the same surreal sense of humour. A steamroller grinds towards a mound of earth shaped like the outline of a human face. A man sits in his underpants eating breakfast from a newspaper-covered table, with a choice of two outfits hanging on the wall – a devil's and an angel's (with a pair of flip-flops on the floor beneath the latter). A woman hangs up her dripping smile to dry on a washing line. A statue – a man in a Soviet suit but with Roman laurels on his head – has removed his shoes and is quietly tiptoeing away from his pedestal . . .

We sat down to watch the new television programme, *Vzglyad* (*View*), which had just been launched and broke every rule set out by the Party propaganda department. Garik and Inna punctuated it with gasps of disbelief and snorts of derision. Until now Soviet television had had newsreaders, who read out exactly what the Party dictated. This programme – a mixture of studio discussion, down-on-the-street reporting and pop music inserts – had real 'hosts', young dudes who spoke without notes, and reporters who went out and stuck their camera everywhere that Soviet TV had previously avoided. It was astonishing – and all the more charming for its shambolic lack of sophistication. The studio set just looked like an office, with cluttered cupboards and plastic chairs, typewriters and anglepoise lamps on the desks, bits of paper pinned to the walls, and a 'chat' area with dowdy old furniture and a grey telephone on the coffee table, presumably so the Kremlin could call in to put a stop to their sedition. But it didn't! Russians were now glued to their TV sets every Friday night at 11.30.

'Bastards!' said Garik, as a *Vzglyad* reporter tried to force his way into the grounds of the Kremlin's élite hospital and got the gates pushed shut in his face.

'*S uma soiti*! – Crazy!' said Inna, as we watched a TV crew arrive at the scene of a traffic accident where the police prevented them from filming. The report went on for five minutes, showing the police ignoring the accident and demanding to know the names of the reporter and cameraman, while the reporter – pointing out that he worked for *state* television, demanded in turn that the officers give their names. 'Quite right!' said Garik. 'Let them know they're being monitored. Otherwise these bastards think they're above the law.'

The young presenters became household names, and revolutionised Soviet television. One week they filmed the enormous queues that snaked around shops all over the country, trying to work out why it was that more goods suddenly appeared at the end of each month. A reporter stood on Red Square jerking his thumb in the direction of the Kremlin, defiantly denouncing the broken Soviet system. In another edition they interviewed Andrei Sakharov: Russian people for the first time saw and heard the shy, faltering boffin, with his speech defect and his too-big suit, talking about how he helped develop the hydrogen bomb, but now understood the horror of nuclear war and was dedicated to his human rights work. Another programme discussed whether Stalin and his henchmen should be put on trial. Another showed graphic images of gangland murders, and victims having horrific wounds stitched up in hospital. We saw footage of police raids on the homes of corrupt officials, turning up jewels and diamonds and cash. There were secretly filmed pictures of police arresting black marketeers. In short, *Vzglyad* showed the grubby, lurid, hidden side of Soviet life which had never been shown on television. The pretence that Soviet society was an advanced form of civilisation was blown to smithereens.

When we visited Volodya and Seryozha, they apologised for the poor fare they had laid on for dinner. 'There is almost nothing in the shops these days, I'm afraid,' said Volodya. Neilian and I felt a squirm of guilt at the thought of our Stockmann's deliveries. 'But we don't even notice,' Volodya went on: 'There is so much for our brains to feast on!' Like Garik, he gestured to a pile of thick journals.

'Ehngus,' he said, 'do you receive *Friendship of Peoples* at your office?' And immediately he wanted an English lesson. 'Is it "receive" or "acquire"?'

'I think I would just say "get",' I replied.

Volodya sniffed. 'Well, I was always told to avoid "get" if there was a more precise alternative . . .'

'Well, anyway, we do subscribe to the main thick journals – including *Druzhba narodov.*'

'Ah, "subscribe", of course. So . . . have you seen the April, May and June issues? It's wonderful, simply wonderful . . .'

Seryozha took up the story: 'You see, they published *Children of the Arbat*. It's simply fantastic. This is more important than making speeches about Stalin. This is how it was. How it really was!'

Anatoly Rybakov's epic novel told the story of young friends living in the Arbat district of Moscow in the 1930s. They end up variously in exile, or in the NKVD (secret police), or simply drowning in the swamp of fear and denunciation that accompanied Stalin's Purges. Volodya had been a small boy in those years, but felt the terror stalking his parents' generation. Seryozha had grown up in the bleak but less terrorised age of 'advanced socialism'. Now both of them, through Rybakov's novel, were able to immerse themselves in Russia's awful past. Millions of Russian readers learned what everyday terror had been like. The book describes an age when a misspoken word – or a misunderstood poem in a wall newspaper at school – was seized upon as proof of disloyalty to the Party or Stalin; an age when a perfectly innocent person could end up having a Kafkaesque conversation like this with an NKVD interrogator:

'I want to know why I have been arrested.'

'We want *you* to tell us that.'

'Tell me what you suspect me of, and I will answer.'

'Who did you have counter-revolutionary conversations with?'

'Nobody.'

'So who had them with you?'

'Nobody had them with me.'

'So you mean you've been arrested for nothing at all? We put innocent people in prison, do we? Even here you continue with your counter-revolutionary agitation!'

The most famous thick journal was *Novy Mir*, whose pale-blue cover became an icon of Khrushchev's Thaw, when it published Solzhenitsyn's labour-camp novel, *A Day in the Life of Ivan Denisovich*. Now it was thriving once more, and at the end of 1987 announced that its first four issues in the New Year would include the celebrated Pasternak novel, *Doctor Zhivago*. This had been published in the West in 1957 and earned its author the Nobel Prize, but had been strictly forbidden in the Soviet Union. I had to smile at a secret memory of mine . . . At university I had bought a miniature edition of the novel in Russian which had evidently been produced by the CIA specially for the purpose of smuggling – it was printed on Bible paper, in two thin volumes, small enough to fit into the pockets of a jacket. Later, on one of my visits to Moscow when Andropov or Chernenko was in power, I had brought it with me, intending to give it to Volodya. For some reason I left it until the last day of my trip to take it to him. He was so horrified by my present that he barely dared even to whisper his refusal: 'If they find this in our flat I will be sacked immediately!' I had no alternative but to put it back in my pocket and take it home, thus becoming probably the only idiot in history to have smuggled *Doctor Zhivago* into *and out of* the USSR.

Seryozha was right when he said novels about life under Stalin were more effective than political speeches about his crimes – and the same went for telling the truth about Soviet history. Gorbachev struggled to work any meaningful criticism of the past into his speeches (and constantly insisted that if only the country had stuck to 'pure' Leninism, everything would have been all right). But the thick journals took up the cause with gusto, no holds barred. *Novy Mir* published a play called *The Peace of Brest-Litovsk* by one of the country's leading historical playwrights, Mikhail Shatrov, which included portrayals of Stalin's erstwhile comrades (who became his enemies), Trotsky, Bukharin and Zinoviev. He had written it in 1962, but that was too early to rescue these figures from the Party's memory hole; only now, under Gorbachev, was he able to publish the play. A friend from Progress days, Svetlana, knew Shatrov, and offered to introduce me to him.

The arrangement was that I would pick up Svetlana, and then Shatrov, from their flats in Moscow, and drive them out to his dacha. I was a big disappointment to him from the outset: I rang his doorbell, waited for him to come down to the street, shook hands, and led him to my car – a brown, mud-spattered, boxy Lada hatchback. Shatrov took one look at it and asked me: 'Are you sure you're from the *Sunday Times*, not the *Morning Star*?' I later used this comment to try to shame the newspaper into buying me a new car (other correspondents had Volvos and Saabs), but to no avail.

It took me about an hour to drive out to his dacha – an hour he spent trying to impress our glamorous mutual friend, while I prayed hard that my jalopy would not break down or fall to pieces as it hiccupped along the bumpy, ice-covered roads. Having to dig it out of a snowdrift would have been the ultimate ignominy. Shatrov's house was in a writers' colony, lost in a wilderness of snow. Eventually I persuaded him that I was almost as interesting as Svetlana (though less eligible to become his third, or was it fourth, wife), and was planning to write an article about him in A Major Foreign Newspaper.

After reprimanding me for turning up without a bottle of whisky, Shatrov served cognac (his cognac), and tea from a samovar, on the veranda, and somehow it didn't feel cold sitting there among the snow-clad pine trees. Looking back at my notes from the day, it seems surreal that we spent time discussing arcane details of arguments made by Russian revolutionaries in the 1920s – and yet the fact that we were doing so (or rather, the fact that Shatrov was able to do so in his plays) went to the heart of the political debate in the 1980s. 'I've never written historical plays,' he said. 'They're all about today – trying to understand today through history.'

'In what way?'

'Lenin, for example. I show him in *Brest-Litovsk* as a great pragmatist who broke old dogmas and accepted others' points of view – that's a model for today.'

The Peace of Brest-Litovsk was due to be premiered in early December 1987, but already Shatrov had written a new play, *Onward! Onward! Onward!*, which he hoped to see in print early in 1988.

'I won't say it "will" be published, but I hope so.'

I asked him why he was so cautious, and he brought out the manuscript to give me a preview. 'Look,' he said, 'here is Bukharin, speaking just before his execution, explaining his loyalty to the Revolution, and why he could not possibly be an enemy of the people.'

In the next scene one of Stalin's associates, Ordzhonikidze, complains to the dictator that the NKVD has searched his flat and reminds him that Lenin had called Bukharin the Party's favourite, not Stalin. An argument develops, during which Stalin tells Ordzhonikidze, who was responsible for planning the USSR's massive industrialisation programme in the Thirties, that one day people will be proud of his achievement, to which Ordzhonikidze replies: 'It wasn't me that carried out industriali-sation but all those people who you are now lining up against the wall . . . Your only passion is power and cruelty.' At the end Ordzhonikidze commits suicide.

I asked Shatrov why getting such plays performed was so difficult.

'Because they – *they* – don't want the truth to be told, because it undermines their own authority. The Soviet people have been told for decades that there were no purges, no mass terror, that Bukharin was an enemy of the people – like they're doing with Yeltsin now, by the way.'

As we spoke it became clear that Shatrov was a staunch Bolshevik. That was why his explorations of Soviet history fitted perfectly the mood of *perestroika*, which was not about ending communism, but making it work better, making it more humane. Like Gorbachev, Shatrov used the key figures from Soviet history to debate where things went wrong, and what lessons could be learned. When Lenin died in 1924, his New Economic Policy (NEP), which signified a retreat from full-on state-controlled communism, was still in force; it was Stalin who ended it and began the murderous collectivisation of the farms. 'The methods used to socialise agriculture were not Leninist ones,' said Shatrov.

Sitting in our overcoats, with the snow gently falling in the garden, I tried to digest what he was saying, and understand why it was so controversial today. Before moving forward, it was clear, the Men of the Sixties felt they had to sort out the past. They were not ready to junk the communist idea yet. Reforms, at this stage, were still justified in terms of 'what would Lenin have thought?' What if Lenin had not died in 1924? Things could have been different. Maybe things could still be different – maybe the Party can still go back to what Lenin 'really' wanted, the Bukharin route instead of the Stalin route, and try again to build socialism . . . If the 'socialism lite' of NEP was okay for Lenin, surely it was okay for Gorbachev?

History would soon show that this was a lost cause. It would not be the Men of the Sixties, in the end, who would shape Russia's destiny.

My work wasn't all diplomatic parties and writers' dachas. I spent a lot of time at the end of 1987 in less glamorous locations, seeking out other heroes of *glasnost*, men and women who had been jailed under Brezhnev for 'anti-Soviet propaganda and agitation', and who now emerged as leaders of a new wave of dissent. 'Leaders' is an odd word, for they were still forced to live in the shadows. They worked as boiler attendants and caretakers, as janitors or labourers, while secretly publishing carbon-copied journals or political tracts at home. Occasionally they organised seminars and news conferences in their apartments – monitored, but not usually impeded, by the KGB.

I set off early one November afternoon in the Lada, hoping to find an address so far away in the northern suburbs of Moscow that I could find no trace of it at all on my street plan. (Maps were not the Soviet Union's strongest point – unless you were in the military or KGB, of course. The rest of us had to make do with 'tourist schemes' which intentionally distorted where things were and depicted outlying districts of the city with a certain artistic flourish.) 'The tongue will lead to Kiev,' goes the Russian proverb, and indeed by stopping and asking half a dozen times I eventually reached my goal – a long, nine-storey apartment block with five porches. Just inside the double doors of one of them was a little caretaker's room, a tiny cell just big enough for a rickety chair and a little desk, an electric heater, and a narrow bed along the wall, on which was seated the man I had come to see.

Boris Kagarlitsky was an earnest twenty-nine-year-old, with a youthful strip of beard circling his jaw like a chin strap. He was an unusual kind of dissident – a leftist who considered himself more Marxist than the Soviet government. In the late Seventies – the period I described at the beginning of this book – he had applied to join the Communist Party, but was imprisoned for anti-Soviet propaganda after publishing an underground magazine called *Left Turn*. 'I was a Euro-communist,' he explained. He had studied theatre criticism, but his political activities made him unemployable, even after his release from jail.

'Actually, I prefer this,' he said, indicating his little janitor's office. 'This gives me time to think, and to organise our next activities.'

I thought of the concierge in our own block of flats – a retired woman, of the kind generically referred to as *babushka*, whose knitted mohair hat never left her head and whose social activities amounted to her daily admonishments to keep Ewan wrapped up more warmly. I wondered if the inhabitants of this particular apartment block realised that their concierge was in fact a covert revolutionary.

Since *glasnost* made it possible, Boris had organised a lot. He was one of the heads of the Club of Social Initiatives, which brought together about a hundred different groups – environmentalists, conservationists, radical poets, and clubs with names like Che Guevara Brigade and Crazy House. Nothing stood still, though. Never mind that all this activity was only semi-legal, and diverse to say the least, the CSI was already banding together with other groups to form a Federation of Socialist Clubs, which was planning a big founding conference in the near future.

It's hard to overstate how subversive this was. Until a year ago, the Communist Party had controlled everything. There was no activity in the country, apart perhaps from sex, that the Party did not initiate, organise, monitor and monopolise. Now there were said to be thousands of 'informal' clubs – known as *neformaly* – all striking out on their own.

Boris's wife, Irina, arrived with their little son, Gosha, to deliver sandwiches and a flask of tea, plus some fresh carbon paper that she had managed to procure. These were the basic tools of the Soviet dissident movement.

Boris was beginning to make my head spin. Soviet politics had seemed reasonably straightforward, with hardliners like Ligachev and firebrands like Yeltsin pulling Gorbachev in two directions, but all within the bounds set by the Communist Party and its sclerotic central committee. Now Boris was rabbiting on about Scandinavian social democracy, 'the need for a profound democratisation of the decision-making process to mitigate the side-effects of the emerging market', and why he disagreed with so-and-so in such-and-such a club because Marxism never envisaged this-or-that . . . It reminded me of the tiresome student union debates I had attended at university. Except our student debaters ended up in the pub, not in prison!

The authorities tried to get in on the act. Two days after I met Boris Kagarlitsky, one of the official news agencies, APN, organised a news conference to help the foreign press 'understand' the burgeoning *neformaly* phenomenon. An official explained that there were now hundreds of groups, from hippies and punks to human rights organisations. He insisted that 'all of them recognise the leading role of the Communist Party'. Either that was wishful thinking, or – more likely – it was part of the great pretence that the slow dismantling of the communist system was actually its 'improvement'.

What made these first months in Moscow so exciting was the total unpredictability of everything. Gorbachev's idea had been merely to sweep clean the road ahead – the road to a better socialist future. But *glasnost* was like a torrent of water: it didn't just wash the road ahead but gushed off into side streets and alleyways, rooting out filth and exposing all sorts of fresh possibilities. Apparatchiks could complain all they liked that this wasn't where it was supposed to go – but there was no way to call it back. It was almost comic to watch things spinning out of control. I spent most of November and December 1987 flitting from one underground meeting to another. I could feel in my bones: this was where the revolution was happening.

I went to a meeting with veterans of the Afghan war, which for eight years had been sending back thousands of unsung dead soldiers in zinc coffins. Those lucky enough to be only maimed returned to a stony, uncaring silence. But now they had got together to found a nationwide veterans' society to lobby for their rights. Men with leg-stumps wrapped in dirty bandages told me about the problems they faced: no proper housing or compensation, no care for their psychological problems, a struggle to obtain something as simple as a wheelchair. The shroud of mendacity cast over the war itself had meant that for eight years the very existence of disabled war veterans was denied. Now they demanded rights for themselves, and a monument to their brothers who died in Afghanistan. But they still believed they had fought for a just cause.

'Was it all a waste of time?'

'No! This is not like Vietnam! We were there giving internationalist aid. We were invited in by the Afghan government.'

One Thursday evening I went to Babushkinskaya metro station to meet Gena Katsov, the 31-year-old organizer of a poetry club known as *Poeziya*. 'We've got about fifty members,' he told me as we trudged across the snow to the district *dom kultury* (cultural centre). 'Usually we hold our readings in squares, all over the city, but tonight we're indoors.'

'So is this an *official* club?'

Katsov laughed and mimed a 'neither this nor that' expression. 'Babushkinsky district council is quite liberal . . . they give us a "roof".' I understood the word to mean both 'premises' and 'protection'.

An audience arrived, left their bulky coats and hats with the cloak-room attendants, and shuffled into a little hall. I am no great judge of the quality of the verse, but it certainly played its little part in the steady erosion of the Soviet lie. The first poem, delivered in the declamatory Russian style, was an expressionist vision of Moscow, its dreadful subur-ban sprawl and soulless life. The second began with the words, 'The day smelt of apples and sperm', and there were uncomfortable looks in the hall as the young poet explored the mysteries of sexual awakening. Next came a tragicomic tale of how drunkards behaved under Stalin, Khrushchev, Brezhnev . . . and Gorbachev (guzzling eau-de-cologne in the bathroom). Katsov himself performed a poem about a blood-drenched Stalin.

At the end of November I visited a gentle bearded man of about fifty called Lev Timofeyev at his apartment in the newish southern district of Tyoply Stan. We drank tea in a gloomy living room where every surface was covered with books and manuscripts. Timofeyev was a leading human rights activist, who had stolen Gorbachev's watchword, *glasnost*, and made it the title of his own *samizdat*[1] magazine. He gave me the latest edition to read while he took a call from Pentecostalist protesters in some other city. Issue number 8 of *Glasnost* consisted of 41 A4 sheets, typewritten on both sides and stapled together. It contained essays, polemics, open letters addressed to Gorbachev, short news items, and even poems, all on the general topic of human rights – including national minorities, religious groups, anti-Semitism and ecology.

After asking the Pentecostalists to write a news note for the next edition of *Glasnost*, Timofeyev told me briefly about himself. He was an economist and journalist; started off in various Soviet magazines, then published dissident articles in *samizdat* and abroad; was arrested in 1985 and sentenced under the infamous Article 70 ('Anti-Soviet agitation and propaganda') to six years in a labour camp and five in exile. In February 1987, however, after two years in the 'strict regime' Perm-36 camp (for 'especially dangerous state criminals') he was released, along with many other political prisoners.

I had never met an especially dangerous state criminal before, and I wanted to learn more about Perm-36 – but for Timofeyev this was already history, and he wanted to talk about the future. (It was a feature of all the dissidents I would meet that they were rarely bitter or angry about their treatment, and seemed to view what they had suffered as just part of the job – which they now continued, doggedly and persuasively battering away at the Soviet system, convinced that one day it would break.)

Timofeyev was busy preparing for the country's first independent human rights conference, to which they had invited activists from all the countries that signed the Helsinki Agreement in 1975. 'It will open on 10th December – Human Rights Day – and we've booked a banqueting hall on Altufyevskoe Chaussee for the main events. There will be three plenary sessions, and five days of break-out groups in apartments around the city . . .'

At this point the doorbell rang and we were joined by Timofeyev's co-editor of *Glasnost* and joint organizer of the coming conference, a meek-looking man of Armenian descent called Sergei Grigoryants. He was also a veteran of the camps, also freed under Gorbachev's political amnesty, also gentle and dogged. We exchanged numbers, and agreed to

---

1 *Samizdat*, literally 'self-publishing', was the name given to underground literature secretly printed and distributed in the Soviet Union.

meet at the conference. 'By the way,' said Grigoryants as I was leaving, 'Some refuseniks [Jews who were refused permission to emigrate] are planning a demonstration on Sunday. You might want to go. It'll be on the little square opposite the foreign ministry building, at midday.'

'It's two days before Gorbachev goes to Washington for talks with Reagan, so they're hoping for maximum exposure,' Timofeyev added.

This would be my first opposition demo in Moscow. I took the metro to Smolenskaya and emerged onto the little square under the Stalinist-Gothic towers of the foreign ministry. It was a beautiful sunny day, the temperature just below zero. I could see the protest as soon as I emerged from the underground. It was much bigger than I had expected – hundreds of people jammed into the little square with banners and placards. But as I got closer I realised that these were not refuseniks – the placards were all about peace and nuclear arms cuts, and the coming Washington summit. Moreover, many of the protesters looked like thugs, wearing leather coats, and they seemed to have arrived in a dozen or so buses that were parked along the road. I pushed my way into the crowd, guided by where television camera crews were working. It soon became clear that about fifty or sixty Jewish protesters had indeed turned up, but their action had been swamped by a 'peace demonstration', evidently organised by the KGB.

The refuseniks stood in quiet little groups, talking to newspaper reporters and TV crews. The 'peaceniks' were noisy and violent – chanting slogans and jostling the refuseniks and reporters. I saw one of them talking into a folded copy of *Pravda*.

I joined some American journalists interviewing some of the Jewish protesters. 'We have nothing against the Soviet people,' one of them was saying. 'We only want the right to go to our homeland.'

'I applied to emigrate eleven years ago,' said Yelena Dubyanskaya. 'My daughter applied separately two months ago . . . but they tell us we have relatives who "have secrets".'

'What kind of secrets?' I asked.

'Ha! About the "Soviet economy".'

Suddenly there was a commotion a few yards away. A posse of 'peace protesters' had barged into a television interview, knocking the Jewish speakers aside with their wooden placards, and sending the camera and its tripod crashing to the snow-covered ground. The reporter – CNN's correspondent, Peter Arnett, whom I knew from the foreign ministry press briefings – was manhandled towards a car and driven away.

The atmosphere was now horrible, as the 'peaceniks' chanted louder. I walked with a man called Leonid Grossman to the edge of the square, where we could talk quietly. 'I've been waiting since 1979. There are four of us in the family – my uncle is in Israel. I worked as a radio engineer but was sacked when I applied to emigrate. That meant I was now unemployed so they accused me of "parasitism" and threatened to evict me from Moscow. They gave me a month to find work. So I got a job in the end as a watchman. In September I applied again, but there's no reply.'

'What reason do they give for refusing to let you go?'

'"Secrets". But ten years have passed since I did any secret work . . .'

Now we were spotted by some KGB 'peaceniks'. Two men with bulldog faces approached us, pushed Leonid aside and started haranguing me: 'Why the fuck are you talking to these people? They're parasites – what have they ever done for our country?' Then he stuck a gloved finger in my notebook and demanded to know: 'Who are you working for? The CIA?'

Moscow seemed to be alive those days with protests big and small, as Human Rights Day – 10 December – approached. The day after the refusenik demo I watched as a man named Viktor Sergeyev stood outside the Lenin Library with three friends holding a poster that said 'Freedom to leave the USSR'. After 25 minutes they were arrested, taken to a police station and charged with 'malicious disobedience of the police'.

The KGB took steps to prevent Grigoryants and Timofeyev from holding their 'International Seminar on Humanitarian Problems'. They, and all the leaders of the planned break-out sections, received visits from prosecutors and police who informed them that permission for holding the conference had been denied. All refused to sign the papers thrust in front of them.

When the day came I made my way to the banqueting hall on Altufyevskoe Chaussee for the opening plenary session, only to find the hall padlocked, and a sign on the door that read *Sanitarny den* – 'Closed for Cleaning'. Two days later, the second planned plenary session was thwarted by a locked door and a sign reading 'Closed for technical reasons'. And the hall booked for the closing session faced an unexpected 'fire hazard'. So instead, the participants decamped to various apartments around the city, where we crammed ourselves into tiny rooms, sitting on chairs, window ledges, boxes, or the floor. At the closing session, Grigoryants reported that about 400 people had managed to attend, against all the odds, including a few observers from abroad.

Many, however, were not even allowed to reach Moscow. 'Genrikh Altunian was pulled off the train in Kharkov,' said Grigoryants. 'The same thing happened in Lvov. A whole group of Ukrainians including Vyacheslav Chornovil were not allowed to board the train, and even had drugs planted on them. Yesterday a group of Crimean Tatars arrived from Uzbekistan – but they had to drive to an airport in Kazakhstan lying on the floors of cars, to avoid arrest!'The room broke into applause.

Timofeyev summed up, reminding the activists that despite Gorbachev's warm reception in theWest, much remained to be done – as the harassment of this seminar had shown. 'There are still 360 political prisoners in the USSR. Our work won't be over until all of them are released, and the articles under which they were imprisoned are repealed.'

By the end of 1987, only two months after arriving in Moscow, I was in no doubt: I had the best job in journalism! No story in the world was more important than the crumbling of the Soviet edifice, and nothing less certain than what was going to be built in its place – always assuming it didn't just crash to the ground unleashing chaos everywhere. Not surprisingly the Moscow press corps was rather smug; we all felt we were writing tomorrow's history books today.

Gorbachev returned from Washington with his ears aching, after a tongue-lashing from President Reagan (and the entire American press) over human rights and Jewish emigration – but with a glittering prize in the form of the Intermediate-Range Nuclear Forces treaty, which did not just reduce but *eliminated* all ground-launched nuclear missiles with a range of less than 5,500 kilometres. That was an astonishing achievement, never matched either before or afterwards.

The West's awe for Gorby, with his intriguing blood-red birthmark on his forehead (which Soviet newspapers continued to retouch even though it was visible on television), was only intensified by the precariousness of his position back home. I wrote a piece that noted how, while Gorbachev was in Washington, his deputy, Yegor Ligachev, had publicly undermined his boss by pouring cold water on some of his policies and suggesting that the two men virtually shared the leadership. This appeared as the *Sunday Times'* lead story, considerably hyped up, under the headline: 'Rival sours Gorbachev's summit triumph'. I was rather put out by this, and complained to the foreign editor that my story had been rewritten. He replied that this was done by the editor himself, Andrew Neil. 'He always takes a close interest in the splash. And, you know, he does run a pretty successful newspaper . . .' As it turned out, history proved Neil to be right. Only two months into the job, I was far too cautious, and afraid of getting things wrong. Two weeks later I wrote a page-long profile of Gorbachev, whom the paper named as 'Man of the Year', listing the innumerable ways in which the Soviet Union had become a quite different place in the space of just one year. Above all, he had achieved something unimaginable: he had utterly changed the way people in the West viewed the USSR.

As 1988 began, I queued with hundreds of Russians for more than an hour in deep snow – not to buy a chicken or bananas (*perestroika* had done nothing to conjure up such luxuries) but to see a new 90-minute documentary film, called *More Light*. It was the most truthful account to date of the Soviet Union's history. 'We are all tired of the silence,' said the narrator. The audience froze as the film showed the explosion that blew Moscow's church of Christ the Saviour to smithereens in the Thirties – to be replaced by an open-air swimming pool. There were gasps as the narrator coolly recounted how many military officers had been purged by Stalin, and the camera ran down a long list of names, all with the same years of death: 1937 and 1938. And we laughed at a montage of pictures showing the late Leonid Brezhnev at his favourite occupation – pinning medals on other people's chests, or receiving them himself. 'We were hypnotised,' said the voice-over, 'by all the false propaganda under Brezhnev.'

And then I went to a different kind of movie. *Assa* was not your standard Soviet melodrama about wistful love affairs and the foibles of communist living. This was Soviet noir, surreal and experimental, about mobsters, the KGB, and rock music. It became the sell-out movie of the year. In the iconoclastic final scene, the famous rock star Viktor Tsoi is told by the manageress of a restaurant why he is not permitted to sing with the house band. She explains, in the dead tones of the Soviet bureaucrat: 'Employment is not possible without a certificate from your local housing administration and a diploma of higher and secondary musical education. Do you have that?'

'No,' says Tsoi, slumped in a chair, wearing a tartan scarf.

'So where do you actually work?' asks the manageress.

'In a boiler-room.'

Tsoi's friend butts in: 'It doesn't matter where he works. He's a musician. A born musician.'

'So where's your certificate?' asks the bureaucrat.

'I don't have one.'

'Where do you live? Where are you registered?'

'Nowhere.'

The manageress continues to read from the rule book: 'Paragraph 3. Sub-section b. Duties of a member of a musical ensemble: to perform wearing the approved uniform of the given collective; to appear on stage in the manner approved by the ensemble's leader; to ensure the quality and correct tuning of the instrument; it is forbidden to . . .'

As she drones on, Tsoi stands up and slopes off to the restaurant hall to join the other members of his band, who are playing a pulsating, grungy riff. He grabs the microphone and sings a raw, muscular lyric, straight into the camera:

> Our hearts demand change.
> Our eyes demand change.
> In our laughter, in our tears,
> In the pulsing of our veins – change.
> We are waiting for change.

The camera slowly swings round to reveal that Tsoi is singing not in a restaurant but in a huge open-air venue, where hundreds of young people are dancing and waving little lights in the darkness.

19

The KGB Makes Friends

THERE WERE PROBABLY some Moscow correspondents, back in the days of the USSR, who longed to be spies. There were undoubtedly those who *were* spies. As for me, it didn't even dawn on me, until it was too late, that I was being lined up for a part in the last major espionage scandal of the Cold War.

The KGB's efforts to recruit me were far too subtle. They didn't give me a secret camera, or invisible ink. They didn't slide an envelope of cash across the table, or bury it under a designated bush in Gorky Park. A good old-fashioned honey trap with some Siberian temptress might have done the trick – but there was nothing like that . . . How the hell was I supposed to know the Motherland was calling?

I guess they knew that, like all new correspondents, I was keen to build up a network of useful contacts. But if they'd been observing me closely they would also have noticed that I was wary about who I trusted. Moscow correspondents received all sorts of propositions. Often callers would refuse to give their names or tell me anything about themselves, but demand to meet because 'it will be very interesting to you'. Others wanted to meet because they thought I could help them leave the country. Every time one had to weigh up the possibility of acquiring a world exclusive against that of being set up by the KGB.

The safest thing was to follow up leads that came via trusted sources. And so it was that I became friends with Yura Shvets, who was introduced to me by my old friend Grisha, the one who had taught Russian in Scotland. 'I've known Yura for years,' he said. 'He works for the TASS news agency so maybe he'll be a good contact for you . . .'

Yura, who was about my age, had previously been stationed in Washington for several years and acquired excellent, twangy English and an Elvis quiff. Now he worked out of the big concrete cube that was the TASS headquarters on the corner of Herzen Street and the Boulevard

Ring, and claimed to have good contacts inside the Communist Party central committee. Of course I knew that as a TASS Washington correspondent he had almost certainly been a spy, but that did not necessarily mean he could not be a good source of information for me. He became an occasional dinner guest at our flat, sometimes together with Grisha, sometimes with his Barbie-doll wife. But most often we met in the open-air – on park benches or under bridges. We would meet at pre-arranged times, look around furtively, and walk slowly together, chatting about the political situation. He would throw me a few tasty scraps that were at least as good as any other correspondent's scraps and sometimes made their way into my next article.

During one meeting, in March 1988, we discussed something that had been published in the hardline newspaper *Sovetskaya Rossiya*, and caused a huge stir. The so-called 'Nina Andreyeva letter' was perceived as a frontal attack on *perestroika* by supporters of Ligachev. It condemned the 'distortion' of Soviet history by men such as Shatrov, poured scorn on the new 'informal' political clubs and the 'left-wing liberal intellectuals' in charge of *perestroika*, and denounced the desire of Soviet Jews to emigrate as 'treason'. Gorbachev left the country for a state visit to Yugoslavia the day after it was published.

'Ligachev practically took over the central committee while Gorbachev was away,' Yura said. 'He called all the newspaper editors together and told them they should be "guided" by the ideas in the Andreyeva letter. It was a coup, Angus. He was trying to put an end to *perestroika*. But at last week's Politburo meeting, he was put back in his place. My sources say it was a real confrontation – and Gorbachev won!' Needless to say, that kind of insider information was invaluable (and proved to be true).

It was only when Yura defected to the United States in 1993 and wrote his memoirs that I discovered what his real task had been in befriending me. He had indeed been a KGB agent while working as a 'journalist' in Washington, and when he returned to Moscow his job, he wrote, was 'to pinpoint people who I believed would be willing to cooperate with the KGB. My job was to screen the people I would meet this way and if I had a feeling that they were "promising" for recruitment, I would pursue further contacts with them.' He revealed that a whole section of the KGB had been devoted to trying to recruit a certain 'Antosha' to their ranks. Yes – I even had a code name!

'Angus had a flawless command of Russian,' Yura wrote (with some exaggeration), 'and he knew the Soviet Union too well. Before long he developed extensive contacts with Soviet citizens, which naturally included a liberal sprinkling of KGB informants. They diligently supplied reports on the British journalist, whose KGB file was swelling at an unprecedented rate. The file contained absolutely no dirt on Angus, but that didn't matter. The RT Directorate of the KGB also had a file on him started a few years back when he had come to the Soviet Union for the first time as an exchange student. Now he reappeared as the *Sunday Times* correspondent, and Deputy Chief of Directorate Bychkov ordered me to establish contact with him.' Shvets described in detail how he courted me, and reported to his bosses that I was 'unrecruitable', upon which I was 'singled out for particularly nasty treatment' – of which more later.

Through all these months when I was being secretly measured up for my spy uniform I was blissfully unaware of Yura's mission. At no point did he ever ask me to do anything in exchange for the information he gave me.

I was worried less by him than by some of the other oddballs who pressed their attentions on me. There was a strange young woman from Ukraine, Lida Karitskaya, for example, who met me several times to speak of her weird ordeal at the hands of the secret police in collusion with some murderous doctors: they had killed her son, she claimed, and she herself woke up one day to find microscopic cuts in her eyelids. She was convinced they were trying to kill her and didn't dare go back to her hometown for fear of being locked up in an asylum. She eventually handed over a folder of 'evidence' to me during a clandestine meeting near the Danilov market, but I never got round to investigating her story properly.

After I published an article about links between the KGB and the church, I had calls offering me more 'interesting material'. Once I was offered documents and photographs (nothing political – in fact they were of George Bernard Shaw!) by someone I trusted, but when I met her husband in the street to receive a plastic carrier bag containing the materials, I was terrified. Was it all an elaborate ploy? Was I being secretly photographed?

Once I was visited in my flat by a group of Ukrainian hippies whose only desire was to be able to leave the country and settle in the Canaries. 'We want to work, though,' they insisted, 'not like *your* hippies.' They had been rearing silkworms in the Krasnodar region and had just been sacked and diddled out of thousands of roubles. That was the final straw.

In this system there was no place for them even though they wanted to work. The Canaries it had to be!

Then there was Boris (I won't give his last name). He, like Grisha, had spent an exchange year in the UK, teaching Russian at Glasgow University. Neilian and I had spent several evenings with him in pubs or at home. That was in the early 1980s, and since then we had lost touch with him. But suddenly he appeared at our door one evening, and explained that he had heard me being interviewed on the BBC World Service. Realising we must be based in Moscow he had gone out of his way to track down our address. It turned out Boris was now a university lecturer in Stavropol – Gorbachev's home region down in southern Russia. He began to visit us quite regularly, whenever he was in Moscow, and he invited me to go down and visit him some time, so I could write a piece about Gorby's home town.

On one of his visits he offered to introduce me to a friend who worked in the foreign ministry – a mid-ranking diplomat who might be useful to me. We met for lunch – Boris, me, Neilian, and the diplomat, Yuri Romanov – at the National Hotel, overlooking the red walls of the Kremlin and the traffic jams on '50th Anniversary of October' Square. The National today is luxurious and over-priced, and even in communist times, despite the threadbare red carpets and limited menu, it was a chichi place to be taken to.

Romanov looked just like a hedgehog, and my eyes kept flitting up and down between his bristly head and little sharp snout. We chatted over the usual range of *zakuski* or hors d'oeuvres, and a bottle of vodka. When I asked Romanov what he did – a fairly natural question to a new acquaintance – he unaccountably bristled, becoming more hedgehog-like than ever. When he recovered he said he worked in the foreign ministry's 'policy planning department', then at once toasted 'our friendship'. He was pretty close to the foreign minister, Eduard Shevardnadze, he said, and toasted my wife. He could even procure me an interview with Shevardnadze, he said, and toasted Boris.

My attempts, over the beetroot soup, to find out a little about his 'foreign policy planning' yielded nothing. He just kept proposing more toasts and slurping vodka through his thin hedgehog lips. I felt like pouring some into a saucer and giving it to him to lick up like milk.

The chicken Kiev passed uneventfully, in the sense that I managed not to squirt the little glob of scalding butter that is the essence of chicken Kiev over his dowdy suit. Then, as the afternoon sun began to sink over the towers of the Kremlin, and we had decided what excellent friends we were, the waiter brought ice-creams, and Romanov steered the conversation to the upcoming visit to Moscow of the American president, Ronald Reagan. Romanov wondered what I thought about it. I asked him what he thought about it, hoping finally for a quote from an insider for Sunday's paper.

'You know,' he said, leaning towards me as if just struck by a great idea. 'You have friends among the American journalists here, don't you?'

I nodded.

'I'd be very interested to know what they are thinking about the Reagan visit. Maybe if we meet again you can tell me something about what they're thinking . . .'

I was truly baffled. If he wanted to know what American journalists thought, why didn't he just read their newspapers? It's not as if they kept their ideas secret. And anyway, I thought to myself, I couldn't recall ever hearing any of them say anything particularly memorable about Reagan's visit, other than wondering whether the old duffer would remember the name of the country he was in. We were all frankly more interested in Gorbachev's internal battles to push through his reforms.

But Romanov wasn't deterred. 'So, you know . . . I'll be very glad to help you with interviews, or access – maybe there's somewhere you would like to visit? – and, you know, we can . . . help each other . . .'

I smiled wanly and we agreed to meet again a week later, just the two of us. Again it was the National Hotel, same inedible food, and this time a promise of help. Gorbachev had recently toured a huge 'model farm' in the district of Ramensky, outside Moscow, and I was vaguely interested in visiting it. To my surprise – after all, he was a 'foreign policy planner' – Romanov said he could arrange it for me.

Meanwhile Ronald Reagan took Moscow by storm. He strolled on Red Square with his friend Mikhail, he spouted a few memorised Russian proverbs, and – in the full knowledge that he had only seven months left in office – he daydreamed aloud about achieving a world without nuclear weapons. He even declared that he no longer viewed the Soviet Union as the 'evil empire' – words that had shocked Russians five years earlier. 'I was talking about another time, another era,' he said.

I began to forget about the vodka-slurping Yuri Romanov. He was proving to be rather less useful as a contact than our maid, or the concierge who sat at the door to our building and at least could tell you what weather to expect outside. The snippets of information he gave me all turned out to be rubbish, as did his boast that he could arrange an interview with the foreign minister. I didn't expect his promise of a trip to the Ramensky model farm to materialise either – and anyway, there were far more interesting things going on during that glorious summer of 1988.

The KGB Closes in

IT WOULD BE fair to say that, at this stage in the proceedings, Mikhail Gorbachev was scoring most highly with, in descending order: Russian intellectuals; Western governments and ordinary people; admirers of bald men with interesting birthmarks; and the remainder of the Soviet public. The first group revelled in their freedom to read and discuss almost anything they wanted. The second had found a Soviet leader they 'could do business with', as Mrs Thatcher put it. The third group went on and on about how Nostradamus had predicted that Russia would be ruled by 'Michael the Marked', who would finally make friends with America. And the final group rolled their eyes and complained that Gorbaty ('the hunchback') was a disaster and the shops were emptier than ever before.

As the Kremlin's acerbic spokesman, Gennady Gerasimov, remarked, when Gorbachev was later awarded the Nobel peace prize, 'it certainly wasn't the prize for economics!' Gorbachev's economic 'reforms' had so far left the state sector floundering, while the new private (or 'cooperative') businesses catered mainly to the wealthy. Neilian and I tried lunch at a new Italian-style restaurant on Gagarin Square. The ambience was unpleasantly formal, and the food was mediocre, but still cost about sixty US dollars. I paid with two fifty-dollar bills – and waited, and waited, for the change to come back. Eventually I had to summon the manager and explain that, no, I wasn't actually offering a forty-dollar tip. He cast me a disgusted look, as if to say, 'You're a bloody foreigner yet you don't understand capitalism!'

Like a sailing ship in a storm, though, Gorbachev was steadfastly tacking his way forward – though to what distant shore was never quite clear. His next port of call, after acceleration and *glasnost*, was democracy – though he didn't quite dare to tell his Politburo colleagues about it yet.

Throughout Soviet history, major policy changes had been announced once every five years at Communist Party congresses, at which thousands of snoozing men in suits applauded enthusiastically whenever a small electric current was passed through their bottoms. Gorbachev had already held one congress, in February 1986, but at that stage he had been in power for less than a year and was not yet strong enough to push through radical changes. He was far too impatient to wait till 1991, so instead he called a special conference for the end of June 1988. In the weeks leading up to it, politicians and journalists ramped up the ever more surreal debate in the press about how best to achieve Lenin's vision of socialism, while more and more protesters began to take to the streets to demand an end to the whole damned communist experiment.

On the last Saturday before the conference I went to a thousand-strong demo on Pushkin Square. Until then, political demonstrations had been small and brief, broken up within minutes by KGB plainclothes men. But this was much bigger and bolder, and the police seemed overwhelmed – and perhaps confused by the fact that anti-government protesters were holding up portraits of the country's leader! Scores of police linked arms and tried to kettle the two main groups of demonstrators. At the height of the protest, under a blistering sun, the sound of traffic was blotted out by the noise of chants, shouts, applause, and the metallic snarl of police loudhailers. When the officers dragged protesters to waiting buses, the crowd chanted 'Hangmen, hangmen!' and 'Down with the KGB!'

Hundreds of people gathered to listen to a well-known dissident, Valeria Novodvorskaya, who had recently founded the Soviet Union's first opposition party, the Democratic Union (as yet, of course, illegal). She was soon grabbed and pushed into a car, and the crowd started arguing with the police, using impeccable *glasnost*-era logic: 'We just wanted to listen to Novodvorskaya! How come you arrested her?'

'We're protecting you,' came the Soviet-logic reply.

'But she wasn't attacking us!'

For the first time, I felt the shiver of revolution, and literally ran back to the office to file a report for the next day's front page.

Finding superlatives to describe the spiralling revolution was becoming increasingly difficult – especially as (unknown, I think, to the *Sunday Times*) I had now become the *Economist*'s Moscow stringer too and needed to describe events using entirely different phrases on Tuesdays (for the *Economist*) and at the end of the week for the *Times*. Not content with that workload, I also agreed to help out the BBC's team, who arrived to cover the Party Conference. We based ourselves at Ostankino, the Soviet television centre, where I could watch a live feed of the debates being streamed from the Kremlin Palace of Congresses. Late in the evening before it all kicked off the BBC's foreign editor, John Simpson, flew in and arrived sweating at Ostankino.

'Andrew,' he gushed. 'How wonderful to see you.'

'Angus.'

'Oh, I'm so sorry, old chap. [Dramatic pause.] Listen . . . I've got to go live on the *Nine O'Clock News* in ten minutes. What do you make of this? What do you expect tomorrow?'

So I chatted with him for five minutes, and then watched him stand in front of a camera and repeat it word for word on the *Nine O'Clock News*. So that's how TV works, I thought.

What no one could predict – least of all me, and therefore not even the BBC's foreign editor – was that we were about to experience four astonishing days of political theatre. Gorbachev stood up on Tuesday morning to address the 5,000 delegates, and didn't sit down again for four hours. The reforms he proposed would, eventually, overturn the entire communist system. I listened open-mouthed, but the overwhelmingly conservative audience kept their teeth clenched: they didn't applaud at all during the first 90 minutes, and when they did it was to cheer Gorbachev's reference to the selfless work of Soviet soldiers in Afghanistan. The centrepiece of his planned reform was for a new kind of parliament to replace the Supreme Soviet, which met for only two or three days a year to rubber-stamp Politburo decisions. The Communist Party would be reduced to a shadow of its former self: it would, it's true, be able to nominate candidates for a third of the seats in the new parliament, but the other two-thirds would be filled in free, competitive elections. The Soviet Union would no longer be run by an unelected party and its all-powerful, secretive Politburo, but by a president, and an elected parliament. Jaws dropped everywhere, most in horror, some in admiration.

For the rest of Tuesday and all of Wednesday, delegates debated this. And they were not happy. So on Thursday Gorbachev took the floor again, to 'explain better'. This in itself was a phenomenal break with the past – the very idea of a Communist leader having to explain and cajole, rather than making a speech, followed by a unanimous show of hands. Television broadcast only extracts from the debate – but it included a

Siberian party secretary demanding that hangers-on from the Brezhnev period should be sacked. Nothing like this had ever been broadcast on Soviet TV since it was invented!

Friday brought Act Four of this thrilling drama, as the disgraced Boris Yeltsin, no less, clambered out of the grave like Banquo's ghost. The leadership, of course, had no intention of letting him speak. His career was officially over. But when his written request to take the floor was rejected, he left his seat on the balcony, went downstairs and strode up the central aisle towards the platform waving his red conference card above his head.

Yeltsin went straight up to Gorbachev and demanded the right to address the conference. Gorbachev motioned him to sit down in the front row, which he eventually did. When he was finally given the podium, Yeltsin delivered a barnstorming speech, demanding the complete demolition of the one-party state. Then he paused, theatrically, and said he now wished to raise a 'delicate question'. His voice croaked with emotion as he tried to continue and the hostile audience in the huge hall started barracking him. He folded up his notes and made to leave the rostrum, with a peevish 'Well, if you don't think you've got the time . . .' But Gorbachev – no am-dram slouch himself – intervened: 'Let's hear him out, comrades.'

Never was there a politician so unafraid to show his feelings in public. Yeltsin went on, to a stunned hall: 'It's become customary in our country to rehabilitate people fifty years after their deaths . . . I wanted to ask for my personal political rehabilitation now. While I'm alive . . .'

The old guard would have none of it. The rest of the conference saw a succession of hardliners take to the podium to rubbish Yeltsin – thereby boosting his heroic stature in the country at large. Maybe it even played into Gorbachev's hands, because the 5,000 apparatchiks in the hall seemed to forget that the main point of the conference, contained in Gorbachev's proposals, was to sweep them out of power. On the final day they all voted in favour, probably assuming that this was just another silly plan that they would toss into the long grass. And then . . . Gorbachev pulled off a masterstroke. Just when the delegates thought it was all over, and they could head off to the special Party food shops and restaurants, Gorbachev pulled a piece of paper from his breast pocket.

His voice was unusually nervous – because he knew he hadn't discussed this with anyone. This was almost literally something he had just scribbled on the back of a cigarette packet. Coughing and twitching, he announced that elections to the new parliament would be held in the spring. 'So . . . that's, um, what I propose. Any objections? Allow me to put it to the vote.' Before they even had a second to reflect on what this would mean for them, and their lifelong Party sinecures, 5,000 men and women obediently raised their hands. On the massive stage-curtain behind the 'presidium', a thirty-foot red profile of Lenin looked out at the hall in horror.

I couldn't quite believe what I was watching on the live feed at the TV centre. I certainly wasn't going to explain to the BBC how important it was. I rushed off to pen 4,000 words for Sunday's paper.

Then something strange, and ominous, happened, for which even my meetings with Yura Shvets and Yuri Romanov had not prepared me.

On Sunday we were due to fly down to Crimea for a few days' working holiday. The business tycoon Richard Branson had just taken over a historic hotel in Yalta for Virgin Holidays. I planned to write a big travel piece for the paper – and relax for a few days with the family after the excitement of the party conference. The flights and the hotel had been booked several weeks in advance – by the *Sunday Times* travel desk – so I hadn't given it much thought until the morning we were due to depart.

That was a big mistake. The rule for foreign journalists was that if you wanted to travel out of Moscow you had to give the foreign ministry 48 hours' notice. I remembered about this only a few hours before the flight. So on the way to the airport we stopped at my office and I sent a grovelling telex to my 'minder' in the foreign ministry's press department. Dear Andrei, really sorry, completely slipped my mind to let you know . . . going to Yalta for a few days' holiday, leaving on flight number such-and-such, staying at Oreanda Hotel, telephone number such-and-such. Apologies for late notification. Hope that's okay . . . Back on Thursday. See you then.

Yalta did not disappoint. It is the jewel of the Crimean coast, the health resort where Anton Chekhov spent his consumptive, dying years and wrote some of his most famous plays and stories. It was where Stalin, Roosevelt and Churchill met at the end of the war and carved up Europe, gobbling up the smaller nations of east and west like portions of caviar. Now it was the centre of the Soviet holiday industry, with magnificent dachas for Party leaders strung along the Black Sea cliff-tops, and more mundane high-rise establishments for the toiling classes.

The art deco Hotel Oreanda, built before the communist revolution, sat at the southern end of the town, beautifully restored and ready to receive British tourists with red Virgin beach towels. It had its own private beach, complete with a little café that used to be called Bar Grot but had hastily been renamed Richard's Bar.

Some of the Brits had strange ideas about how to behave on a beach. They wanted to move their sun-loungers to face the sun, but the beach attendant soon scotched that idea: 'Put that back where it belongs!' Richard's beach was fenced off from the 'Soviet' section, where hundreds of holidaymakers made the most of the limited space by sunbathing standing up, turning slowly like doner kebabs dripping on to the pebbles below. I asked some of the Virgin tourists what they made of it all. Their biggest complaints were about the Russian language ('I just can't get me head around that Acrylic alphabet') and the food ('You get the meat today, and the potato pancakes tomorrow').

It was a very Soviet experience for tourists more accustomed to the Costa del Sol. Yalta's beautiful parks and gardens were dotted with huge portraits of Politburo members, and red banners bearing words from the Soviet Constitution that appeared to have become the town's motto: 'Citizens of the USSR have the right to rest'. The hotel, despite Branson's involvement, wasn't really adapted to Western needs. You had to finish your evening meal and vacate the restaurant by 7.30 each evening, because that was when the entertainment started – and *Soviet* citizens were served! The only exception was for the Ukrainian food evening once a week, when the holidaymakers could stay, and enjoy the live music. There was also a beach party once a week, till 11 pm – but the hotel director insisted the music had to be vetted in advance. The staff weren't very happy either, it has to be said. The beach party was 'too much work for them', and they were only paid two roubles extra for serving. The woman who ran a little bar in the hotel foyer complained that the Brits were not drinking enough, so she was failing to fulfil her plan. 'When the Finns used to come here they spent all their time at the bar!' The Virgin rep urged her tourists to approach the week 'with a sense of humour'.

We loved it. Neilian and Ewan and I took an old wartime public bus up to the Uchan-su waterfall, and then to a mountain restaurant set in beautiful woodland by Lake Karagol. It specialised in game dishes, service so slow you thought the waiters had gone home, and frogs. The frogs were in the lake below the veranda, and kept the customers amused while waiting for their wild boar or quails. It was one of those Soviet establishments that had all the makings of something really wonderful, but you longed for it to be taken over by Germans, or at least by the three young *kooperatory* who ran a little private restaurant called Gourmand on the Yalta seafront.

We spent two wonderful days strolling among the acacias and magnolias, eating, tasting Crimean wines, and chatting to Richard's tourists. On the Tuesday afternoon, around five o'clock, we staggered up from the beach, red-skinned and rather sore from lying on the uncomfortable pebbles, and were unexpectedly confronted by the hotel manager. He ushered me into a little room, where I was introduced to the head of Yalta's visa department and the head of the Crimean board of Intourist (the state tourism organisation). They told me I had committed a grave violation of the regulations, and showed me what they said was the relevant paragraph of the Ukrainian administrative code. They had been told 'by Moscow' to call me in. I read the Code and noted the prescribed penalties.

'So what did Moscow tell you to do with me?' I asked.

'To give you a warning,' the Intourist head replied, and then, before I had time to sigh with relief, added, 'and to ask you to leave Yalta. You have been rebooked on to the next flight back to Moscow.'

I wasn't quite handcuffed and frogmarched back to Moscow, but they still managed to make me feel like a criminal. I was allowed to go to our room and inform my wife and son that our holiday was suddenly over, and then they bundled me into a car and drove me to the Intourist hotel on the other side of Yalta to have our plane tickets changed. From there they escorted me back to the Oreanda. We packed, and around midnight we were all taken to Crimea's airport, two hours' drive away, and accompanied right to the steps of the plane under KGB guard.

Out of sheer bloody-mindedness, we went back to Yalta the following Monday to complete our holiday, this time giving the requisite 48 hours notice. But it was not the last I would hear of my illicit trip to Crimea.

A couple of weeks later Boris reappeared in Moscow. 'Yuri Romanov is unhappy with you,' he told me. 'He'd arranged the trip to Ramensky for you, but you didn't get in touch.'

That was just typical, I thought. He arranges a trip, but instead of bothering to tell me, he waits for me to call him, and then complains because I somehow fail to pick up his thought-waves and divine that something has been organised for me. In any case I was getting tired of

With friends in their Moscow apartment. From left, Seryozha, Angus, Volodya and Neilian

Volodya aged four with his mother and aunt and the President of the Soviet Union, Mikhail Kalinin

Garik and Inna Basyrov

'Couple' by Garik Basyrov

A crowd gathers to watch me performing on a ladder . . .

. . . and how the piece to camera appeared in the report

Filing a report by satellite telephone from Chechnya

Russian troops pose in front of the destroyed presidential palace in Grozny

My friend Nikolai Vorontsov, the geneticist (white shirt and black tie), with Boris Yeltsin on a tank in front of the Russian Parliament during the attempted coup

My children, Ewan, Duncan and Katie, on the BBC car near Red Square (around 1996); and Ewan playing under Lenin's watchful eye in 1989

Soviet soldiers raise the Red Flag above the Reichstag in Berlin at the end of the Second World War

Yevgeny Khaldei, the photographer of the Reichstag picture, reunited with the then 18-year-old soldier who raised the flag, Aleksey Kovalyov (left)

Consulting the shaman in Siberia

With Mikhail Gorbachev

On a plane with the man who might have been president, Boris Nemtsov

. . . and meeting the man who did become president, Vladimir Putin, at a Valdai Club dinner

our meetings and was trying to avoid seeing him again. His tip-offs were useless, and there were strange things about him that unsettled me. Unlike almost every other Soviet official, Romanov had no secretary and always picked up the phone himself when I called him – very quickly, too, as if he spent his entire day at an empty desk just waiting for my call. Where his office really was, I didn't know, because when I offered to give him a lift to the foreign ministry in my car, he refused, saying he would rather go by metro.

So now he was miffed, was he? I called him and arranged to meet him for coffee at the Intourist Hotel on Gorky Street on Monday 26 July.

The weekend before that was gorgeous, and we had an outing planned. An old friend, a teacher called Varya, wanted to take us to her aunt's dacha on Sunday afternoon. The dacha was in a special Academy of Sciences settlement in a beautiful spot called Vyalki, just south of Moscow. (In Soviet times, scientists, musicians, artists, and other professionals enjoyed many perks – not just nice apartments in town but country houses with all amenities, including a cinema, a sports hall, and a shop that stocked not just tins of sprats but fabulous treats, like jars of plum jam or pats of Vologda butter.) Aunt Katya had been visited by foreigners before, but she took the precaution anyway of asking the Academy of Sciences' permission for our trip, which was granted.

We set off in my car, with Varya giving directions – but we missed the turn-off from the main highway and had to turn back, and then double-back again, to reach the required exit. In retrospect I guess that might have looked a little suspicious, as if we were trying to throw off a tail. My car may have been a battered brown Lada, but it was identifiable as belonging to a foreigner by its special plates, starting K001 (K for correspondent, 001 for British). Still, we were well within the 40-kilometre area around Moscow that was nominally open to foreigners, so we felt there was nothing to worry about.

Just as I turned off at 'Kilometre 27', however, a policeman leapt out from behind a tree at the side of the road and waved us down. This was the dreaded, tedious GAI – the State Automobile Inspectorate, whose only function was to extract bribes from drivers for made-up offences. Your car might be a bit muddy, or the tyres too soft or too hard, or the paintwork scratched, or the wrong colour for a Monday – whatever it was, you would be pulled in, have to show your papers (which would naturally have something wrong with them too) and be expected to slip a few roubles (dollars if you were foreign) into the pages of your passport if you didn't wish to spend the entire day discussing just how dirty your windscreen actually was.

But in this instance, the policeman – a certain Lieutenant Zhemalo – had a different concern. He informed me at once that he had stopped me because I was 'attempting to penetrate a zone closed to foreigners'. I was taken into the GAI office, a large booth set back from the roadside, where Zhemalo spent the next two hours writing out three 'protocols' and four 'reports', without carbon paper. While he sat writing, I studied a big framed map on the wall, which turned out to be the very map that we foreign correspondents had been begging in vain to be issued with: it showed in big patches of pink those areas that we were not allowed to enter. When Zhemalo spotted me studying it, he leapt up, removed it from its hook and placed it on the floor, face to the wall. Obviously I was not meant to know the rules I was being accused of violating.

Finally, like a schoolboy proudly holding up his homework, he showed me his 'protocol' and asked me to approve it. It read:

'I, Inspector of service BSBDMS, militia lieutenant M. M. Zhemalo, have composed the present protocol about the fact that Citizen Angus Roxburgh at 13:00 on 25.07.88 was driving a V-2104 car, number-plate K001 835 heading for the populated point of Vyalki without having the appropriate permission for the trip, by which action he violated the established procedure for travel on the roads of the USSR, article 184 of the RSFSR Code 'On Administrative Violations of the Law'. Place of report: REO GAI No. 3, Moscow.'

Now it was my turn. I was required to write my own 'Explanation', also in triplicate. I insisted on pointing out, in the most supercilious tone I could muster, that I could not possibly have known I was entering a closed zone 'since no maps are published which show where foreigners may or may not go'.

Eventually all the work was done, and we were allowed to return to the car and head back into Moscow. It was now mid-afternoon, but I was buggered if I was going to miss the chance to visit Vyalki. The Academy of Sciences, after all, had given permission! So we parked the car near a station, and caught a train instead, arriving in plenty of time for a lovely afternoon in the sunshine, with beer and barbecue and a quick splash in the lake. Hee-hee, nobody had spotted a thing!

Next morning with a sigh I set off for my appointment with Romanov, steeling myself for the reprimand Boris had warned me to expect, for failing to call him about the trip to Ramensky. Sure enough, over coffee and obligatory eleven o'clock Georgian cognac, he told me off, adding that he didn't think I was 'very active'. I was still figuring out what that meant when he steered the conversation towards our mutual friend Boris, and his long-standing invitation for me to visit him in Gorbachev's homeland, Stavropol.

'Yes,' I said. 'Boris seems a bit worried about it . . . he says I must arrange the trip through official channels.'

'Really?' The bristles pinged a little on the top of his head.

'Yeah . . . I don't know why he's worried. I always arrange my trips officially.'

'Oh yes?' Romanov drawled. 'What about Yalta then?'

My heart gave such a leap it almost knocked the cognac glass out of my hand. How the hell did he know about that? He's a foreign policy planner. Why would . . . ?

Okay, okay, I thought, trying to slow my breathing. So he's been informed. Yeah, after all, he's in the foreign ministry, he's a kind of unofficial minder . . .

I started trying to justify what had happened. 'Well, look, that was exceptional . . . there'd just been the Party Conference . . . so much to do . . . right up to the last minute . . . I just clean forgot about sending the telex in time . . . and I did send it before we left, after all, telling them exactly where I was going to be staying! It's not as if I just got up and went there without telling anybody!'

The hedgehog was ready. His little beady eyes bored into me: 'Yes,' he said, and then, after a dramatic pause and a little sniff: 'Not like yesterday, eh?'

I nearly collapsed. I could feel my face flush bright red and the sweat break out all over my body. Within less than 24 hours the information from the GAI had gone straight to the 'foreign policy planner'.

He started joking about Vyalki, speaking in such a way that I couldn't tell whether he knew we had gone there by train in the end, or whether he was just trying to find that out: 'Yes, Vyalki . . . it's an infamous collective farm! A millionaire loss-maker! Yes . . . nice woods there, nice pond . . .'

I just nodded. Now I knew exactly who Romanov was, and he certainly wasn't planning Russia's foreign policy. I rushed home and did the old classic – turning on the taps as loudly as possible, radio up full-blast, so I could tell Neilian what had happened. We decided I should never see Romanov again. And what about Boris, who had introduced us? He still kept turning up, but I could never trust him.

21

Baltic Rebirth

THE SUNDAY AFTER that creepy meeting with Romanov I flew to Latvia. The Baltic republics were always the best place to escape to when Moscow was being an arse. The salty air sweeping off the sea and the aroma of coffee and cake in medieval streets were enough to dispel the reek of the greasiest KGB spook. And this time Latvia did not merely not disappoint, it overwhelmed all expectations.

I met up with an old Latvian friend, Velta, and she and her husband drove me to Turaida, a medieval castle set in primeval forest, half an hour from the capital, Riga. The view from the round red-brick watchtower was wonderful. 'You know what the Russians call it?' asked Velta. 'Our Russian Switzerland!'

'It's neither Russian nor theirs,' her husband chimed in.

Latvia had been part of the Russian empire for 200 years, but it enjoyed a brief period of independence between the two world wars. In 1940 it was seized by Stalin and incorporated into the Soviet Union. In 1941 it was invaded by the Nazis, and in 1944 'liberated' by the Red Army, opposed by many Latvians who saw the Nazis as the lesser evil.

'We were tossed back and forth like a shuttlecock,' said Velta. 'But it's the way the Russians enslave us that irks us most.' We leaned on the rampart, gazing out at the forest and the sandstone banks of the Gauja river. 'They pretend to protect our language and culture, but in reality we are becoming a minority in our own country. Latvians only make up half the population now – and only about a third in Riga! Do you know, just last year alone 18,000 immigrants from other parts of the Soviet Union flooded in to work in new factories here. And of course the newcomers go straight to the top of the waiting list for housing.'

'We don't even want those factories!' said her husband. 'They're really just a means of tying us even more closely to Moscow . . . And the pollution they cause – do you know they had to close all the beaches around

Riga this summer because of all the effluent flowing into the sea from cellulose plants and cement works that we don't need? The Baltic used to be able to cope. But the shit that goes into it now is just too much. By the way, I mean that literally – half a million cubic metres of untreated sewage from Riga empties into the sea every day!'

Velta told me about her father, an elderly man in poor health. 'He goes to the doctor and can't even explain his symptoms in his own language, because the doctor only speaks Russian. Can you imagine that?'

We walked from the castle down to the river and crossed a bridge into the town of Sigulda, where the republic's infant Green movement was due to hold a rally that afternoon. Ostensibly the protest centred on the pollution of the Gauja river – some held placards saying 'We want to swim again in the Gauja' or 'Save our fish' – but I quickly realised that this was just a cover for the real story: it was the Latvians themselves, not sea-trout or salmon, who were the endangered species. What I was witnessing here, in early August 1988, was the very earliest sparks of a movement that would soon tear the Soviet Union apart.

Two petitions circulated at the rally. One was against a planned atomic power station. The other was to bring back the traditional dark-red and white Latvian flag, which Stalin had banned. (The official flag of Soviet Latvia was just the usual communist red with a hammer-and-sickle, plus some condescending blue and white waves along the bottom.)

The crowd of a thousand people – one-tenth of the population of Sigulda – broke into song. 'It's called *The Blue Forests of Latvia*,' a middle-aged man whispered to me. Then he told me about his parents. 'I was a boy during the war. When the Red Army invaded they came for my father. They said he was a Nazi sympathiser. He was no Nazi! He was just a Latvian patriot – he hated the fascists and he hated the Soviets too. They took him away and shot him in the head. Then they came back and grabbed my mother and deported her to Siberia. We never saw her again. That's what they did. Thousands of us . . .'

A huge cheer went up as someone hoisted the illegal claret-and-white flag on a building.

'We would have been like Finland,' said Velta. 'Before the war we were on the same level, and had the same history . . .'

This environmental rally was most definitely not about the environment! The Greens' leader made a speech, which Velta translated for me. He spoke about plans for the foundation of a Popular Front later that month, which would 'support *perestroika*' by demanding

decentralisation, economic independence for the republic, and the restoration of Latvian as the state language.

No, I thought, as I went to sleep that night: this is a revolution – in
fact, a mass revolt, even bigger than what is happening in Moscow.
Sometimes when I had travelled around the Soviet Union during my
years at Progress Publishers I had noted the apparent lack of tensions in
such an ethnically diverse country. There were few outward signs that
people resented speaking Russian, and there were rarely reports of
ethnic conflict. In the Caucasus, nominally Muslim Azeris married
nominally Christian Armenians; Georgia's vibrant capital, Tbilisi, was a
melting pot, with a church, a synagogue and a mosque within metres of
each other; in Ukraine's capital, Kiev, Russian, not Ukrainian, was
spoken everywhere. Most people actually thought of themselves as
'Soviet'. But it turned out that the 'indestructible union of free republics,
united for ever by great Russia', as the national anthem had it, was
mainly held together by the police state. Once the straitjacket was loos-
ened, the veneer of harmony cracked. The most powerful force unleashed
by *glasnost* was the rekindling of national identity.

The next day, in Riga, I discovered that Latvia's national revival was
by no means confined to small groups of protesters, or even to the
planned Popular Front movement. It had infected the entire political
class. I walked through the dead government quarter of the city, typewriters clacking behind open windows, to the foreign ministry. In
Moscow, diplomats lectured journalists about Communist Party policy
(and reprimanded you for breaking rules), but here Alberts Liepa, a first
secretary in the ministry, took up the refrain from Sigulda without missing a beat. He described what was going on as *zemdega*, which I
understood to mean the embers glowing under a layer of ash. 'Blow on
it gently, and it will burst into flame,' Liepa said.

He assured me that the meeting I had attended in Sigulda was 'only
one of many that took place yesterday'. He went on: 'Every nation who
felt like it has occupied us. It has left its stamp on the Latvian character.'
He blamed much of the country's woes on Stalin. Tens of thousands of
Latvians emigrated after the Soviet takeover in 1940, and again after the
war, to avoid being deported to Russian labour camps. 'As a rule they
were the brains of the Latvian people – engineers, doctors, artists, architects. The vacuum was filled from the east.'

I popped into the city's 'Dome' cathedral, founded in 1211. For seven
and a half centuries Latvians had congregated here to pray, preserving

their dignity as invaders swept in and out of their country. Under Soviet rule, the communists banned religious services, removed the altar and turned the cathedral into a concert hall. But people still came, to listen to the magnificent organ. Bach was also a great antidote to communism.

The following week I went to the neighbouring republic of Estonia, and was so astonished by what I found there that I felt I had stumbled upon a secret society. Estonia was like a chunk of Baltic cliff that was about to break off from the mainland, yet neither the Western press nor the Soviet seemed to have noticed this – the Western perhaps because it was preoccupied by events in Moscow, the Soviet because the implications were too big to contemplate.

In Tallinn I met an economist, a writer, a Communist Party ideologist, a diplomat and lots of 'ordinary' people, and without exception they all sang from the same rebel hymn-sheet. Valle Feldman was the foreign ministry's official spokesman, but it would have been easy to mistake him for the spokesman of Estonia's Popular Front, which had been founded in April (several months before Latvia's). 'We're hoping to publish our programme on 20 August,' he said, 'and in October it'll be adopted by a People's Congress.' The date, he pointed out, was important – three days before the anniversary of the infamous 1939 Molotov-Ribbentrop Pact. The crucial 'secret protocols' of the Pact, by which Stalin and Hitler divided eastern Europe into spheres of influence, had never been published in the Soviet Union – indeed their existence had been denied. 'Our radio station,' said Valle, 'has already read out the protocols! And they'll be published tomorrow in the Party paper, *Rahva Haal.*'

Valle was drinking lots of strong coffee, and it was either the caffeine or the politics that made his speech very fast and nervous. 'For the first time, Angus, the Estonian people have a great goal,' he gabbled. 'Everyone is working towards it. The pressure for change from below is so huge that it will be difficult to stop.' Then he clattered his little cup onto its saucer and said quietly: 'It could be a wonderful conclusion. But it could be another Prague Spring . . .'

He said this with such emotion I could already imagine the tanks of the Warsaw Pact rumbling down Toompea Street and taking aim at Tallinn's medieval castle.

Once again, the events in Estonia demonstrated that Gorbachev's 'genius' was to initiate changes without knowing how to control them. Responding to the obvious popular dissatisfaction with the communist old guard, he had plucked an old college friend, Vaino Väljas, from his post as Soviet ambassador to Nicaragua, and installed him as Party leader in Estonia. Within weeks, the national flag – a blue, black and white tricolour – was legalised after a 48-year ban. The new Popular Front was allowed to publish its own uncensored newspaper. There were firm plans to take Estonia out of the Moscow time-zone and align it with Finland, for Christmas to be made a public holiday, and for the Russian spelling of the capital (Tallin) to be given a double 'n', as it is in Estonian. And following the publication of the Molotov-Ribbentrop protocols, it was now possible to speak openly about a Soviet 'occu-pation' in 1940, instead of a 'popular Estonian revolution and vote to join the USSR'.

Valle explained that Estonians were pressing for the 91 per cent of industry currently run by Moscow to be put under local control, and introduced me to one of the republic's leading economists, Tiit Made, who had come up with the concept of 'regional self-accounting'. He gave me his business card, which featured a cartoon of a rampant cockerel abandoning one hen and chasing after another, with the caption: 'Always ready for a new business'.

So, this 'regional self-accounting' idea, I asked him, what would that mean, exactly?

'Well,' said Made, and proceeded to name a list of measures that read like an extension of the joke on his business card. 'Estonia should have its own convertible currency, shift towards Western trade partners, invite Western banks and companies to finance the rebirth of the Estonian economy, and encourage the re-emigration to Russia of the hundreds and thousands of non-Estonian workers who have flooded the republic as a result of Moscow's central management. As for our defence indus-tries,' he said, 'Moscow will be free to procure defence equipment from our factories. Paying for it, of course, in hard currency.'

'Um . . . do you think the Russians will get the joke?' I said.

Tiit Made smiled and clasped his hands under his chin. These guys really didn't give a shit what the Russians thought!

As I walked with Valle past Tallinn's Russian-language theatre, my un-diplomatic friend took another swipe at the 'occupiers'. Their theatre was usually empty, he said, because the Russians here were uncultured. The Estonian theatres were always full.

He took me to the Communist Party headquarters to meet Peeter Sookruus, the deputy head of the propaganda and agitation department.

Surely he, at least, would put an end to all this seditious talk. But no, he too turned out to be a reckless anti-communist, and admitted happily that all the initiative was now with the people, and the Popular Front, not with the Party. 'You want my personal opinion?' he said. 'We have pluralism of opinions now. It doesn't really matter what the Party's view is.'

Next stop – the Writer's Union, and coffee with novelist and poet Jaak Jõerüüt, one of the founders of the Popular Front. He explained that the Party could no longer act without the consent of the Front. 'We have a dual power situation,' he said. 'People say a second cabinet sits in this room!' Then he added wistfully: 'But we don't want that, we are writers, not politicians ... But recently it's been impossible to write – there's too much going on, we're constantly on TV, in the papers, on radio ...'

In the evening I attended a meeting at the Political Education House, where representatives of the Popular Front, the Communist Party and the city council answered questions from a packed hall of about 600 people. Together, they hammered out ideas for the forthcoming Popular Front programme. At the end, a choir of boys and girls with straw-blond hair and neat uniforms marched onto the stage, led by flag-bearers carrying the blue-black-white ensign, and sang folk songs.

My short week in Tallinn in the summer of 1988 left me in no doubt that it was only a matter of time before Estonia (and with it the other two Baltic republics, Latvia and Lithuania) would become independent. I wrote a rousing piece for the *Sunday Times*, in which I wondered whether the Kremlin was really aware of the tide of popular feeling washing its Baltic outpost. I was glad that the paper published it under a bold headline: 'Rebirth of the Estonian nation'. I felt like a trumpeting angel announcing the death of the Soviet Union. For the first (maybe the only) time, I felt I was reporting something that no one else had yet spotted.

I visited the third Baltic republic, Lithuania, in October. Here too they had a popular front, known simply as the Movement, or Sajudis, and it was about to hold its first congress. My first port of call was the communist youth paper, *Komjaunimo tiesa*. Its editor, Gedvydas Vainauskas, quickly recognised me as a would-be hero of the Baltic renaissance and insisted on interviewing me when my interview with him was over.

'We were the only paper that wrote about Sajudis when it was founded,' he boasted. 'Our paper sells half a million copies every day – in a country of three and a half million people!' He claimed his paper was the first in the Soviet Union to bring up many forbidden topics: 'The Party tried to stop us printing an article about Stalinism.'

A huge rally on 23 August, to commemorate Stalin's victims, was the moment, Gedvydas said, when the Lithuanian communist chiefs failed to spot the public mood and got left behind. 'They can't speak to ordinary people,' he said. 'They lack purely human qualities. It's only a matter of time till they will be thrown out.'

Another key moment, he said, was on 28 September, when riot police had broken up a big demonstration organised by the Free Lithuania League. 'They had shields and enormous batons. That was the first time we'd seen such violence. It was a *huge* mistake! The crowd shouted and whistled at them – "Dogs!" "Occupiers!". It caused an uproar. The Party held a special meeting and immediately agreed to restore our independence-era flag, our anthem, the use of Lithuanian! They knew that if they didn't make these concessions the people would come out in the streets to demand the head of the Party chief.'

Gedvydas was confident that Sajudis would get further concessions. 'Our movement uses Gandhi's methods of non-violent resistance. It makes it impossible for government conservatives to object.'

In the next few days it looked as if Lithuanian television had already been taken over by the Movement. I watched the Communist Party chief, Songaila, humiliated on air for his part in ordering the police crackdown on 28 September. On the eve of the Sajudis congress he was sacked.

The congress itself was an ode to joy and freedom. Sajudis leaders – mainly writers and other intellectuals – spoke eloquently of their plans, as if it was taken for granted that they would form the next government. The thousand or so delegates inside, and thousands watching in the square outside, interrupted speeches with cheers and chants, and burst periodically into song.

In the evening I joined half a million Lithuanians in Cathedral Square for what, I guess, must have been the biggest spontaneous gathering ever seen at that time in the Soviet Union. Candles sequined the dark sky, and thousands of red, green and yellow flags swayed in time to hymns and folk songs. When it was announced that Vilnius Cathedral was to be given back to the Catholic Church – after 48 years as an art museum – and

Cardinal Sladkevičius would celebrate mass in the square the next morning, people wept, hugged, crossed themselves, and gazed into the starry sky in disbelief. It would be almost three years before Lithuania truly gained independence, but for me, it all happened that evening. There was no way back – even though the thugs in Moscow would keep trying.

22

Triumph and Tragedy

WHAT A HEAD-SPINNING time this was to be in Russia. Even when the spirit soared, the heart kept sinking. Everything was changing, but no change was assured. Every flight of fancy came with its own ball and chain. The intelligentsia desperately wanted *perestroika* to succeed, but the masses saw it already failing – so while some queued to see the latest films, most joined the ever-lengthening lines for food. All the lofty talk about 'improving socialism' was only making it worse than ever. Gorbachev had taken to deriding the Brezhnev period as the 'era of stagnation', but there were many who thought it had been the best time of their lives.

Our friends didn't. Garik's art was proving popular abroad. He had an exhibition in Zurich, and he spent two months making a series of colour lithographs in Paris, with a graphics studio and a hotel room provided for him and Inna by a French art dealer. The Vorontsovs had new freedoms, to travel abroad for scientific conferences and exchange fellowships. Volodya and Seryozha clung to their faith in *perestroika*, but were fearful as the pendulum swung back and forth between Gorbachev and his enemies.

In the autumn of 1988 a movie called *Little Vera* took the country by storm. Fifty-five million people went to the cinemas to watch their own dismal lives played out on the screen. The film depicted the utter alienation of Soviet youth, a world of sleaze in a crumbling industrial town: crummy discotheques, forbidden dollars, unhappy romances and loveless sex, a paralytic father and domestic violence, homemade tattoos, boorishness and tears – plus the inevitable Russian laughter seeping through those tears. 'What's your aim in life?' Vera's boyfriend asks her as they cuddle on a beach. 'Seryozha,' says Vera, 'we all have one aim – communism.'

Even Gorbachev was getting frustrated with his inability to turn the Soviet Union around. I watched him on television, in the Siberian city of Krasnoyarsk, arguing with townspeople who were complaining that their toilets didn't work. 'Why do you run to me with your petty problems? Don't ask the general secretary, complain to your council! You may not have sausage, but you've got *perestroika*! Take things into your own hands!' But the people wanted a tsar, not *perestroika* with no sausage. Nobody had ever urged them to take power into their own hands before, and they were nonplussed. I was reminded of a Vysotsky song about a prisoner released from jail: 'Yesterday they gave me my freedom. What the hell am I going to do with it?'

Where they did take power into their hands, of course, it immediately threatened the very basis of the state. I had cheered the national revival in the Baltic republics, but there was an ominous side to this too. Ever since February I had found myself reporting ethnic unrest and bloodshed from far-flung parts of the empire. In Armenia, demonstrations that started out as exuberant protests against Stalin's crimes and local corruption soon took on a nationalist tint as the majority Armenian population of Nagorny Karabakh – an enclave within neighbouring Azerbaijan – demanded that their region be transferred to Armenia. In response, Azeris in the city of Sumgait carried out a pogrom against local Armenians, leaving 26 dead. Suddenly, *glasnost* turned bloody. The harmonious cohabitation of Soviet nations collapsed, as hundreds of thousands of Armenians fled from Azerbaijan, and Azeris from Armenia. The headlines over my *Sunday Times* stories became more and more portentous, as the entire country seemed on the brink of cracking up.

Nonetheless, Gorbachev seemed to be winning. In October 1988 he ousted several hardliners from the Politburo, established himself as 'president' of the USSR, and promised to release all political prisoners by the New Year. Shortly before Christmas he set off like Santa with a big sack of presents for the world, flying over the North Pole to the United Nations in New York.

I joined a few dozen Moscow correspondents on the accompanying press sleigh. The Kremlin spokesman, Gennady Gerasimov, changed into a tracksuit for the long Aeroflot flight, and mingled with the journalists, promising a historic speech to the General Assembly, and then a groundbreaking trip to Cuba and a stopover on the way home to see Maggie Thatcher in London. After many hours we made a refuelling stop at Gander, Newfoundland – an airport that seemed to exist only to service Aeroflot flights and prospective Soviet defectors. We lolled in a drab airport lounge for three hours, drinking beer. A Christmas tree twinkled, and Bing Crosby crooned, but otherwise it might have been the middle of Siberia. In a corner of the waiting hall, next to a neon sign that read 'Bacardi Rum welcomes you to Gander, Newfoundland, Canada', was a little desk with a discreet notice informing Soviet citizens that they could apply here, if they wished, for political asylum. Our Aeroflot crew filed past in a tight group, the pilots and stewardesses as if handcuffed together.

When we finally got to New York it was so many hours and so many time zones and bottles of beer away from Moscow that I could neither think nor sleep. Manhattan's canyons sparkled with frost and festive glitter. Steam rose from chestnut-grillers' stands. I drifted into sleep for a few hours, forty floors up in some flashy hotel, then rose to see what Father Christmas had brought.

His speech to the United Nations on Wednesday morning was a brave attempt to do to world affairs what he had already done to Soviet politics. There were gift-wrapped initiatives for all. He was going to slash Soviet troop numbers in Europe, even if the West didn't reciprocate. Whole tank divisions would be disbanded, the army cut in size, and top-secret radars opened up to the world. The old Soviet shibboleths of class war and the inevitability of the victory of communism over capitalism were thrown out. Gorbachev preached 'new thinking' – cooperation for the sake of 'the universal human idea'. It was massive – effectively the renunciation of the Soviet Union's global ambitions.

Then Gorbachev launched himself on Manhattan like a film star.

The Soviet leader may not have been pleasing all of his own compatriots, but in New York he and Raisa were bigger than The Beatles. A neon billboard on Times Square showed a hammer and sickle and the words: 'Welcome, General Secretary Gorbachev.' Raisa was said to have bought a diamond bracelet at Bloomingdale's, which only proved how down-to-earth and loveable she was. I hung about on Broadway with thousands of New Yorkers waiting for a glimpse of the great man with the red birthmark. 'What do you think of him?' I asked a middle-aged woman. 'He. Is. Juss. Wunnerful,' she replied. Traffic ground to a halt as his motorcade advanced from Wall Street, and 'gridlock' was instantly dubbed 'Gorbylock'. The New York police, and Gorbachev's security detail, had no idea what to expect next, as he jumped out of his Zil limousine at will to shake hands with his fans. The Big Apple was conquered. First, to paraphrase Leonard Cohen, he took Manhattan; soon he would take Berlin.

While we all felt the earth shifting politically in New York, what none of us knew at that moment was that it was literally shifting 9,000 kilometres away. Right then, a massive earthquake was destroying whole towns and killing tens of thousands of people in Armenia. In the middle of the night I was awoken by someone from the Soviet delegation saying Gorbachev's trip to Cuba and London was cancelled and we would be returning immediately to Moscow. Gorby's New York triumph dissolved at once into tragedy.

It's worth recalling, almost thirty years on, that Armenia was not then a separate country: it was part of the USSR, as much as Florida is part of the United States. Gorbachev was its leader – and he had to take charge. He *really* had to take charge because, despite his urgings to people to sort out their own broken toilets, even earthquake relief was not properly started without his personal presence.

By Saturday he was picking his way through a wilderness of rubble where up to 50,000 had perished. The world statesman and hero of Manhattan was almost reduced to tears. 'I find it unbearable to see so many people suffering,' he said. 'I find it hard even to talk about it.' But what he found even more unbearable than the sight of the suffering was the attitude of many of the Armenians, who – quite incredibly, given the circumstances – started haranguing him about Nagorny Karabakh, demanding that it be restored to Armenia from Azerbaijan. At the airport, as he prepared to fly back to Moscow on Sunday, his grief turned to fury: he fulminated against 'demagogues and adventurists' who were inflaming nationalist passions at a time when cooperation was needed. 'What kind of morals do these people have? They are waging a battle for power, and they must be stopped.' Six members of the 'Karabakh Committee' – moderate and respected members of society who had been helping to organise relief work – were promptly arrested and given 30 days' imprisonment.

We Moscow correspondents could only watch all this playing out on television, because the rule still applied that we could only travel out of Moscow with official permission – and none was forthcoming. Then on Tuesday, the Kremlin spokesman, Gerasimov, gave his usual afternoon briefing at the foreign ministry press centre. I was sitting near the back, next to Jonathan Steele of the *Guardian*. Somebody asked what would happen to journalists who violated the travel rules. Gerasimov gave a hazy answer, something like, 'Well, this is a very unusual situation . . .' Jonathan and I looked at each other.

'Do you think he meant what I think he meant?' I said.

'Yes,' said Jonathan. 'I do.'

We both bolted from the hall so we wouldn't hear if the end of Gerasimov's sentence contradicted what we hoped he meant. We rushed home to collect a few clothes, then met up and drove together to Sheremetyevo airport. There, we channelled our inner conmen and somehow blagged our way past border guards and onto an Ilyushin-76 transport plane that was being filled with tents, army rations, hypodermic syringes and medicines. It helped that eight doctors from Manchester, and British firemen with their dogs, were also on the plane, so we could plausibly claim to be 'covering' their rescue mission. Nonetheless, this was unprecedented: never before in the communist state had journalists just hitched a ride on a cargo plane, with no visas or written permission (though they did make us buy tickets, as though this were just a regular passenger flight to Yerevan).

The names of the devastated towns, Spitak and Leninakan, are seared in my memory. Until I went there – like most people – I had never witnessed the total, utter, unimaginable rupture of modern civilised life. Everything you took for granted, every comfort, every basic amenity – was gone. The lives of more than a quarter of a million people – smashed to pieces by the hand of God.

In the city of Leninakan the main square was a parody of Soviet vanity. Scores of pinewood coffins were piled up, waiting for corpses, around the obligatory statue of Lenin. A little khaki tent was marked 'Headquarters of the District Party Committee', while the actual Party headquarters – a huge, pompous building with a classical pediment – stood crushed and lopsided, still with three red agitprop placards on its façade, and a long banner with the words 'Let us implement the decisions of the 27th Party Congress'. People warmed their feet at bonfires. Vans delivered bread. Street after street of nine or twelve-storey housing was now a vast landscape of rubble, on which lonely people moved around, prodding with sticks, hopelessly lifting chunks of concrete or wood as if by some miracle they might find a wife or a husband underneath. The rescue operation was so monumental, so overwhelming, that while a few desperate souls dug purposefully, moving debris with their bare hands, most just stood and stared, with no idea where to even begin. A crane lifted a bathtub, and placed it somewhere else, but the effect was like moving one pebble to different spot on a beach.

I stood on the edge of a volcanic crater that had once been an apartment block. Men, some wearing masks against the stench of rotting flesh, pulled beams and slabs of concrete apart. I watched a young man, his face drained of expression, as a crane lifted a panel to reveal the crumpled bodies of his mother, his wife and his child, still in its mother's arms, all already dead for almost a week. The humanity of the rescue workers (who in fact were just ordinary townspeople) brought me to tears. How carefully they removed the wreckage, lest they hurt the dead. When they uncovered a woman's legs they protected them with wooden planks in case more debris fell while the crane winched up another concrete slab. I saw a little stone fall onto the young woman's face, and a man leaned over and carefully picked it off, preserving the dignity of a human being whose living light was long since extinguished.

Concrete panels crumbled as they were lifted – proof that they contained too much sand and not enough cement. Most of these apartment blocks had been built in the Brezhnev era. I thought of my brand-new flat in Moscow, back in 1978, where the windows had to be screwed tight and the newly installed plumbing leaked. What hope was there for Soviet buildings in an earthquake zone? Everyone, from the local people to the Politburo, blamed the corruption and shoddy workmanship that had epitomised the communist era. The authorities belatedly decreed that no buildings higher than three or four storeys should be built here in future, and that 'more care' be taken in construction. As the Russian saying goes, the peasant only crosses himself after the thunder peals – when it's already too late.

A local man who still had petrol in his car offered to drive me from Leninakan to Spitak, the small town at the very epicentre of the earthquake. As he crept around fissures that had opened up in the road, he thanked us ('us' being the West) for the aid we had sent, and blasted his own government: 'And what's the Soviet army doing? Ah? How come they don't have the special equipment, and trained dogs, that you have? Ah? Thank you Frenchmen, thank you British, thank you Canada . . .' But soon he forgot the chaos around us and began an unforgiving assault on the Azeris, who had killed dozens of Armenians ten months earlier in Sumgait as the dispute began over Nagorny Karabakh. 'We don't want any aid from Azerbaijan. We are turning it back. We don't want their cranes. They are murderers. We hear so many reports of their barbarism and sadism . . . what they did to Armenian babies! We Armenians are Christians! We are the second oldest civilisation in the world, after Egypt. Do you know that? Where were the Azeris then? Ah? Ah?'

Now I understood Gorbachev's anger when he was confronted with this kind of talk. It was astonishing that the survivors of a devastating natural disaster were so consumed by ethnic hatred. Even the crash of a Yugoslav transport plane that was bringing aid to the region was blamed on the Azeris.

The rolling dun-coloured hills outside Spitak were dusted with snow. New graveyards were marked out with string. Thousands upon thousands would be buried here. The quake struck at 11.41 in the morning, when people were at work, children at school. While in Leninakan a few buildings survived, here in Spitak nothing did. Here the rescue effort was listless and forlorn. A brazier burned outside a hut. A man lay sleeping on the ground, his head propped on a plastic bucket.

23

The KGB Gets Me

NOBODY PREDICTED THE convulsions that would occur in the world in 1989. I certainly didn't predict those that would happen in my own life. Though perhaps I should have seen the warnings – like the unexpected appearance at our door in January of our old friend Boris, with a bouquet of flowers for Neilian's birthday.

'How did you know it was her birthday?'

'The all-knowing Yuri told me.'

So Yuri Romanov – and his stooge, Boris – were still on our tracks.

Life was too busy, and too much fun, to bother with them.

We went for a family weekend at Zavidovo, where UPDK, the diplomatic services organisation, rented out wooden dachas to foreigners. Somewhere nearby, behind tall green fences, the Politburo had their own dachas, and a hunting reserve. This is where they used to ply bears with honey and vodka, or tie them to a tree, so that an old dodderer like Brezhnev might have a fair chance of potting one.

On some other weekends we went sledging with our friend Varya in the Moscow suburb of Kuzminki. In a clearing in the woods, hundreds of children and grown-ups, muffled against the frost, enacted a Bruegelesque winter scene – skating, tobogganing and throwing snowballs.

Then there was the day when Ewan, now two-and-a-half-years-old, almost had his appendix out. He was violently sick one night and by morning had a fever, so we took him to the local polyclinic. Two matrons in white overalls prodded and poked him, and recommended, first, that we rub down his body with vodka, and second, as a precaution, that we take him to hospital for a second opinion. We drove to a hospital in the centre of town, where another pair of motherly but utterly clueless doctors prodded him some more, muttered darkly to each other, then pronounced that he had acute appendicitis and must have an operation at once. The thought of our son going under the knife in a Soviet hospital was terrifying, so we said we'd 'be back' but wanted to go and get a second opinion. It was Sunday, and the British embassy doctor's surgery was closed, but a notice directed us to the US embassy, where a GP was on duty for Western citizens. There we were quickly seen by a doctor who immediately did something that none of the four Soviet medics had done – he took an otoscope and looked in Ewan's ears. He had an infection. It was this that had caused the vomiting and fever.

'So he doesn't have appendicitis, then?' we asked.

The doctor stifled a laugh and assured us that an ear infection was not a sign of appendicitis. He prescribed some penicillin, and by the end of the day, Ewan was fine. And still had his appendix.

A friend called Slava Cherny, who worked on the newspaper *Sovetskaya kultura*, invited me to a theatre performance, based on Yevgenia Ginzburg's memoirs of the Gulag, *Into the Whirlwind*. The production, at the Sovremennik theatre, used a sparse set that served to represent prison, court, convoy or camp, as required. Its depiction of the degradation of Soviet women as they were pressed through the meat-grinder from tribunal to cattle-truck to jail or firing squad was harrowing, to say the least. It was one of those occasions where you knew, without turning, that the people sitting around you were swallowing back tears and clenching their fists to try to stop themselves wailing with anguish. When the lights went up at the end, it felt like being at a huge funeral. And, in a way, we were. Events like this signalled – we thought – the passing of an era. Talking about the horrors of the past, surely, would ensure they did not happen again.

And yet at the same time, all these revelations, I sensed, were also having a demoralising effect on the population. The jubilation of the intelligentsia (that the truth was finally being told) was mixed with a surge of revulsion at the sheer enormity of the crimes, and the creeping realisation that almost all Soviet citizens, to a greater or lesser degree, were complicit in this terrible history. Some had participated willingly, some unwillingly, some only in a small way; many had committed little treacheries, almost all had turned a blind eye, and only a few had stood up to the terror. And a great many people, those millions who had genuinely believed they were building a better society, now felt betrayed and befuddled, as they struggled to accept that they had lived their lives in vain.

*   *   *

I travelled a lot in those first months of 1989, almost as if I sensed that my time was running out.

I watched the last Soviet troops pulling out of Afghanistan, marching over the Amu Darya river at Termez in Uzbekistan. The West, with its customary lack of imagination regarding what might follow, celebrated the defeat of the Soviet army. Within a few years the country, where girls went to school and women trained as teachers and doctors, would fall into the hands of Islamist extremists, who would ban music, stone adulterers, end women's rights, and set about terrorising the West.

In February I went back to Estonia, where the drive for independence was now way beyond the point of no return. The Estonians were no longer *calling* for independence – they were just *doing* it. Three months earlier, their parliament had declared the country's 'sovereignty' and rushed in laws that declared its land and air, and banks and natural resources, to be Estonian – not Soviet – property. Now they were fighting to make that a reality, after Moscow declared the moves unconstitutional. I watched their president, Arnold Rüütel, make a speech about Estonia's 'just goal': it was merely a question of 'what we can achieve today, and what only tomorrow'. 'The blue, black and white tricolour of independent Estonia now flies over this city,' I wrote. 'Each day at dawn, the flag is solemnly raised on the medieval tower on Toompea hill above the government building in Tallinn. Each evening it is lowered again. It is already a much-loved tradition, although only three days old. Until last Thursday, the red Soviet flag flew there.' I loved this brazen defiance – and the fact that the Estonians didn't just hoist their flag and leave it there, but repeated this middle-finger gesture every single day.

I went to Kiev, where Ukraine's communist chief, in power for seventeen years, mouthed his support for *perestroika* while not lifting a finger to change anything, and to Lviv in western Ukraine, where – as in the Baltic republics – *glasnost* and national revival were intertwined.

In Georgia, Soviet troops waded into a peaceful nationalist demonstration with clubs and sharpened spades. Twenty people, mostly young women, were killed. My contacts brought me photographs and eyewitness testimonies. The massacre was the first such action against a nationalist movement, and would do more than any other event to spur Georgia to independence.

Not that I had to travel far for news. My office became a magnet for dissidents, nationalists and malcontents. I still have folders full of the kind of things people would bring me – manifestos, open letters, dossiers of abuses, self-published magazines, unpublished poems and plays. They placed more faith in the powers of a Western journalist than in the Soviet system, but in truth I had no idea what to do with most of them. They wouldn't like to hear me say so, but the grievances of tenants in some provincial Soviet town shocked me less than the sight of 200 people queuing for three hours along the pavement of Kalinin Avenue in the centre of the Soviet capital to buy a half-kilo of *karameli* – caramel candies. Even the carefully typed and stapled samizdat journals, such as *Glasnost* and *Referendum*, were beginning to pile up on a chair, unread, as the Soviet Union's first genuine parliamentary election kicked off, providing much more exhilarating political action.

One morning in January 1989 I was walking up the broad steps to the Academy of Sciences building when a gust of wind blew the beret off the head of a man hurrying up the steps in front of me. I picked it up and ran after him. It was Andrei Sakharov, the dissident nuclear physicist. He quietly thanked me for returning his hat, but to be honest didn't look as if he had noticed its absence. It was hardly surprising that the distrait old boffin was preoccupied with weightier matters: he was on his way to a session of the Academy's presidium which was to choose its candidates for the coming parliamentary election. Sakharov had the support of a huge majority in the scientific community. At the session, however, the presidium, kowtowing to the Party's conservative wing, decided not to register him as a candidate.

There was an uproar. A few days later I went with my old friend Nikolai Vorontsov, the geneticist, to a protest rally, where hundreds of scientists demanded Sakharov's inclusion on the ballot paper. 'The Presidium must resign!' and 'If not Sakharov, who?' said the banners. 'Sakharov is the conscience of our nation,' said Vorontsov, addressing the crowd through a bullhorn. 'Our Academy is in crisis. For decades the members of the presidium have been elected primarily for their spinelessness – they don't represent us!' Members of said presidium were literally peeping out through the curtains at a balcony window, their spines temporarily keeping them erect as they observed the insurrection unfolding in the square below them.

When it came to election day, the scientists resorted to subterfuge. A huge number of them crossed out all the names on the ballot paper, necessitating a second round of voting – in which Sakharov was finally nominated. He won one of the twenty seats reserved for the Academy in parliament.

The incident was typical of the chaotic election process that brought Gorbachev's new parliament into life. Since the Soviet Union had never held a proper election before, nobody really knew how to do it – especially since Gorbachev had come up with a bizarre system whereby some candidates were elected from normal constituencies while others, like Sakharov, were elected by organisations (which included not just lofty bodies such as the Academy of Sciences, or the Communist Party itself, but the Stamp-Collectors' Union and Friends of the Cinema).

The Party tried hard, of course, to rig the nomination process and prevent as many undesirables as possible from standing. But since anyone could nominate themselves, at public meetings held throughout January, the wily Russian people – the *narod* in whose name the Party pretended to rule – often outfoxed the apparatchiks. It was open democracy season, with rules made up on the spot. I went to a nomination meeting in the Krasnopresnensky district of Moscow which was chaos from beginning to end, partly because the inexperienced chairwoman insisted on demonstrating how fair she was by putting every trivial procedural matter to a vote of the 600 people present. Straight off, someone else wanted to chair the meeting, so she put this to the vote, and lo and behold, we now had two chairpersons, who couldn't agree on anything. It then took half an hour to elect seven more officials to sit behind the seven bottles of mineral water at the long table on the stage, each one carefully explaining why he or she was worthy of this honour before being voted upon. Who would take minutes of the meeting? Nobody knew, so everyone shouted. Someone from the hall jumped up to speak at the rostrum. 'Who the hell are you?' shouted the crowd. Others joined in the chorus from two microphones at either side of the hall.

The chairman tried to quieten them: 'Comrades, I am old and in ill health. I can't shout above this noise.'

'If you're ill, why the hell are you chairman?' came the response from a man at the back of the hall. His neighbour reprimanded him for being so rude, and the two came to blows, like Popeye and Bluto.

Eventually some would-be candidates were able to present themselves, including a radical journalist.

'Who's your agent?' asked the chairwoman.

Nobody replied, so the chairwoman said she would do it, 'just to get things going'.

'You can't do that – you're supposed to be neutral.'

'Okay, let's vote on it. Those in favour of me nominating the candidate?'

Two hours later, after all the candidates had spoken, the chairman suggested they vote on them.

'How?'

'By a show of hands.'

'No!' shouted a white-haired man in the centre of the hall. 'There are people here who haven't registered.'

'Alright, then, only those with pink entrance cards can vote.'

A chant went up: 'We want a show of hands. We want a show of hands.'

'Quiet, please. Quiet. Now. Let's have a show of hands on who wants a show of hands . . .'

In the end, they chose the radical journalist – but that was just the start. His name would go forward to a constituency meeting along with others nominated by enterprises and other residents' meetings. Eventually two or three names would appear on the ballot paper for the vote on 26 March.

The really big name in this election was, of course, Boris Yeltsin. He'd been sacked as Moscow boss, had his plea for rehabilitation rejected by the Party Conference, and was routinely dragged through the mud by the official press. But the people loved him. He stood as a candidate in the country's biggest and most important constituency – Moscow city, with six million voters. His rival for the seat was Yevgeny Brakov, director general of the huge Zil car factory, which among other things produced limousines for the elite – precisely the kind of perk that Yeltsin railed against. At the evening meeting where the two men were nominated, in the grand Hall of Columns near Red Square, the glittering chandeliers tinkled as Yeltsin's voice boomed out, challenging the very foundations of the Soviet political system. Here I was again, I congratulated myself smugly, witnessing history being made. Definitely the best job in the world.

Over the next few weeks I went to several hustings with Yeltsin and Brakov, at factories and public halls, and had no doubt at all that, however biased television coverage was, and however hard Gorbachev himself tried to do down his rival, Moscow's electorate were in thrall to the big man from the Urals who dared to challenge the establishment. Thousands took to the streets in his support. Wherever he spoke, throngs would mass outside the building, asking for 'spare tickets', as if his meetings were box-office hits. Opinion polls did not exist in the Soviet Union, so one day during the week before the election I walked down Dorogomilovskaya Street, near my office, and asked a hundred Muscovites how they intended to vote. More than 90 of them said they would vote for Yeltsin. That was far more than I expected – and turned out to be incredibly accurate. On polling day Yeltsin trounced the Party's man with 91.5 per cent of the vote, on a turnout of almost 90 per cent. As slaps in the face go, this was a whacking great right hook.

Overall, the results were mixed. Needless to say, the Party (and the strange voting system) ensured that hundreds of its loyal servants were elected. But dozens of pampered Party barons also received satisfying kicks up the arse. In many constituencies where they had arranged to be the only name on the ballot paper, thousands of voters flocked to the polling stations for the sheer pleasure of drawing a big fat pencil stroke through their names. The entire Party elite of Leningrad was rejected. More importantly, dozens of recognisable radicals – the *intelligenty* who were the real drivers of *perestroika* – won seats, ensuring that the parliament, when it met for its first session two months later, on 25 May, would be a humdinger.

May 21st started off as a normal Sunday. It was the one day of the week when I was unlikely to receive any requests from the paper. We had scarcely woken when the telephone rang. It was Rod Lyne, number two at the British embassy. He said the ambassador wanted to see me at eleven o'clock. That was a fairly unusual time for a dinner party, so I asked whether there was anything to worry about. Rod replied only that the ambassador would not ask me in at eleven on a Sunday morning for no reason. With a growing sense of foreboding I got dressed, had breakfast, and got into the old Lada to drive to the embassy, directly across the river from the Kremlin.

I arrived together with Ian Glover-James, the ITN correspondent, which both cheered me up a little (at least it wasn't just me being told off for some misdemeanour) and worried me even more, since it was now clear something bigger was going on. The BBC's man, Jeremy Harris, also turned up, and the three of us sat in the embassy foyer discussing what the story might be, and why it was being given exclusively to us. It was either very exciting or very frightening.

The embassy's press attaché showed us in to see the ambassador, Sir Rodric Braithwaite. Rod Lyne was also there, together with the ambassador's wife, Jill, and Tony Longrigg, a boozy pal of mine who was then political counsellor and would later end up as governor of the island of Montserrat, shooing the natives away from an erupting volcano.

We sat down in a little circle, and the ambassador said he had 'distressing news' for us. By way of a preamble, he told us that on Friday the British prime minister, Margaret Thatcher, had taken the decision to expel eleven Soviet spies from London. The government had wanted to do this quietly, with no fuss, but . . . I remember the hairs at the back of my neck rising at this 'but', and sure enough, the 'distressing' bit of the ambassador's news was still to come. He said he had been summoned late on Saturday night to the foreign ministry, where first deputy foreign minister Kovalyov had given him a list of eight diplomats and three journalists who, he said, had been working in the interests of the British special services and engaged in impermissible activities. It was a straight tit-for-tat, he said. We were the named correspondents and had been given two weeks to leave the country. 'From 10.15 last night.'

So we did have a scoop. It was us.

Never have three journalists been so lost for words.

It was the most shocking moment of my life. Usually you take your own decisions – they may be wrong, you may make mistakes, you sometimes regret them . . . but at least you are responsible for them. Now, for the first time, someone else was making a major decision on my behalf, without so much as asking what I thought about it. It was like some gigantic mechanical grabber picking me up by the head, swivelling round, and dumping me on a pile of rubble somewhere else. Career over. My life as a Moscow correspondent over – right in the middle of the biggest story of the late twentieth century. How ironic! A sting from the tail of the old Cold War, just when democracy was dawning.

Within hours I became a little celebrity – *in* the news rather than reporting it. I gave interviews to umpteen newspapers that rang, from Stockholm to Saragossa. I mumbled something incomprehensible to my friend Martin Sixsmith, the BBC television correspondent, for the Sunday night news bulletins. Everybody was asking me, as if I was some kind of expert: 'Why do you think this has happened, now?' I hadn't a clue. I just wanted to cry. I migrated from sadness and incomprehension, to betrayal ('Don't they know I love them, for Heaven's sake?'), to anger, to numbness.

The next morning I drove to my office. The KGB officer who sat in a little booth guarding the foreigners' compound saluted me and began the usual Monday-morning chit-chat: 'Hello, how are you, how was the weekend . . . ?'

I tried to give the usual Monday-morning answer: 'Fine, thanks. And you . . . ?' But instead found myself blubbing uncontrollably: 'They're expelling me! Expelling me! I don't understand it! Waaah!' The poor man's chin dropped in astonishment. All those years of secret-service training, but he was unprepared for this.

During the day I wrote a letter to the head of the press department. I still thought I had a chance to change their minds. But by that night I began to realise I was caught up in a deadly serious game. Around 11.30, my old friend Nikolai Vorontsov, who had just been elected as a member of the new parliament, rang and said I must come and see him immediately. I drove down Leninsky Prospekt to his apartment, that intelligentsia den, stuffed from floor to ceiling with books, that I loved so much. We sat together in his kitchen till one in the morning debating what I could do to avoid deportation. He said he would bring it up the next day with Gorbachev's foreign policy adviser, Georgy Shakhnazarov, a fellow liberal who would surely help, and he advised me to write a personal letter to Eduard Shevardnadze, the foreign minister.

Before I got home it became clear the KGB were not taking things lightly. I was nominally accused of espionage, and it seemed their agents were under orders to treat me as a spy – to tail me, to intimidate me, and to terrify me. As I drove back up Leninsky Prospekt – a vast ten-lane thoroughfare, almost empty at this time of night – I saw two figures in the distance ahead of me, stepping out into the road. As I got closer the men stopped in the middle of my lane, right in front of my car, brandishing champagne bottles. I was certain they were going to smash my windscreen, ducked to avoid them, and swerved to the side. Their hands touched the windows, but they didn't use the bottles. My hands went numb with terror. I drove on a few hundred metres, then stopped to recover. Oh my God, I thought, this is not a joke.

The next day I visited Volodya and Seryozha in the afternoon. As a precaution I parked my car a bit away from their block and continued on foot, even though it was pouring with rain. When I came out a couple of hours later and returned to the car, still in torrential rain, I saw at once that a tyre had been punctured. I had no choice but to get out the spare and spend fifteen minutes down on my knees changing the wheel, the rain splashing off the tarmac and pouring down my back. Twenty yards down the road I could see two goons sitting in their car, laughing at me.

During the two weeks until our departure from Moscow I was followed everywhere I went – on foot, on the metro, by car. I might not have noticed the cars had I not been tipped off by Yura Shvets, who said he remembered how it was from his time in Washington, where he had been tailed by the FBI. The spooks were always about five cars behind, he said. And true enough, I began to spot them – a variety of white Ladas, about a hundred yards behind me, usually in a different lane. I noted the numbers of the cars I saw, and discovered that at least three were on constant duty, following me everywhere I went. I tried to shake them off by turning into side streets unexpectedly, but they always found me again. If I was on foot they were there too, sometimes taking my photograph from across the street. They were almost beginning to convince me I really was a spy.

I continued to work. On Wednesday, the day before the opening of the new parliament, I went to Luzhniki, a wide open area near the Olympic sports stadium, to cover a massive rally in support of democracy. The speakers, and the crowd, were exuberant, demanding that the radicals who had been elected to parliament must make their voices heard. Yeltsin appeared, cheered to the skies like David setting off to slay Goliath. I wandered through the crowd, interviewing people and writing in a little notebook – and every time I turned round I found the same two thugs, in flat caps and leather jackets, just a few feet away from me. I couldn't take it in: I was witnessing the greatest upsurge of democracy Russia had ever known . . . and at the same time I was being thrown out of the country.

That night I wrote a personal letter to the foreign minister, Eduard Shevardnadze, asking him to reconsider the decision. It was not the normal sort of missive one would send to a Soviet official, far less the foreign minister. I dispensed with formalities and spewed out an emotional love-letter about my affection for Russia and desire to help them be understood properly in the West: let them realise, I thought, how an innocent man feels when he is punished.

But the next day the KGB got tough. It turned out that the world's most secretive espionage outfit had a 'press officer', never before seen or heard, and on Thursday afternoon he held his first news conference. I missed it, because I was too busy following the debates in the new parliament, but in the late afternoon a producer from the BBC called me and asked if they could interview me about the 'new allegations' made about me. It turned out that the KGB was accusing me of very specific crimes to 'prove' I was a spy. I asked the producer to read me what was running on the news wires.

Well, guess what? I had broken Soviet travel restrictions by going to Yalta and by 'trying to penetrate' a closed area near Moscow. That much was true, though having a Virgin holiday and going to a barbecue were hardly proof of espionage. But there was a further mysterious accusation: I had also 'tried to engage a Soviet citizen as an informant about closed facilities'.

'For this purpose,' the spokesman said, 'the foreigner handed over to the Soviet citizen special equipment for listening to and recording telephone conversations, and promised him a monetary reward for any information of interest.' It's a shame I wasn't there, because the spokesman apparently showed the 'technical device which Roxburgh had handed over to the Soviet citizen'. He continued: 'The gadget has no trademark. We are of the opinion that the instrument has been camouflaged as a household appliance and can be used for recording telephone conversations, and, most importantly, for intercepting low-frequency magnetic fields dispersed by various sources, specifically, telephone lines and cables and electronic systems.'

I explained to Neilian what I had just heard, and we both immediately came to the same conclusion. Boris! Our old 'friend' from Glasgow and Stavropol had once asked us for a favour: next time we were in the UK, could we bring back a little Dictaphone, one of those new ones with small cassettes, for him to use at work, at the university? That must be it. Boris's bloody Dictaphone! They must have adulterated it to make it look like some sinister listening device.

Now I was really scared! If they were saying this was not just a tit-for-tat expulsion, but real espionage, anything could happen. I could be arrested and formally charged with spying. That had happened just three years earlier to an American journalist, Nicholas Daniloff.

We decided we should go to the British embassy and ask for advice. But what could we do with Ewan, our not quite three-year-old? Well, how convenient! Boris himself suddenly turned up at the door, for one of his unannounced visits. So we set off to the embassy, leaving our child in the tender care of a KGB spook.

This time they took us into the 'inner sanctum', the embassy's safe room, protected from prying listening devices by electronic jammers and double-skinned walls. 'I just want you to know,' I said, 'that I am not a spy!'

The ambassador laughed gently and exchanged a wry glance with the MI6 station chief, sitting opposite. 'It's okay. You don't actually need to tell us that. We would know.'

But what if I had to prove it to the KGB? I began preparing myself mentally for arrest and questioning, and knew I would do badly. I can hardly follow the plot of an Agatha Christie novel, so how would I handle interrogation under blinding lights in a Lubyanka cell? I imagined myself breaking down and confessing everything. Yes, I went to Richard Branson's hotel in Yalta to put a bug in the beer grotto. Yes, I planned to blow up the Oreanda Hotel. Yes, I swam in the lake at Vyalki – and tried to find out what fuel a member of the Academy of Sciences used to light a barbecue. Yes, I tried to recruit Boris as a spy and gave him a bloody Dictaphone. In fact, I disguised my own son as a listening device and left Boris in our living room with it . . .

Life went on. While seeing to all the practical arrangements – packing, finding a removal company, arranging somewhere to live back in Britain, visiting friends for the last time – I also covered the first astonishing days of the new parliament – the 'Congress of People's Deputies'. It surpassed all expectations. The first speech was made not by Gorbachev or any Communist Party hack, but by Andrei Sakharov, the 'conscience of the nation'. He was followed by a procession of other radicals, and their speeches – without exaggeration – changed Russia for ever. No topic was avoided. All the views previously aired at kitchen tables, or at meetings attended by a few hundred liberal intellectuals, were now debated in the national parliament, and broadcast live to the entire nation. For several days, the country stopped working. Industrial production fell by 20 per cent, and in most offices and academic institutions no work was done at all. As one anti-communist followed the other to the rostrum, the country's old leaders – the Politburo – sat quietly on a side balcony, like crows on a telegraph wire.

The Communist Party still had what one liberal deputy called a large 'passive-aggressive' majority in Congress, but these first two weeks of wild, open debate marked the moment they effectively lost power. Every time I hear someone claim that Russians are somehow 'not ready' for democracy, and only long to be led by a strong leader, I remember the atmosphere of those days. In my final dispatch I described it as the moment the Soviet Union turned from a totalitarian state into a fledgling democracy. The *Sunday Times* printed the piece with a photo of me stamped with the word EXPELLED. Most gratifyingly, the *Moscow News* reprinted my article in Russian the following week, which I took as a sign of solidarity from my Soviet colleagues.

Being associated with a British 'spy' could not have been easy for our friends, but they were not deterred from visiting us. Varya and her husband came to see us at our October Square flat, and were photographed as they left by a man with a long lens on the other side of the road. We went for a last drive in the country with Volodya and Seryozha in their beloved orange car. Garik and Inna, and Grisha and Zoya, came for a last meal. And the Vorontsovs were welcoming right to the end. Nikolai raised my case directly with the most liberal Politburo member, Alexander Yakovlev, who promised that if I left the country now he would make sure I got a visa to return soon. It occurred to me that Nikolai – not just an eminent scientist but now a member of parliament – had no computer. I left him my Amstrad word processor.

Only a few acquaintances took fright. Slava, who had taken me to see *Into the Whirlwind*, apologised when I suggested we meet: 'You know, it's a bit awkward . . .' Boris finally disappeared out of our lives altogether; mission accomplished, I guess. As for Yura Shvets, he positively revelled in it all. We had lunch with him and Grisha in a French restaurant on a riverboat, after which, as I drove home, he hunkered in the back seat, telling me which KGB cars were following me.

Grisha remained the enigma in our lives. He was one of my oldest and best friends in Russia. We must have drunk gallons of vodka together. I would never have suspected him in a million years . . . yet it was he who introduced me to Yura, and then turned out to be a friend of Boris too. It could all be a coincidence, of course. Or it could be that the KGB's spidery web went everywhere, enmeshing friends and acquaintances and workmates and everyone else you ever came into contact with, until in the end you had no idea who was who – who was saying what about you, who was for you and who against, who was a real friend and who a secret agent, and who was both at the same time. In some eastern European countries, after the fall of communism, they had a process of 'lustration', which exposed everybody who had ever worked with or for the secret services. If they did that in Russia it would,

I think, destroy millions of friendships and families. Sometimes it's better not to know.

We left Moscow the following Saturday on a British Airways flight, plied with champagne by cabin crew who clearly thought we were real celebrities. I realised how naïve I had been during my two years as a correspondent. I had never been bothered by the idea that the KGB was watching me. I hadn't been careful about what I said on the telephone, or about who I met, or where. Garik had a good explanation for my expulsion: over the two years I had got rid of the office driver and secretary, and also our maid. 'That's it,' said Garik. 'You sacked too many KGB majors!'

The allegations made against me were, of course, absurd, and my banishment from the Soviet Union was brief. I applied to return to Moscow for a short trip in 1990, and Alexander Yakovlev made sure I got a visa, as he had promised. During the trip, though, I met Yura Shvets for one of our furtive conversations under a bridge, and he told me the KGB were furious. It was they who had insisted on my expulsion, he said, and they were incandescent that I had now returned.

After this, I become a small pawn in a vicious battle going on in Soviet politics, between the liberals around Gorbachev and the hardliners surrounding the KGB chief. The next time I applied for a visa, in January 1991, the KGB were in the ascendant again – they had just sent tanks against independence supporters in Lithuania – and for the first time my application was turned down. When the liberals got the upper hand again a few months later, I got back in.

Yura told me the KGB had made a fourth allegation against me, in addition to the three they made public. It was that I had once 'tried to persuade a Soviet citizen to defect'. I have a feeling that this might actually be true. I have vague memories of a very drunken night in Glasgow, The Curlers bar perhaps, with that group of visiting Russians from the balalaika orchestra, when I was a post-grad student. The conversation went something like this:

Russian: 'I really love thish beer.'

Me: 'S'good, ishn't it? 'S'called Tartan Shpeshial.'

Russian: 'But we have very good vodka . . .'

Me: 'Yesh, you do.'

Russian: 'But thish ish very, very good. I like it here.'

Me: 'Tell you what! Why don't you just shtay in Britain? Eh? If you like the beer . . .'

My drunken jest was dutifully noted by one of the Russian minders who accompanied the balalaika players on their trip to Glasgow. That was almost forty years ago. But KGB files don't burn. I expect the account of my dastardly plot remains in the Lubyanka vaults to this day.

24

Spitting Live Frogs

THERE IS SOMETHING I haven't mentioned yet: I had somewhat carelessly managed to have myself evicted not only from the Soviet Union but also from the *Sunday Times*. It happened after I went to London in April 1989 to cover a visit by Gorbachev. At his press conference a *Sunday Times* colleague took me aside and revealed that a new newspaper was being set up, to be called the *Sunday Correspondent*. He was to be its foreign editor and he wondered if I would like to move with him to the new paper, as its Moscow correspondent. They would give me great opportunities, he said; it would be 'a writer's paper'; there would be no interference in what I wrote; I'd have much greater scope than at the *Sunday Times* . . .

Thus I came to make one of the more baffling decisions of my life. The *Sunday Times* already gave me every opportunity I could dream of, and I had all the freedom and scope I could wish for. The new paper (contrary to speculation in *Private Eye*) didn't even offer me more money! And yet, never known to have resisted flattery, I succumbed. My expulsion, which followed within a month, was evidently divine retribution for my vanity. I was now the ex-Moscow correspondent of a newspaper that didn't yet exist. Try putting that in your CV.

However, the sun shone on me: I had just spent two years covering the best story in the world in the Soviet Union; and now, as I moved to the *Sunday Correspondent*, the best story in the world shifted to a new locus. I became Eastern Europe correspondent, just in time to cover 1989's year of miracles – the fall of communist dominoes in Poland, Hungary, East Germany, Czechoslovakia, Romania and Bulgaria.

For a year I shuttled around east European capitals watching what happened when people finally grew sick of swallowing too many live frogs. I borrow the expression from the Polish Nobel laureate, Csesław Miłosz, who wanted to express what it felt like for an intelligent human being, living under communism, to be force-fed a mendacious ideology all his life.

> A man may persuade himself, by the most logical reasoning, that he will greatly benefit his health by swallowing live frogs; and, thus rationally convinced, he may swallow a first frog, then a second; but at the third his stomach will revolt.

Miłosz wrote this in 1953, but it was not until 1989 that there was a mass vomiting all over Eastern Europe. Only in two countries, Poland and Hungary, did the communist governments have a presentiment of the impending deluge, and – with Moscow's assent – start reforming. The others ignored Gorbachev's gnomic warning to them that 'he who is late will be punished by life', and the people took things into their own hands. Three cameos stay with me, from East Berlin, Prague, and Bucharest.

As a student, in the 1970s, I had lived for a few months in West Berlin – the capitalist, decadent, free half of the city, entirely surrounded by the Berlin Wall and communist East Germany, known as the German Democratic Republic. The Wall was an ever-present, eerie reality: streets suddenly came to a dead end; underground trains travelled from one part of West Berlin to another underneath the eastern sector, passing through darkened, unused stations. Tourists climbed onto observation platforms on the western side of the wall to gawk at the dowdy lives of the poor sufferers in the East. I didn't find it particularly dowdy, because compared to the Soviet Union this was Kodachrome communism, where shops actually had stocks of food on the shelves. I often went for day trips to the East, to escape from the sparkle and sleaze of the Ku'damm and stroll in a world that was old-fashioned and unpretentious. Once when I was returning through Checkpoint Charlie I was arrested and held for two hours when border guards accused me (accurately) of having changed money illegally. They refused to accept as a mitigating circumstance the honourable fact that I had used the money to buy handsome volumes of Goethe and Schiller. My favourite Berlin song from communist times was by Udo Lindenberg, called *Mädchen aus Ost-Berlin*. A boy from the West goes on a day trip and falls in love with an East German girl; they dream of a time when the Wall will be gone and 'the Rolling Stones and a band from Moscow' will play together on the Alexanderplatz;

but at midnight the boy must hurry back across the wall, before his day pass expires.

In June 1987 President Reagan went to West Berlin and, standing at the Brandenburg Gate, issued this challenge to the Soviet leader: 'If you seek peace, if you seek prosperity for the Soviet Union and Eastern Europe, if you seek liberalisation, come here to this gate. Mr Gorbachev, open this gate. Mr Gorbachev, tear down this wall!'

Nobody in their right mind expected this to happen, but in early October 1989 I went to East Berlin and watched as Gorbachev literally sparked a popular revolution that within a month would achieve exactly what Reagan had demanded. He came to take part in celebrations of the fortieth anniversary of the German Democratic Republic. His host was the abominable Erich Honecker, best known for a 1979 photo of him enjoying a full-on-the-lips 'fraternal' kiss with Leonid Brezhnev. He tried to do the same with Gorbachev, but the days of the Brezhnev smooch were over – and also of the Brezhnev doctrine that had crushed the Prague Spring in 1968. Now, according to the Soviet spokesman, Gennady Gerasimov, 'We have the Frank Sinatra doctrine.' The countries of the Soviet bloc would be allowed to do things 'their way', even if they wanted to abandon communism.

Gorbachev's speech to Honecker's congress included his prophetic warning to those who resisted change. The ardent young communists of the *Freie Deutsche Jugend* were supposed to stage a torchlight procession that evening to celebrate forty years of socialist triumphs in eastern Germany, but – with Gorbachev in town, demanding changes – it turned instead into a mighty protest against communism. I found myself swept along in a tide of thousands of demonstrators who surged through the city's central streets, chanting 'Gorby, Gorby'. Their numbers swelled minute by minute, as East Berliners came down from their apartments to join in. It was a Saturday night – the paper was about to go to press – so I had to run from hotel to hotel to phone in frantic updates to my copy. The protesters chanted the great motto of the East German revolution, 'Wir sind das Volk' (We are the people) straight into the faces of the Volkspolizei ('People's Police') as the latter blocked their path and thwacked them with heavy batons. After a month of gathering pressure, on 9 November, it was all over: the Berlin Wall came down, and I walked freely through the border where once I had been arrested. Germany was reborn. I thought of Udo Lindenberg's song, his 1970s ode to freedom. Finally, the dream had come true – love prevailed over politics.

At the end of October I saw a repeat of the Berlin protest in Prague. When crowds of peaceful demonstrators gathered on Wenceslas Square a small army of riot police with long truncheons moved in and started beating them up. The crowd splintered and headed off into dimly lit side streets where they played cat and mouse with the police all evening, chanting 'Freedom!' and 'Havel to the castle!' Two months later their hero, the dissident playwright Vaclav Havel, would indeed be installed as president, as another domino fell. At least my hotel was right on the square this time, so I was able to nip indoors to update my story every hour or so, as the clashes escalated. There was no internet or email in those days, but it was possible to hook up a laptop computer to the newspaper's server in London, to read news agency wires and file copy. This did, admittedly, involve vandalising your hotel room telephone. You had to expose the wires, identify the two correct ones, and attach your modem to them using crocodile clips. Then, by inserting a cunning sequence of commas in the dialling code you could circumvent the hotel's switchboard and establish a (very slow) connection to London. The KGB would have been proud of me. I now felt I fully justified the headline – 'With a pen and a picklock' – that had appeared a few months earlier in a Soviet newspaper, over an article denouncing me as a spy masquerading as a journalist.

In fact, my next encounter with the KGB was a rather pleasant one, involving plenty of vodka and fried fish. This was in November 1989, when I was the only British journalist covering what would turn out to be the last Romanian Communist Party congress presided over by the country's mad dictator, Nicolae Ceausescu. I ended up one night with four Soviet journalists, who were presumably KGB agents, in their little flat near my hotel. There had been no heating in Bucharest for weeks, and their apartment was quite literally freezing. The only provisions they had were bottles of vodka, bread, and large amounts of fish, which the TASS correspondent fried up over a tiny gas flame, filling the kitchen with clouds of steam and rivers of condensation. They may have been KGB, but they had no time whatsoever for Ceausescu, who was determined to face down all the Gorbachevian nonsense that was spreading from Berlin and Prague. *Glasnost* was definitely not a Romanian word. His speech to the Party Congress was the most spine-chilling political oration I have ever seen – a throwback not to Brezhnev's days but to Stalin's. Ceausescu called himself the *Conducător*, meaning Leader (as in Führer), and he conducted the audience as if they were an orchestra.

He spoke in short segments, a few minutes long, each one starting out quietly, and slowly rising to fever pitch, at which point the audience – thousands of robotic apparatchiks – sensed that it was the moment to leap to their feet and applaud wildly. They continued, each individual terrified to be the first to stop clapping, until the *Conducător* motioned to them to sit down. Then he continued with the next movement – adagio, piano, then accelerando, swelling to a great crescendo . . . cue tympani and the entire hall was on its feet again, palms smashing together like cymbals.

I was surprised it took so much as a month before the masses chased Ceausescu from his palace. On Christmas Day, he and his wife, still in their thick winter coats, were dragged, kicking and screaming, to a court-yard wall, where they died in a hail of executioners' bullets.

The *Sunday Correspondent*, though an excellent newspaper which launched the careers of some of Britain's most influential journalists, proved to be short-lived – pushed out of the market by the *Independent*'s launch of a Sunday edition. I bailed out early, in May 1990, in the same manner as I had joined it – lured away again by providence, or perhaps vainglory. This time the siren voices belonged to Norma Percy and Brian Lapping, who were embarking on a series of six television films about *perestroika* for the BBC. Would I like to join the production team as series consultant? Silly question. Would I mind if they also paid me to write the book to accompany the series? Even sillier.

Norma's approach to historical documentaries was to relate political events through the eyes of the protagonists – no interviews with journal-ists or experts, only with people who were actually in the room when decisions were taken. Her films took a long time and a great deal of money to produce, because her method involved interviewing everybody twice. First we spoke to as many players as possible off the record, to find out what stories they had to tell. Then we sifted through hundreds of hours of interviews, and only when we had compared all the different accounts, and mapped out how we would tell the story, did we go back for second interviews on camera. The trick was to bring history alive by getting politicians to stop talking about politics (directly, at least) and to recall instead the anecdotes surrounding the events in which they took part. It worked like this: Politician X would recall getting 'a little angry' with Politician Y, but wouldn't elaborate; then we would ask Politician Y about it, and he would say: 'Angry? X walked out and slammed the door!' So then we would go back to Politician X (with camera this time) and say: 'Can you tell us again the story about how you got up and slammed the door when Y was demanding such-and-such?' And invariably Politician X would forget that he hadn't actually told us this the first time round, and confirm it on camera. In this way we coaxed blood from quite a few grim-faced stones and were able to put together the first insider account of the wheeling and dealing in Gorbachev's Kremlin.

The Second Russian Revolution, as the series was titled, could never have been made even one year earlier, because the Kremlin was closed like a clamshell. But the timing was perfect. Suddenly it was in vogue to speak openly about things; and many of the protagonists were full of grudges, and glad to get them off their chests. We persuaded a large number of senior Soviet politicians, most of whom had never even shaken the grubby hand of a Western journalist until then, to sit down for hours and tell the inside story of Kremlin politics in forensic and colourful detail. Gorbachev himself did not take part, but when the series was shown on Soviet television, he saw it and was so impressed he demanded to be in it – so two more films were made, including the main hero himself.

The stars continued to align themselves in my favour. My friend Martin Sixsmith, the BBC's Moscow correspondent, was leaving for a new posting in Washington – just as my year of work on the documentary was coming to an end. He suggested that I apply for his job. The very thought of standing in front of a television camera, talking to millions of viewers, made my knees rattle like bamboo chimes. But Martin insisted there was 'nothing to it', and eventually I applied. Only after I got the job did I realise he was a lying bastard.

I was due to join the BBC in September 1991, and then, after a few months of training, go out to Moscow permanently towards the end of the year. In the meantime, I hoped to enjoy a relaxed summer. Thanks to *perestroika*, our old friends Volodya and Seryozha were finally able to visit their beloved Britain. In August they came to stay with us in Caversham. We showed them around London and Oxford, and then we all drove to Scotland for a holiday on the Hebridean island of Islay, where we often rented a cottage in summer. We disembarked from the ferry in the early evening, and drove along one of the most beautiful roads in the world, skirting the shore of a sheltered inlet on the Atlantic Ocean. Sheep wandered over the road without a care. I stopped near the strand and switched the engine off, so we could listen to the whisper of marram grass and the gentle splash of waves. The green meadow turned to velvet in the softening rays of sunset. It was so magical, we barely breathed. Nothing – nowhere – could be farther from the hubbub and chaos of Moscow than this island, this temple of peace and permanence, where nothing changes in a thousand years.

On Monday, 19 August, I woke early and switched on the radio, as usual. My heart somersaulted, and I turned on the TV to see if it was saying the same thing. Then I ran up to our guests' bedroom and hammered on the door. 'Volodya, Seryozha, get up, come downstairs. Something terrible has happened!'

We watched the pictures from Moscow in disbelief. Tanks on the streets. *Swan Lake* on Soviet television, as though a death had been announced. An 'Emergency Committee' had taken power. Gorbachev had been overthrown and was under house arrest at his holiday villa in Crimea. It was a coup d'état, a putsch by the dinosaurs of the KGB and military. Volodya and Seryozha, marooned on a Scottish island, felt as if their homeland had been swallowed by an earthquake.

The BBC Russian Service got in touch and asked me to come down to London. I caught a plane from Islay's tiny airport to Glasgow, then another to London, and by evening I was ensconced in a studio at Bush House with the great broadcaster Masha Slonim, analysing what was happening for a Soviet audience that suddenly grew by millions as their own media were silenced. I had never broadcast live in Russian before, but emergencies produce miraculous skills. We spent hours on air, sifting through every scrap of information coming in, and watching the coup leaders as they held a press conference that was so feckless we felt sure they would not succeed. Apparently Gorbachev himself, all his communications cut by the KGB, was listening to us on a shortwave receiver: 'The BBC came in best of all,' he said later.

The next day I rang the *Guardian* to see if they would take a comment piece from me. 'What we really need,' they said, 'is extra hands in Moscow. But nobody's got a visa.'

'I've got one,' I said.

'When can you go?'

'Now!'

Next morning I was on a plane to Moscow. I arrived too late to witness Boris Yeltsin's most famous photo op ever, as he climbed on top of a tank in front of the Russian parliament building, leading the resistance to the coup (with my friend Nikolai Vorontsov right by his side). But I did arrive in time to join the crowds gathered outside the KGB's headquarters, jubilantly celebrating the felling of the hated statue of 'Iron Felix' Dzerzhinsky, the founder of the murderous machine that had kept them in check for seven decades. I drank Soviet champagne out of any plastic cup that was proffered to me, and was swept away, like all the revellers, on a wave of euphoria.

The *Guardian*'s chief Moscow correspondent, Jonathan Steele, was not there. He had wangled his way, brilliantly, on to a flight down to Crimea for the news scoop of the year – an interview with Gorbachev, still under house arrest. So it was left to his deputy, John Rettie, and myself to sweep up everything that was happening in Moscow. I had an entirely free rein, covering events that shook the world.

By Wednesday night the coup had collapsed, and Gorbachev was back in Moscow. But not in control. For things had changed – irreversibly. It was Boris Yeltsin who had rallied the nation and defeated the coup, and now he was calling the shots. He had been directly elected as president of the Russian Federation in June, and now it was he who set the pace of reform, not Gorbachev. Over the next few days power steadily leached from the Soviet government, led by Gorbachev, to the Russian one, led by Yeltsin. Boris was at the peak of his power. I watched him address a quarter of a million people from the balcony of the Russian parliament, while signing decrees with a great flourish between sentences. There, I've just banned the Communist Party from operating in the security services. Now ... this decree removes all of Russia's resources from central government control and puts them under the Russian government. Now let's see ... ah yes, *Pravda* – we'll ban that!

There were victims, too, in this putsch. Some of the plotters committed suicide, and weren't mourned. But three young men were killed defending the barricades near the Russian parliament. They were buried, as martyrs, on Saturday. I joined a crowd of thousands who gathered on Manezh Square by the walls of the Kremlin to bid the three men farewell. Gorbachev came out to thank them, in an unsteady voice, and declared them Heroes of the Soviet Union – then hurried off for consultations with the handful of men left whom he could trust. The three coffins, on the backs of lorries, draped with the white, blue and red Russian flag – not the Soviet one, of course – moved slowly out of the square towards the Lenin Library, surrounded by a vast but orderly crowd. Order was kept not by the police, but by thousands of young men, punks and hippies, veterans of the Afghanistan war, many of their faces unshaven, some wearing camouflage fatigues and medals, others with headbands. These were the people whose impromptu 'self-defence units' had defended the Russian parliament, the White House, during the putsch.

As the procession moved along Kalinin Avenue, I noticed that the statue of Mikhail Kalinin – Stalin's one-time henchman and lover of Volodya's Aunt Sonya – was gone. It must have disappeared during the night, following Dzerzhinsky to a graveyard of Soviet statues.

We reached what was now called Free Russia Square, on the embankment in front of the White House, and waited for Yeltsin to appear on the balcony. The crowd was buzzing with rumours. 'Did you hear that bastard Kryuchkov [the former KGB chief and one of the conspirators] on TV last night? He said that when everything "blows over" he'll come back and "work for the good of the people again".'

'Like hell he will! Did you hear? Just before the putsch he ordered a factory in Pskov to produce 250,000 pairs of handcuffs.'

Yeltsin appeared. The putschists, now in prison, were eating each other like cockroaches in a jar, he said, each trying to blame the others. Turning to the parents of the dead men, he asked forgiveness for not being able to protect and save their sons. 'Sleep well, our heroes. May the ground be as soft as down.'

After the funeral I went to see Garik in his studio and found him crouched over his wireless set, listening to a new station that had just started up – the first independent radio in the Soviet Union, called Echo of Moscow. He motioned me to keep quiet: 'Every item's a sensation!'

I listened. 'President Yeltsin has recognised the independence of Estonia . . . This afternoon Ukraine declared itself independent . . . The Ukrainian president has resigned from the Communist Party's politburo and central committee . . . There is an unconfirmed report that Mikhail Gorbachev will today give up the post of general secretary of the Communist Party . . .'

'*S uma soiti!*' Garik whispered his traditional expression of wonder: 'Enough to make you crazy!'

Echo of Moscow was in full flow. 'Last night the red flag was removed from the central committee building on Old Square and replaced with the Russian one. The building has been sealed, but a car was apprehended as it tried to leave with a batch of incriminating documents in its boot . . . Other documents have been found proving that the central committee sent orders to the republics to fulfil the decrees of the putschists . . . The mayor of Moscow, Gavriil Popov, has personally ordered that Gorbachev's office in the central committee be sealed . . . Volunteers for Moscow's self-defence units are requested to report to entrance number two of the city council . . .'

This was like 1917. The people had taken power into their own hands.

Garik and I headed out into the streets. It was a warm, sunny evening. Knots of people were standing discussing the developments. Opposite the Bolshoi Theatre, the statue of Karl Marx, fashioned from an enormous slab of granite, was splattered with ink, paint and swear-words, but was still standing. Across the road, the monument to another Bolshevik leader, Yakov Sverdlov, was gone, but a group of deaf-and-dumb youths were attacking its marble pedestal with crowbars and chisels, apparently hoping to make some pocket money by selling chunks of it to tourists. The lessons of the Berlin Wall were everywhere.

We strolled up the road to Lubyanka Square, where the party that started on Thursday night with the toppling of Iron Felix was still going on. A few hundred yards away, all was quiet at the Party's central committee. Inside, lead seals dangled from the locks of a thousand doors. Outside, volunteers from a self-defence committee kept onlookers away from the once-forbidding entrances. 'All the underground passages are guarded too,' said one of the guards, proudly adjusting his khaki peaked cap.

I left Garik and took a taxi to the Vorontsovs. On the way I drove past my old flat on October Square, and felt a twinge of disappointment to see the big Lenin statue, where Ewan used to play, still standing. Nikolai and Yelena had guests, and we all sat down to watch *Vremya*, the nine o'clock news programme, on TV. 'President Gorbachev has appointed a new interim government, led by the Russian premier, Ivan Silayev,' the newsreader said.

I noticed the Russians were drawing in their breath and holding it through each new story. 'We have just heard . . .' began the announcer.

'Oh God, what's coming?' my friends whispered.

The newsreader stopped and picked up her telephone. Our hearts started racing.

First, there came a string of decrees by Boris Yeltsin, which effectively stripped Gorbachev of most of his powers. All Communist Party and KGB archives were to be put in the hands of Russian Federation officials. In the absence of a central Soviet government, the Russian government was assuming all responsibility.

Someone off-screen whispered to one of the newsreaders. He cleared his throat, preparing to make the most important announcement since the Bolsheviks seized power in 1917. Gorbachev, who just the day before had been defending socialism and the Party, was disbanding its central committee, resigning as general secretary, banning Party activities in the army and security organs, and ordering all of its property to be handed over to local councils – effectively consigning to oblivion the organisation that had run the Soviet Union for almost 74 years.

On another channel, the owlish liberal, Alexander Yakovlev – the man who had helped me obtain a visa against the KGB's wishes – hinted in an unassuming way that it was he who had changed Gorbachev's mind and persuaded him that the game was up. 'Gorbachev's statements when he returned after the coup were all wrong in the new situation,' he said. 'All that stuff about socialism and defending the Party . . . I told him about it today.'

Things had come full circle: the revolution that started in Gorbachev's Kremlin had swept from Moscow to the Baltics and Berlin, gathering strength like a hurricane as it arced down through central Europe, and returned now to blow itself out in Moscow. For me, it was all part of the same movement – the people rose up in all those places and defeated the totalitarian monster. The Russians spat out the live frogs and finally embraced freedom, just as the east Europeans had done two years before.

At midnight I looked out of the window. A full moon had risen in the sky. Suddenly we realised we hadn't eaten anything all day. Some food appeared on the table and a bottle was opened. Following the Russian tradition at a funeral, we didn't clink glasses. The Party's corpse, after all, was still warm. But a corpse nonetheless. Sleep well, may the ground be as soft as down.

25

Turning off Gorbachev's Lights

MY REBIRTH AS a television correspondent took place in the BBC's World Affairs Unit, where I was delivered into the capable hands of a brilliant producer, Neil Everton, who looked after me for a couple of months before I took up my posting in Moscow. I was not his first baby. He had already nursed several other reporters struggling to make the transition from print to screen.

'So, what shall we do with him, Brian?' he said to Brian Hanrahan, the BBC's top foreign correspondent, who was sitting in the corner. Our paths had already crossed as Moscow correspondents. I also knew him from several beers drunk together in eastern Europe during the year of revolutions, and enjoyed his dry humour.

'I suppose he could try scripting an obit of Yeltsin,' said Brian. 'He's supposed to know a bit about Russia, isn't he?'

Excellent, I thought, I can do that standing on my head. I sat down (nonetheless) and wrote what I thought was a sparkling account of Yeltsin's career, priding myself on the fact that I knew of footage that existed for every event I mentioned – it was all about 'writing to pictures', after all, wasn't it?

Neil took my script, pursed his lips and handed it to Hanrahan. 'What do you think, Brian?'

'Hm . . . How are you going to cover that?' said Brian, meaning, 'with pictures'.

'Easy,' I started. 'I know there are pictures of everything – I've seen them.'

But that wasn't the problem. It was the way I had written the story. It turned out that 'writing to pictures' was not exactly what was required. *Thinking* in pictures was, and creating *sequences* of pictures – and only after that deciding what words to write to them. What I had produced was a newspaper article, which has its own rules and logic. Just sticking random pictures over those words would not turn it into a television report! In fact, it would look ridiculous.

The grammar of television, Neil explained, was quite different. You began with the best, most arresting picture sequence, and built up the whole report from further sequences, based around a single person or scene, and often leading to a sound bite. Even a short report followed the basic rules of film-making: characters didn't pop up randomly: you set them up visually, then let them walk out of shot before they appeared in a clip; if you had two interviewees one after the other they needed to be filmed facing in opposite directions, or else separated by another shot. The trick was to allow the pictures to speak. There was usually no need to describe what was on the screen, other than to identify people or indicate what was going on, because the images were already saying more than a thousand words. You could let the pictures tell the story of what was happening, while you used your script to *add* meaning, to comment or analyse. In short, it was the pictures, not your ideas, that dictated the way the story was told.

'It's very simple,' said Neil. 'If the viewer isn't grabbed by the first twenty seconds – and I mean grabbed by the pictures, not your lovely, profound words – they might switch over to another channel.' So, if the story was that ministers had met to discuss what to do about an outbreak of rioting, you wouldn't start with ministers sitting round a table; you would start with the riots, and then move on to pictures of the talks.

We dug around in the archives and picked out the sequences we needed of Yeltsin at various stages in his career, and arranged them roughly in an order that made sense . . . and then, with Neil's and Brian's help, I wrote a script.

Then there was the problem of my reedy, weedy voice. Even the picture editor couldn't conceal her laughter as I spoke into the microphone for the first time, trying to pronounce my words ever so genteelly and carefully. I sounded like the teacher's pet at a Scottish primary school, who was about to get beaten up by the guys smoking ciggies in the playground. Neil coached me in producing sounds 'from the diaphragm', forcing me to 'project' my speech – so loudly the viewers could have switched off their tellies and just opened their windows.

'*He's* not doing that,' I grumbled, watching Hanrahan recording a script without the slightest effort.

'He is, actually,' said Neil. 'He's just been doing it for years, so it's completely natural.'

Eventually I learned to boom like all TV reporters – most of them even when they're just having a quiet drink with fans, I mean friends.

'*Now* you've got authority,' said Neil proudly, as though removing a nappy, sniffing it and finding it clean. Off you go into the big, wide world.

Arriving back in Russia in November 1991 was a big shock. The scenes I witnessed were astonishing. I had seen the Communist Party lose power in August, but only now did the brutal reality hit me: the place was in freefall, a superpower dropped from a great height, reduced to the state of a developing country. Gorbachev's frantic attempts to inject vitality into the communist economy by allowing state-run enterprises to trade with one another were now exposed as unworkable. The system was in its death throes – and working in television allowed me to see it close-up and in high definition. (This was one of the unexpected benefits of moving from newspapers to TV. Of course as a print journalist I had visited factories and hospitals – but the magic of television, and especially the BBC brand, gave me privileged access. A television camera, I discovered, cast a spell on people in a way that a man with a notebook did not. I was allowed to poke my nose in . . . just about everywhere!)

One of my first reports featured a vegetable depot on the outskirts of St Petersburg (as Leningrad had just been renamed, after a referendum). Its function was to take in supplies from collective farms across the country, store them and distribute as required to all the state shops in one of the city's districts. It was the *sole* distributor of fruit and vegetables for hundreds of shops – and maybe half a million people.

First I watched teams of women sorting through huge crates of potatoes, which were so rotten they'd become a semi-liquid, stinking, dark brown sludge, like pigswill. Wearing rubber gloves up to their elbows, the women clawed through the mush and picked out the few potatoes that might be usable, and tossed them into a separate cart. The rest of the gunk was shovelled into enormous rubbish bins.

'The potatoes were in a bad state when they arrived,' explained one of the women, 'and within two weeks they were completely rotten.'

'Why didn't you send them to the shops before they got rotten?'

'Well, we have a plan to stick to . . .'

'And you'll distribute these to the shops?' I asked, looking with disgust at the 'saved' potatoes.

'Well, no, but if they're not too bad, we can send them to pig-farms . . .'

Finally, I understood why the carrots and potatoes I used to queue for in Yasenevo and Chertanovo were of such poor quality – and that was in the good old days when the system more or less worked! Now the system was broken. The depot looked like the graveyard of the Soviet economy. Only the agitprop department had worked well here: a sign in the manager's office read: 'Let us not allow a single kilo of produce to go to waste!'

'I've worked here for twenty years,' a woman told me, 'and I've never seen so much rotten stuff, before the winter even starts.'

In another part of the depot, women were trying to save beets that arrived four weeks earlier from Ukraine. 'They're supposed to last all winter,' said the depot manager with the hangdog look of a schoolboy handing in his homework late, 'but they're mostly rotten. We'll have to buy more.'

We drove to a fruit warehouse, a cavernous hangar which was entirely empty apart from a few dozen boxes of imported lemons.

Then we went to see the city's newly elected mayor, Anatoly Sobchak – a lawyer by profession and one of the democrats whose speeches had set the new parliament alight back in May. Now, in the city that half-starved to death during the Second World War, the prospect of starvation was once again real. As winter approached, food stocks were at half their normal level. Sobchak's solutions for the crisis ranged from the ingenious to the desperate. He had introduced ration cards for all foodstuffs in state stores. He had set up control points at the city limits to stop food being taken out. He had struck direct barter deals with other Soviet republics. He had contacted factory managers and asked them to send lorries out to parts of the country where there were potatoes 'going spare', to buy them up and distribute them to their workers. And he was arranging 'oil for food' deals with Germany and other countries. To be precise, these deals were being arranged by one Vladimir Putin, a former KGB spy in East Germany, who had returned to St Petersburg and found work with his old law professor, who put him in charge of the city's relations with foreign countries. Later, Putin would be accused of personally profiting from these deals, which saw Russian resources disappear abroad but not much Bratwurst or Sauerkraut appearing in St Petersburg's shops.

The rushes of our BBC shoot in the city show Putin as a shadowy, timid-looking bureaucrat, lurking in the background of a meeting with Sobchak, but of course he was unknown at the time, so we did not interview him.

My first reports in Moscow itself were all about the food shortages. The cliché about 'empty shelves' in Soviet shops established itself at a time when they were in fact merely poorly stocked and erratically supplied. Now it wasn't a cliché. I filmed the longest queue I had ever seen, on a street near the BBC's office, leading to a milk shop, which had nothing in it at all – not even the leaking squishy pyramids of reconstituted milk we used to buy in the old days. Women in the line told me they had special ration cards giving them the right to buy milk for their infants . . . but they were useless since there was no milk for anyone at all. And still they queued, patiently stamping their feet for warmth in the grey slush, hoping for a miracle.

The thought occurred to me that if Russians didn't rise up against their leaders now, in such desperate conditions, they must be the most docile, or most stoical people in the world. Who else would stand for this? The trouble was, I guess, they didn't know who to rebel against. The Communist Party had already been banned. Gorbachev, still nominally the country's president, was universally hated, but he was on his way out. And Yeltsin was their one-time hero, now threatening to unleash market-driven prices on them. Around the corner, we filmed one of the first communist demonstrations, with red banners and Soviet slogans, denouncing Gorbachev as a traitor and Yeltsin as a Judas. I interviewed old women in headscarves who shook their fists and swore that the best days of their life had been under Brezhnev or even Stalin. It gave us terrific sound bites to use, always with the implication that these hoary old fossils were misguided Luddites who didn't get how awful communism had really been for them . . . but in retrospect it was wrong to have portrayed them as clownish or deluded: these were good Soviet citizens who had been wrenched from the relative comfort and stability of the old system and plunged into poverty and confusion.

Bells tolled day after day for President Gorbachev. He was still desperately trying to stitch together a new union, or confederation, that would hold the twelve remaining Soviet republics together (minus the Baltics) – however loosely. But in early December Ukraine voted to confirm its independence from the USSR. And then Yeltsin met the leaders of Ukraine and Belorussia at a hunting lodge near the Polish border where they signed a deal that effectively consigned the Soviet Union to history. They established a new 'Commonwealth of Independent States' and invited the other republics to join them. There was no place for Gorbachev, or Soviet power, in this arrangement.

The TASS newswire clacked out this momentous news on the telex machine in the BBC office on the evening of 8 December. I tore off the page and read it. And read it again. Then I called the editor of the *Nine O'Clock News*. 'Um, I think something pretty big has just happened,' I said. 'Yeltsin and the Ukrainians and Belorussians have just disbanded the USSR!'

The response from the duty editor was: 'Oh . . . they're always saying things like that, aren't they?'

'Well, up to a point,' I said, almost adding, 'Lord Copper'. 'I don't think they've actually done this before. They're setting up a new Commonwealth of Independ . . .'

But before I reached the end of the sentence I could sense the boredom settling in at the other end of the phone, confirmed by a tart, 'Listen, mate, we're pretty full tonight, so we'll probably pass on that one.'

If I hadn't been only one month into the job I would probably have sworn at him and demanded to lead the bulletin. But I was green, and in awe of programme editors, so I meekly gave way. And thus the BBC failed to report the dissolution of the USSR on the day it happened! Next day, of course – once newspapers and newswires had reported the event – they were all over it, and over the next weeks we chronicled the Soviet Union's agonising death.

Yeltsin helped himself, day by day, to Mikhail Gorbachev's last remaining powers. One day the plaque on the Soviet foreign ministry was taken down, and it became the Russian Federation's foreign ministry. Other government buildings followed suit, until Gorbachev had no fig leaf left to hold in front of him save for the title of 'President of the USSR'. On 25 December 1991 he bowed to the inevitable, and in an emotional speech on television he conceded it was all over. The country of which he was president no longer existed. The Soviet flag, red with its yellow hammer and sickle, the fluttering beacon of hope for workers' parties around the world, was lowered from its spotlit place on top of the Kremlin. The white, blue and red flag of Russia shimmied up the pole – and Boris Yeltsin shimmied into Gorbachev's room in the Kremlin, ensconcing himself with all the levers of power before his predecessor even had time to clear his desk.

I interviewed the ex-president a few months later in his new office – a think-tank known as the Gorbachev Foundation. He was a broken man, full of venom for Yeltsin. After the interview was over, he crossed to his desk and started gathering various papers into his briefcase. I left the cameraman and producer to de-rig the lights and pack up the equipment, and walked over to chat more informally with the ex-president – my idol since the earliest days of *perestroika*. I gave him a copy of my book, *The Second Russian Revolution*. He thanked me – but the cover, with its picture of himself flanked by Ligachev and Yeltsin, sparked off a fresh tirade. Yeltsin 'only knew how to destroy, not to build,' he complained, and began pulling out documents from his desk, leafing through them and jabbing at various sentences that evidently proved how he had been betrayed. He looked as if he could do with some counselling, like a loving father who had just been served with divorce papers informing him his evil wife was to have custody of his children. It was taking some time for my colleagues to pack away the hot TV lights, and eventually Gorbachev shut his briefcase and walked, with a heavy gait, towards the door. We shook hands, and the former president of the USSR, once the second most powerful man in the world, sloped away, without even a bodyguard, leaving us alone to tidy up in his office. 'Don't forget to turn out the lights, please,' he said, with that gentle smile that had charmed the world, 'and shut the door properly when you leave . . .'

26

Humiliated and Insulted

I BRIBED. FINALLY, I bribed. I did it for the sake of my wife and two small boys, Your Honour.

We were living in the BBC's smallest flat, really intended only for an unmarried cameraman or producer, and four of us were crammed into a single room – Neilian and I, Ewan, and our second son, Duncan, who was born in the year of revolutions, 1989, between Prague and Bucharest. Renting apartments to foreigners was still the prerogative of the foreign ministry department known as UPDK. My written requests for a bigger flat, notwithstanding the BBC notepaper and the official stamps (without which no Russian bureaucrat would even look at a document) all appeared to have been recycled as toilet paper. So I made an appointment, and walked into Mrs Я.'s office with a plastic carrier bag containing two bottles of whisky and one of French wine. This was a Goldilocks bribe, I was advised – not too much, not too little. I didn't mention it, of course, but merely placed the bag on the floor beside her desk, while I told her briefly about my family's needs and she told me at great length that accommodation was in very short supply. As I got up to leave, I sort of nodded shamefacedly at the bag on the floor and coughed '*Pozhaluista*', which means 'There you go' or 'You're welcome' or 'Please'. Mrs Я. ignored both my nod and the bag – to the extent that I wondered whether she had actually noticed what I was doing. I walked towards the door in a panic: what if she hadn't grasped that I was bribing her, and only saw the bag after her next supplicant came – and assumed that *they* had left it? Should I go back and explain? I reached the door and turned, planning to cast another meaningful glance in the direction of the bag, but instead just murmured, 'Bye, then . . .' and walked out. It was another two months before we got a bigger flat.

*   *   *

I loved the collegiality of working in television. Newspaper reporting was a fairly solitary profession, whereas in TV you worked in a team. The BBC office had locally hired producers (a Russian, and two or three Russian speakers from Britain who were glad to gain experience for not much money). There were two cameramen, Bob Prabhu and Dave Skerry, and a picture editor, Duncan Knowles (later succeeded by Duncan Herbert) who all became my gurus, guiding me through the mysteries of television writing and editing. I was one of two television correspondents, the other being Ben Brown, a BBC star who could easily have made me feel like his unglamorous sidekick, but in fact was a great colleague, happy to share the work, and generous with good advice to a TV novice.

I still squirm when I recall my first 'two-way', as live interviews with the news anchor are known. They take some getting used to: you sit facing directly into a camera, with an earpiece through which you hear the presenter's questions – but you can't see her. Nowadays the questions and answers are often scripted, or at least carefully prepared, but in those days you just took whatever questions the newsreader threw at you – live in front of ten million people. The hardest thing, though, was not what to say, but how to keep your eyes focussed on the lens. On my first live outing, Bob helpfully put a tape in his camera and recorded my performance, so I could see how I looked – and I discovered that my eyes had been repeatedly darting to the side throughout the interview. I looked like a shifty criminal doing a polygraph test. Amazingly, the BBC continued to use me, and I learned to keep my eyeballs under control.

Another ordeal was the 'stand-up' or 'piece to camera' – the fifteen or twenty seconds in a report where the correspondent speaks directly into the camera. It's an essential element of the television package, which adds credibility by showing you are actually at the centre of events, and allows you to speak directly to the viewer. They can take an hour or more to record, for a variety of reasons. You have to find the right spot. You have to deal with passers-by getting in the way or policemen telling you you're not allowed to do that there. And the reporter has to remember his lines – which can be hard, especially if you've written something so complicated or boring that you yourself can't even memorise it. In those early days in Moscow, we did many stand-ups at big demonstrations, and to achieve a good perspective the cameraman would often raise his tripod to the highest level, and then ask me to stand on a step-ladder, so the crowd would be visible behind me. This was invariably a cause of great ribaldry among people in the crowd, who usually assumed that I was on a ladder not for the sake of a good picture but because I was preposterously small. They would barrack me every time I forgot my words or started again because I wasn't happy with my delivery. Brian Hanrahan had warned me that television news was 'eighty per cent logistics, twenty per cent journalism', but he never mentioned the bloody humiliation!

A two-minute package on, say, the food shortages, could take an entire day (or sometimes more) to put together. One of the office assistants would set up an interview with a politician or an expert, and it could take an hour and a half just to drive there and film the interview. Then we would scour the city looking for good shots to illustrate 'poverty', film in shops (which sometimes required advance negotiation), and perhaps attend a demonstration, where we would do vox pops and record the piece to camera. Then we would return to the bureau, where the picture editor and I would view all the rushes, decide how to structure the piece, pick clips from the interviews, write a script (a tiny number of words, compared to a newspaper article, but much more deliberately chosen), edit it all together, and feed the cut story by satellite to London . . . in time for the *Six O'Clock News* (nine pm in Moscow).

It was great fun – but there were uneasy moments too. A print journalist only needs to walk past beggars in the street in order to write the words: 'The number of beggars in Moscow is growing.' He might even take a couple of minutes longer to write an evocative sentence. In television, you can't get away with that. You need to show them, and that has to be done sensitively. Bob and Dave were discreet and brilliant cameramen. One beautifully composed shot, of an old woman crouching in a bleak windswept underpass – hand timidly outstretched, cowled head nodding in silhouette – was used again and again in programmes about Yeltsin's Russia. We didn't just grab the image: it required the tripod to be set up, the shot to be framed, and the right moment to occur, as a passer-by placed a coin in her hand. I gave her a decent amount of money as if to atone for preying on her plight, but it still felt horribly intrusive and awkward.

Most of our work in 1992 involved intruding on the lives of the unfortunate. On 2 January, Yeltsin ended the state control of prices, allowing the market to dictate the cost of everything, including food – as the first step towards recreating a capitalist economy and stimulating the market. He was guided by Western economists, who had seen 'shock therapy' work wonders in Poland and other East European countries. I sometimes wondered whether they had really studied Russia's society at all before unleashing the unbridled forces of the market on it. Reviving Eastern European economies after 40-odd years of communism was one thing; reviving Russia's – after 74 years of state control, total war, purges and stagnation – was quite another. In Poland, older people still remembered what it was like to live in a thriving pre-war economy; in Russia, whole generations had come and gone, obliterating even the memory of free enterprise and full shops. Of course, there were a few wide boys and spivs who grabbed the chance to make a quick buck, but there were many millions who saw their life savings disappear in the bonfire of inflation, and suddenly discovered that capitalism was even worse than its portrayal in Soviet propaganda films had suggested.

Our filming took us from dosshouse to orphanage to soup kitchen to street market, like Stations of the Cross on a post-Soviet *via dolorosa*, providing an almost daily menu of despair to the news bulletins.

We filmed in the huge concourse of the Kursk railway station, where passengers were outnumbered by people sleeping rough. And in a distant suburb we filmed in a dosshouse, Russia's first since the 1917 Revolution, where a few of those desperate people were given a proper bed – after being searched for lice and scrubbed down with carbolic, a process that we dutifully filmed and showed to a teatime audience back home.

In one square, we met ordinary people selling off the most extraordinary things, in what must have been the world's biggest-ever flea market. There were elderly people, whose 300-rouble-a-month pension had suddenly become almost worthless. And there were also professional people – teachers, office workers, doctors – whose salaries were left standing when Yeltsin fired the starting gun to liberate prices. A research scientist was selling a hairdryer. An engineer was holding three or four items in his hands – not nice gadgets or even second-hand clothing, but rusty padlocks, screws and hinges that looked as if they must have fallen off some shed, maybe at his dacha. A physicist with six published scientific papers to his name was standing in the snow selling an old brass doorknob. He himself realised the absurdity of the situation: he just grinned with a lopsided smile when I asked him what he hoped to be able to buy with the proceeds. 'For me it's nothing,' he said, 'but somebody might need it – and I'll have a bit of money for a beer ...'

'How much can you get for it?

'For this?' He giggled. 'Maybe ten roubles.'

The West responded to Russia's distress by sending planes loaded with humanitarian aid – which was welcomed, even if it was humiliating for a great country to be holding out a begging bowl. The European Community dug into its food surpluses – the infamous butter mountains and milk lakes – and dispatched them to Russia. The official in charge of distributing supplies in Moscow told me that about four million people in the city would soon be on the breadline. He was prioritising the most vulnerable – old people, invalids, children, single mothers. But Russians didn't lose their pride: this was the time of mad cow disease in Britain, and officials in the northern port of Murmansk refused to unload a delivery of British beef, suspecting that contaminated meat was being offloaded onto them. They held out for three weeks, but eventually relented, and served it up to 100,000 children.

We filmed one night at Moscow airport. Every few minutes ghostly lights appeared in the darkness and another cargo plane swooped down through the blizzard, bringing random consignments that were usually a surprise to the recipients. Ella Pamfilova, the minister of social care, told me: 'We've no idea what they're bringing or where the aid is intended for. We just have to open the boxes and look!' Many Russians wondered whether 54 American planes, full of army rations left over from the Gulf War, were just a meaningless show. For weeks afterwards I came across brown MRE ('meal, ready-to-eat') packs lying unsold at street markets. The Russians were probably nonplussed by bags marked 'Menu 15, Beef Enchilada, Warfighter Tested', and almost certainly had no idea that before eating you had to warm the food by adding a small amount of water to trigger a chemical heater inside the bag. Or maybe they just found them disgusting.

The Salvation Army, banned for decades in the Soviet Union, were back – with prayers, hymns, and a big recruitment drive. General Eva Burrows told me she 'sensed' that the Russian people could fit into a 'military-style church'. They also set up soup kitchens, and of course we were there, sticking our lenses in the faces of desperate old people dribbling food down their chins. There was nothing we wouldn't do to jerk a few tears back home.

As well as liberating prices, Yeltsin made street-trading legal. What used to be black marketeering now became a full-time occupation for hundreds of thousands of people. They lined the pavements all the way from the Lubyanka KGB headquarters, past Children's World, down to the Bolshoi Theatre and the Kremlin. Many were selling home-made items – knitted hats or gloves; others new goods apparently bought in the shops – bed linen or underwear, or a kettle or light bulb. I met Sergei, a former policeman, selling shiny new shoes and boxes of chocolates, which he bought at the Lubyanka, then walked down the street and sold for a profit at the Bolshoi. He was doing a roaring trade. He couldn't possibly survive on his policeman's salary of less than 1,000 roubles a month, he said, but by trading like this he could earn 20,000. He took me home to show me his lifestyle. He had a very comfortable flat, and owned two TV sets and two video-recorders – 'because technical goods like that keep their value, and if the government suddenly devalues the currency I won't lose out.'

Every day brought some new horror for us to film. Dysentery, salmonella, botulism, trichinosis (whatever that was) – Moscow was rife with them . . . well, not quite, but filming disgusting chunks of meat being sold from hand to hand, fish lying on the ground, and piles of rubbish infested (one was told) with rats, could certainly create that impression. Did we over-egg it, I wonder? Sometimes, probably. The medium of television requires strong images, which inspire strongly worded scripts. You came back from a shoot with two hours of rushes, and from them selected the most eye-catching pictures, totalling no more than 100 seconds. The more appalling the story, the more likely it was to get on air. Plus, you really felt sorry for these people, and hoped that sympathies evoked in the West would encourage governments to provide more aid. It wasn't that we ever reported something that was not true – but by showing isolated incidents, chosen because they offered the most striking pictures, one could give the impression that the whole of Moscow was engulfed in disease, poverty and chaos – which it wasn't.

Thus, capitalism was reborn in Russia – spontaneous, unruly, unregulated and unhygienic. Watching it grow over the next months and years was amazing, like a quick course in economic history. What developed over many centuries in mankind, happened over a couple of years in Russia. First there were individuals, bartering or selling goods from hand to hand. Then they got tables to display their wares on, then stalls. Then the richer ones got several stalls and hired workers. Then they banded together and formed small companies. They didn't pay taxes, but they did pay protection money to thugs who found that threatening stallholders was easier than buying and selling. Thus the Russian mafia was also born. At the same time state shops were sold off to their employees – and instantly the new owners had an incentive to beautify the premises, install smarter display counters, find better suppliers, and price their goods in accordance to supply and demand. Prices soared, but suddenly everything was available. Those who became rich enough could set up a café, or a repair shop, or a small bakery. It wasn't long before real supermarkets appeared, with groaning shelves (and guards at the door carrying Kalashnikov rifles). At first much of the produce was imported, but eventually Russian farms began to catch up, and even learned to package their foods attractively.

Selling required marketing. So now the great communist-built avenues of Moscow were lined with billboards, almost all (at first) advertising trading companies rather than the goods they sold. We went to film in one small electrical goods store. The story was typical. The young men had started out by driving to neighbouring countries to sell scrap metal, bought on the black market. On the first trip they made enough to buy two computers which they brought back and sold for a very high price in Moscow. With the cash – and more scrap metal or timber – they went abroad again, and this time came back with ten computers, and a couple of televisions or cassette recorders. The revenue from those sales was ploughed back into more purchases, and within weeks they had a thriving electrical goods business – and employed others to do the travelling for them.

It struck me that the one thing never in short supply was business acumen – which made me fume with rage about the kind of aid supplied by the West, much of it predicated on the patently false notion that Russians had to be taught how to sell things. Billions of dollars poured into the coffers of scoundrels such as Arthur Andersen, whose consultants flooded the country training people to do what they were already doing very successfully. A woman who had a little bakery on New Arbat told me she had been on a management course in Oxford. 'All I really need is a new micro-oven, so I can produce fresh bread right here in my stall . . .' Simple, you would have thought, but that wasn't the focus of Western aid at all.

Jeffrey Sachs, the Harvard economics guru who helped devise Russia's 'big bang' reforms, said at the time that the country would need from the West a $5 billion stabilisation fund, plus $15 billion of assistance *per year* for many years to provide a financial and social cushion for the Russian people. What happened?

In early 1993 Yeltsin flew to a summit in Vancouver to try to persuade Western leaders to provide real support. He reminded them that after 1989 tiny East Germany had needed $100 billion 'to get rid of the communist monster'. Russia had ten times the population, and 160 times the territory. He came away with a promise of just $1.6 billion, mostly in the form of loans that would have to be repaid, food aid, and cash that went not to Russian companies but to pay the exorbitant fees charged by Western mega-consultancies for 'technical assistance'.

Russia's industrial capacity was as useless at the end of the communist era as Germany's was at the end of World War Two. If it wasn't physically destroyed, it was crumbling, outmoded and hopelessly inefficient. But while Western Europe got the Marshall Plan – billions of dollars to rebuild the economy – Russia in the 1990s got the 'Marshall Plan of the Mind'. This was a cheapskate, hare-brained scheme, designed to demonstrate how concerned the West was without having to spend very much.

It included Britain's Know How Fund, which was meant to teach Russians about democracy and freedom. Under its auspices producers from the BBC helped Russian radio to make a soap, modelled on *The Archers*, called *House 7, Entrance 4*. Just as *The Archers* was originally sponsored by the Ministry of Agriculture as an educational programme, so its new Russian equivalent was supposed to help listeners understand how a Western society works, by gently introducing 'Western ideas' through everyday stories of Russian life, with characters that included the obligatory *babushka* (granny), an intellectual whose job was under threat, a factory worker, and a plumber who drank too much. I didn't say so in my report, but it was hard to think of anything more patronising. If the project helped Russian radio produce an entertaining, professional-sounding soap, then fine, but the idea that it was going to help them behave like Westerners was absurd. And in any case – why should they behave like Westerners?

27

No Static at All

EVERYTHING WAS CHANGING. Even the FM radio band used in the Soviet Union was abandoned in favour of the frequencies used in Europe, and suddenly my Western car radio burst into life with new Russian commercial stations. That scorching summer of '92 I drove around with the window down, radio blaring, 'following the Moskva, down to Gorky Park,' as the Scorpions' hit of the year put it, 'listening to the wind of change'. The first new station was called 'Europa Plus' – what else? – after all, Russia's destination was clear. You had to hold on to that thought – that Russia's painful transition was . . . a transition, not the final goal. And the political elite, the intelligentsia and most of the population in those days all believed that Russia's destiny lay with the fellow Slavs of Poland and Czechoslovakia, rejoining what Gorbachev had called 'our common European home'.

Of course, you couldn't have all this going-back-to-capitalism stuff without also bringing back its bourgeois accoutrements – stockbrokers wearing crimson braces, tiny children learning ballroom dancing, a noblemen's club, casinos, and a national lottery to con the poor into believing there was always a small chance that they might become millionaires too. I did reports about all these things, watching the encroaching Westernisation with mixed feelings of pleasure and horror. Having lived through the late communist era, how could I not love the fact that little cafés were appearing, which did not serve rancid meatballs to be eaten with a buckled aluminium fork? But it was distressing to see that the first things Russians chose to import from the West were the trashiest: Mexican soap operas, Big Macs, translations of Barbara Cartland novels.

People stopped addressing strangers in the street as *tovarishch* or 'comrade', but struggled to find a better expression. Some tried *grazh-danin* ('citizen') for a while, but that too had a strange, Soviet sound to it. The equivalents of 'sir' and 'madam' (*gospodin*, *gospozha*) took a long time to take hold, because until now they had only been used for foreigners and they sounded truly Dostoyevskian when applied to a Russian. Most Russians just stuck with the more down-to-earth terms they had used in Soviet times: 'Man!', 'Woman!', 'Girl!', 'Young man!', however vulgar they might sound.

Etiquette was taken seriously, though, in some circles. I visited the new Assembly of the Nobility in a beautiful pastel-green mansion on Pokrovsky Boulevard, where fledgling aristocrats – anyone who could definitively prove their lineage – were being schooled not only in how to address each other correctly, but in manners, elocution, gait, attire and general poshness. The assembly's founder, Prince Andrei Golitsyn, told me its purpose was to revive the spiritual and moral values that were typical of the noble class in Russia, and which were lost for seventy years. 'Our task is to bring up a new generation, and for that purpose we're opening grammar schools where boys will have to learn the skills of oratory, and the art of social intercourse.' I kept thinking back to that song that had struck me a decade earlier when it was used in a Soviet propaganda film about wastrel émigrés: 'Don't lose heart, Lieutenant Golitsyn, Cornet Obolensky, pour out the wine!' The building used to belong to the Institute of Marxism-Leninism, and the commies ripped up the parquet and nicked the chandeliers when they saw the second revolution coming – just as the aristocracy had done in 1917 when the Reds were rampaging. Soon there would be a fine restaurant here, and a ballroom. Little Natasha Rostovas were already practising a polonaise in the communists' former library. Their teacher, of noble marrow but a product nonetheless of the communist age, sometimes addressed her debutants as 'comrades' by mistake.

Just one rung down the social ladder from the aspirant aristocracy was the burgeoning bourgeoisie. You didn't have to prove your ancestry for this, just build a successful business. The key to that was generally to have been in charge of some Communist Party assets at that crucial moment of lawlessness when the Party collapsed. Failing that you could steal, swindle, bribe, murder – or find yourself a good thief-in-law to do the murdering for you. 'Thief-in-law' was the title given to bosses in the Russian underworld – experienced jailbirds who had organised daily life in the Gulag and now emerged as a newly minted Russian mafia.

I once spent some time with mafia bosses in Tbilisi, the capital of Georgia – just to find out how it all 'worked'. One, who suggested I call him Irakli, took me to a restaurant which was closed that evening, but produced a sumptuous banquet at the snap of Irakli's fingers. He didn't pay for the meal. On the contrary, the manager drooled over him, thanking him for coming. Over the meal Irakli told me about the 'thieves' law' and ethical code. They were scrupulously honest with one another, he said, and had only come into being to compensate for the total failure of the Soviet planned economy. 'There were thieves at every level,' he said, 'from government minister to factory manager to shop-floor worker. Each thief was on a salary appropriate to his level in the network. You see, the kickbacks and payments simply made sure the system produced something, at least.'

'And ... do you ... murder people?' I ventured.

Irakli laughed. 'We are not like the American mafia! If a boss comes into the neighbourhood who threatens our livelihoods, we don't kill him – we just buy him off and make him one of us. Salaries might have to go up a little, but, you know ...' He shrugged.

Irakli was a relatively junior mafioso. On another evening I was whisked off through the darkest Tbilisi alleyways to meet a 'real' boss, in a mansion he was building for himself. Geno was a slight figure in a black silk shirt and white trousers. He showed me round his home and told me: 'It is worth millions! But I never paid a kopeck. Every ounce of cement, every piece of wood, every nail, was donated by my friends.'

'What did you give them?' I asked.

Geno looked at me with great solemnity: 'I stand by them every minute. Any time of day or night, if they're in trouble or need help, I am there.'

The other men around the table referred to Geno as 'our elder brother'. As we sat in the garden under the stars, Geno shuttled back and forth bringing bottle after bottle of champagne, and little plates of food. Some of the men exchanged glances, and one of them whispered to me: 'It is a sign of respect that the great man should serve you himself.'

Even Western businessmen who came to make their fortunes in Yeltsin's Moscow soon learned who really ran the country. A Russian friend of mine worked as *maître d'* in the restaurant of the beautifully restored Kempinsky Hotel, just across the river from the Kremlin. Most days she had to deal with a large group of 'businessmen' who spent all afternoon picking at a meal, snapping their fingers to order wines worth hundreds of dollars, abusing the staff, and leaving without paying. The Austrian manager received 'offers' from mysterious men who wanted to protect the hotel from 'dangerous people'. The manager turned down

the offer, repeatedly . . . until the mysterious men offered a little induce-
ment: his BMW went up in flames one night. 'You see,' they told him the
next day, metaphorically wiping the petrol from their hands, 'you really
do need some help.'

When all around was in flux, our oldest friends' apartments still provided
the sanest refuge. The only difference was that, with the possibility of
having to do a live two-way at any moment constantly hanging over me,
I couldn't indulge in the quantities of vodka that we consumed together
in the old days. Our friends were not among those who were forced to
sell off their belongings at market to make ends meet, though none of
them was particularly well off. Most of them took advantage of one of
the few Yeltsin-era reforms that really had no adverse side-effects – the
right to own your own flat. Everybody in Russia was given the chance
to 'privatise' the apartments they were living in – simply acquiring, overnight, valuable property which they could then modernise, sell or rent
out, as they wished. As a result most Russians became owners of their
own apartments, paying only for utilities – which left a considerable
share of their income for everything else.

The Vorontsovs acquired their big double apartment from the
Academy of Sciences. Yelena, it's true, still working at the university, had
a laughably small salary. But Nikolai was enjoying a new life in politics.
Having served as environment minister in Gorbachev's government, and
stood alongside Yeltsin to face down the hardliners' coup in August
1991, he was now a member of the Russian parliament – and a busy
activist. He sat, smiling through his thick spectacles, still puffing on cigarettes in long holders, recalling his protests against nuclear testing in the
northern Russian region of Novaya Zemlya, which helped to bring about
a moratorium. Then he showed us photos of his japes in the Pacific
Ocean in the spring of 1992, where he joined a Greenpeace ship protest-
ing against French nuclear tests on Mururoa Atoll. He was arrested by
French marines and deported.

Varya and her husband struggled with money, but with their knowledge of foreign languages were able to take on second jobs. Volodya was
still translating, and Seryozha found a job at a new economics institute
set up by the architect of Russia's reforms, Yegor Gaidar. Garik and Inna
felt freer as artists than they had ever done.

All our friends were still broadly supportive of Yeltsin and were just
glad to see the back of the communist system. But I noticed how our

conversations were changing. After the splurge of *glasnost*, it seemed, everything had been said – and all the once-banned literature had been read. People were even getting bored with politics and just longed for a normal life. What surprised me most – and maybe epitomised the change – was Garik's art. Ever since I had known him he had depicted *sovok* – Soviet man – in hundreds of tragicomic situations: reading unending tracts of propaganda, taking to the countryside in search of privacy, disappearing into a subway that led nowhere, undertaking surreal contortions to survive in Soviet society. The *sovok* would survive for many years in Russian thinking and behaviour, but already Garik, it seemed, had lost his subject-matter. Now he was producing only abstract art – collages comprising fragments of paper, children's drawings, or scribbles where he had tried out a crayon. At first, I was taken aback, and asked him why he had done this.

'It just happened,' he said. 'I didn't actually take a decision. Maybe I was tired of those deep, philosophical compositions. The new works completely lack any social dimension or exploration of our Soviet way of life – they're quite different.'

They certainly were – and they would become even more different. A few years later, when Garik and Inna finally acquired a dacha in the countryside, Garik began collecting odds and ends that he found lying around – pieces of wood, old chunks of ironmongery, hinges, bolts, screws . . . and from them produced a brilliant series of little sculptures which he named *Inkubusy* – 'Incubi' – which he described as 'little dolls or toys or deities made some time in the next millennium and discovered even later, but exhibited now!' The Latin word *incubus*, he said, meant 'nightmare', but he wasn't too interested in the precise translation – for him it was a capacious word that was just right to describe his figures. They were displayed, at the Museum of the Orient, on boxes painted black and white, light and dark blue, and grey, just like exhibits from an archeological expedition in some far-away future.

Maybe this was Garik's way of saying 'the end of history'. Russia, for all the imperfections of this transition period, was becoming a normal country: the age of oppression was over. No need to portray people sleepwalking, or bending double or standing in corners. It was time to look up from the dirt, forget about Soviet reality, and think about the bigger mysteries of life.

28

Siberia: The Shaman's Curse

IT'S OF TURKIC origin – *chiber*, meaning beautiful. Or perhaps *seber*, meaning snowstorm. Or it's from *shibir*, the word used by Genghis Khan's marauding descendants to designate the marshlands, seeded with birch trees, that they encountered when they first moved north and west out of Mongolia. Or maybe it's from *sabyr*, the Tatar word for patience, but also apparently the word they once used to describe themselves and their own territory: the land of the Sabyrs. Whatever its origins, when Yermak's Cossack army conquered the powerful Tatar Khanate of Sibir in 1582, its name went into the Russian language, and thence into English – Siberia – and came to mean the entire tract of land that stretches right across northern Asia from the Ural mountains to the Pacific Ocean. More than any other word in the Russian language it also became synonymous with punishment and labour camps.

I had long wanted to go there, preferably not as a convict. In January 1993, when the BBC was hungry for anything from its Moscow correspondents, the more exotic the better, I arranged a week-long trip to the blasted ice-fields of Yakutia, a huge territory right in the centre of Siberia. It promised to yield a cornucopia of feature stories about diamonds, shamans, reindeer, pollution, near-extinct tribes, and endless shots of me looking extremely cold. All of this would provide welcome relief from the daily news diet of spiralling prices, poverty, crime, and Russians looking extremely cold.

If you look at Yakutia on a globe of the world, and let your eye slip down to India, you will see that they are more or less the same size. But whereas India has 1,200 million inhabitants, Yakutia has just one million. One million souls spread out across a massive, deep-frozen chunk of Siberia. It was conquered around 1632, as the Russian empire clawed its way towards the east, guzzling up lands whose vast resources of natural gas and oil, timber and coal, were scarcely even guessed at. It gained notoriety as a particularly nasty place of exile for political prisoners, both under the tsars and after the communist revolution. Things began to look up only in the 1950s, after diamonds were discovered here – and not just a few, but one quarter of all the diamonds in the world. It was hardly surprising that when Yeltsin came to power declaring that Russia's regions should 'seize as much sovereignty as they could swallow', the Yakuts spotted a chance to dig themselves out of centuries of poverty and misery. In 1990 they declared sovereignty, and the following year renamed their republic 'Sakha', using the Yakuts' own name for themselves.

A six-hour overnight flight from Moscow delivered us to Mirny, a town that would not exist were it not for the diamonds. Its name means 'peace', and was chosen not just as one of the approved Soviet names for just about anything, from cinemas to candies, but because a diamond mine is known as a 'pipe'. This allowed the local bosses to inform the Politburo that they had started production in 1957 with a witty coded message that must have had Khrushchev and his friends chortling in the Kremlin: 'We have smoked the peace pipe. The tobacco is excellent.'

Until just a few months before our visit, Mirny had been a 'closed city', off-limits to foreigners. Now, in honour of the BBC, the vice president of Alrosa, the republic's sole diamond extraction company, took three entire days off work to make us welcome. There was something relentlessly communistic about his attentions. A journalist would be lucky to get half an hour, I imagine, with the vice president of the huge South African diamond company, De Beers, but Gustav Yakovlev abandoned all other duties to act as our guide and host. In those three days Alrosa would produce rough diamonds worth a cool eight million dollars.

Gustav whisked us in his official car straight from the airport to the peace pipe – though we could easily have walked, since the mine sits right at the end of the runway. If your plane overshot, you would end up at the bottom of a very deep hole.

'*Takogo nigde ne uvidish*,' said Gustav proudly: 'You won't see anything like that anywhere.' And he was right. Standing on the edge of this gigantic kimberlite mine was an awesome experience. It was the second-largest man-made hole in the world, a gigantic inverted cone, 1,200 metres wide at the top, and spiralling 500 dizzy metres into the frozen ground. An icy wind blasted stinging pellets of snow across the open plain. My red-tipped nose shone out from under a woollen hat and the upturned hood of my sheepskin coat to illuminate a spectacular piece to camera.

Gustav had laid on a show for us. When Dave, my cameraman, was ready – his tripod rapidly becoming unusable as the lubricant in the swivel-head began to freeze up – Gustav murmured into a walkie-talkie, and a series of explosions snaked around the side of the mine, deep down near the base of the cone, and threw a rusty cloud of dust, rocks, ice and diamonds into the air. When it all settled, little dinky trucks set off down the slopes to scoop the stuff up and bring it to the processing plant, about twenty kilometres away in a tiny settlement called Almazny. Almaz means rough diamond.

'We used to send all the uncut diamonds to Moscow,' Gustav explained as we drove there in his chauffeured car. 'It was all marketed by the South Africans. Russia and De Beers shared the profits, and we saw nothing. But now we are allowed to keep twenty per cent of the rough gemstones.' Gustav put his arm on the back of his seat and craned his neck round to speak to me. 'Ha-ha!' he cackled. 'Twenty per cent! Can you imagine?'

A brittle emptiness filled the streets of the little village. A few fur-clad bundles shuffled along the frozen dirt pavements. Some dogs yelped and prowled among the snowdrifts in an empty lot. Dim street lights struggled to brighten the winter afternoon. Low, barrack-like houses puffed streams of smoke into the sky, like ocean liners sailing in a vast white sea.

'Soon we'll be cutting and polishing our diamonds ourselves,' said Gustav, grinning manically like a Klondike millionaire, 'and selling them directly on the world market.'

We arrived at a sorting centre, where the raw kimberlite ore was being crushed and washed in great clanking machines to free the diamonds. Women in white lab coats weighed chunky gemstones worth thousands of dollars and placed them with tweezers into a variety of beakers, chipped china teacups and enamel cooking pots. In their raw state the diamonds looked dull and unimpressive. Only when cut and polished would they turn into glittering jewels to adorn elegant necks and fingers around the world.

As we left the factory the soles of our shoes were inspected.

The following day we set off before dawn in Gustav's official car, not quite certain where we were headed. But Gustav had a plan for us. His plan was to make us love everything about his native Yakutia.

We drove eastwards out of Mirny along a narrow road slashed through the taiga. Spindly larches were etched against the sunrise. The ground was frozen so solid that many trees had keeled over, their roots unable to suck any sustenance out of the soil. Those that survived did not grow tall. The entire stunted forest, every needle and frond, was silvered with hoar-frost.

'*Takogo nigde ne uvidish*,' said Gustav: 'You won't see anything like that anywhere.'

The warmth inside the car and the steady thrum of the studded tyres on the snow-covered track made me sleepy. Gustav seemed to have eyes in the back of his head, or perhaps a secret camera hidden in his sable hat. Every time I dropped off he would call: '*Speesh, Angoos*?' Are you sleeping, Angus?

After a few hours we came to a little village named Krestyakh. The night before I had asked where the first diamonds were found, and this was it. Just outside the village we reached the spot on the Vilyui river where geologists discovered the first gems in the summer of 1949. Now, in midwinter, the rapids were frozen into fantastical shapes, as though an immense frost had suddenly snapped the jumping water into solid ice. Waves were suspended in mid-splash. Great chunks of chiselled ice protruded from the snow-cover – like outsized representations of the precious crystals that were found beneath the surface.

Filming this scene, at twenty-five degrees below freezing, was not easy, but soon Gustav was hustling us back into the car, complaining that we were falling behind our timetable.

'But we need time to make beautiful pictures,' I explained.

'But we must fulfil our programme,' countered Gustav, although the only programme we had was the one that he had apparently created for us.

At the next stop, a herdsmen's wintering place called Toibokhoi, two hunters, straight from a Genghis Khan film set, appeared from some-where to show us how they set traps for foxes and minks. Dave's camera was full of condensation after being brought into the warm car from the freezing cold outside. Gustav scowled when I explained that we would need to wait at least ten minutes before the fog on the lens would clear.

In the centre of the village – a Wild East settlement of clapboard shacks and barracks – we were introduced to Boris Ignatiev, chairman of Suntar district council (an area much bigger than Wales), who it turned out was also going to spend two full working days with us. Boris wore thick, darkened glasses, as though his eyes were damaged from living in a landscape that glares white at you for most of the year.

'Good thing there's no frost today,' he said, without irony, as we set up the camera in the street for an interview. I didn't translate this to

Dave, who was alternately wiping the camera lens and his own spectacles with a cloth, only to see them mist up again immediately.

'Until we gained our autonomy,' said Boris in heavily accented Russian, 'all our riches went to the centre. We were run by Moscow, and lived off the crumbs from Moscow's table. But now that we're going to have control of our own wealth, everything will change.'

He promised to show us the republic's first diamond-cutting centre, equipped and run by a joint venture with the Japanese, in the district centre, Suntar. But before that, the programme envisaged lunch – the reason we had been hustled through our filming all morning.

It began with a concert. A girl in Sakha national costume – an ornately embroidered frock and silver filigree headdress and breastplate – sang a kind of yodelling song. Then a whole troupe of players and dancers performed, while waiters brought dozens of dishes to the table and Gustav explained: 'We Yakuts are celebrated for our hospitality. You won't see anything like that anywhere.'

Most of the meal consisted of things I would prefer not to see anywhere. Blood sausage – 'made from *pure* blood,' Gustav insisted. Foal's sweetbreads. Reindeer tongues. Reindeer brains. Skewers of roasted bear-meat. Bowls of fatty ursine broth. Not a vegetable in sight. And the *piece de résistance*: a platter of hard dark-brown slices that I fondly imagined might turn out to be chocolate-covered after-dinner mints. As the meal continued, however, the hard slices thawed in the heat and turned into a soggy warm mass of raw horse liver, some of which Gustav scooped onto my plate with his usual aphorism.

There was little alternative but to ward away the horrors by drinking as much Yakutian vodka as was humanly possible. I proposed extravagant toasts to the people of Sakha and their great hospitality: 'You won't see anything like that anywhere,' I said. After a while I found the bear kebab wasn't in fact too bad, and I was glad to think that there was one less predator roaming the streets.

'Angoos!' Gustav's voice pierced my reverie. 'The people here say that when God was distributing wealth around the world, his hands froze when he was passing over Yakutia and he dropped half of the world's resources here – diamonds, gold, gas, and oil. This is why we love to welcome guests here, to share what we have.' He gestured to the dishes that covered the table, still mostly uneaten. '*Takogo nigde ne uvidish!*'

It was dark by the time we continued on our way towards the town of Suntar itself. The headlights of Gustav's car played on lace curtains of billowing snow. On the edge of town our driver saw a human figure lying on the road. He stopped, wanting to help, but Boris pulled alongside in his car and told him: 'Leave him. We've got to get to our next appointment.' We drove on.

Our hosts' unrelenting timetable took us next to an 'ordinary Yakut family'. Their wooden cabin had fancy kitchen units imported from Czechoslovakia, and a microwave oven, but no running water. The father and son dragged home an urn of water on a sledge. I tried to imagine what it must be like nipping to the outdoor toilet in the middle of the night when it's forty degrees below.

Our hostess sang strange ululating songs, and led us in a kind of circular war dance, which involved us all stamping with our left foot into the circle while she improvised lines about events of the day – echoed with gusto by Boris and Gustav. It turned out Maria Yegorova was a *shamanka*, a female shaman. She told us she had only started practising her arts five or six years ago, during *perestroika*. 'Sometimes here, sometimes alone in the forest.' Her beliefs had been outlawed for seventy years, ever since the Bolsheviks had 'civilised' Siberia. *The Great Soviet Encyclopaedia* – that multi-volume compendium of wishful thinking – described shamanism in past tenses, as an early form of religion that arose in primitive times and survived only in class-based societies. 'Professional shamans,' it said, 'were nervous, easily excitable people able to bring themselves to a state of ecstasy and hallucination, which took the form of a self-regulated hysterical fit.' In the classless USSR, it claimed, this nonsense had disappeared. Yet here in the form of Maria Yegorova (and many more like her) it had in fact survived – like a dormant crocus bulb buried under decades of leafmould on the forest floor. It had survived silently, through generations when even word of mouth was perilous.

Over more vodka Gustav said: 'My father was a Bolshevik – and proud of it, like me. He once found a shaman casting spells like that in a circle. It was forbidden in those days. He shouted at him: What do you think you are up to? And the shaman set fire to the bales of hay my father was carrying – by magic.' Gustav leaned in. 'So you see . . . the power of a shaman can humble even a communist.'

Boris chipped in with his own story, about a shaman who predicted to him that his father, who was lost in the war, would return home 'with the big frosts'. 'And that's how it was. My father returned when the winter came.'

These local barons were brought up as communists, and still acted like communist chiefs, stage-managing every moment of our trip, boasting of their own hospitality, shooing us past the embarrassment of a man possibly dying in the snow, but I saw now that they were also simple Siberians, who believed in spells and magic.

Maria Yegorova served the last dregs of tea from a painted pot, and then – half shaman, half priest – addressed the fire spirit and asked it to look after us and send us on our way with goodness in our hearts.

A low yellow moon displaced enough darkness for us to stumble back to our hostel. Boris apologised that it had no running water. 'We would have put you in our best hotel, but the heating is broken there.'

He locked the door and warned us not to go anywhere unaccompanied. Gustav said he would come with us if we needed to go outside for a pee: 'You might get lost.'

'Or mugged,' said Dave, who had seen drunken figures lurching around in the darkness.

The building was paper-thin, made of plywood and cardboard, dimly lit by a dangling light-bulb with a flickering orange filament. It was hard to sleep. Outside, animals snuffled. Bears? Wolves? Dogs? I couldn't tell. A steady wind moaned under the floorboards like a shaman's dying prophecy. We could have been in a prison-camp barrack. But this was Russia's diamond capital, not the Gulag. For forty years people here had been sitting on untold wealth, picking diamonds from the soles of their shoes. In the local store, I had noticed, everything was rationed: meat, sugar, vodka, butter, oil, condensed milk, salt, cigarettes, matches. Rationed, that is, when they were available at all. Would the Yakuts' new-found autonomy finally change their lives, I wondered.

The next morning our planned visit to the Suntar diamond polishing centre was called off after the Japanese bosses of the joint venture forbade it. Apparently they feared generating publicity for their plans to break the De Beers cartel by marketing finished diamonds themselves. The meek acceptance of this by their Yakut co-directors made me suspect these poor people were breaking free of the Russian noose only to fall under the knout of a new master.

Gustav and Boris hurriedly rewrote our programme, and took us instead to a fur farm in the town of Elgyai. Here, hundreds of white foxes were going slowly berserk in tiny cages while they awaited their slaughter at the age of six months and ultimate dispatch to the same elegant necks and shoulders as the diamonds from Mirny. The collective farm would get about 25 dollars for a white fox pelt – a tiny fraction of what it would eventually fetch in Paris or New York. The farm director's upbeat spiel was predictable, and filled me with foreboding: 'Under the old system we never saw any benefit, though we knew our furs went to rich foreigners. Now we can fulfil our potential . . . We'll make millions of dollars . . .'

The Elgyai museum included a mock-up of a stone-age scene, in which hunters dressed in furs were tearing open a dead animal and eating with blood-dripping hands. I thought back to last night's equine entrails. In terms of cuisine, they hadn't really moved on much.

We drove the long, monochrome road back to Mirny, Gustav periodically reminding me to admire the forest and not to sleep. The following morning we finally left him to run his company again, and caught a flight to the republican capital, Yakutsk.

The plane was a 44-seater Antonov-24, a turboprop much used by air forces and airlines around the communist world, with a catastrophic safety record. Sitting next to me was a drunk Aeroflot pilot – off-duty, I presumed, though he was in uniform.

'Deutsch?' he asked me.

I ignored him, and averted my nose from his vodka breath. He was sorry not to be able to hold a conversation with me. 'Oi,' he lamented, 'my mama always used to tell me: Learn a foreign language, son!' Some of the other passengers found him highly amusing and laughed along as he babbled away. 'But I didn't listen to her. Guten Tag. Achtung! Anshantay! That's all I know . . .' He spent the rest of the flight swigging from a bottle and visiting the toilet to smoke foul-smelling cigarettes.

In Yakutsk, a city of 200,000 people, you don't breathe, so much as eat the solid air. A frozen, smog-like haze filled the spaces between buildings. Human forms, clad mostly in furs, with ear-flaps down, loomed out at me from the fog. Everything was in stasis: huge pillows of snow and icicles hung from roof gutters, threatening to skewer passers-by; the river port, from where, for just five months a year, ships can ply a route to the Arctic ocean, was solidified and silent, the vessels gripped by the steely ice; cars with double-glazed windscreens purred over snow-carpeted roads, their headlights barely penetrating the suspended crystals of grey air; a bus stopped to disgorge a dark mass of coats, scarves and hats; inside, passengers rubbed little peepholes on the frosted windows.

Wages here, I was told, were two and a half times higher than in western Russia, but their value had been eaten away by hyperinflation. For the first time I heard the Russian word *materik* – the mainland – used not to describe a landmass as seen from an island, but to refer to the European part of Russia, now all but inaccessible to the people of Siberia. 'They pay us a supplement for living in the north,' one young woman told me. 'But we are marooned here. We used to fly to Moscow regularly, it was so cheap, and we took holidays on the Black Sea or Crimea ... but now that's all gone. We are stranded. I don't know if I'll ever see the mainland again.' She had beautiful blue eyes and her cheeks were flushed with the cold. 'I just want to lie in the sun on the beach ...' She looked at me pleadingly, as if I could take her there, and sighed a stream of breath that froze at once on a lock of blond hair peeking out from her fur hood.

Katya and Viktor 'emigrated' from the mainland to the island of Siberia in the bloom of youth. They were in love, had diplomas from their institutes in Kiev – Katya's in teaching, Viktor's in engineering – and they responded readily and uncynically to the call that went out from the 17th congress of the Komsomol, in April 1974. They danced at student parties to the Soviet Union's top band at the time, Samotsvety (The Gemstones), and their bouncy hit song about the limitless opportunities afforded by the vast, multinational USSR: 'My address is not a house number or a street, my address is the Soviet Union.' Katya was Ukrainian, Viktor Belorussian, and now they would go to Siberia, to work on what Brezhnev had dubbed the 'Construction Project of the Century' – BAM!

The Baikal-Amur Mainline was to be a 4,300-kilometre railway, a twin sister to the existing Trans-Siberian, but running some 200 kilometres to the north, at a safer distance from China. Work had first begun under Stalin, when tens of thousands of prisoners constructed a few hundred kilometres of track while incarcerated in the BAMlag labour camp, a subdivision of the Gulag. Many were worked to death or shot on the spot for trying to escape. The idea was then forgotten until the late Sixties, when a small war with China reminded the Politburo that the Trans-Siberian – which in places ran only a dozen kilometres from the Chinese frontier – was not exactly secure. The vision of BAM was revived as a strategic necessity. It would also improve access to Siberia's mineral resources, and run all the way to Sakhalin island in the far east.

Katya and Viktor were the kind of people Politburo dreams were made of – bright, enthusiastic, too young to know about the horrors of the

Stalin era, ready to set off on a great adventure, like the frontiersmen of America's Wild West, thrilled to be opening up their country, and seeing nothing wrong with the communist propaganda that accompanied the venture.

In 1974 thousands of delegates to the Komsomol congress, all in identical brown uniforms and flat caps, officially adopted the BAM as the organisation's premier project with these stirring words, addressed to Leonid Brezhnev: 'Comrade General Secretary of the Central Committee of the Communist Party of the Soviet Union! We, the ambassadors of the Komsomol organisations of Moscow, Leningrad and all the union republics, are ready to fulfil the most important tasks of the Party, and pledge to devote all our strength, our knowledge and the ardour of our Komsomol hearts to the cause of the Communist Party, and the building of communist society . . . We pledge! We pledge! We pledge!'

Katya and Viktor heard the call and also pledged. They arrived, along with thousands of others, to wield spades and lay bricks, and to take part in the biggest propaganda extravaganza of the Brezhnev period. The BAM was inescapable – it inspired novels, poems, songs, it even had its own film studio, and reports featured night after night on the television news, as every freshly laid kilometre of track was treated as a major event. This was agitprop as it had never been seen before. There were barbecues in forest clearings, red banners, young love, guitars, beautiful girls in workers' padded jackets, young men with chiselled jaws and exhilarated eyes. They were pioneers, mastering the elements, taming the taiga, building tunnels and bridges across virgin land, overcoming monumental challenges for the sake of the motherland. The best brigades and workers were feted with prizes, their faces shone from boards of honour, heroes of socialist competition became heroes of novels and plays. They picked berries and mushrooms, and listened to the Gemstones and the Jolly Lads on tape recorders. Provincial party first secretaries in brown fedoras made flying visits to distribute praise. Building sites were adorned with portraits of Lenin and Brezhnev. Journalists and songwriters vied to coin the best slogans, from Project of the Century to Track of Courage. Every night brought news of another bridge, another cutting dynamited through a mountainside, another branch line, another station or rail switch, another wedding, another child born on the BAM. Cigarettes jutted from clenched teeth, breath steamed, and hearts swelled to the romance of shifting thousands of cubic metres of frozen soil and rock for the motherland. The Soviet

Union had lost the space race, but now they had their own patriotic achievement. They built schools and hospitals, canteens, apartment blocks and houses of culture. It was a melting pot of Sovietisation, where different nationalities worked shoulder to shoulder. Each republic adopted a different town along the track – the Ukrainians built Urgal, the Azeris Ulkan, the Estonians Kicheru – turning the entire railroad into a symbol of Soviet togetherness. It was also a good earner: wages were five or six times higher than the average. But for Katya and Viktor, it was something more: 'It wasn't just the pay, and it wasn't that we were building something for the ministry of defence, something farther away from China – the main thing was the Idea, the fact that we were building something for the Soviet Union's future.'

Living in Moscow in the late Seventies, and also while translating Soviet broadcasts for the BBC Monitoring Service in the mid-Eighties, I felt I got to know every inch of that railway, with its 47 kilometres of tunnels and 4,200 bridges. I could reel off the names of its major stations and junctions like a poem: Taishet, Tynda, Berkakit, Neryungri ... I was there, listening through headphones at my post in Caversham, in September 1984, when the historic Golden Link was finally laid – the last section of the BAM, completing the track from Taishet to Sovetskaya Gavan.

And now, finally, I was going there.

We left the city of Yakutsk and flew south, to Neryungri, a town that only came into being in 1975 after the discovery of coal in the region. For centuries the virgin forest here was alive with reindeer, arctic foxes, muskrats, sables, wolves and brown bears. Now a branch line connected the town to the BAM, and a Lowryesque landscape of pylons, power lines, smokestacks and tiny beetling people stretched from horizon to horizon. On its outskirts Viktor the railroad-builder, now a colliery manager, showed me round the vast Neryungri opencast mine – one of those places that makes the jaw drop, at the sheer scale and audacity of human endeavour. The gentle hillsides of south Yakutia were being carved up, scooped out and carted off in tipper-trucks as big as two-storey houses. I had never seen such enormous vehicles, but showing this on television was difficult: in a landscape devoid of recognisable landmarks, they looked the same as trucks just one-third as big. I should have asked the cameraman to show me standing beside one of the wheels, with my head reaching only to the axle. Equally monstrous excavators, with scoops the size of cottages, were shovelling up coal as though it were sand on a beach and dropping it into the backs of the trucks. I stood on a ridge at the edge of the colliery and surveyed its breath-taking bleakness. We might as well have filmed in black and white. The lorries crawled up and down the snowy man-made canyons in a haze of coaldust. Chimneys at the coking plants and power stations belched clouds of filth that spread like a blanket under the sky, blotting out the weak light from the sun. There was no horizon.

Viktor drove us back into Neryungri. The town's nine-storey apartment blocks jostled together like grey tombstones in a snow-covered cemetery. 'When we first came here, it was a village of a few hundred people,' said Viktor. 'Now we are 76,000.' He himself had helped to build the school where Katya now taught, and their two children studied. Did he regret following the Komsomol's call two decades ago, and ending up here? 'Not at all! People are still coming – the average age here is just 30. It's good pay. But it's also the . . . *romantika!*' And the place had a future, he said, because the coal would last another hundred years. 'Of course,' he added, with a little understatement, 'the air is pretty bad. Most people suffer from bronchitis or asthma. And heart disease.'

I stood still and watched the grime falling out of the sky like pepper. After writing in my notebook for one minute the page was covered with fine dust. I stepped into a snowdrift, pulled out my boot, and gaped at the hole I'd made: the sides were striped like a black and white liquorice mint, the black layers showing the days when the dirt had fallen thicker and faster than the snow.

The next morning we drove south from Neryungri, through the rail junction of Berkakit, to the village of Iengra, where a majority of the 1,600 inhabitants were Evenks. The Evenks, or Tungus, are one of Russia's small – and disappearing – Siberian peoples. In 1993 there were only about 30,000 of them, living mostly in Yakutia. They are, like the Yakuts, oriental in appearance and speak a language related to the Manchu once spoken in north-east China. The creation of a written language in the 1930s failed to defend it against the onslaught of Russian, and sixty years later fewer than half of Siberia's Evenks spoke their own language fluently, while three-quarters of them used Russian as their mother tongue.

We had come to film the way of life of the Evenk reindeer herders. Once upon a time they had been entirely nomadic, following their herds across the taiga. The intense industrialisation of Siberia, plus the Soviet mania for systematisation, had changed all that. Now the herders were employed by *sovkhozy*, state farms, and their children stayed at boarding schools. As we waited for a helicopter at the *sovkhoz* office, its chairman, Vyacheslav Tomtosov, dealt with random problems – whether rakes had been delivered, how to help a man whose relation was too drunk to do any work. He described how the farm operated. It had 21 herds, with 500-600 reindeer in each, and five to six farmers per herd. The herdsmen were paid a salary plus a supplement depending on how much meat they sold to the state, and had small flats in town although they spent their entire working life with their herds.

Then Volodya came in, the Evenk herder whom we would follow for the rest of the day. He had been in town for a couple of days, to collect provisions and visit his children at boarding school. 'Until the BAM came,' he told me, 'Evenks lived in the taiga and never went near the towns.' He croaked a laugh, but I couldn't tell whether he was rueful or happy about this. His breath smelt strongly of vodka. He looked like a red Indian in a cowboy movie, with broad, high cheekbones, long dark hair, and a haggard face. He said he was 35, which put him well on the way towards 45 – the average male lifespan for Evenks. He said he had six children – five at the boarding school and one six-year-old who lived with him in the taiga, with Volodya's mother. Volodya's wife died four years ago. The *sovkhoz* chairman told me she had committed suicide after becoming pregnant for the seventh time. 'We have eight or nine suicides in the village every year,' he said. 'Almost half of all deaths are suicide.'

We boarded a Mi-8 helicopter laden with the bare necessities of life – loaves of leathery black bread, bottles of vodka, and *papirosy* – tarry Soviet-style cigarettes with a hollow cardboard mouthpiece. We flew for miles, low over sparse, stunted larch woods, to herd number 5's base. The rotor blades whipped up a snowstorm as we landed. I stepped out, into the most remote landscape I had ever seen. Volodya and a colleague lit up *papirosy* and began carrying the loaves and bottles to the base, which was no more than a brown military-style tent heated by a small stove with a little metal chimney. An Evenk woman shook a rattle bag and made clucking noises to corral reindeer into a pen, while a man used a lasso to catch wayward ones by their huge velvety antlers. Then Volodya and I set off on a half-hour trip across the snow, pulled on a sledge at high speed by two pounding reindeer.

'*Vot moi dom*,' he declared when we arrived at a lonely canvas tent, and I thought I detected a hint of pride in his voice. Not just 'This is my home', but something more: this is my element, this is how we Evenks live, not in towns or cities, not like you, but like this.

A rusty chimney pipe exhaled a sickly stream of smoke. Volodya drew aside the flap and I crouched to step inside. His mother, a tiny, timid, ancient-looking figure, sat on a log beside a metal stove. She flicked her eyes incuriously towards me. Volodya's little boy jumped up to greet his father. I allowed my eyes to wander around the little circle of their home, perhaps ten feet across. They had a few iron or enamelled pots and mugs, a bucket of water, and an old wooden box that may have contained clothes. A pile of twigs lay near the stove, and the rest of the floor was covered with reindeer hides. More skins were rolled up against the lower edge of the tent to keep out draughts.

I squatted next to Volodya, and Dave somehow squeezed into the tiny space too with his camera to film our interview. Volodya talked of reindeer not just as the beasts he herded, but as though he and these animals were part of an ecology, their lives intertwined and interdependent. 'They are my family too,' he said. 'They clothe us and feed us, and we feed them and tend to them.' I could see that without reindeer, the Evenks' traditional way of life would simply have no sense, and indeed would not be possible. They slept on reindeer skins, and made clothes and shelter from them; they ate their flesh, every part of it, blood, muscle and offal, and ground the bone and horn for medicinal use; they used the antlers as weapons and the skins to make drums; in the past – before Soviet civilisation – the Evenks buried their dead by sewing them into reindeer skins and placing them high up on poles. In death, in other words, they *became* reindeer, and offered themselves to the next world.

I felt ridiculous – the western intruder, with my neatly-trimmed camera-ready hair and expensive coat, come to study an exotic, primitive species that lived with 'so little'. I couldn't stop the thought returning to my mind: how could they exist 'with nothing' – no books, no TV, no possessions at all? What on earth had Volodya's mother and son been doing during the couple of days he had been away? How had they spent their time?

Volodya's mother sat peacefully. She must have been around fifty, or sixty, but looked almost twice as old, her wizened skin stretched over her skull, emphasising her Mongoloid features. Her tiny eyes, like a bird's, silently observed as Dave balanced the big camera on his shoulder, framed his shot, focused and zoomed, adjusted his lights, wiped the lens, and I held out my microphone in front of her son and asked strange questions, about all the wrong things. I was obsessed by the absence of what I took for granted in life, instead of finding out about the presence of the things that shaped *their* existence.

Volodya complained of how cold it could get in the taiga. 'I wouldn't wish it on my enemy,' he said, and spoke admiringly of Alaska where, he had heard, the indigenous people lived in comfortable two-storey cottages. Was it possible at all, I wondered, to preserve the traditions and languages of such people, while also providing them with modern comforts? How could you be nomadic, and at the same time educate your children properly? How could you develop industry, with its cities and factories and the amenities you want, without driving away the animals that were so much part of your life? It wasn't just the Soviets that had made a mess of this. In Alaska, I knew, they also had high rates of suicide and alcoholism, and American culture was slowly – or quickly – destroying ancient traditions.

Back in Iengra the next day, we visited the school – the only one in the whole of Yakutia where the Evenk language was even taught, but only for two hours a week. The 274 pupils, of whom 173 were Evenk, learned everything in Russian. Tatyana, the Evenk language teacher, told me they had no proper textbooks: the few that existed used a different dialect that the children here barely understood. 'A whole generation of children have lost their language. It's only in the taiga that they learn it, from their parents . . . but they spend almost their whole childhood here at boarding school.'

The children put on costumes and performed a reindeer dance for us. It was delightful, but it was play-acting, a cute modern musical about a way of life that was already scarcely a memory for these young Evenks. They snuffled the air with their noses, and pretended to paw the snow with their hands, but it all looked and sounded more like Disney's Bambi than anything I had seen out in the wild. The school was cosy and well-equipped. The walls were decorated with children's paintings, English verbs and pictures of Tolstoy and Pushkin. I could smell dinner being cooked in the canteen. Whatever the loss of their traditional way of life, it was hard to regret that these children had an alternative to the bare tent in which Volodya's mother sat in silent contemplation.

A young man called Vadim Naumov joined us. He was chairman of the local branch of the Association of Northern Peoples, and was fighting a lonely battle to revive Evenk culture. The brutal collectivisation campaigns of the Thirties, he said, had destroyed the Evenks' traditional clans, which his association was now trying to recreate. The BAM had brought disaster by forcibly settling people in new villages. Shamanism, he said, was not the idiotic superstition that the communists would have you believe it was.

That evening Vadim picked us up in his jeep and we drove a long way into the forest, far from the smokestacks and street lights. We came to a tent, lit from inside by a flickering flame. At the sound of our car, two elderly figures emerged from the tent to greet us – Savei Vasiliev and his wife Liza. 'Savei is the greatest shaman in Yakutia,' said Vadim reverentially. 'People come many tens of kilometres to be treated. Yesterday Savei cured a sick girl who came from Yakutsk.'

The tent was similar to Volodya's. We sat on the floor on reindeer skins. Liza, who seemed to be drunk, ineptly washed some metal dishes, containing the sticky remains of their last meal, with boiling water and a dirty finger. She set up a board on logs in front of the stove as a table, and offered us bread, and tea from a filthy enamel mug. Then some strong spirit was handed around, and Liza mocked her husband. 'Baaah,' she said, waving her hand at him dismissively and slurring her words, 'he's a lousy shaman . . . give him more to drink, the fool.'

Savei himself ignored the insults and calmly told me a little about his life. He was born five years before the war, finished primary school, and became a reindeer herder and musher, a dog-sled driver. 'In the winter we hunted, and in springtime we made runners for the sleds.' He was known, however, to come from an ancient dynasty of Evenk shamans. '*Ya – geneticheskiy nositel*,' he said, literally, a 'genetic carrier' of shamanic powers. In 1973, regardless of the Communist Party's views, the village elders decided he must become a shaman, and two years later, on the little river Barylak, he was initiated.

Vadim interjected that Savei treated all kinds of ailments – liver, heart, epilepsy – and had mastered every ritual and method of shamanic medicine. Liza scoffed and knocked back more vodka. Savei said his forebears, from whom he inherited his powers, were 'on the upper planet' now. The performance he would give us would be a repetition – a copy – of the songs they communicated to him.

The table was cleared away and I went outside while Savei put on his performance clothes. I stood still in the frozen, silent night, watching the flames from the stove cast the shaman's shadow onto the skin of the tent, and contemplating once again my own western superciliousness. Was he for real, endowed with special powers, or just a stupid man, steeped in ignorance and superstition? It was easy to mock, to disbelieve, yet I also felt a touch of admiration for people so self-sufficient and oblivious to the outside world. I didn't suppose he had much idea about President Bush or Prime Minister Major; maybe he was only dimly aware of Boris Yeltsin. His life was 'whole', guided by seasons and the rising and setting sun. He communed with spirits and a celestial beat that I could not hear. He was unaware of a million things that I knew, but aware of things that I could not even conceptualise. Ah, there I was, at it again! The conceited luxury of a Western man, contemplating the artless beauty of the savage! The tent-skin glowed in the darkness. Where was this upper planet? Why did I find it so hard to believe in this man's communication with his ancestors? This was something literally beyond my ken: I knew I could never understand it 'from within', but trying to analyse it and fathom it from without also brought no understanding.

I heard jangling and drumming, and went back inside. Savei was now dressed in full costume. His headgear had long deerskin tassels, and he wore a soft chamois bodice with an embroidered breast-piece, and a collection of metal animals, trinkets and charms were attached to his back, clanking and jingling as he moved. He bent almost double, beating a large drum like an Irish bodhran – a wooden frame with hairy reindeer skin stretched over it. As he ducked and gyrated, his eyes closed in concentration, and he chanted – or moaned – some kind of formless laments or incantations. Vadim, our guide, said he was singing about nature, animals, birds, death, life. He splashed pure spirit on the fire, 'to feed the god', and the flames leapt up and sizzled.

When it was time to leave we all went outside and stood wordlessly for a few minutes in the trembling air, lit by the dancing fire flames inside the tent. It felt as if a ghost was standing behind every tree. The upper planet was right here, all around us. Savei shook my hands, then suddenly bounded away into the darkness, and returned with a magnificent set of antlers, which he presented to me. 'It is my gift for you,' he said.

We squeezed back into Vadim's jeep, and set off on the long trip back to Neryungri. I sat in the middle of the back seat, cradling the antlers in my lap and wondering whether Aeroflot would allow me to transport them back to Moscow as cabin baggage. The car slowly warmed up and we all dozed a bit. After more than an hour we reached the town, and the car drew up outside our hotel. In the darkness I had noticed the base of the antlers, which I was holding, growing rather wet and soft, as it thawed out. Now, as I stepped out of the car, I looked at what I was holding, and realised with disgust that the reindeer's entire brain was still attached to the skull. This was what I had felt, growing softer and softer in my hands. I swore, and without a second's thought hurled the revolting object away.

Back home in Moscow a couple of days later, after a good long sleep to recover from the Siberian trip, I had breakfast and got ready to go to the office. I put my coat on, reached up to take my hat from its peg – and suddenly collapsed in excruciating pain. I had ruptured a disk in my upper spine (not a common place for back injuries) and was confined to bed for more than a week before it recovered.

Was this the shaman's revenge, for throwing away his gift, I wonder? I am not so superstitious as to believe such things, and would not have mentioned it were it not for something that happened after my next encounter with a shaman. It was later in the same year, in November. This time we were in Tuva, a remote and sparsely populated republic on Russia's border with Mongolia. The shaman I met there was of a different kind – a fire-swallower, a comedian and showman in Elvis-style trousers, who put on public performances in theatres. We met after his show, and he demonstrated his powers by running his hot palms over my body and diagnosing various ailments from which I did indeed suffer – sciatica, headaches, heartburn . . . But he did not inspire the kind of respect that one had felt for Savei. This one came across as a charlatan, and I joked about him after we finished filming.

On the morning we were due to leave Tuva, I washed, dressed, went down to breakfast in our hotel, and again suddenly collapsed in pain with a herniated disk in the upper spine. Those are the only times in my life I have met shamans, and the only times I have injured my upper back.

'Even a communist,' Gustav had told me back in Yakutia, 'can be humbled by a shaman.' Cocky journalists too.

29

Katastroika

ENDING PRICE CONTROLS and allowing people to trade were only a small part of Yeltsin's grandiose plan to recreate capitalism in Russia, and he had to move fast if the nation was not to gain the impression that the word signified nothing but poverty, soup kitchens and the Salvation Army. Already they had a word for it: *katastroika*.

Free prices did put an end to the shortages, because people could no longer buy huge quantities of subsidised foodstuffs, and hoard them. The shelves in the shops filled up with produce – much of it imported, all of it expensive. The much bigger task was what to do with the vast state-run economy, which produced very little that anyone wanted to buy. Almost the entire economy, remember, with the exception of the new collective and private businesses that had started up in the last few years, was owned by the state. That included hundreds of thousands of small, medium and inconceivably enormous factories.

Moscow's state planners had had the ingenious idea of building enterprises so huge that the cities in which they were located did nothing else: every single person living there either worked in the factory, was married to someone who worked there, or worked in the ancillary industries that fed the factory – plus of course the schools, shops and hospitals that served these workers. As soon as you gave consumers the chance to buy beautiful products manufactured in the West – the things they had dreamed of owning for decades – the old Soviet factories just couldn't compete. And if the factory stopped producing, and laid off workers, then the entire 'mono-city' was doomed.

The country's failing industries could neither produce what people wanted nor afford to pay their workers . . . so they ended up remunerating them with the goods they produced – which became a kind of alternative currency to the rouble. Most of the towels or blouses being sold on the pavement outside Children's World had not been bought – they were the 'wages' received by someone who worked in a towel or clothing factory.

So Yeltsin's team rolled out the next stage in their plan – to privatise the entire economy by allowing ordinary citizens to buy shares in it. They put a value on the total assets of the state (all its factories, farms, transport depots, and so on), divided it by the number of people, and issued privatisation vouchers – one for every citizen – to the value of 10,000 roubles – about $33 or £20 at the time. With these vouchers, which looked like banknotes, you could buy a share in whatever business you chose, or you could sell it for its nominal value to someone else.

I went along to a street market to see what was happening and do the usual 'vox pops', whereby the reporter asks random passers-by what they think, until he finds the range of answers that correspond to what he thinks they should think. 'I don't understand a thing about these vouchers,' said one woman. 'I think it's all just another swindle,' said a man. And then the balancing view from a third who claimed: 'I'm going to invest my voucher.'

It didn't take long, naturally, for these 'privatisation cheques' to gravitate towards those who did know what to do with them. The uninitiated parted with them, in exchange for 10,000 roubles – or nothing at all – while the savvy gathered together tidy sums that they could use to buy up state property. There was one city in Russia where denationalisation was in full swing – Nizhny Novgorod.

It was one of those places I always felt I knew without ever having been there. It was the scene of Maxim Gorky's *Childhood* – a Dickensian world of poverty and floggings, set against the brooding presence of Mother Volga. It was the gaily coloured costumes and abundant produce of the Nizhny Fair, painted in cherry reds and lapis blues by Boris Kustodiyev – a place so celebrated around the world in the nineteenth century that Thomas Hardy referred to his fictional agricultural fair at Greenhill, in *Far From the Madding Crowd*, as 'the Nizhny Novgorod of South Wessex'. And then it was renamed Gorky, after its most famous scion, and became a drab Soviet city – well, I assumed it was drab, because it was off-limits to foreigners, and all anyone knew about it was that it had secret defence installations and was where Andrei Sakharov and his wife, Yelena Bonner, were forced to live. Basically, it stood for everything that was nasty about the Soviet Union. Now, in the 1990s, it was called Nizhny Novgorod again, and was the main venue for the Great Russian Property Sell-Off.

The impresario here was the region's governor, a young curly-haired whirlwind called Boris Nemtsov, who moved so fast you could hardly keep up with him. I met him several times over the years, usually for a quick chat while he was meeting with Western advisers, grabbing a sandwich or a beer, or joking with a crowd of besotted local people. He was genuinely popular – the first leader of a new generation who had torn up the Soviet past and were intent on persuading the rest of the population to come along with them. He made Yeltsin and, especially, Gorbachev look like has-beens, old fuddy-duddies brought up in a different era. At just 33, he was exactly the kind of man Western leaders wanted to see running Russia: full of ideas, quick-talking, smart – and possessed of the charisma needed to drag the population through a horrific upheaval. A few years later, when he was deputy prime minister, I travelled with him on a trip to Krasnoyarsk in Siberia and was so impressed, I described him in a report for the *Nine O'Clock News* as 'the man who might finally lead Russia into a more normal, more democratic and prosperous future'. Watch this face, I said, while warning that his reforming zeal was bound to earn him enemies. When Vladimir Putin came to power in 1999, Nemtsov became one of his fiercest and most eloquent critics . . . and in 2015 he was assassinated while walking across a bridge just a hundred metres from the Kremlin.

In November 1992 I watched one of the first auctions he organised, in the grand resurrected building of the old Nizhny fair, where they were selling off the communist state, lorry by lorry. Not many Russians could see the point of buying shares in huge companies, but this was something concrete – trucks that you could use for your own business. They were lined up for inspection outside in the rain – battered old vehicles that had been abused by too many careless drivers. Oleg Ulanov surveyed them all, decided exactly which one he wanted, and went inside to bid for it. He had only set up his business four months earlier, with 5,000 roubles of capital, but already had a million – one quarter of which he spent on the van, which he wanted to turn into a mobile grocery store. He patted the bonnet lovingly and told me: 'The first thing I'm going to do is get it repaired and repainted, with my firm's name – 'Ulanov and Co'. I had a vision straight from Thomas Hardy – Ulanov's mobile shop puttering around picturesque villages on the Volga, selling pies and cider from linen-lined baskets. Could Russia really become like that? Would

Oleg be foolish enough to fall in love with a married woman . . . that buxom, flighty one in the red polka-dot kerchief? I must warn Oleg what he might be letting himself in for . . .

Nizhny's pioneering new capitalists had already opened up some attractive small shops and restaurants, but their owners were well aware of the fragility of the reforms. 'Things could change at any moment – they could just ban everything,' said one businessman. 'One of my friends just wrapped up his business here and left for Norway. He wanted me to go with him, but I said no. And he said, It's up to you . . . but when the fascists or the communists come back I'll be in Norway. And you'll be in Siberia.'

Out in the countryside around Nizhny privatisation of the farms was also getting under way, but a day spent on the Pravda collective farm didn't inspire me with confidence that the peasants' life would change for the better. All the farming folk I spoke to had meekly handed over their vouchers to the farm director, who had gone to an auction and bought one of the ten lots into which the farm had been divided. 'Well,' said Aunt Dusya, 'we didn't know what to do with them. We trusted him to do the best.' He certainly did: he told me he'd have to sack half the workers to make his new farm more efficient. The auction itself made my flesh creep. Land ownership had always been the most sensitive issue in Russia, and it was not until 2001, under President Putin, that the buying and selling of land (as opposed to farms and property on it) became legal. Yet here, the collective farms were being sold off at an auction run – very visibly – by Americans. A young man and woman, straight from Harvard, and armed with all the insight into the Russian mind that a good American education can provide, sat at the auctioneer's side, efficiently recording the sales on a spreadsheet.

Outside, rural life looked much as it did in the days when Tolstoy had owned an estate and spent his latter days mowing grass with the peasants. Horses, not tractors, pulled ramshackle sledges across snowy, rutted tracks; an old man with a flowing grey beard pumped water into pails from a stand-pipe; the entire village had one telephone; and the cows were being milked by hand. Electricity seemed to be the only concession to the twentieth century. Aunt Dusya put extra logs into the stove in preparation for baking a batch of loaves. She didn't know what privatisation would bring, she said: 'They talk about it all the time on the telly, but it's all too confusing for an old woman like me. It'll be as God commands . . .'

*   *   *

1993 would turn out to be one of the most decisive and fateful years for Russia's fragile democracy, ending in mass bloodshed and the rise of a new and sinister political force – all thanks to Yeltsin's determination to plough on with his ruthless and unpopular reform programme.

The reforms were fiercely opposed not only by millions of ordinary people, but by most members of the Russian parliament. They had been elected in 1990, before the collapse of the Soviet Union, and were mostly members of the Communist Party, but had not always been in conflict with Yeltsin. Indeed, they elected him as Russia's leader, and even when he went on to become the country's first directly elected president a year later, in June 1991, there was no major dispute. Yeltsin did not campaign on a promise to introduce shock therapy – in fact he said he would 'lie down on the rails' if prices soared. It was only when this did happen, in 1992, that a rift grew between the executive and the legislature. A power struggle emerged, and in March 1993 deputies tried (and only narrowly failed) to impeach the president.

A referendum was set for late April which asked people whether they had confidence in Yeltsin and his reforms. In the weeks before it I set off on a road trip from St Petersburg to Moscow to 'take the pulse of the nation'.

The week-long trip was boiled down to three four-minute reports for *Breakfast News*, in which I drove (for visual impact) an ancient Lada from the old 'Westward-looking' capital, through ancient cities and moribund villages, to Moscow, sampling opinions and showing everyday life along the way. Although the finished films appeared to show just me driving an old car, the trip involved a cameraman, a producer, a fixer, and a driver for a second car – and endless doubling back and forth on busy roads to create arty shots of the car passing significant signposts or landmarks. This wasn't eighty per cent logistics, it was almost entirely logistics – but the final result looked and sounded stunning. We had church services and heavenly singing, old village wells, a stock exchange, an auction, a milk shop whose staff didn't know their store just been sold off, extraordinary snow-covered landscapes, a miserable roadside café, boys who earned more by washing cars than their parents did at work, a ballet teacher who shuttled back and forth to Turkey to buy clothes to sell in Russia, ostentatious red-brick villas being built on the outskirts of Moscow, a brass band playing a jaunty wartime tune (which we used as a soundtrack throughout) – and lots and lots of vox pops.

The pro-Yeltsin voices were outweighed by the anti, and the older, headscarved, communist ones were definitely more strident. We came across this lively argument on Petersburg's Nevsky Prospekt.

'We had a wonderful socialist system. Our economy was fine under Stalin,' said one woman, middle-aged but certainly too young to remember the Stalin period. Asked about the West's help, she added, 'We don't need Western aid, thank you. And we don't want this government that's been forced on us by the Americans.'

'I'll vote against Yeltsin,' said a man.

'I won't,' said another. 'I support the reforms he's carrying out.'

'What reforms?' said a third, apparently just passing by and overhearing the argument.

'The transition to a market economy,' came the reply.

'And then what?'

'Then nothing. That's it!'

'Ha! That's kindergarten talk . . .'

A woman walking past in a burgundy knitted hat stopped to speak. 'We don't need Yeltsin. He's ruined our country.'

Another agreed: 'I'll definitely vote against him. He's robbed the Russian people. We live like beggars.'

The woman in the woollen hat wasn't finished. 'We need a military man to run the country,' she said.

Pro-Yeltsin views seemed to be confined mainly to the businessmen at their auctions and stock exchange, and to some of the younger people we met. As I drove from town to village in my green Lada, listening to the *cri de coeur* of a nation pitched into turmoil, Russia felt like a boiling samovar, the lid poised to explode under the pressure.

The summer was a great escape. We spent a month living in a dacha that belonged to one of the era's great war cameramen, Rory Peck. He and his family were away for the summer and we were glad to take up his offer to look after the house – and his dog, Boris. The dacha was in the village of Peredelkino, where Pasternak wrote *Doctor Zhivago*. It was an idyllic retreat – a slightly ramshackle wooden house with a huge rambling garden, a big veranda and old Soviet posters on the walls.

Rory had trained as an army officer, but he never served, preferring the life of an independent cameraman. He made his name covering wars in Afghanistan and the Gulf. Once when we visited his dacha some of his old Afghan friends turned up and we played cricket among the birch trees – an incongruous sight in rural Russia. When wars started breaking out on the periphery of the disintegrating Soviet Union, Rory was always at the front line, and would turn up at the BBC office with stunning pictures – and the whole story sketched out. All I had to do was put words to his images, and produce a tremendous report without ever leaving the BBC cutting room. This trick was another of the conceits of television: a correspondent couldn't always be where the action was, but with the help of cameramen like Rory you could give the impression that you were (although the last words in the report – 'BBC News, Moscow' – would tell any attentive listener that you were in fact safely in your office, probably drinking a cup of tea as you edited some piece about slaughter and mayhem).

Many Russian freelancers, or stringers, also brought their pictures to us from trouble spots. Their images were often brilliant, and obtained only by putting their lives at risk – but we were horribly cynical about them when they would turn up at the BBC office, straight from a war zone, still covered in mud from some stinking trench. I don't know who coined the disgraceful phrase, but they became known as 'video smellies' – such is the callous banter of a BBC newsroom. A producer would come to my room and say, 'Angus, there's a video smelly here. Do you want to come and see what he's got?' Once when a stringer overheard the remark, he gave a puzzled look, and the quick-witted producer explained: 'It's what we call you – you know, *smely*.' *Smely* is Russian for brave – and that's certainly what they were. Even when we ourselves were actually in a war zone, we would often incorporate stringers' pictures into our reports: they were (and presumably still are) the unnamed, unacknowledged heroes of some of the most striking BBC coverage.

Later, in 1995, I did a report from Moscow about three old Russian women trapped in their home for days in war-torn Chechnya, afraid to go outside. One of the sisters had lost her mind from terror. They were confined to the bathroom of their ground floor flat, the only room not yet destroyed, and hadn't eaten for five days. The pictures were superb, capturing the fear in the women's eyes, their flinches as bombs exploded nearby. My report was moving, and attracted favourable comment in the newsroom, but apart from the words it wasn't mine. It was all a video smelly's work – his pictures, his interview, his initiative for finding the story in the first place.

The referendum went in Yeltsin's favour, but protests against him continued, and the conservative parliament began a legislative battle with the president – until on 21 September 1993 Yeltsin dissolved it by presidential decree. Deputies refused to leave the building. Yeltsin cut off their electricity, phones and hot water.

I spent several days, and nights, down at the 'White House', the great cruise-ship of a building where members of parliament huddled for warmth, in overcoats and hats, holding debates by candlelight. Illicit arms – Kalashnikovs, pistols, grenade launchers, gas masks – were smuggled in, in anticipation of an assault. Tens of thousands of pro-parliament demonstrators took to the streets. Hundreds stayed all night outside the building, lighting bonfires to keep warm. Police tried to block access by rolling out razor wire and parking trucks bumper to bumper around the entire building. Protestors constructed barricades across roads from whatever they could find – paving slabs, rubbish bins, wooden pallets, railings and commandeered trolley-buses. The great Russian musician Mstislav Rostropovich turned up to support Yeltsin by conducting a fiery performance of Tchaikovsky's 1812 overture, complete with booming cannon fire, on Red Square. The massive crowd that filled the square was good-humoured and confident of defeating the 'dinosaurs' cowering in their freezing White House. But I wasn't so sure. The tension grew by the day. At the end of September I did a night-time piece to camera with helmeted police behind me hauling away the makeshift barriers and beating up protestors with batons. Would Yeltsin dare to storm the White House, I wondered.

As the story neared its climax, I had a dilemma. My wife was back in England, about to give birth to our third child. I called Vin Ray, my foreign editor, and he laughed at my indecision: 'Are you mad?' he said. 'Being present at your child's birth is a million times more important than any news story.' I went back to our house in Reading, and watched the tragic denouement in Moscow on television.

Yeltsin brought his army into Moscow and bombarded the White House, engulfing it in flames and forcing his enemies out. The night before, *spetsnaz* troops clashed with armed protesters who tried to seize the central television studios. More than 200 people were killed in the two incidents, including my friend Rory Peck. He was caught in crossfire as he filmed the pitched battle raging at the TV station. He was always close to the action. This time too close.

Three days later, my daughter Katie was born. I was there, and Vin Ray was right.

*   *   *

Although I was not directly involved in covering the final days of Yeltsin's assault on his own parliament, I did choose, rather inexplicably, to get embroiled in a dispute over the BBC's coverage with the journalist John Pilger. 'The BBC,' he wrote in the *New Statesman,* 'has led the propaganda barrage, constantly referring to Yeltsin's draconian methods as reforms and his parliamentary opponents as hardliners and extremists. Boris the Good, on the other hand, is the democrat whose patience finally snapped: such a generous description of a man whose troops had just burned the nation's parliament.'

I took issue with this in a letter to the same magazine – but in retrospect I think Pilger was right. It wasn't that we had failed to show the catastrophic effect of Yeltsin's reforms on ordinary people, but we definitely fell into the trap of suggesting (mainly, as Pilger indicated, through our choice of words) that despite all the hardship Yeltsin's reforms were 'right' and the democratically elected deputies in parliament, who opposed the reforms, were 'wrong' (although I am sure the BBC never referred to them as 'extremists'). Given that I myself was appalled by the reforms, and felt they should have been introduced much more slowly and with massive Western assistance to cushion the effects, I am surprised that I found myself sucked into the 'establishment' view. Maybe it was because so often the anti-reform voices came from people who blithely opined that everything had been better under communism or even under Stalin.

In any case Yeltsin's victory was a Pyrrhic one. When a new parliament, now called the State Duma, was elected in December 1993, voters overwhelmingly rejected the reformist parties – effectively overturning the verdict they had given in the referendum nine months earlier. And there was a big surprise. They did not turn to the communists, who only scored twelve per cent, but to a neo-fascist nationalist party led by Vladimir Zhirinovsky, a man dismissed in the West (and indeed by most people in Russia) as a buffoon and a populist. His party was known as the Liberal Democratic Party, but it was neither of those things. With 23 per cent of the popular vote, he swaggered into the BBC office for his first interview as though he already ruled Russia. His 'policies' were nothing short of bonkers – recolonise the 'lost' territories of the Soviet Union, dump nuclear waste in the Baltic states, bring back cheap vodka and sausage. He was a man who had blamed Jews and ethnic minorities for Russia's ills, and sent his paramilitaries to support Saddam Hussein in Iraq.

The architect of Yeltsin's reforms, Yegor Gaidar, compared the new situation in Russia with the Weimar Republic of pre-war Germany, in which Hitler was able to rise to power by making populist gestures at a time of economic instability. It was the first time I had heard that comparison being made.

In fact, Zhirinovsky proved to be more of a disrupter in the new parliament than a leader. But he did begin to set the tone of Russia's political discourse, stoking popular discontent with the country's weakness and humiliation.

30

Chechnya

THE FIRST INTIMATION of war was mundanely unexciting – a slightly disturbing drone, no more threatening than the sound of the cameraman snoring on the floor a few yards away. The growling waxed and waned as the bombers flew through the dark night. The window panes, taped diagonally against bomb blasts, rattled. I heard some distant thuds, and some crackling that sounded like fireworks, turned over and tried to sleep on. It wasn't frightening, just ordinary, just another strange event to find oneself covering. You did a soup kitchen, a ballet school, a demo, a privatisation auction, a news conference . . . and then you did a war, because that's what came up next.

This one didn't come up just once, though. The war in Chechnya went on from December 1994 to the autumn of 1996, and I spent so much time there it became a part of my life. I came to know Chechnya's little roads and villages better than those around Reading, and developed a soft spot for the Chechen people – who unfailingly gave us their bedrooms, floors and food. In Moscow they were universally despised as crooks, gangsters, or just 'blacks' – the very incarnation of evil. For a hundred years Russians had scared their children with a lullaby about wicked Chechens, crawling around with their daggers, and nothing had changed.

In 1991 the Chechens had taken it into their heads to declare independence from Russia. But while nations like Armenia, Georgia and Azerbaijan, in the southern Caucasus and outside the Russian Federation, were able to secede, Chechnya lay on the northern slopes of the Caucasus range, inside the Russian Federation – and Moscow had no intention of losing even an inch of 'Russian' territory. Chechnya had belonged to the empire since the middle of the nineteenth century.

I first went there in September 1994. Grozny was still a normal Soviet city, with its theatres and concert halls, its university and stadiums, its long broad avenues, lined with southern trees. Well, not quite normal, as Russia had imposed an economic blockade, so there was no heating, no telephones, and no electricity half the time. Even cold water was a problem. Rickety pumping stations could only coax it to reach the lower floors of apartment blocks, so workmen trundled around the city with water-carts, from which people filled pails, and struggled with them up many flights of stairs. At least the marketplace was thriving: you could buy almost anything here, including Kalashnikov rifles, from young men in dark aviator shades.

Most Chechens blamed Russian vindictiveness for this situation; some also blamed their own president, General Dzhokhar Dudayev, who used to fly nuclear bombers in the Soviet air force and now commanded his tiny independent nation of one million people, slightly more than half of them Chechens. He specialised in making bloodcurdling threats to the Russians. Chechnya's symbol was the wolf. They would rule the mountains, fight in packs, and tear the Russian sheep to shreds.

Our translator, Aslan, a lecturer in English literature at Grozny university, and probably the most lamb-like Chechen you could ever encounter, took us into the mountains to meet some of his family in the village of Vedeno. We sat in their garden, under the shade of lime trees, as the sun's afternoon rays crept over the hillside. His aunt recalled the terrible day in 1944 when Stalin exiled the entire population, for allegedly collaborating with the Nazis during the war. 'The Russian soldiers came to our village and grabbed everyone, put us on cattle trains, and sent us to Kazakhstan. Everyone! Half the people died on the way there. I can't think of it without crying.'

One of Aslan's cousins told me: 'Our revolution in 1991 was intended to establish Islam here.' She was wearing a small kerchief on her head, like any Russian peasant in the summer; no sign of deep faith.

Another cousin smiled mischievously as she admitted: 'Well, yes, relations with the Russians are not too good right now . . . but I'm not very sorry that so many of them are leaving . . .'

Aslan's neighbour, a man wearing a skullcap, said: 'Not everyone here likes President Dudayev . . . but we all want to have a completely independent, Islamic country.'

I wondered what the *Great Soviet Encyclopaedia* had to say about the Chechens' ruthless deportation in 1944, and rehabilitation under Khrushchev in 1957, after which they were slowly allowed to return to their ancestral lands. This is all it said: 'During the Great Patriotic War the Chechens fought on the frontlines and took part in the partisan war against the fascist invaders. Several thousand people were awarded honours and medals, and 36 were given the title of Hero of the Soviet Union. In 1944 the Chechen-Ingush Autonomous Republic was abolished. It was restored by decree of the USSR Supreme Soviet on 9 January 1957.' It turned out, moreover, that the Chechens had benefitted hugely from Soviet rule: 'In the years of Soviet power the culture of Chechens changed radically: illiteracy was wiped out, a written language created, a national intelligentsia grew, and various forms of art and literature were widely developed.'

By December, the Kremlin's patience with the wolf-people of Chechnya had run out, and an invasion was inevitable. So here we were, lying in a house in the outskirts of Grozny, some on beds, others in sleeping bags on the floor, listening to the bombers' night-time 'softening-up' raids on outlying villages and parts of Grozny. In the daytime we went to film the damage. There seemed to be no discernible plan to the Russians' attacks. In one village several houses were smashed to bits by bombs – the villagers laid out the dead for burial and showed us the remnants of enormous shells. In another, sheep had been set on fire, and lay dead or scampered around with their fleeces burnt brown. In Grozny, two women were killed as they alighted from a bus. Bystanders vowed there would be 200 years of vengeance for the attacks. Chechen fighters, dressed from head to toe in white, patrolled the snow-covered fields and roads leading to Grozny, laden with grenade-launchers, and keeping their spirits up with cries of 'Allahu Akbar' – God is great! In the centre of the city, outside the presidential palace where Dudayev had decamped to a bunker, people performed a *zikr* every evening – a wild, rhythmic dance, in which old men with long beards tore round in circles, whipping themselves into a frenzy.

We watched long columns of Russian tanks and military vehicles draw up just outside the borders of Chechnya, and on 11 December they began their slow invasion, as frantic telegrams went back and forth between the Kremlin and Grozny, offering, and rejecting, peace talks. Some commanders were apparently reluctant to march straight into Grozny, but Russian bombing raids on the capital grew in intensity. At a certain point it became too dangerous to sleep in the city, so we moved our base out to Khasavyurt, a town in Dagestan, just across the border from Chechnya, and from there drove in each day to film in the capital.

For this, incidentally, I was derided by ITN's gung-ho correspondent, a man I once saw screaming at his poor cameraman to 'get on that fucking bus, Oleg' – a bus heading into a besieged village that was about to be hammered by Russian helicopter gunships – while the correspondent himself stayed at a safe distance. We all took risks, of course, and were under considerable pressure to do so from our bosses in London, who on the one hand told you every day *not* to take risks but at the same time were ecstatic if you did. I remember a phone call from my deputy foreign editor one morning, in which she steeled me for action by telling me in a special confidential tone: 'Angus, we see this as a potential award-winner', which was code for: 'try and get as close as you possibly can to being killed – without actually getting killed, of course . . .' On TV, news gets bigger, the closer the correspondent is to danger. Stories would move up the running order (and be nominated for awards) if the reporter appeared to be under threat, or an explosion went off during his piece to camera. (These days, this has become intolerable: reporters embedded with a British or American army unit now routinely use the word 'we' – as in, 'we came under fire as we entered such-and-such a city' – and the distance between reporter and combatant has vanished. The *reporter* didn't come under fire, for God's sake – the troops did! The reporter was just stupid enough to be with them.) In Grozny, we all took risks – particularly my friend Ben Brown, during the mass assault on the city on New Year's Day 1995 – but we also relied hugely on those unacknowledged stringers who stayed in the most horrendous circumstances to get the best pictures, and ferried them out to our producers. One stringer remained inside the presidential palace in Grozny during the bombing until there was almost nothing left of it.

Even our 'safe' house in Khasavyurt wasn't exactly a haven of tranquillity. It had been found by one of our ever-resourceful producers, and was big enough not just for the BBC team but for several other journalists and satellite teams. (Wherever there is news, a team of satellite engineers and producers appears, for without a 'sat dish', none of our reports would ever reach home.) The house belonged to a divorced or separated Dagestani woman. One night we were all asleep, like children squeezed into a dorm, when the woman's estranged husband came back, apparently having heard that his ex was making a lot of money from foreigners. We heard shouting, and threats of violence . . . and noises that seemed to indicate he had a canister of petrol and was planning to burn the house down. We all froze. I think we probably all had the same thoughts: we must stop this . . . but this crazy drunk man almost certainly has a gun. I am ashamed to say that I was hugely relieved when an American reporter, David Stern, finally got up and went out to try and reason with the man. David wasn't a smoker, but he grabbed a pack of cigarettes anyway, and managed to take the man out into the garden, give him a smoke, and heroically talked him down from his crazy plans. The rest of us just lay there in the dark, scarcely breathing, until it was all over, and the man went away.

Grozny, meanwhile, nineteenth-century villas and communist tower blocks alike, was slowly turned to Swiss cheese. And then grated Parmesan. The pictures you see on television – of Dresden after the Second World War, or Aleppo in Syria more recently – cannot convey what it actually feels like to walk around a pulverised city. Streets and shops that I had strolled in a month earlier were now just empty shells, cascades of debris, wastelands of rubble. A few thousand people still lived there, in the cellars or on balconies that somehow hung on the sides of destroyed buildings. They were almost all Russians, for unlike the Chechens they did not have families they could stay with in the villages. Hundreds of thousands of refugees had streamed out of the city. I spoke to them just across the border in Ingushetia, where train wagons had been brought onto a siding to provide temporary accommodation. These were families who had had decent jobs and apartments. Life in a sunny southern city in the Soviet Union wasn't too bad, with its open-air cafés and leafy parks. They had escaped with just a bundle of belongings – and maybe an icon or two if they were Russian. Everything else they once owned now lay in the dust of Grozny.

Back in Moscow, all my friends were incensed by the war. They had no particularly warm feelings for Chechens as such (and were slightly sceptical about my tales of how hospitable they were), but the brutality of Yeltsin's invasion sickened them. They were able to witness it thanks above all to a new television station, NTV, which had been started up by some of Russia's most talented and courageous journalists. The war suddenly brought out something new in the Russian press. Most of the media had supported the 'shock therapy' inflicted on the economy, doing the government's job by portraying it as a necessary transitional period of pain, and most had even gone along with Yeltsin's bloody storming of the White House. But the war in Chechnya stuck in their gullet.

War reporters emerged of a kind that Russia had never seen before. Like most Western correspondents, they tended to sympathise with the Chechen cause, and were appalled by the savagery of the Russian assault, the indiscriminate killing of civilians, and the self-evident lack of preparedness of the poor Russian conscripts sent into battle. Yelena Masyuk's hair-raising reports on NTV made her a nationwide star. Her live broadcasts from the battlegrounds spared nothing, and flatly contradicted the official government story – that the war was going according to plan, with few casualties. NTV was privately owned, but even the state-owned channel RTR was relentlessly critical of the campaign.

'You see,' said Volodya over herring and boiled potatoes, 'this is the great thing that has happened. They can't hide things from us now! We learn more from the box (he pointed to their little television set) than we do from the BBC World Service nowadays!' He looked at me carefully, to check that I wasn't offended by his remark.

'People don't like Yeltsin now,' said Seryozha. 'He's shown he is an old communist – he only knows one way to solve a problem.'

'But Gaidar . . .' said Volodya, referring to the cherub-faced former prime minister who had introduced the shock therapy reforms. 'He is an *intelligent*. That's the difference, you see. He is fantastic – we go to every rally, and he always speaks out against the war.'

'There will be another rally this Sunday,' said Seryozha.

'Tfu!' Volodya spat his traditional gesture of disgust. 'Those generals! Grachev, you just look at him. *Morda*! That ugly mug! They say he was drunk when he took the decision to invade.' I had rarely seen Volodya so agitated about anything.

The promised anti-war demonstration took place, on an icy January afternoon, and the next day Seryozha telephoned. 'Angus, Volodya has passed away. He died in his sleep. His heart gave out.'

A few days later we pushed his coffin on a little sledge across the dappled dove-blue snow of a Moscow cemetery. Before he was lowered into the deep-frozen ground, they removed the lid of the coffin, and Volodya's dead face was exposed to the softly falling snowflakes. The little group of friends paid their respects. Seryozha spoke, and asked me to say something. I praised Volodya's perfect command of English: I knew that was what he would want to hear. Then we all approached the coffin and kissed him. I really didn't want to, but forced myself to follow the Russian tradition. His forehead was cold and bony, like a stone. That wasn't how I wanted to remember such a warm, loving man.

Afterwards, back at the flat, as we quietly drank to his memory, some-one described Volodya as the archetypal *intelligent* – not just brainy and erudite, but profoundly decent, committed to fair play and justice, a man who took the world's woes to heart so strongly that it ultimately killed him.

'Yes,' said another friend. 'Yet another victim of the Chechen war.'

By February the 'action' had moved from Grozny, which was more or less under Russian control, to the villages (which the Russians kept attacking on the pretext that Chechen fighters were hiding there), and to the mountains (where fighters were really hiding). We based ourselves mainly in Nazran, the capital of Ingushetia, just to the west of Chechnya, and used an armoured Land Rover to travel in each day to see what was going on. It was usually driven by Makhach, one of the BBC's drivers from the Moscow office, who was Dagestani and therefore a 'local' in this part of the world. It was the most uncomfortable vehicle I have ever subjected my spine to. The back was full of equipment – boxes of lights and other gear, camera tripod, batteries, satellite phone, flak jackets, some food supplies – and we perched on two narrow iron benches along each side, as the car rattled over shell-pocked roads (and sometimes open fields, to avoid going through military checkpoints). If there had been a shaman in the vicinity, I'd have been a goner.

There were usually five or six of us: the cameraman, the producer, the picture-editor and two correspondents – myself for TV plus a radio reporter. Sometimes a newspaper hack would cadge a lift with us too. And what a merry crew we were, rollicking around the byways of Chechnya like a travelling comedy act. Two of my radio colleagues, Malcolm Brabant and the late Bob Simpson, kept up a brilliant stream of gallows humour through the very worst atrocities. The only time we stopped laughing was after a gunman at a checkpoint fired at us when we pulled away – and we found the bullet lodged in the Kevlar armour, just beside Duncan Knowles' head. And he was our picture editor – how could we have filed a story without him?

Outside the bullet-proof skin, there wasn't much to laugh about. I'll never forget the little family group in the mosque in the village of Goragorsky – mother, father and small son – he was probably about eight. The mother was wearing the traditional brightly coloured dressing gown that so many Chechen women wear even out of doors. I don't remember much more about her appearance, only the gaping red hole in her head, and the tatter of an arm sticking up into the air. The son and the husband, equally mutilated, were laid out beside her on oriental carpets. They'd been killed the previous day when their car was hit by a rocket fired at it from a Russian helicopter. Against Muslim tradition, though, they had not been buried that day, but brought to the mosque and exhibited. Crowds of local people wandered in and out to look at the horror show, using it to keep their hatred of the Russians on the boil. Outside, villagers harangued me with desperate lectures and pleas. 'It's part of a policy of genocide,' they said. 'They want to destroy our nation. Why doesn't the West help? You must tell the world about what is going on. Only tell the truth,' they said, and added: 'This is what the Russians call humanitarian aid – they send us rockets!' I had heard the same sick joke so often in Chechnya it had almost drained my compassion: all I wanted to do was get away from them. Bob filmed the scene, but we couldn't possibly show it on television.

The village of Samashki always seemed to be in the news. After a convoy of Russian tanks was attacked in the area, the village was subjected to a ferocious bombardment. We went to see the aftermath – dozens of destroyed houses, dead animals, families on the edge of unreason. Hiding in cellars was no defence against incoming shells. A woman showed me the basement where her mother and sister were both killed. Their bodies were laid out, wrapped in rugs. With guns rattling all around the village, the remaining family members were too scared to risk going to the cemetery to bury them.

As usual, this unbelievable human tragedy became just a sixteen-second sequence in a report. Every day – no, ten times a day – you were racked by the thought that you were scavenging among people's misfortunes. How surreal it was, to intrude on a family's mourning, to film whatever they showed you, the fragments of shells, the ruined houses, the bodies, and then to place a bereaved woman in front of a huge camera, with an appropriate scene of destruction nicely framed behind her, and ask her to tell you about it; you would press her to talk until you obtained a usable sound bite – and then you usually allowed her to talk on, until she shed tears, and you filmed that too, because that would be the most moving part of your report. We did that again and again, but not callously: it was what you needed in order to tell this horrific story and bring its horror into people's living rooms. But I wasn't proud of it, even if the stories were often very powerful.

At least this felt like real journalism. You set out each morning with no idea what you would find that day, but knowing that the news needed a report from you by teatime. The fear of not finding anything newsworthy was greater than the fear of being killed – because that, for some reason, didn't normally occur to you. In fact, there was always plenty to report, and indeed much that we had to leave out. But throughout each day it was a race to film scenes, interview people, understand the story, and knit it all together into a report – and then get to a satellite point where you could feed it back to London by 6 pm. Much of that depended on chance, and on the willingness of men with guns to let you do what you wanted to do. The conscripts manning checkpoints usually demanded cigarettes, glue, or photographic film – not because they were all amateur photographers but because, if you boiled the film, you got damned good hallucinations. When the Russians discovered that reporters often had satellite phones with them, they would sometimes let us pass in exchange for a few minutes to call their mothers and tell them they were safe.

On one occasion we were stopped as we tried to get to a recently bombed village. We knew that ITN had just been allowed through. But we weren't. The usual bribes didn't work, and I ended up arguing with an officer.

'You've just let ITN go through! Why not us?'

'Turn around and leave.'

'But we're the BBC. We're more important than ITN . . . and anyway, that's not fair – they're our competitors! Surely you understand.'

'Get back in your car and leave. Now.'

'Look. Let's be reasonable. We only want to do the same as our colleagues are doing . . .'

'I'll give you ten seconds to leave.'

'We want to show how the Russian army is bringing peace to the region.'

The officer took out a pistol, cocked it, aimed it at me, and started counting: 'Ten, nine, eight . . .'

'Okay, fine!' I said, with an incredibly brave look of derision that must have chilled the soldier's blood. That would show him! Then we drove away. Pretty quickly.

The country was a patchwork of villages controlled either by Russians or by Chechens. Mostly we tried to avoid crossing lines, but sometimes we made mistakes. One night we were returning to Nazran in our white armoured Land Rover after a day in Grozny, and took a wrong turning in the village of Samashki. Makhach turned the vehicle round and we headed back towards the road for Nazran. But our manoeuvres were spotted and Chechen fighters, weighed down with Kalashnikovs and grenade launchers, flagged us down. As the 'leader' of our team, I was ordered out of the car, and surrounded by hostile bearded faces. Why were we out so late? Were we working for the FSK, the Russian intelligence service? How come it happened that every time the village was visited by a TV crew, it was shelled the next day?

The fighters escorted us to Achkhoi Martan, the district centre, and a stronghold of Chechen resistance. The local security chief – aka chief thug – strutted in, a young, confident-looking man in a leather jacket and white scarf. In a tiny room thick with cigarette smoke and full of fighters balancing rifles on their knees or juggling with grenades, he lectured us about the unacceptability of being in the Chechen state without a Chechen visa. I politely told him there was no such thing as a Chechen visa, and added that he ought to treat Western journalists better since it was thanks to us that the world knew about the Russian invasion and the suffering of Chechen civilians. That was a bad mistake. For such impertinence, he said, he could have me shot. And there was no doubt about it, the gunmen suddenly looked delighted at the prospect of having such an interesting command to carry out.

My cameraman helped to defuse the situation by claiming to be a Muslim and reciting a few words he knew from the Koran. He told the commander in his broken Russian: 'If you do not trust me, your Muslim brother, then shoot me first and let Allah be the judge of your action.' I also decided a less combative stance was my best option, and stopped contradicting the man. After an hour or so, our host calmed down and gave us an escort back to the Chechen roadblock where we'd been arrested. It was almost midnight now, and the road between here and the next checkpoint, a Russian one, was pitch-black and menacing. The Chechen fighters, seeing our doubts about crossing the front line, suddenly became paragons of gentleness, as if their earlier ferocity was merely a uniform they put on to frighten foreigners. Akhmed, who described himself as an entrepreneur, with business in Moscow, said we could stay at his place till it got light. His house, on the edge of the village just a mile from Russian artillery, was not exactly reassuring: the roof was full of holes from the last Russian bombardment. He fetched food for us, and we were joined by three other fighters for a late candlelit supper. The Chechens showed great discipline, offering us vodka but abstaining themselves, this being the month of Ramadan. 'If we die with alcohol on our breath, it will be a disgrace,' they said. The house was impressive – one of those red-brick mansions that Russia's new rich were erecting all over the place. It rang true when Akhmed insisted that they were not bandits, as Moscow claimed, but just ordinary people defending their families and homes. We laid out our sleeping bags in the barn, and fell asleep to the gentle pluffing sound of distant explosions.

A few nights later, it was the Russians' turn to demonstrate their hospitality and their aggression. I had driven into Grozny with Bob Prabhu and producer Jamie Coomarasamy, and we found ourselves stranded near the city centre after dark – not in the armoured Land Rover but in an ordinary car. Here, curfew meant curfew. The city was deserted, there was total silence broken only by gunfire, and total blackness lightened only by Russian army flares sent up to illuminate the sky and help them pinpoint snipers. Troops were under orders to shoot anything that moved. Some Russian interior ministry troops stopped us and escorted us to their base in an armoured personnel carrier. We drove slowly through the dark streets, the only light the blinking of our left-turn indicator – a sign to other Russian troops not to fire on a friendly vehicle. We reached their checkpoint in the city outskirts, where they gave us shelter in their little wooden hut.

These young men from Novosibirsk, professional soldiers with families back home, couldn't have been kinder to us. Around their wood-burning stove they shared their food and drink, and sang sad songs to a badly tuned guitar. But as the night wore on, the demons gathered. The talk turned to the enemy. 'The only good Chechen,' they all agreed, 'is a dead Chechen.' 'Don't trust their hospitality . . . They'll embrace you by day, and stab you in the back the same night.' As the drink took hold of them, the atmosphere turned hostile, and Jamie suggested I should try to calm them by singing some songs. I took the guitar and sang 'Yesterday', which lulled them into misty-eyed confusion, and then Status Quo's 'You're in the Army Now' which, whether they understood it or not, seemed to win them back onside.

At this point, however, I began to feel extremely unwell, and regretted having touched the disgusting tinned meat they had offered us earlier. I broke out in waves of sweat. The senior officer immediately ordered one of his men to take me to the officers' cabin across the road. I was given a bunk, with plenty of blankets, and my batman stayed in the anteroom, coming in periodically to stoke up the stove with firewood. In the middle of the night my stomach was churning like a cement-mixer and I knew I would have to go outside. I told the soldier, who said he would accompany me into the trenches beside the little army camp. As we stumbled through the darkness he called to the sentries: 'Don't shoot, it's just a colleague who needs a shit.'

We reached the place where I could perform, and I squatted down, emptying my bowels in a rush, while the good soldier stood guard just behind me. It was possibly the strangest moment of my life. Above me, the sky was dotted with stars; the rat-a-tat of gunfire sounded from every direction, and flares occasionally illuminated the horizon; and there I was, pants around my ankles and a Russian soldier watching me shit.

And yet, the strangest thing of all was: I kept wanting to go back to Chechnya. Because I actually loved it there. I loved the amazing hospitality of the people. I was humbled by their ability to keep going. I admired their resistance. I was awed by the doctors I saw performing operations in hospitals with almost no medicines or power. I loved the way that even in the manmade moonscape of Grozny, people kept their dignity – women still took the time to dress smartly and put on lipstick. (I was criticised for saying this in a report, but for me those red lips, carefully painted, were a potent symbol of resistance, as if to say, 'No, you bastards, you can bomb the shit out of us, but I will not stop being a human being.')

At the start of the war there was a restaurant in central Grozny called Lozania, which became the foreign journalists' hang-out. The owner managed to procure daily supplies of canned beer, and occasionally played a battered piano in the basement-level bar. I'm sure I was not the only journalist there who experienced a creeping, unsettling realisation that, actually, you preferred being here, in this smoky beer bar with war-junkie colleagues, and bombs exploding above, to being at home. Here, and in other lodgings that we rented in Chechnya over the months, we would joke, laugh, drink and discuss. I drank 20-year-old Lagavulin for the first time, and never looked back. The one thing we never did was ask each other how we were coping. There seemed to be no need – we were all having such fun, in this human sewer. There was more companionship and good sense here, it seemed to us, than at dinner parties back in Moscow.

Not asking each other was probably a mistake. Post-traumatic stress takes many forms, and I think we all suffered from it, one way or the other – possibly for years to come.

*　　*　　*

I have already mentioned the tyranny of the image in television journalism, and the guilt one felt, knowing that a woman who was visibly in terrible distress was likely to be the star of one's report. On the other hand, television is by far the most powerful medium, and just occasionally you felt it was all worthwhile – not because an editor praised your report, but because it stirred a few viewers to action.

I once showed an old Russian woman living in a bombed-out apartment block in Grozny. Maria, 78-years-old, took me to what remained of her flat – just a charred shell, with one outside wall smashed to pieces. 'Everything was burnt,' she said, 'my sewing machine, the fridge, the bed, the sofa, the wardrobe, the bedside table – everything. Nothing was left.' The report showed the appalling conditions people had to survive in, collecting water from a pipe, or from puddles, while Russian soldiers careered around in their armoured vehicles. From all of this, one detail caught the eye of a viewer in England, who wrote to me to ask how she might be able to get a new sewing machine sent out to Maria. (I replied to her letter, and had to warn her that nothing sent to poor Maria in her destroyed building was likely to arrive.)

On a different occasion I visited an old people's home in the Chernorechye district of Grozny where a single carer – a Chechen woman called Malika – did her best to look after the patients, in the most appalling conditions: no heating, no hot water, no clean linen, and food cooked up in a squalid kitchen from rations donated by the Russian army. Many of the bedridden patients had lice, and lay wheezing and coughing on damp, stinking sheets. In her little sound bite, Malika said this: 'We need help. We need a generator to give us light and heat. We need bed linen, blankets, clothes, slippers.'

She didn't mean this as any sort of 'appeal', to be broadcast on the BBC. But one viewer of the *Six O'Clock News* took it exactly that way. Joan Capp, a retired nurse in her mid-sixties, who had already delivered humanitarian aid to Bosnia, rang me to check some details, and then devoted the next year or more of her life to trying to help the poor people of the Chernorechye old people's home. I called her the Angel of Grozny. From her house in Bootle, Cumbria, she spent five months fundraising, buying food and equipment, and organising a phenomenal personal aid effort, which involved taking a forty-ton truck full of goods across Europe to Grozny. One day she rang me again, from Kiev, where the truck had broken down, local customs officials had impounded the cargo, her Chechen escort had absconded, and she had run out of money to continue. Despite her age, she was spending the freezing nights in the cab of the truck. Undaunted, Joan pressed on to Grozny and visited the old folks home – with war still raging around it. She even met Malika and promised her that, somehow, the aid would get to them. After many more months of fundraising and chasing after unscrupulous intermediaries, she eventually received news that the hard-won aid (or at least some of it) had finally reached the people who needed it – though what happened to the Chernorechye old people's home when war resumed in Chechnya, she never found out. I still find it hard to believe that one of my reports sparked off such a great, selfless endeavour. Joan is now well into her eighties, very frail, and blind, but still runs her Cumbrian charity, looking for ways to help the unfortunate around the world. Since Chechnya, she has organised aid convoys to Pakistan, Lebanon, Syria and many other places.

Individuals like Joan were moved to action by our reports, but our governments were not. Sometimes it felt to me that we must be doing a poor job in Chechnya, because despite broadcasting horrific images and stories of atrocities being committed there, the world scarcely reacted. Grozny was just as much a cesspit of human cruelty as Sarajevo was at the same time, or Aleppo recently – but the world just turned a blind eye. I don't think it was our poor reporting. It was the indifference of the West to a massacre carried out not by a recognised dictator but by their darling, the great democrat, Boris Yeltsin. As I recall, no British diplomat even travelled to Chechnya to witness the carnage with their own eyes.

I can't say that I was always as even-handed in my reporting from Chechnya as a BBC correspondent is perhaps supposed to be. In the face of such indiscriminate destruction of people's lives, it was hard not to show pity for the ordinary people caught up in a conflict that was beyond their control. The Russians, with their overwhelming air power, had rendered part of their own country unfit for human life, killing and displacing just as many Russian citizens as Chechens. It was they who ran the 'filtration camps', where Chechen suspects were held indefinitely and subjected to torture. How could you show a man with scars all over his body, where Russian soldiers had burned him with cigarettes, and be balanced about that?

Only once – but I still feel uneasy about it – did we allow the tyranny of the television image to push us too far. We were with a group of hard-line Chechen fighters in their hideout, drinking tea with them in an ornately decorated living room. The place was full of beautiful carpets, weapons and ammunition boxes. The men vowed to introduce sharia law in Chechnya, and boasted about their intention to go out and destroy the market stalls of traders who were selling vodka and beer.

Our TV ears perked up. I asked: 'When are you planning to do that?'

'Now ... in a few minutes ... when we finish ...'

We carried on chatting, and the men continued to promise action. Their leader kept returning to the sin of selling vodka. 'They even sell it to Russian soldiers! We have to stop this.'

For an hour there was a great deal of talk, but no sign of action, so I said something to the effect of: look, if you're going to show us what great zealots you are would you mind doing it while it's still light enough for us to film you?

The fighters finally agreed, but I noticed them exchanging doubtful glances which suggested they might have been bluffing – but could not back down without looking weak or stupid. We all headed down to the market, and the men held their Kalashnikovs like sledgehammers and went from stall to stall smashing all the vodka bottles from the shelves – leaving the poor female vendors holding their faces in horror and begging them not to destroy their livelihoods. The shots made an extremely powerful sequence in our film, perfectly demonstrating the fanaticism of these Islamist fighters ... but I have never forgiven myself for precipitating an event that might not have happened without our intervention. At least not that day.

The leader of the Chechen rebellion, General Dzhokhar Dudayev, was the most unstable, maniacal person I ever encountered. You know that feeling you have when you are talking to a man who is cackling like a psychopath, and he suddenly stops, and stares at you as though he's decided he's bored with you and is now going to pin you against the wall and slit your throat? You never had that feeling? Neither had I.

Dudayev had been in hiding, somewhere in the mountains, ever since the Russians drove him out of Grozny at the end of 1994. A year later, we set out to find him. We spent weeks sweet-talking his propaganda chief, Movladi Udugov, a young man who became more and more devout the longer I knew him. One night he slept in our little room, and I woke in the morning to find him already on his prayer mat, and the sign from Allah seemed to be that Dudayev was ready to receive us. We spent a very long day driving from safe house to safe house in different villages, being passed from one 'presidential representative' to another. We drove in a four-wheel-drive ambulance to smooth our passage through Russian checkpoints, escorted by Chechen fighters who naturally had left their weapons at home. In the afternoon we had tea with a field commander named Doku Umarov, a long-bearded terrorist who said he wanted to take the war at once to the streets of Moscow, 'but Dzhokhar won't allow us to do this – yet.' Umarov later became the most wanted man in Russia after masterminding many atrocities, but on this occasion he was the perfect host, passing round freshly baked pastries, honey and cream.

Now we had to leave normal roads and travel on forest tracks to avoid Russian checkpoints. In the village of Roshni-Chu we found ourselves in a room with the supreme Islamic leader in Chechnya, Mufti Akhmad Kadyrov. He wondered whether many British people were converting to Islam. I mentioned Cat Stevens, but he hadn't heard of him. Outside in the darkness, local children danced and clapped their hands, chanting the names of field commanders and appealing to Allah to protect them. At around ten in the evening word came that we should move, but first they confiscated any cigarette lighters, penknives, keyrings and tape-recorders: we could take only what was needed for the interview. We travelled not in our ambulance, but in a jeep driven by Abu, Dudayev's security chief. He drove in complete darkness with no lights on, only flashing them occasionally to see the way as he darted down dirt tracks, over flimsy bridges and across fields. Russian tracer fire streaked the sky. Eventually we reached a village, and a house with huge iron gates, guarded by heavily armed Rambos in black tunics and berets. Inside it looked like something from a Chechen Ideal Home exhibition, with unused pots and pans on display, and beautiful carpets on the wall.

We unloaded our equipment, Movladi spoke on a walkie-talkie, and then Abu took us for another little ride in his jeep, allegedly while the equipment was searched, but apparently just to add to the mystification. After a fifteen-minute wait in a dark gully, listening to the shelling, we returned to the house. Suddenly, at midnight, Dudayev swaggered in wearing military fatigues and forage cap, with those crazy eyes glinting like daggers and his moustache clipped like Clark Gable's.

We sat down at a table – not in front of the blue wall-carpet preferred by the cameraman, because Dudayev deemed it 'too interesting'. I remarked that he was looking very fit, purely so the sound-recordist could check the voice level.

'I suppose you'd rather see me dead!' came the ready repartee, followed by a manic chortle. During our talk his mood lurched about, from grim humour to bloodcurdling menace.

I expressed my sadness at how Chechnya had been destroyed.

'Everything is fine in our country.' He smiled at me pityingly. 'Everything is fine in our country,' he repeated. Should I laugh, or just nod in sympathy? Mustn't get it wrong. What about the Russian occupation?

'Yes, we have occupiers,' he said, in the same deadly-serious bantering tone. 'But that's temporary. We intend to leave a limited contingent here – those who are dead already and those who are prepared to die on this land.'

The Russians, he elaborated, were all schizophrenics, crazed with a mania for world domination. Slowly it emerged that Dudayev was less interested in merely freeing Chechnya from Russian control than in doing mankind a huge favour by freeing it of Russians.

'I need a little war,' he said, because he had 300,000 unemployed, homeless men who knew only how to fight.

I was edging towards the door by now, but he was enjoying himself. 'I have a programme – not to separate from Russia but to enter it and destroy it from within.'

Oh yes? Er, how?

Well, you remember Budyonnovsk? Ah, yes, the place where a Chechen fighter named Shamil Basayev took 1,000 innocent people hostage in southern Russia last summer . . .

'I wanted to show Russia that it would not go unpunished. I sent Shamil to take the Kremlin, but he only took a maternity hospital in Budyonnovsk!' He laughed heartily, his eyes bulging with delight. 'That doesn't count! We'll have to have a replay!'

When? How?

Dudayev narrowed his eyes. His chest rocked with silent mirth.

'There's a time for everything. War is a special art form, a terrible one. You need patience. Patience is courage in war.'

So his threats to unleash terrorist acts in Russia remained in force?

'I have never threatened anyone, merely predicted. And so far my predictions have been justified.'

It wasn't Dudayev's words that frightened me so much as his erratic behaviour: the smile that morphed into a sneer, the laughter that creased his face and brought tears to his eyes – but abruptly vanished, leaving a murderous grimace in its place. There was absolutely no doubt in my mind that one ill-advised question or misplaced joke could earn me a place in front of a firing squad, probably led by the 'commander of western forces', the comic-book Rambo with a massive handlebar moustache and dark shades who was guarding the room.

We talked for an hour and a quarter, at the end of which Dudayev invited us to visit him later in his secret bunker: 'But it's at your own risk, ha-ha-ha-ha-ha, because the Russians shell it every hour ha-ha-ha-ha . . .' The next day Movladi explained that the bunker was actually in an old Soviet missile silo. The 'normal' road to it was constantly under attack, but there was a secret route we could use, only with Dudayev's personal permission, and only if we were blindfolded for the journey. For several days we were shunted from place to place waiting for the moment to go in . . . and then the deal collapsed.

Five months later Dudayev was killed by a Russian missile as he spoke in the open air on his sat-phone. For all his precautions, he hadn't reckoned with the Russians' ability to lock on to a satellite signal and pinpoint his whereabouts.

31

The Fear of War

MY FIRST-EVER TRIP to the Soviet Union was in the summer of 1974. My memories of it are about as sharp as the fern on a trainee barista's first cappuccino. I do recall that it was in the city of Krasnodar, down in the south of European Russia, not far from the Black Sea, and that it involved attending Russian classes for a month. There were discos on the roof of the university refectory, where we danced the night away under southern skies to the big hits of the day – 'My Address is the Soviet Union' by The Gemstones and 'How Wonderful This World Is' by The Jolly Lads. My capitalist advances were firmly rebuffed by a Komsomol goddess called Nadya, but the girls in our group seemed to be luckier, and a certain amount of international snogging went on in the dark corners, under the pretext of discovering more about Russian verb endings. The rest of us drank the vodka we had smuggled up in carrier bags, while pretending to enjoy glasses of Baikal, a Soviet concoction distantly related to Coca Cola.

Other than that, the only thing I can remember is that we visited an inordinate number of war memorials and museums and were treated to endless statistics about casualties and military operations. It struck us twenty-year-old Brits as odd. We were the tail-end of the hippie generation, gentle people with flowers in our hair, whose immediate concern was to stop the war in Vietnam – yet our counterparts in the USSR were still harping on about the Great Patriotic War, which had ended a whole 30 years ago. The usual thing in the West was to discount this fixation as Soviet propaganda. Well, the Soviets may have exploited it, but they didn't invent it. It took a few more decades of meeting countless Russians for me to understand the profound difference between our perception of war and theirs.

Brought up in a country where Second World War on the home front means *Dad's Army*, our senses were – and are – truly numb to the reality of total war. The battles on the eastern front were the most devastating in all human history. Between 1941 and 1944 the Germans occupied or destroyed major Soviet cities: Kiev, Minsk, Smolensk, Stalingrad. Almost half of the entire population of the USSR experienced occupation by Nazi forces. In Leningrad, which was besieged and bombarded for 900 days, a million civilians – a third of its population – *starved* to death.

In Britain, we were never invaded, never occupied, never forced to live under a foreign power, never subjected to executions and marauding by Nazi troops. We didn't have gallows in our town squares, people hanged from trees and lampposts, we didn't endure mass starvation with people reduced to eating rats and grass, we didn't have the Gestapo searching our attics and cellars, we weren't subjected to forced labour. We didn't have villages where the entire population was rounded up and burned alive in some barn. By contrast, in the countries of the former Soviet Union – especially Ukraine, Belarus and Russia – war is part of every family's life and recent history, an event so traumatic that it altered the nation's DNA. Yes, Britain suffered tens of thousands of casualties, and the Blitz, and Dunkirk and the D-Day landings with all their sacrifices . . . but war did not come to our own shores, and that's the huge difference in our vision. Britain had 67,000 civilian deaths, mainland USA none, the Soviet Union 16 million. For military deaths the figures are 380,000, 400,000 and around 10,000,000, respectively.

Of course, you can blame some of the Soviet Union's suffering on Stalin's blunders and purges of his generals – but that doesn't change the reality of what ordinary people went through. And yes, the Soviets themselves committed atrocities – from Katyn to the Baltics – but again that does not diminish the suffering of those who lived and fought in occupied or besieged territories. It was a hell like nothing any British or American family could even imagine.

What we commemorate on Armistice Day each year is the heroism and sacrifices of those who went to war; what they remember in Russia on Victory Day is the indescribable suffering of those to whom war came.

I think the divergence in our experiences does much to explain why the Americans and British do not 'get' Russia's concerns today. Other Western nations, such as France and Germany itself, which did experience the devastation of war on their own territories, tend to understand Russia's experience better. The Poles and Balts, who also suffered hugely in the War, might also have been sympathetic to Russia, had their liberation from the Nazis not ended in occupation by the Soviets. Instead, they ended up clamouring for membership of NATO – an issue that soon began to sour the relationship between Russia and the West.

Victory Day in May 1995 – the fiftieth anniversary of Hitler's defeat – was giving Boris Yeltsin a headache. He wanted to celebrate it in grand style, with leaders of all the wartime allies, and more, present on Red Square. The trouble was, few of them wanted to salute a display of Russian military might and a march-past by troops who were currently massacring civilians in Chechnya. (Such embarrassment was as close as the West came to condemnation of Yeltsin's war.)

A solution was found: hold two parades. President Clinton, and the British prime minister, John Major, stayed away from the militaristic one, at which modern tanks, missiles and troops staged a great show of virility, but attended the historical one on Red Square, at which 5,000 World War Two veterans and vintage vehicles tottered across the cobbles in an appropriately unthreatening manner.

This was, Yeltsin hoped, a winning combination. On the one hand he showed that Russia was still a superpower to be reckoned with; on the other he reminded his guests that we had once been allies in the fight against Nazism – and could be allies again, now that communism was dead and buried. To prove the point, they draped lots of ivy on Lenin's mausoleum in Red Square to hide the word 'Lenin', and put up a huge poster showing a Russian soldier and an American GI with their arms around one another.

Yeltsin glowed with pride as President Clinton, in a short speech, dealt with the common Russian complaint that the West no longer remembered the sacrifices made by the Soviet people in the War: 'The Cold War,' Clinton said, 'obscured our ability to fully appreciate what your people had suffered and how your extraordinary courage helped to hasten the victory we all celebrate today.'

But in my report on the day's celebrations, I pointed out that Yeltsin brought up in his talks with Clinton what I called the Russian leader's 'prime obsession' – Nato's plans to expand eastwards, which had 'contributed to Russia's growing sense of isolation in the post-Cold War world'.

As I write these words now, more than twenty years later, I can't help but note that most 'experts' in the West today believe (or claim) that it was only with the coming of Vladimir Putin that Russia became 'obsessed' with NATO's expansion. But Yeltsin – and Gorbachev too – were equally baffled by the alliance's decision to move into eastern Europe. Putin has become a handy excuse, I think, to justify a policy that began long before anyone had ever heard of him.

A producer in London had come up with an excellent idea for a short documentary feature to mark the anniversary. We would track down the photographer who had taken one of the most famous shots of the entire Second World War – the moment when Soviet soldiers raised the red flag above the Reichstag in Berlin – and also one of the soldiers in the photograph, and bring them together for the day. The photographer was Yevgeny Khaldei, now 78 years old. We found him in his Moscow apartment, delighted to reminisce about his celebrated photo and even to develop it again in a chemical bath in front of our eyes, waving his hand briefly under the light to make the smoking city in the background more dramatic. He had arrived in a devastated Berlin with the victorious Red Army in May 1945. The Reichstag had already been taken, but there was no photo of the moment, so Khaldei, a war photographer for TASS, arranged for the flag-raising to be re-enacted by three soldiers. 'We didn't actually have a flag,' he said, 'so I sewed a yellow hammer and sickle onto a red table cloth.' An 18-year-old private from Kiev, Aleksei Kovalyov, climbed onto a statue on the roof and stuck the flag there. Khaldei climbed even higher for the picture, so that the burning ruins of Berlin could be seen below. There was one little catch, Khaldei told us. 'When I developed the photo I saw that the soldier stretching up to support Kovalyov was wearing a watch on both wrists! I had to airbrush one of them out, so it didn't seem like Russian soldiers had been looting!'

Meanwhile we had contacted Kovalyov and paid for him to travel up to Moscow from Kiev. Then we arranged for him and Yevgeny both to be strolling around on Red Square and to 'happen' to bump into each other. It was hilarious.

'Hello,' said Khaldei. 'Lovely day for it, isn't it.'

'It is,' said Kovalyov, his medals clinking on his chest. 'Where were you in the war, then?'

'Well, I ended up in Berlin.'

'Really? Me too.'

'What were you doing?'

'Oh, I was just an ordinary soldier. Ended up at the Reichstag.'

'Hm.'

'And you?'

'Well, I was a photo-correspondent . . .'

There was a long pause, followed by: 'You wouldn't know the chap who took that photo on the Reichstag, I suppose? Khaldei?'

'Khaldei? That's me.'

'What?'

'I'm Khaldei.'

'Well, you were a lot younger in '45!'

'Hm!' said Khaldei, still not recognising the old soldier.

'We need to have a talk, my dear!' said Kovalyov.

Khaldei did a double take: 'What? You're not Kovalyov, are you?'

'Of course I am!'

What a great moment that was. The two broke into broad grins, kissed and hugged. We ended up in the Metropol Hotel, where they got nicely drunk, living through the war all over again – and cursing Yeltsin for killing innocent people in Chechnya.

I made two trips in 1995 to try to understand both sides of the NATO enlargement story. First – any old excuse to go back to my favourite place – I went to Estonia. At the Paldiski nuclear submarine base, which I was smuggled into by Green Party activists, I saw the destruction left behind by the departing Russian forces: you could understand the Estonians' anger at the visible legacy of Soviet occupation – ground saturated with paraffin and toxic chemicals, stores of nuclear waste, scuttled warships, a wilderness of buildings smashed up as the Russians departed. On the other hand, tens of thousands of Russian troops were suddenly gone, just as the Estonians had dreamed – pulled out so fast by a compliant Kremlin that they had nowhere to live when they arrived back home. As for the hundreds of thousands of Russians who had moved to Estonia, or been born there, during the years of Soviet occupation – we filmed some of them at language classes, learning to speak Estonian. But many did not bother to learn, causing resentment among the local population. Most of them could not even vote, because they could only become Estonian citizens after passing a language test. Even the European Union had to warn the government (here and in Latvia) to stop discriminating against the Russians if they wanted to become members.

But it was NATO membership for these countries that worried Russia more than their plans to join the EU. I went to Kaliningrad, the little exclave of Russian territory sandwiched between Lithuania and Poland, both of which were in line to join NATO. We filmed a new border post being built between Kaliningrad and Lithuania, and Russian soldiers with dogs patrolling a new barbed-wire border with Poland. I found the whole thing depressing, as did all the Russians I spoke to.

Yevgeny Shaposhnikov was the very last Soviet minister of defence, one of the 'good guys' who had supported Gorbachev and opposed the coup that briefly overthrew him. He told me he felt Russia was being left with no say in Europe's new security arrangements: 'The West is trying to build a new world order, but it'll be a one-sided, unstable world order that will lead to new disorders in the world.'

The old Iron Curtain had disappeared, but Europe's new dividing line was now appearing, 600 miles closer to Moscow. Russians were perplexed. 'We don't threaten the Poles,' they said to me, 'so why do they need NATO's protection?'

I shared their sense of betrayal – because four or five years earlier I had celebrated the end of communism both in Russia and in the Baltic states and Poland, and really believed that Gorbachev's vision of 'a common European home' was destined to come into being. In my piece to camera by a watchtower on the new fortified border with Poland, I said: 'Seen from here, NATO's expansion sends all the wrong signals. It tells the Russians they're still not really accepted by the West. It tells them they're still seen as the enemy. No matter how sweetly NATO tries to sugar the pill, Russia's going to feel once again like a pariah in Europe.'

I pointed out that East Europeans were worried by the surging popularity of communists and nationalists in Russia, and that this was 'one reason NATO feels it needs to expand'. But, I added, 'by doing so it may also be cornering the bear, making him more likely to lash out in anger.'

I've probably only ever said one prophetic thing in my entire life, so I might as well boast about it. That was it.

32

Life Is Getting Better, Comrades

PROBABLY THE BIGGEST controversy I ever caused in my life concerned the fact that I reported night after night from Moscow on the BBC news without a hat on my head.

The *Independent* published an article in December 1995 by a wag called Magnus Mills, which began with the conversation that allegedly occurred in his house every time I appeared on the *Nine O'Clock News*.

'Why doesn't he put a hat on?'

'He never wears a hat.'

'But he's in Moscow. Look at the guy, he's practically freezing to death. He should put a hat on. Everyone else has got a hat on.'

The point was, Magnus went on, that nobody listened to what I was saying because all they could think about was the icicles developing at the end of my nose.

It was very amusing, and I replied to the letters section with what I thought was an equally amusing rejoinder, in which I blamed BBC bosses for not allowing correspondents to wear hats. I joked that I pleaded with them, but they were so callous they didn't even care if I caught a cold.

Before I knew it, the story was splashed across centrefolds in several tabloid newspapers. 'BBC's Man in Moscow in Bitter Feud with Bosses' – that kind of thing, complete with mock-ups of me wearing the hat I longed for. And hot on the heels of that came a missive from an extremely senior BBC boss, accompanied by a klaxon and flashing neon lights saying SENSE OF HUMOUR FAIL. He warned me sternly never again to make statements to the press without his prior approval.

Twat. He must have been the only person in the entire country who didn't realise it was all just a bit of fun.

* * *

When I wasn't on screen, of course, and I felt sure that my boss wasn't looking, I did wear hats in winter. Days off with the family were wonderful. Sometimes we spent the weekend at a dacha on a former Communist Party estate, now owned by a Western oil company, where British friends of ours had a little mansion. The estate still had its ex-KGB security guards, who opened the huge steel gates to let you drive into the fenced compound, plus gardeners, drivers, maids and groundsmen to clear the snow from the driveways that swept up to each impressive porch. Each house had its own nuclear bunker, and though you couldn't see your neighbour's house through the screen of trees, you could walk there along a series of interconnecting pathways, with street lighting for evening strolls and benches on which the Soviet Union's geriatric leaders must once have rested their bones and admired the stunning view across the river. We stayed in what passed – for communist bosses and oil executives – as little more than an outhouse, but was in fact a wonderful Scandinavian-style cabin complete with sauna (from which you could leap straight out into the snow). The setting was idyllic: soaring pine trees, complete silence, thick snow on which to sledge down through the trees to the Moskva river. And in the summer, we sunbathed on the bank of the river, abuzz with insects and heavy with the drowsy scent of wild flowers.

One of the BBC drivers, Vasily, also took us out in winter to his rather more modest dacha, north of Moscow on the Volga, where we walked out onto the ice, drilled a hole, and waited for tiny fish (called, if I remember rightly, *yorsh*) to snap at our bait. A few did, and with them Vasily cooked delicious *ukha* – a soup made with the fish (heads and all), onion, potatoes, bayleaf, dill and a splash of vodka.

In the city too, to borrow Stalin's phrase, 'life was getting better, comrades, life was getting happier' – for foreigners like us, I mean. Finally there were places to take the kids for Sunday brunch or an after-school treat: Patio Pizza, Santa Fe for fajitas, and the Starlite Diner – a real chrome-and-Formica American burger joint, where they had taught the waiters to smile and enjoy their work as they served baked potato skins, tuna melts and banana splits (mainly to foreigners, but it was catching on).

All of the new Western-style eateries were so much better than the poker-up-the-arse Russian places that were also appearing, with their starched white tablecloths and condescending waiters. Only the Georgian restaurants didn't feel the need to pretend they'd been around since the nineteenth century. Mama Zoya, in the basement of an ordinary apartment block, served the most delicious *khachapuri*, *tsatsivi* and *khinkali* this side of the Caucasus mountain range. (For the few unfortunate readers who have not yet tried Georgian food, those are cheese-bread, chicken in walnut sauce, and meat-filled dumplings – but the description doesn't even hint at the tongue-zinging flavours of Georgian food.)

Life was slowly becoming better for more Russians, too. Inflation dropped from 1000 per cent in 1993 to a mere 20 per cent in 1996–1997, and a new middle class was emerging with enough money to eat out occasionally, or to have a '*euro-remont*' (European-standard renovation) done to their flats: out went the cracked pale-green tiles and leaky pipes, in came Finnish or Austrian bathrooms and kitchens. Some could afford to install satellite television, and go abroad on holiday. Nothing convinced me more of the changes that had come about than the sight of Russian families, queuing to show their passports at the airport, ready to fly off to a European beach – something that had been denied to them for seventy years.

And then there were the super-rich – the 'New Russians' – and all the things they 'needed': casinos, 'gentlemen's clubs', rip-off restaurants, cosmetic surgery, cruises and yachts, country villas with turrets and swimming pools, property and money-laundering companies on Cyprus, bodyguards and Grand Cherokee jeeps. Moscow remained a not particularly dangerous place for ordinary people, but if you were a banker or businessman you probably had enemies.

The BBC office was now located in the Radisson-Slavyanskaya Hotel, near the Kiev railway station. The hotel was a joint venture owned by an American called Paul Tatum and a Chechen named Umar Dzhabrailov. One day in 1996 Tatum was shot eleven times in the head and neck, and after that the hotel was no longer a joint venture. (The BBC remained there, though, paying exorbitant rent for its ever-expanding operation, with TV and radio now brought together, and the website about to be launched.) I personally witnessed mafia-style shoot-outs or hold-ups on three occasions – in the foyer of the Radisson hotel, in a restaurant, and on the pavement outside another hotel near the foreign ministry, where a man was pinned to the ground by Kalashnikov-wielding masked men. The manager of our favourite Santa Fe restaurant suddenly disappeared, presumed dead. Every time you went into a supermarket, such as '7th Continent', near our home, you walked past an armed guard in camouflage fatigues.

In March 1997 we made a short documentary about a St Petersburg mafia boss who insisted we call him Viktor. With his bodyguards two steps behind at every moment, and a firm promise to obscure his face in the report, we toured some of the casinos and cafés where he provided the *krysha* – the 'roof' or protection. He had started his career in the *perestroika* period. 'Some of my mates started up cooperative businesses, but they were all crushed by red tape and gangsters. I realised it was better to be on the side of the gangsters, so I joined one of the appropriate structures. Then, when the elders got killed, I found myself at the top . . .' He took me to the Okhtinsky cemetery to visit the grave of one of his mates, who had been shot dead at the age of 35 – 'ten times in the head with a TT pistol'.

Was the killer caught? I asked.

'We don't want the killers to be caught, because they'd be put in prison. We want to find them ourselves.' For that purpose, Viktor's gang had several bent cops on its payroll, providing intelligence, but doing nothing to prosecute criminals.

Over a game of pool in one of his gaming palaces, he told me he preferred pool to roulette because it required calculation and training, not just luck. 'Like in life – it's better to work things out. You sleep better.' Unfortunately I beat him, even though it was the first time I had ever played pool. Viktor took the humiliation calmly. We went on to his riding club where he reassured me that he himself did not do murder: 'I don't consider myself a gangster, just a man with a taste for risk and adventure. I'm not into banditry. The "wet stuff" [murder] is for specialists – hired killers.'

Later we went to an airfield. Before he soared into the sky in a little sports plane (like the one he was planning to buy soon, for a quarter of a million dollars) he told me of his dreams. 'Everyone wants to live well. You know, I wouldn't mind becoming president of the country . . .'

33

What Kind of Russia?

BY THE MIDDLE of 1997 Moscow and I were growing a little tired of each other. I had spent almost six years in Russia for the BBC, and almost ten years of my life in all. Yet I was still not much the wiser. Every time I thought we were getting close to some kind of understanding, she would wriggle free of my embrace and appear behind me, with hands on hips and a coquettish smile, saying, 'Uh-uh! Not yet!'

Nothing did more to make me feel the eternal outsider than a brilliant satirical show on NTV, called *Kukly*, or 'Puppets'. Like the British *Spitting Image*, it used grotesque rubber puppets of politicians to poke fun at them. But unlike the British show it did not just do 'sketches' based on the week's events; rather, every episode was a reworking of some fairy tale or children's story or opera or historical event . . . in which the characters were replaced by the politicians. In other words, this was pretty sophisticated: even if I understood the language (mostly) and the political context, I was exposed as an uncomprehending foreigner by all the allusions to obscure stories that Russians learned from their mothers or at school. I would sometimes go to see Garik and Inna the next day for an explanation.

For all my friends, *Kukly* became the centrepiece of Saturday night's viewing – just as the highlight of Sunday's was another NTV programme called *Itogi* ('Conclusions'), a long review of the week's politics that included hard-hitting reports and live interviews conducted by its moustachioed presenter, Yevgeny Kiselyov. Now that the bonanza of buried literature and historical revelations uncovered by *perestroika* was exhausted, these two shows became the new talking points for Russia's chattering classes.

NTV was Russia's first entirely private television network, owned by a media and banking tycoon, Vladimir Gusinsky, who also sponsored theatres and productions at the Moscow Conservatoire. It was much more professional than its rivals, and fearless in its criticism of the Kremlin. But not being state-run didn't make it like the BBC. This was *commercial* television, and its need to drum up revenues went beyond the designated advertising slots. Over coffee in the Radisson Hotel, Kiselyov told me about the pressures television producers faced, constantly being propositioned by businesses or interest groups who were willing to pay big money for an appearance on air. He admitted that NTV was not immune from this: if a business was featured on a news programme it was probably because it had paid for it; even interviews were not done solely on the basis of newsworthiness. If you paid enough, you could guarantee a spot on primetime.

The West fawned on Boris Yeltsin as a great democrat, who had brought freedom and the free market to Russia. It was the Western dream come true: the Soviet Union had shrunk in size and influence to become just Russia, bereft of its outlying colonies; it was militarily weak and could safely be ignored by a rampant United States that truly believed history had 'ended' with the triumph of liberalism; above all, it was a market of 145 million people, sucking in Western products.

Russia had certainly gained both freedom of speech and private property, but in the mid-Nineties the media and big business conspired together to 'save' democracy – by completely undermining it! The problem was that Yeltsin, while feted abroad, had become so unpopular at home that he no longer mustered double digits in opinion polls. There was a strong chance that he would be defeated in the 1996 presidential election by the communist leader, Gennady Zyuganov. The president had become an embarrassment – often appearing drunk in public, scarcely able to speak during interviews, and probably less likely to win an election than the corpse of Lenin, embalmed in its Red Square mausoleum. The prospect of a return to communism terrified not only the West but also Russia's intelligentsia, middle class and, above all, the small number of phenomenally wealthy oligarchs who controlled the economy and media. What happened was a spectacle that made a mockery of democracy. Yeltsin's team effectively handed Russia's great resources – oil, timber, coal, aluminium – to the oligarchs, who returned the favour by bankrolling Yeltsin's campaign and using all their influence, including the TV channels they owned, to transform him from utter loser into miraculous victor.

And there was another actor at work here. A team of American political strategists or 'election gurus', including a man who had worked on

Bill Clinton's own campaign, sat in an office in the President Hotel, across the corridor from Tatyana Dyachenko, Yeltsin's daughter and chief adviser, and brazenly manipulated the election to ensure 'our man' won. (Not that I reported on this at the time, of course. The US mission was entirely secret – the American 'advisers' were not even allowed to leave their hotel for fear of being spotted.) The head of the international election monitoring group later admitted he had his arm twisted to avoid any criticism of what was in fact a completely fraudulent election – in which even the people of Chechnya, still reeling from Yeltsin's hideous war, supposedly voted en masse to keep him in power.

The plan worked faultlessly. Yeltsin duly won the election, which the West deemed 'free and fair'. 'Democracy' was saved. Capitalism was saved. But both were fatally undermined in the nation's eyes. Russians found simple word-play could sum up their views. *Demokratiya* became *Dermokratiya* – incorporating the word *dermo* or shit. And *privatizatsiya* became *prikhvatizatsiya* including the word for 'grab'.

I found myself looking at my beloved Russia in despair as she fell prey to every con trick and sick joke that 'freedom' threw in her path. We filmed a report in a dating agency on Tverskaya, as Gorky Street was once again known, where American men with toupees and personality disorders were allowed to inspect dozens of Russian women and choose a bride. They could even 'try them out' for a few days while in Moscow, before deciding whether to take them back to adorn their sad lives in the States.

Millions of people watched the get-rich-quick squad building their villas and dining in fine restaurants – and fell for criminal schemes that promised them the same. A financial investment firm called MMM ran TV ads featuring a worker named Lyonya Golubkov whose acquisitions (or dreams) progressed, over the weeks, from new boots for his wife, to a fur coat, then furniture, a car, a house, and 'maybe a flat in Paris' – all by virtue of investing in MMM shares, which promised annual returns of 1000 per cent. Sadly, MMM didn't really exist, except as a receptacle for gullible people's money. The astonishing thing was that, even though the ads were basically comedy skits, which portrayed Golubkov as a naïve simpleton verging on complete idiocy, millions and millions of people went out and bought MMM shares, only to find their money disappear in a puff of smoke when the pyramid scheme went bust and its founder, Sergei Mavrodi, was arrested for tax evasion. I filmed them in July 1994, standing outside MMM's office shaking their fists and blaming . . . no, not the crook who ran the company, but the government, which had promised them a glorious capitalist future and – once again – let them down.

Every quack and charlatan rushed in to fill the space vacated, I suppose, by Marxism-Leninism. If 'scientific communism' and 'dialectical materialism' no longer seemed to provide the answers, and capitalism turned out to be a chimera, who could one believe? Let's see now, how about that chap who came on television and merely by moving his lips could 'energise' a jar of water that you placed in front of the set, so that it could cure your illnesses? That was Allan Chumak. Anatoly Kashpirovsky was even better, because you didn't need the jar of water: he just spoke to you from the screen – and *ten million* viewers were cured during his first six programmes, can you imagine that? Cured of common sense, maybe.

Chumak and Kashpirovsky won devotees in inverse proportion to the Communist Party, reaching their peak just as the USSR collapsed. By the mid-Nineties there were so many healers around it was a wonder anyone still needed a hospital. I went to see Anjelika Effi, a 'third-generation Russian witch' (and host of 'Anjelika Effi's World of Wonders' on TV) at her downtown white magic salon. Having a cameraman by my side, my appointment didn't cost anything; otherwise it would have been 255 US dollars just for a twenty-minute consultation. There were supplements for specific services: bringing back an estranged husband or wife cost 550, a 'simple spell' cost 155, and a full-blown correction of the karma would set you back 1,000 dollars. The salon looked like a high-class doctor's surgery, with receptionists making appointments and taking your dollars, and a cabinet of amulets and talismans to spend your cash on once your karma was fixed. Some of the clients in the plush waiting room vouchsafed their problems to me.

'I've had the evil eye put on me,' said one lady, carefully avoiding mine.

A man told me people mostly came to Anjelika when they had tried and failed to solve their problems elsewhere. 'Some might have sexual problems, things like that. Not me, I mean . . .'

Anjelika herself, a large woman with backcombed hair and a dress covered with symbols of wizardry, spoke to me from behind her desk, which was decorated with orbs and scarabs engraved with hieroglyphs. 'Stop anyone in the street and ask them whether back in Soviet days they used to go to old women who cast spells or lifted curses,' she said.

'Everyone will tell you, they existed even then.' It's just that I've worked out how to make a bloody fortune from it, she might have added.

There was only one soothsayer who merited serious attention – Alexander Solzhenitsyn. The bearded sage of Vermont, as he became known after 20 years in exile, finally returned home in the summer of 1994. He had been the darling of the West in communist days – when his three-volume history of the Gulag won him the Nobel Prize and his fierce criticism of Soviet power made him a hero. He turned out to be just as hostile to Western society's consumerism and decadence, however, and was sickened by the advance of precisely those Western values in post-communist Russia. He believed Russia had its own, deeper values, and was given his own fifteen-minute slot on television to preach them. His ratings plummeted as he ranted like John Knox at the pulpit, and the show was soon taken off air. Only when Vladimir Putin came along did Solzhenitsyn finally find a leader, and policies, he could admire – which put him even more at odds with his one-time supporters in the West.

It was definitely time for me to go. I was feeling dissatisfied both with Russia and with the job I was doing. The BBC's interest in what was going on was beginning to flag. I seemed to spend an inordinate amount of time reporting on Boris Yeltsin's health and drunkenness, and knew more about heart surgery than I did about the Kremlin by the time he underwent his quintuple bypass operation in November 1996.

Russia was changing in so many ways, not all for the better. Even kitchen-table conversations had taken on a new character. People talked about money now, and what they could buy; holidays, a new bar that had opened up, finding a better job, repairing the flat. The old intellectual chat seemed to be disappearing. Oh God – it was the worst of all outcomes! Russians were becoming more like us!

My friend Varya showed me her seven-year-old son's school note-book, in which he had drawn dollar exchange rates going up and down, and arrows showing taxes going up. His teacher asked him what he was worried about, and he replied: 'Pensions not being paid.'

In the summer of 1997 I made a nostalgic trip down to Krasnodar, to see whether I could track down any of the people I had met on my first trip to Russia. I couldn't, but I did meet friends of friends – Sasha and Sveta, who had also been students back in the Seventies and now ran a small business. They took me to a new private restaurant, and then we took a trolleybus to the university, picking up a third friend – Yuri, a local journalist – on the way. He happened to have a bottle of vodka and some plastic cups with him. Some things didn't change! It was dark now, and we crept, like students again, into a park and found a bench under some chestnut trees. The first mosquitoes of the summer were buzzing around. I asked Yuri what he missed from the old days.

'You know,' he said, 'it was more humane then. People were less self-centred. There was more of a sense of being together, being part of a collective. Nowadays we've become disunited – less sociable.'

Then Sveta said something that made me feel sad, for the loss of something that really had made Soviet society very special. 'We don't even socialise the way we used to. We often used to get together in the evenings at each other's apartments. We'd have a bite to eat – nothing elaborate – maybe sing songs, drink a bit . . . and just talk, for hours and hours . . .'

'Why don't you do that now?' I asked.

The three pondered their plastic cups.

'We're all too busy with our own lives,' said Sveta.

'It's different now,' said Sasha, her husband. 'You have to work hard to get on. There's just less time for meeting friends.'

'Most people are preoccupied with getting by in life,' said Yuri. 'How can you philosophise when you don't know where your next meal is coming from? And there's another thing . . . There's such a gap now in wealth, many people are embarrassed to have old friends round – you never know how they're going to judge you . . .'

Everybody was asking themselves where Russia was headed. But in reality she was going nowhere, because – as John Lennon might have put it – how could she go forward when she didn't know which way she was facing?

It was Yegor Gaidar who had hinted at the disturbing similarities with Weimar. It wasn't just the economic situation – hyperinflation, unemployment, impoverishment. There was also Russia's loss of great power status, and the demoralisation that caused. American leaders just would not shut up about having 'won the Cold War' – which implied to every Russian that they 'lost' it. Just as Germany was humiliated by the Versailles Agreement, so Russia felt humiliated by her 'defeat' – a feeling exacerbated by NATO's consolidation of every other country in Europe into an alliance against Russia.

Russia had lost a quarter of its territory, not just the countries grabbed by Stalin (the three Baltic states), but territories that had been part of Russia since Tsarist times. The end of the USSR was perceived by Russians not as the end of 'empire' in the sense of losing some distant colonies, but precisely in the way the English (and most Scots and Welsh) would perceive the sudden break-up of the UK – with all the chaos that would entail for families, trade and centuries-old cultural links. What made it worse was that about 25 million Russians who had lived in other republics were now stranded 'abroad'. Foreigners! Crimea – the jewel of Russia, where everyone loved to take their summer holidays, where Chekhov had lived, was now in Ukraine! How stupid was that, people asked? No one in Yalta even spoke Ukrainian! It was a fluke, an administrative error – but Russia was too weak to challenge it.

This swamp of disquietude was a breeding ground for insect-life – ultranationalists, neo-communists, populists and demagogues. Democracy itself was weak: parliament was fragmented among many small, squabbling parties, and the new Constitution bestowed sweeping powers on the president – the current one and whoever would come after him.

After decades of manipulation and social engineering, Russia didn't even know who she really was. People were searching for a national identity, a sense of purpose, a destiny, a redefinition of the nation. I was asked to take part in a discussion on Russian television about 'The Russian Idea'. For an hour the participants argued and fretted about the fate of their country. It looked like a scene from a nineteenth-century Russian novel – a gathering of earnest intellectuals: almost all the men had beards – some goatees, some neatly trimmed like Tsar Nicholas the Second's, some long and Tolstoyan, one was positively Aristotelian, and two had strange necklaces of fuzz strung under their chins from earlobe to earlobe. The hair-styles cast them as latter-day Dostoyevskys and Gogols. The captions on screen identified them variously as journalists, philosophers, priests and 'people's artists'.

My modest contribution to the debate was to say that looking for a national idea was a pretty strange thing to be doing in the first place. I seem to remember saying that nations were what they were, defined by a variety of historical, cultural and linguistic influences, and there wasn't a lot one could do to change that. And anyway, why should one want to? The new Russia, I suggested, would emerge naturally. To try to invent – artificially – a 'Russian Idea' – was extremely odd. No other country bothered ...

Well, I was promptly told, what other countries did was their business. I came under particularly vehement attack from the writer Eduard Limonov – who, I should point out, was a self-confessed admirer of Hitler and Stalin, advocated a new Iron Curtain to keep all foreign goods out of Russia, and wanted to ban abortions to boost the size of the Russian nation. Otherwise he was a very reasonable fellow. He objected to the very idea of a foreigner daring to pontificate about the Russian Idea – and I suppose he had a point. It was up to Russians to find a dream to follow.

I couldn't help feeling that there were at least a few things that could safely be imported from the West without jeopardising the uniqueness of the Russian soul. The Protestant work ethic, for instance, which was still sorely lacking, five years into the rebirth of capitalism. I went for a haircut in one of Moscow's top hotels, the Metropol, thinking they would do a speedy job there. Three barbers were lolling around in chairs. They ignored me, so I asked if I could have my hair cut. One of them stirred himself to inquire whether I had an appointment. 'No,' I said, 'I was hoping you could just do it now.'

'We're busy,' came the reply.

I looked around the room, wondering if some customers were perhaps lurking in corners I couldn't see. 'It wouldn't take . . . long . . .' I began to plead.

'You need an appointment,' they said. Clearly the profit motive meant nothing here, never mind the Protestant work ethic.

'So can I make an appointment then, please?' I said.

'If you *want*,' one them said, like Basil Fawlty.

'Maybe this afternoon,' I said.

'*We* don't make the appointments,' said one of the barbers. 'You have to go to the office.'

I was about to ask where the office was when another barber actually said something rather helpful. 'It's closed,' he said.

I decided perhaps my hair wasn't that long after all.

I paid a visit to Mikhail Shatrov, the playwright who had been at the forefront of *perestroika*'s rewriting of Soviet history, to see what he made of the new Russia and where it was going. Astonishingly, he didn't really care. Sitting in a plush Western-style office, he was writing neither plays nor political speeches. 'I've left public life altogether,' he told me. 'I don't want to take part in it: it's just a stream of words and demagogy. Of course I wanted to change things, but I failed. What we dreamed of in the *perestroika* days has not come about. They've thrown the baby out with the bath-water.' (The baby, he meant, was socialism, in some improved, humane form.)

Shatrov was now a businessman, president of a multi-million-dollar enterprise, in charge of a project that would regenerate a piece of inner-city wasteland and give Moscow a new complex of theatres, concert halls, exhibition rooms, restaurants and offices, to be known as the Russian Cultural Centre. His job involved procuring credits, finding sponsors, and coordinating the work of designers and builders for the project. This, he said – with a touch of sadness that doubtless was compensated for by his bank balance – would be his memorial, not the political works of theatre to which he devoted all of his creative life.

Shatrov turned up late for our meeting, and while waiting for him I browsed through the latest issue of *Moscow News*, once the flower of *glasnost*. In it I found an article by another playwright, Alexander Gelman. 'We were waiting for springtime,' he moaned, 'and instead there came autumn. I wrote one page, then tore it up; wrote another, tore it up too. I'll probably tear this one up as well!' Gelman, like Shatrov, had been a mover and shaker under Gorbachev. His plays were staged at the Edinburgh Festival in those days when everything Russian seemed so wonderfully exciting. Now, he talked like the archetypal 'superfluous man' – a Chekhovian ditherer, beating his breast in despair, wishing he could change things, but powerless to do so. 'We had hoped that freedom would be joyful and bright,' he wrote, 'but it turned out to be painful, brainless and bloody. The freedom of evil is blooming, the freedom of goodness is vegetating. We hoped that new, marvellous people would come, and rebuild our country in a new, rational way. But the people who came were no good: one was too cunning, the next clapped-out, the third smart but too submissive, the fourth capable but a misanthropist, and so on and so forth . . .'

So did the intelligentsia have no say in Russia's future? Before I left Moscow, I had to make a very belated call on one of my heroes – a man I had never met but whose songs had taught me so much about the Russian language, and the Russian heart – Bulat Okudzhava.

He was exactly as I expected – except older and frailer. He was 73 and had spent most of the past year in hospital with breathing problems. (He passed away only a month after we met.) His flat was like that of every Russian intellectual: lined with books and paintings, and manuscripts scattered on occasional tables, every scrap of wall-space filled with higgledy-piggledy framed photographs of family and friends.

'I remember the 20th Communist Party congress in 1956,' he said, 'when Stalin's personality cult was exposed in Khrushchev's famous secret speech. There was euphoria among the intelligentsia, and we thought everything would change – there would be a completely new life now. Two years later we realised we'd been mistaken. Thirty years later Gorbachev came along and there was *perestroika*. Again we thought: tomorrow there will be democracy and everything will be marvellous. Nothing happened, and the euphoria passed. You see, we don't learn.'

Okudzhava didn't blame Boris Yeltsin, though, for the failure of democracy, nor Gorbachev. 'Russia's misfortune,' he said, 'is not due to having some stupid guy at the top who can't run the place. No, the misfortune is in Russia itself.' And then he gave me a little Russian lesson, explaining the difference between two words that both mean 'freedom': *svoboda* and *volya*. 'Such was its fate and history,' he said, 'that Russia never knew what *svoboda* was; it knew what *volya* was – the complete freedom to do whatever you like; whereas *svoboda* means "do what you want but obey the laws" . . . and in Russia people have never liked laws, never respected them. In Russia they never respected the individual.'

And intellectuals – he went on – were respected even less than any other individuals, which was why after their brief tilting at windmills under Gorbachev they had now gone back into hibernation. Under *perestroika*, he said, the intelligentsia had all the bright ideas: they went out and made speeches, thinking: right, I'll tell them, people will understand, we can *change things*. But they just got kicked in the face – by the people, and by the authorities. So now they had gone back to their own business, of being *intelligenty*.

We sipped tea from china cups, and I looked longingly at Okudzhava's guitar, which was propped against a wall, and wondered fleetingly if I should play him one of his songs. Instead, I asked whether he was disappointed in Yeltsin.

'No . . . he has weaknesses and virtues. He's an ordinary person like the rest of us, his psychology's the same . . . so what's the point of crying, "Yeltsin's bad"? What are the rest of us?'

So where, for God's sake, was Russia going?

'Russia has a penchant for authoritarianism, for strong power. It's our slave psychology, it's in our genes, transmitted from generation to generation. A man might drive a Mercedes, and put on modern clothes, but in his soul he's a slave, and doesn't even understand that's what he is. He has the desire to subjugate himself, to see a god above him . . . We'll see what happens.'

We shook hands warmly. His mind was still grappling with my question as we walked to the door; you could see the shadows flitting over his deeply lined face.

'You know,' he said, 'Russians didn't know what freedom was when we were given it, or how to use it. Such people need to be kept on a tight rein. Otherwise they'll destroy everything.'

34

Watching from a Distance

BRUSSELS, I CONFESS, had never really come-hithered me the way Moscow had. Midday briefings at the European Commission weren't at the top of my foreign correspondent's bucket list. But it was there that the family moved at the start of 1998, when I was appointed BBC Europe Correspondent, and to my surprise I became nerdily obsessed with the minutiae of European Union decision-making, and determined to fulfil the mission given me at my job interview – to 'explain Brussels'. Unfortunately the people who appointed me with that lofty aim were not the same people who edited the news programmes, and the latter had little interest in spoiling their shows with anything that might help people understand even the most basic facts about the EU's legislative system. They mostly wanted us to follow up all the tedious hyperbole in the press about 'interfering' Brussels regulations and decisions taken by 'unelected' Eurocrats – ignoring the inconvenient truth that the European Commission merely proposes laws, whereas they are *passed* by elected governments and members of the European Parliament. They loved it when I chased the French commissioner, Edith Cresson, down a corridor hurling accusations of fraud and nepotism at her, but when I suggested covering the European Parliament's four-day sessions each month, during the *Today* programme's 'Yesterday in Parliament' slot, they looked at me as though I'd been struck down by some awful euro-sickness that had clouded my vision of what public service broadcasting was.

The result of the British media's disregard for the European political process was there for all to see when Britain voted to leave the EU in June 2016. Why would anyone want to stay in a political system whose workings were a total mystery?

Still, it was an exciting time. I took up the job eight months after Tony Blair was elected as British prime minister, and soon all of the major European countries had centre-left governments, heralding, we thought, a new happy-ever-after 'Third Way' in politics. Instead, I soon found myself covering the rise of neo-fascists in Austria and the Netherlands. A Europe correspondent's job also entailed covering earthquakes, avalanches, school shootings, cable-car disasters, football hooliganism, mad cow disease, and whatever other bit of nastiness God chose to bestow on the continent.

I loved the unpredictability of it all, though it was certainly a surprise to emerge from a debate about phthalates in the Strasbourg parliament one evening to be called by the foreign editor and asked not to go back to Brussels but to fly instead to the other side of the Earth, to cover the bloody end of Indonesia's occupation of East Timor. Towards the end of 2001 I went twice to northern Afghanistan at the start of America's 'war on terror'. I can't deny that I relished the return to news that didn't involve qualified majority voting – though flying back to Brussels from a war zone was even harder than returning to Moscow from Grozny. I came home from Afghanistan one Saturday evening in December and went with my wife, more or less straight from the airport, to a dinner-dance at the British school, where people naturally were all agog at what I had been doing. 'Gosh, you're just back? What was it like there?' they asked me. Of course, it would have been nice to tell them a few tales of journalistic derring-do – but I hadn't done any derring, and all I could think was that two days earlier I had almost tripped over two dead Taliban fighters whose bodies were slumped around the base of a lamp-post on a street in Qala-i-Jangi, their faces the colour and texture of the foie-gras on the table. How could you talk about that, in a room full of people enjoying a Christmas ball?

I even felt myself getting angry, to be back in the comfort and safety of a European city. I found it hard to concentrate on conversations about 'ordinary' things – pension plans, the school Christmas concert, or where to buy the best Flemish cheese. My mind was still shackled to the poor, dispossessed people of Chechnya or Afghanistan – places where human life was an afterthought, where people convulsed by unspeakable horrors grabbed your sleeve and dissolved into tears. It was in those dark places that the human spirit shone most brightly.

My head was swimming with images of Chechnya – women and babies huddled in dark cellars while bombs crashed above them, open trucks of villagers escaping with a little bag of possessions, others stumbling around in rubble, trying to cope with the fact that they had just lost every single thing they ever owned. Several years after I saw her I was still thinking of a ten-year-old girl called Alekhan (maybe it was worse that I knew her name, and that she was the same age as my son, Ewan). We filmed her being carried across a half-destroyed bridge, with Grozny in flames behind her. She had been hit by a shell and was concussed and moaning with pain. I helped her mother carry her to a car that took her away somewhere that could provide medical aid. But I doubt that there was any such place.

It occurred to me that I might be suffering from post-traumatic stress disorder. I emailed a new unit the BBC had set up to help journalists who might be traumatised . . . but they didn't reply – so I did what most journalists do. Bottled it up.

None of this squashed the Russia bug, and luckily the foreign desk sent me back to Moscow several times during my six years as Europe correspondent. And guess who I met on one of those trips?

It was October 1999, and I was back in Chechnya, which had become a lawless, semi-independent state since the rebels forced out the mighty Russian army back in 1996. I had sympathised with their cause then, but now they had gone crazy, and the republic had become a no-go area for foreigners after Red Cross workers and others were kidnapped and murdered. In the autumn of 1999 a series of devastating bomb attacks inside Russia were blamed on the Chechens, and Moscow seized the chance to launch a second war, even more merciless than the first, to bring the place back under control. I flew on a Russian military helicopter to a base in Znamenskoye. President Yeltsin had recently appointed a new prime minister, who flew in on a separate helicopter, and came to talk to our little group of journalists. He was wearing a cream polo-neck sweater and a tweed jacket, as though he was off for drinks at the golf club, and marched in with a jaunty, lopsided swagger, evidently pleased with a recent hole-in-one at the eighteenth.

Vladimir Putin was an unknown quantity – apart from one humungous quantity that everyone knew about, which was that he had spent his entire career in the KGB, before hanging around in the shadows in St Petersburg in the early Nineties, and then rising quietly to the top of the Kremlin, only breaking cover in 1999 when Yeltsin officially appointed him as prime minister and his chosen successor. Why Yeltsin did this, no one could quite fathom, though there was a little clue in the fact that Putin had just helped the president's family avoid prosecution. Russia's prosecutor general, Yuri Skuratov, who was investigating a massive

corruption scandal involving the Yeltsin family, was filmed by the Federal
Security Service (aka KGB) with two prostitutes. The FSB was headed
at the time by Putin, who made sure the film was shown on television,
thus destroying Skuratov's career and his attempts to compromise the
Yeltsin family.

Putin loved to play the tough guy. He promised to 'liquidate' the
terrorists, even if he had to swat them 'in the shithouse'. So when I
found myself face to face with him in Chechnya I asked him how he
could retake the shithouse of Grozny from the terrorists without killing
thousands of civilians at the same time. He looked at me with a hint of
recognition, I thought (could he really be the guy who tried to arrest
me in Leningrad all those years ago?), and promised that no civilians
would suffer. So I came back with a second question: 'You mean you'll
wait till all the civilians have fled, and *then* flatten it?' A little smile
played on his lips: 'I'll . . . discuss that with you . . . separately,' he said.
Discuss? With me? Separately? What did that mean? His smile was
almost angelic. Who would have guessed that this dapper little man
from the golf club was about to unleash a war of such ferocity that tens
of thousands of civilians would perish in Chechnya over the next few
years, as well as hundreds more in retaliatory terrorist attacks on
Moscow and other Russian cities?

A few months later I was back in Russia for the presidential election,
at which Putin's triumph was guaranteed, thanks again to the efforts of
oligarchs and their media toys. I went to St Petersburg to investigate his
childhood. I visited the tenement where Putin grew up with his parents
in one room of a communal flat, and got into fights with other boys in
the courtyard. His old history teacher recalled his fascination as a boy
for politics and heroic espionage stories. A former classmate told me how
the young Volodya, for a dare, had climbed up to a fifth-storey school
balcony and hung there from the railing. From stunt man to strong
man – the promises he made now were just what most Russians, after
the chaos of the Yeltsin years, were longing for: stability, restoration of
Russia's pride and place in the world. He would put a stop to the rot.

But by the time of my next trip, in July 2000, just three months into
his presidency, it looked like they could be getting more than they
bargained for. 'Mr Putin's devotion to democracy is uncertain,' I
reported. He was pushing through legislation that would allow him to
sack elected members of Russia's 'senate', and had appointed seven
regional governors, mostly from the KGB and military, as his enforcers

in the country. A plaque commemorating Putin's old KGB boss, Yuri Andropov, was back on the wall of the Lubyanka. And Stalin's name had been sneaked onto a new plaque in the Kremlin too. Paramilitaries had recently arrested Vladimir Gusinsky, the owner of the most critical television station, NTV. In his first 'state of the nation' speech Putin demanded a strong state, to enforce the rule of law, crack down on crime and corruption, and unify the country. He spoke up for the free market, and for freedom of speech . . . but two years later he would force NTV to drop its hilarious puppet show, *Kukly*, because he couldn't stand the fun it poked at him. That single act of vanity spoke volumes about his personality, just as the imprisonment of the outspoken oil tycoon Mikhail Khodorkovsky was an early omen of how he would deal with his political opponents.

Given what did come – Putin's authoritarian rule, his crackdown on human rights and backsliding on democracy – I am often asked how it could have happened that I ended up, from 2006, working for three years as a media consultant to his press secretary. Indeed, an old journalist friend from Moscow looked at me with something close to disgust at a presentation of my last book, *The Strongman*, and blurted out: 'How *could* you do that?' This begged two questions: what did I actually *do* – and I'll get to that a few pages from here; and, before that, how did I end up doing it in the first place. Unfortunately the only way I can explain this weird aberration in my career is by describing – as briefly as I can, because it's rather painful – some of the events that led up to it.

The writer Clive James wrote, about himself: 'Excessive conceit and deficient self-esteem are often aspects of each other.' So it was for me, as I blundered blithely through a prospering career, damned pleased with myself but also haunted by the fear that I wasn't really good enough for it, and thus slowly but surely preparing the ground for its humbling demise.

As noted at several junctures in this book, my career as a journalist – once I got past the profession's initial reluctance to let me in at all – had succeeded without much effort or forward planning. New jobs fell into my lap, often just as the last one was coming to an end. Even the black cloud that swirled above me when I was turfed out of the USSR in 1989 had a series of East European revolutions tucked away in its lining, keeping me fruitfully and joyfully employed for the next year. Not any more – and when it came to making my own decisions I proved ridiculously bad at it!

I was never much good at schmoozing important people, and had sailed through my dozen or so years as a BBC foreign correspondent without even being sycophantic to the corporation's bosses, indeed despite sometimes being the opposite. I was taken aback one day when my foreign editor, Vin Ray, prefaced some remark to me with the words: 'I know you don't think I'm any good at my job, but . . .' This shocked me, because I actually thought he was brilliant at his job – I just didn't understand it very well, and in particular I didn't appreciate why the BBC had begun to throw enormous amounts of money at projects that in my view got in the way of good news reporting. Vin was carefully preparing the ground for the advent of 24-hour news channels and bi-medial, multi-skilled reporting (which needed individuals who unlike me were capable of writing, filming, editing, producing and brushing their teeth, all at the same time – while also being live on air, on TV and radio, all day long). That obviously required huge investments – in new technology, in bureau chiefs to manage the complex new operations, in people who were willing to move with the tide. I guess he saw the future, and I didn't. Anyway, the future soon saw me coming – the brontosaurus of journalism crawling out of a swamp.

The whole direction of TV news was getting me down. What I had loved about the job was the human side – getting out and meeting ordinary people, spending an entire day, or even several days, gathering material for a crafted, original package. Now the stress was more and more on instant, live reporting. The new 24-hour news channel was voracious. You could spend an entire day meeting no one at all, just standing in front of a camera saying the same thing over and over for different bulletins, most of it regurgitated from wire reports. Sometimes a producer in London would whisper a line from Reuters in your earpiece, just as you went on air – and that would be your new 'line' for that hour, even though you hadn't even had a chance to check it out. 'So what's the reaction been to this in Brussels, Angus?' they would ask. 'I don't bloody know, I've been standing here all bloody day,' I wouldn't answer.

Working in television is a fickle business. One day your face doesn't fit any more – and not just if you're a woman. Suddenly, I found myself being dropped from the main news programmes, and not being sent to cover stories that were on my 'patch'. One editor on the *Six O'Clock News* replaced me several times, at the last minute, with a younger (blonde, female) correspondent. My confidence stumbled. I began to dry up sometimes during live interviews, forgetting my train of thought.

For four years based in Brussels, during which my bosses had dangled various possible future postings in front of me – Delhi, Washington, Middle East – I assumed I would remain in the corporation until I retired. But when my time in Brussels came to an end, and no specific new job was offered, I took a fateful decision to stay in Brussels and go freelance. I negotiated a part-time contract as BBC Scotland's Europe Correspondent, but had to find a huge amount of other work to replace the missing income. My plan to make award-winning documentaries received a polite smile in the BBC's documentaries department. I found myself doing things that were anathema to me as a journalist, such as media training – which amounts to teaching people how to evade journalists' questions.

I tried, and failed, to convince myself that being BBC Scotland's Europe Correspondent was 'a great new opportunity' rather than a demotion – especially when it turned out that while they loved the idea of having their own man in Brussels, they didn't really care much about having him on air. In the next two years I only did a handful of TV reports, and initial interest on radio dwindled to 'Can you do us a funny review of what's in Europe's papers tomorrow morning?'

In short, I'd left a well-paid, permanent, high-profile staff job at the BBC, and found myself flapping like a haddock on the deck of a trawler. The simile comes to mind because one of the few jobs that was guaranteed for me was the one no one else wanted – sitting through an all-night council session every December to report on the EU's exciting fisheries quotas. 'Well, Sophie, I can tell you that in the last few minutes – this is news just in that I can break to you – what we're hearing is that total allowable catches for *psetta maxima* and *sprattus sprattus* (that's turbot and sprats to likes of you and me, Sophie) are to be *increased*. Quite a surprise development, that. But there's good news for sand eels in the Skaggerak – those pesky Danes will be catching less of them this year. Pelagics are up this year, anchovies down. Jellyfish floating on the top. As for haddock, well, I plan to go and eat a full quota, Sophie, battered, fried and with chips, just as soon as I get away from this effing microphone . . .'

It would have driven a lesser man than me to drink and depression – and unfortunately I was a much lesser man than me. I shrivelled up like a potted plant without water, and for six whole months I did almost nothing except stare mindlessly out of the window into our beautiful Belgian garden, slug red wine, contemplate the throw-weight of trucks at busy road junctions, and write songs. One of them was about Alekhan, the little Chechen girl we filmed because she was dying. When a psychiatrist tested me for depression, I scored top marks.

That was the situation in March 2006, when I got a call from two former journalist colleagues who now ran a Brussels PR company, GPlus. Together with a New York firm, Ketchum, they had just secured a phenomenally lucrative nine-month contract with the Kremlin's press office – and had no one on their staff who spoke Russian, knew about Russian politics, and also knew about the media. They wondered if I happened to know anyone like that. If I am being honest, Russia hadn't even loomed small in my befogged mind for at least a year, and I was only dimly aware of what was happening there. But the prospect of using my skills and thinking about Russia again, not to mention the mere fact that someone out there actually needed my experience, was irresistible. I warned them I knew nothing whatsoever about PR, but they assured me there was nothing to it. They offered me the same salary as I had once been on at the BBC. How could I refuse?

It certainly wasn't a future I had ever imagined for myself, and I didn't like the idea of it. But if I tried hard, I could persuade myself there was a positive side to it: if I was going to sell my soul to the devil, I could at least use the time to find out what the devil was like.

35

In the Kremlin

STAND ON RED Square, in the heart of Moscow, and Russia's history and national character leap out at you from every stone and hue. Those soldierly ranks of granite cobbles, laid to withstand ferocious winters, and also the grind of tank-tracks during military parades. Saint Basil's cathedral, with its crazy, spinning-top domes – a kind of frenzied, idiotic beauty, a unique, beguiling work of art created for the satisfaction of one of Russia's cruellest tyrants, Ivan the Terrible. Lenin's mausoleum, carefully preserving the corpse of an old and discredited ideology, visited by the curious and the still faithful. Just behind it, a city-centre graveyard for communist dictators. And the great secretive fortress itself, the Kremlin, with its Orthodox churches and classical European palaces, surrounded by enormous dark-red walls – beautiful, crenellated and impenetrable, forever shielding the workings of power from the eyes of Russians and foreigners. The twenty exotic towers along the Kremlin wall were all designed by Italian architects over five hundred years ago, but were modified – Russianised – over the succeeding centuries. Here is all you need to know, really: five centuries of beauty, creativity, faith, oppression and resilience, in one quick *tour d'horizon*.

Tourists enter the grounds of the Kremlin, to see its splendid museums and churches, from the opposite side. We went in through the tradesman's entrance, the Spassky Gate, next to St Basil's, where a guard ran his finger down a typed list of approved visitors to the Presidential Administration. Suddenly we were inside that red-brick wall, walking along the space between it and the first Kremlin office building – it's in that claustrophobic alleyway that you suddenly experience the forbidding height of those walls that have protected the Kremlin for centuries. Security at the entrance was as tight as you would expect – but inside, everything was disappointingly drab. There was more opulence on the tourist side of the Kremlin than in this office building. The carpet runners looked as if they had not been changed since communist days, the paintwork on the skirting boards was chipped, and the smell of boiled cabbage wafted from some hidden canteen; the toilets were like those I remembered at Progress Publishers thirty years ago – smelly, yellow-stained urinals and the stink of stubbed-out cigarettes from ashtrays next to the cracked sinks. We were squashed into a tiny lift and taken up to the third floor, told to wait for a few minutes in an anteroom . . . and then entered the office of Putin's spokesman, Dmitry Peskov.

Dmitry, and his deputy, Alex Smirnov, were our points of contact in the Kremlin – both tall men, fair-haired, confident, fluent in English, Dmitry sporting a sandy moustache and the perfect manners of an experienced diplomat (which is what he was before becoming Kremlin spokesman). On my first visit to Dmitry's office, I was part of a group of senior Ketchum and GPlus executives, keen to hear exactly what he hoped we could do for them, beyond the broad goal of 'improving Russia's image'. He sat us around a long conference table, and I surveyed his office while his secretary brought in black tea in china cups, and little hard biscuits. His windows looked out across the Kremlin ramparts to Red Square. The wood-panelled room was decorated with a big Russian flag and a map of the country, little jokey posters on the walls, and a wooden club: 'I need it sometimes to deal with journalists,' he joked. He had about a dozen telephones, on and beside his big desk, apparently a different one for everyone he might wish to call – plus one with no dial, which I guessed must be a hotline to somebody important. The array of old-fashioned telephones turned out, however, to be a low-tech anomaly in Dmitry's life. Both he and Alex were obsessed with Apple products, and upgraded to every latest iPhone, iPad and MacBook the moment they appeared.

Russia held the presidency of the G8 group of leading industrialised nations during 2006, and Dmitry made it clear that this was to be the main focus of our work – or at least its starting point. 'We want the presidency to be a big success. This is what the Boss wants,' he said. The 'priorities' of Russia's presidency, he said, were 'international energy security, the struggle with infectious diseases, and educa-tion' . . . but it soon became clear that this was only the formal agenda. They were more worried about the reluctance of foreign investors to come to Russia, and . . . 'You know, people in the West don't understand us . . . The things they say about us, well, it's crazy.' Dmitry raised his shoulders and his eyebrows simultaneously, in a gesture I would see again and again – his little round eyes so incredulous at the West's obtuseness, they almost popped out of his head.

The West was indeed failing to 'understand' Russia at that point. It wasn't just the steady rollback on human rights and democracy in Putin's first six years: 2006 had started with Russia cutting off gas supplies to Ukraine – supposedly because of non-payment, but also clearly in retaliation for Kiev's increasingly anti-Russian stance since the Orange Revolution in 2004. In retrospect I wondered if the main reason they took on a Western consortium to do their PR for them was because their own 'political technologists', as they called them, had been completely outshone by the Americans during the Orange Revolution.

I came to this as a complete novice. My entire experience of PR until then had amounted to deleting annoying emails with a well-practised mouse-click and a muttered curse. Soon I would find myself sending journalists emails with a well-practised click and a muttered curse. My views on PR should certainly be taken with a large pinch of salt, tainted as they are by three years of wishing I was doing something else, but I'm afraid I saw little to change my perception that it was all charlatanism. Almost everybody I worked with, in the GPlus team in Brussels and Ketchum in New York, was absolutely charming – all extremely intelligent, diligent, dedicated individuals, with whom it was a delight to work. But why, oh why, did they do this? All I could think, through three years of PR nonsense, was: what a waste of talent!

GPlus essentially did two types of work. It had a very knowledgeable group of specialists in European affairs, who advised clients about changing or upcoming EU legislation and how it would affect them. For any company unable to afford its own specialist EU unit, this advice must be invaluable. GPlus also carried out more conventional public relations – media training, events and 'communications strategies' for clients whose coffers were bigger than their brains.

The general concept of PR was explained to me with these words: 'It's just a case of holding the client's hand. Reassurance. Manage their expectations . . .' That explained nothing, but it only took me a few weeks to understand that it really was as simple as that. The chief task of a PR company is not to promote the client, but to promote itself in the eyes of the client. For that reason, a low-risk strategy is essential – no big promises, just a steady, reassuring stream of paperwork that convinces the client you are working very hard for them. And if, at the end of a year, there have been no terrible headlines – which, after all, there *could* have been! – then you have been successful, and (so long as you can convince them that many potential pitfalls still lie ahead) you can hope to renew the contract for another year. It became clear to me from early on that the main concern for GPlus and Ketchum was to win a longer contract at the end of 2006. For that reason their advice contained nothing that might offend the Kremlin. It was like a teacher praising a useless or disruptive child to his parents so as not to hurt their feelings, pointing out the 'strong points' instead of the faults.

The power of a PR company's *self*-promotion is quite astonishing, as became clear when the head of GPlus appeared in a list of the thirty most influential people in the EU. The *Financial Times* named him as one of the 'prime influencers of policy and legislation in Brussels'. I couldn't for the life of me think of a single thing he had ever influenced, other perhaps than the choice of restaurant for a splendid lunch, or the size of the consultancy fee extracted from the Kremlin. The paper described him as 'efficient, straight-talking and well-connected' – and I couldn't agree more. I would even add: affable, witty, self-made, clever, and such a thoroughly nice chap that he wouldn't even be offended by what I am writing here. But influential? As proof of his 'influence' the *FT* cited the fact that his company was 'famously hired to cover Russia's priorities during the country's 2006 G8 presidency'. Famously, indeed. And a fat lot of good his influence did there! Over the next few years Russia's international reputation slumped from merely execrable to satanic. It did however, make his company extremely profitable. Which is, after all, the whole point of PR.

We returned from Moscow to our offices in Brussels and New York, and set about preparing 'strategy documents' and media analyses which, being written by transatlantic committee, ended up like instructions for a washing machine. Much of the work involved preparing a daily press review – a massive compilation of everything printed in the Western media about Russia each day, together with a covering note summarising the issues and, if necessary, pointing out any 'action' that required to be taken. It was also our job to prepare briefing notes for Russian ministers who were travelling abroad or planning to give a news conference. Here, Dmitry's brief was baffling, because we were never informed in advance of any Russian policy or initiative. When we asked what 'line' the minister wished to take, Dmitry would tell us just to write what *we* thought he should say. This was like writing an instruction manual without knowing whether it was for a washing machine or a refrigerator, and needless to say, ministers rarely if ever used a single word we suggested. Some, such as the formidable foreign minister, Sergei Lavrov, were positively dismissive of our efforts: he certainly didn't require any foreign *piarshchik* to prompt him! We did draft some op-ed articles for the Western press, but again, these were usually radically rewritten, and our job mainly came down to placing the pieces in a newspaper. Lavrov, incidentally, was the coolest of characters, the most unflappable diplomat I ever met. I once set up a telephone interview for him at a summit, which he did from the Soviet delegation's room, where he first poured himself a large whisky from a decanter (while cracking jokes about 'Ketchup' as he called Ketchum), then slumped into a comfortable armchair and expounded Russian policy in perfect English for half an hour, live on air with some radio station.

On one visit to St Petersburg Alex took a Ketchum colleague and myself aside and told us directly that we should effectively be telling journalists what to write – and paying newspapers to print more flattering stories. 'We know,' he said, 'how political technology works. We need you to do this.' We explained that in the West paying newspapers just wasn't done, but they didn't really believe us, because they assumed that what was done in Russia must be the norm everywhere. I think they remained unimpressed by our efforts, which did not involve a single bit of arm-twisting. They put up with what we did, but our endless roadmaps and PR-babble about 'deliverables' and 'reaching out to stakeholders' were not really what they had hoped for.

Most of our interaction was by telephone, including weekly Moscow-Brussels-New York conference calls, but groups of us from GPlus and Ketchum also flew over frequently to Moscow – or met Dmitry and Alex in New York, London or Brussels. It quickly dawned on me that a large portion of the consultancy fee seemed to disappear on flights, hotels and telephone calls. My parsimonious Scottish heart used to jump out of my chest when I observed my American colleagues during trips to Moscow, where they would – each, individually – call New York on their mobiles, racking up stupendous roaming costs (no Skype in those days) to join a conference call, during which for the best part of an hour they merely listened to their colleagues rabbiting on about other work that had nothing to do with the Kremlin account, but which nonetheless apparently required these executives to chip in 'Uh-huh' and 'Sure' at regular intervals.

Gruesome stories began to pile up. In October 2006 the journalist Anna Politkovskaya, a fearless critic of Putin and of the Chechen leader, Ramzan Kadyrov, was murdered in Moscow. A month later the former Russian FSB agent Alexander Litvinenko was fatally poisoned in London, accusing Putin personally in his deathbed statement. Opposition groups started organising demonstrations in Moscow – and were habitually arrested or beaten up. The oil tycoon Mikhail Khodorkovsky was put on trial for a second time, on fatuous charges.

Our advice to the Kremlin on all these occasions was simply ignored. Putin had his own reasons for reacting as he did, and we were neither privy to these reasons nor had any way to influence him – though we tried hard. Within hours of Politkovskaya's murder becoming known, we suggested that Putin should express his shock and order a full investigation – and we pointed out that since foreign leaders (and many Russian politicians) had condemned the murder, it looked bad if Putin remained silent. Then the first headlines came out: 'US shocked, Kremlin silent as journalist killed.' It took three days before Putin finally said anything at all – and then it was a mealy-mouthed statement that deprecated Politkovskaya as a journalist of little importance. When Litvinenko died, Dmitry Peskov made some meaningless comment to the effect that 'the death of a person is always a tragedy'. In PR terms this was like spreading your palms and shrugging – because the PR agency working for Litvinenko's friends, run by Margaret Thatcher's old spin-doctor, Lord Bell, was in overdrive, issuing pictures of a hairless and suffering Litvinenko on his deathbed and the full text of his last 'testament' in which he blamed Putin personally for the murder. On the second Khodorkovsky trial, we dutifully warned the Kremlin that it would hugely undermine their alleged efforts to improve Russia's investment climate. But the wheels were in motion to convict the oligarch and keep him incarcerated. Our words – as we knew perfectly well even as we went through the motions – were pointless.

The GPlus/Ketchum consortium managed to renew the Kremlin contract each year – but it was never a foregone conclusion. The last quarter of each year was spent producing expensive glossy brochures to illustrate how successful they had been. They took credit for everything, including *Time* magazine's nomination of Putin as Person of the Year in 2007, even though they had not merely done nothing to achieve it but weren't even aware it was in the pipeline, and were completely taken aback when Dmitry told us about it on a conference call. We produced exhaustive lists of all the arses we had licked, or merely approached with outstretched tongue – roll-calls of every journalist and 'influencer' we had ever discussed the weather with (or 'reached out to', to use the vernacular), lists of conferences we attended and articles we had drafted (never mind if they were never published), lists of conference calls we had arranged, and pictures of op-eds that appeared in newspapers. And of course, '100-day strategies' and '30-day plans', full of 'primary communications goals', 'policymaker outreach' and 'third party engagement'.

It is a mystery to me that, since our task was to change the way the West thought about Russia, we never conducted a single poll or focus group to try to find out exactly what it was that Western people or governments feared, so that the Kremlin's messaging could be tailored to have the best impact. The advice we gave was sucked out of the air by people who knew little about Russia and simply assumed they knew what bothered the West. The Kremlin would have been better off hiring the American spin-doctors who brilliantly reinvented Boris Yeltsin for the 1996 election, precisely on the basis of focus group studies. (It was the 'scientific' nature of their advice that had convinced the Russians to follow it.) A real PR strategy might have involved carefully reading the mood in the West and advising subtle shifts in emphasis for Putin and his entourage, who would have been ordered to stick to our guidelines, and stay on message. But we didn't do any of that at all – and neither, as far as I could see, did the Russians themselves. Putin acted on instinct, not sociology – and his instinct apparently told him that the best way to counter bad news was to take his shirt off and pose for manly photo shoots on horseback, fishing, flying a fighter jet or doing butterfly stroke in an icy Siberian river.

I was shocked by the murder of Anna Politkovskaya. I had had coffee with her in Moscow just the previous year. She was a beacon of brave and admirable journalism in a world of forelock-tuggers. I couldn't quite believe that Putin would have personally ordered her elimination (she just wasn't that important to him), but her murder took place on his birthday, as though someone had arranged a nice 'present' for him. Moreover, just two days earlier, in a restaurant in Moscow, I had overheard Dmitry Peskov telephoning the odious Chechen leader, Ramzan

Kadyrov – prime suspect for ordering the murder – to congratulate him on *his* birthday. It was as if the entire apparatus was involved in some dirty cabal.

I started looking for ways to get back to journalism before my conscience was entirely shredded. But PR was like a swamp – easy to sink in, but very hard to clamber out of. I approached all my friends on Fleet Street and got the same reply everywhere: it's a bad time, we're actually laying off staff . . . Only the *Independent* said it could use me as a stringer in Brussels – but could pay no more than £100 for a 'page lead' and less for any other article. Moving the family to live in a shed wasn't really an option. When GPlus renewed its contract after the first year, I had little choice but to stay on and make the best of it.

Sadly, some of the lights that used to guide me in Russia were slowly going out. Volodya Korotky had died during the first Chechen War. Nikolai Vorontsov, the scientist and environmental campaigner, died in 2000. And in 2004, on the eve of his sixtieth birthday, Garik Basyrov was sitting quietly in his kitchen with Inna, enjoying a cup of tea and a laugh, when his head suddenly tilted forward – and he was dead. I visited his grave, marked by a small, unassuming stone, lying like a pillow among fallen leaves in the Novodevichye cemetery.

Now I was mixing in different circles – and performing mental and moral contortions like some of the characters in Garik's drawings. I gave Dmitry Peskov some media training, and helped him prepare for many meetings with journalists and for live television interviews. We could do nothing to influence what he said, far less what the government did, but we did at least persuade him that talking to journalists as much as possible was the best way to get your point across. If you didn't speak, your opponents certainly would – and it would be their views that would then dominate the press. Nothing showed that more starkly than the brief war with Georgia in 2008. The Georgian president, Mikheil Saakashvili, who started the conflict by attacking South Ossetia, was on TV non-stop from the very first day, claiming Russia had started it; Russia took so long to catch up that no one believed them, and to this day the prevailing narrative is that Russia simply invaded Georgia because that was Putin's 'plan'. Only when Saakashvili stuffed his necktie into his mouth while waiting to go on air for the BBC did a few viewers begin to suspect he was a little nervous about something.

In reality, Peskov did not require much training. He was exceedingly pleasant and fluent – and totally in tune with his master's voice, so you knew you were always hearing Putin's views. He might have been more persuasive if he had occasionally given a glimpse of the internal debates that went on inside the Kremlin, but he had iron discipline. Unfortunately we could never persuade him of the benefit of briefing off the record, giving journalists little titbits that they could use without attribution. We began a tradition of small dinners with Dmitry in fine restaurants for a dozen selected Moscow correspondents. Most journalists highly appreciated the better access that we secured for them – though not all. When I took Dmitry to a meeting with the editorial board of the *Economist* in London, their chief Russia 'expert' sat opposite him with a little notebook, but not because he was at all interested in learning the Kremlin's opinion about anything. No, these were his own 'lecture notes', and he spent most of the hour interrupting Dmitry and expounding his own views about Russia. Sadly, many of the most influential commentators on Russia close their ears to anything that might confound their own prejudices – much as their Russian counterparts do when describing the West.

Among the other officials I 'trained' was the energy minister, Sergei Shmatko, who was occasionally called upon to explain Russia's decision to shut off gas supplies to Ukraine – which had brought power cuts and freezing cold to many countries further west. The only way to improve his public appearances would have been to lock him in a cupboard until the event was over. I began a session with him by showing the introduction to the British comedy quiz show, *Have I Got News For You*, which included a cartoon sequence showing Vladimir Putin turning a huge tap on a gas pipeline, and all the lights across Europe going out. The point was merely to illustrate how Russia's policy was so ingrained in the popular imagination that it could even be used in an entertainment show without further explanation. I wanted Shmatko to grasp just how difficult it would be to persuade people that Russian policy was justified. Sadly I couldn't get him to concentrate on this because he was fixated on an earlier segment of the intro, which showed a Chinese rice-farmer choking as heavy industry grew up all around him.

'He's wearing the wrong hat,' said Russia's energy minister.

'Who is?'

'The farmer.'

'Why?'

'That's a Vietnamese hat.'

'OK, well, never mind that . . . the point is . . .'

'No, but the Chinese don't wear hats like that.'

'Alright, but the point I want you to think about is the section showing Putin . . .'

'But why have they made the Chinese man look Vietnamese?'

'Look, that's just to illustrate the booming Chinese economy, and the pollution it causes.'

'But he's Vietnamese . . .'

Igor Shuvalov, by contrast, was suave, savvy and popular with Western journalists and officials – in fact, he was a case study in how easily people are swayed by appearances and a slick command of English. Shuvalov was the minister in charge of Russia's G8 presidency, and later deputy prime minister, and I briefed him a few times before media appearances. In London, I chaperoned him to a series of meetings at the *Financial Times* and some think-tanks. Because he wore smart suits, had neatly groomed hair, spoke excellent English and could throw in a few jokes, he gained a reputation as a reformer and liberal. In fact, he was little different from the oligarchs the West loved to despise – incredibly rich, with vast properties in London and Austria, way beyond the means of a mere government official, children educated at a British private school, and so on.

At a private gathering I once heard him 'joking' about Ukrainians. 'I don't trust the Ukrainians an inch,' he said. 'Never have. Never will. Putin thinks the opposite – he sees them as our brothers and sisters. But I don't believe it. They break their word the day after giving it. Now they're acting like aggrieved little brothers. They used to think they fed the whole Soviet Union, yet somehow we manage without them!'

The interesting thing, hidden away in that little tirade, was his off-the-cuff remark about Putin's feelings of kinship towards the Ukrainians. Putin allegedly told the US president, George W. Bush, that Ukraine wasn't a proper country, and often spoke about the shared culture and history of Ukrainians and Russians. When Ukraine moved towards severing ties with Russia in favour of closer links with the European Union in 2013, Putin's reaction was exactly as Shuvalov's assessment would lead one to expect: on the one hand, the patronising 'we know best' attitude of a big brother towards a smaller sibling; on the other, genuine feelings of closeness and shared history that he didn't want to throw away. (Incidentally, this was exactly the way many English people – including, ironically, some vocal champions of Ukraine – viewed Scotland's moves towards independence in 2014.)

Shuvalov, with his Western manners and charming English, was a star of the 'Valdai Club' gatherings, which began in 2004 and became an annual tradition, bringing fifty-odd foreign Russia specialists together for debates and meetings with top officials and academics. The very concept of the Valdai Club is derided by the Kremlin's most implacable critics as a forum attended only by 'useful idiots' who return home brainwashed and drooling with admiration for Putin. I attended three Valdai weeks during my time with GPlus, purely as an observer, and found very few Putin droolers among the guests. Indeed the academics and journalists who attended included some of the best-informed (and most critical) commentators on Russia. It beats me how anyone can argue that you can understand Russia better by not speaking to Russians.

A Valdai week normally included a visit to somewhere exotic – one year there was a cruise down the river Lena in Siberia, another year there was a visit to the oil fields of western Siberia, another included a trip to Chechnya (to meet Ramzan Kadyrov) and to the provincial city of Rostov. The programme included seminars with Russian academics, and meetings with Kremlin officials such as Shuvalov, or the equally sociable 'first deputy prime minister' Sergei Ivanov, who in the autumn of 2007 was tipped as Putin's likely successor.

Putin was approaching the end of his second term in office, and was barred constitutionally from standing for a third term. The main contenders to succeed him were Ivanov and the other 'first deputy prime minister', Dmitry Medvedev. Ivanov, a former KGB spy like Putin, was seen as the tough option, while Medvedev, a former lawyer with no history in the secret services, was regarded as a softer, more 'Western-oriented' choice. I had the privilege of walking along a street beside Ivanov at the very moment he learned that Putin had just dropped him from the shortlist. Ivanov was visibly shocked. 'No,' he stammered, 'he didn't discuss this with me . . .' We went on to the meeting with the Valdai Club, where Ivanov did his best to hide his disappointment. His spiel to the group of Russia-watchers included the predictable – 'I categorically deny that we are using gas supplies as a political weapon against Ukraine' – and the disarming: 'Yes, I liked the Beatles. And I really like Pink Floyd. And I went to the square in St Petersburg to watch the Rolling Stones this year. But I don't like rap and that kind of stuff, I'm too old for that.' But the most revealing stuff was hidden in what

Ivanov didn't exactly say. Asked about Putin's 'heir apparent', he said: 'I am not at all sure that he will simply name a successor and that will be that. I don't think it will happen like that. I don't think it is the way Putin would act. But things will get clearer at the United Russia Congress [Putin's party] in early October. The key will be who United Russia will support, and secondly what Putin's options will be, so as not to become a pensioner! He's too young for that. He would never agree to be a lecturer or something like that. He is thinking over his options now. But he will not stay on for a third term, I am sure of that.' The point was: Ivanov – a close colleague of Putin, former minister of defence, and until an hour earlier himself the 'heir apparent' – clearly had no idea what was going to happen. The Valdai meeting was invaluable for this insight alone: one of Putin's closest confidants did not know what Putin's plan was. The president, in other words, took major decisions almost alone, consulting only a tiny number of people – or maybe none.

The highlight of each Valdai gathering was a long meeting with Vladimir Putin himself, either at his Moscow residence or in Sochi. Being in the same room, having a chance to shake his hand and watch his mannerisms, is clearly better than just reading his words. There's nothing like waiting in an anteroom for two hours just for him to turn up, to understand that he sees himself as unconstrained by the niceties of normal social behaviour – a tsar who keeps visitors waiting (whether a foreign president or a bunch of hacks), as a deliberate display of power. Close up, you see what angers or amuses him. He kicked off one of these sessions with a blunt indication that he found the Valdai meetings themselves increasingly pointless – for him – because he didn't see any positive coverage resulting from them in the Western press. The persistence of what he called 'stereotypes' about Russia in the West was one of the things that angered him most. I found his response interesting when one participant asked him about the views of Vladislav Surkov – one of his closest advisers, whom Westerners continually quoted as though he was a mirror image of Putin himself: 'I don't work for him. He works for me,' retorted the president. It was certainly easy, in the presence of such a commanding figure, to be cowed – and some of the academics (more so than the journalists) tended to preface their questions with sickeningly sycophantic verbiage: 'I just want to thank you for . . . it's such a privilege to . . . it's so kind of you to agree to . . .' And the atmosphere was such that hardly anybody dared to ask a follow-up question if Putin had dodged answering the first. But I learned that Putin himself hated this craven behaviour. At the end of one session Dmitry Peskov told me: 'Why do they behave like this? Putin detests it! He comes here hoping for a good argument, and all he gets are these boring, soft questions. They should challenge him.'

The sense of stasis in the Kremlin, as everyone waited to hear what Putin planned to do next, was palpable, even from my conversations with Dmitry. 'We're not sure what our task is going to be,' he confided on the plane: 'ensuring the president's legacy, moving to a new boss, or what.' He said Putin would spend the next few weeks entirely at his Sochi residence: 'He's tired of the Kremlin, and tired generally. He wants to work on his future plans, and the structure of a new government. This will be his way of ensuring the continuity of his policies at least for the early period of the new presidency.' He said Putin was aware that, however he might try to dominate him, his successor would carve out his own path, and this was worrying for him: 'All presidents end up strong. Yeltsin thought Putin would do his bidding, but ended up hardly ever seeing him. Putin is aware of this.'

After months of uncertainty, in December 2007, Putin chose a man whom he evidently hoped he would be able to dominate: his old mate from St Petersburg days, Dmitry Medvedev. He was 'elected' in March 2008 – a not exactly surprising outcome given that the head of the electoral commission, Vladimir Churov, had said: 'Churov's First Law is that Putin is always right'. The new president immediately appointed Putin as his prime minister, and though he was always seen as his benefactor's lapdog, Medvedev did briefly inspire hope that something might change for the better. He spoke about reforming the economy, and seemed intent on improving Russia's human rights record.

Dmitry and Alex stayed with Putin, moving to the prime minister's office in the White House, while appointing trusted colleagues to the president's press office. Our job was to work with both teams – but there was never any doubt that it was Dmitry who called the shots – just as the new prime minister would be the backseat driver of the presidential limo.

However overshadowed he may have been, I soon saw just how much authority the title of president confers on its holder. Within the walls of the Kremlin, the supreme leader commands total respect. In July 2008, two months after Medvedev's inauguration, we arranged an interview with him for half a dozen Western journalists. I was on hand to make things go smoothly, and was soon happily engrossed in BBC-like tasks – helping the cameraman and interpreter to lay cables discreetly around the Presidential Library, where the meeting would take place. The library is in the Kremlin's Senate building, just yards from the president's office. It is a small room, with a beautiful inlaid floor and a round table in the centre, dark-panelled walls and bookshelves all around, and a mezzanine-level balcony where the interpreter would sit, quietly speaking into a microphone. The technical issues took some time to resolve, and Medvedev's team was getting nervous as I kept asking them to postpone by a few more minutes. Eventually, everything was ready, and they called for the president. I was astonished by the sudden change in atmosphere: everyone had been joking, bustling around, getting things ready; now all the courtiers snapped to attention and – literally – held their breath as we heard presidential footsteps approaching down the corridor. It could surely have been no different in the days of Ivan the Terrible. I looked out, and saw Medvedev striding along, swinging his left arm furiously, exactly as Putin did. When he sat down with us, I saw that he also mimicked some of Putin's facial expressions and verbal tics. The poor chap really wasn't doing very well at being himself. It wasn't a great surprise when, four years later, Putin announced that they'd be swapping jobs again, and Medvedev (who had been desperately trying to distance himself from Putin and drum up support among liberals and businessmen) nervously agreed, pretending that he thought relinquishing the presidency was a sterling idea.

Medvedev's Achilles heel – according to the absurd Western press which condemns racism, sexism and homophobia but sees nothing wrong with mocking a person's height – was that he was an inch or so shorter than Putin. As a minuscule (and shrinking) five-foot-sixer myself, who can scarcely reach the table to type these words, I was outraged by the almost universal scorn poured on Putin's size. As if it wasn't enough that he had lousy policies, you also had to ridicule him as some sort of dwarf. Since Medvedev was even smaller, he really belonged in a freak show. Masha Gessen, one of the most unrelentingly critical commentators on current Russian politics, described Putin as 'a small guy in every sense', and of his successor she wrote: 'Medvedev made Putin look charismatic. At just over five feet (his exact height was a closely guarded secret), he also made Putin look tall.' Unlike Gessen, I have stood right beside both men, and can categorically state that Medvedev is scarcely any shorter at all. But even if he was, so what? And how exactly can a president's height – when he appears in public every day, standing beside other people – be a 'closely guarded secret'?

The real trouble was not Medvedev's tininess, but the fact that Putin was still hanging around in the background. We should have advised him to go into retirement and become a heartthrob on *Strictly Come Dancing*. Instead, he kept on making speeches and giving interviews – including one that made me suspect the Kremlin was actually trying to sabotage poor Medvedev's chances. Within a few days of each other, Putin gave an interview to Bloomberg television, and Medvedev to Russian television. The difference, in sheer production terms, was embarrassing. Bloomberg placed Putin in a beautiful room, artily lit, with potted plants as props. The Kremlin's TV team, by contrast, chose a brashly lit hall and sat Medvedev in a huge ugly seat that really did make him look like a little boy. I sent off a blistering memo about how to set up a TV interview to show even a truncated president in a favourable light.

I was getting good at blasting off pointless memos. I sent some to old colleagues at the BBC to try to get them to pronounce the president's name correctly. Say 'Invade ye', and then change it to 'Mid –VADE – yev', I instructed. Really, there was no end to the silly things I could find to fill my time while pretending to be a PR guru.

Much of the time I felt like a mole, working in the interests of my journalist mates rather than the Kremlin. I lobbied especially hard for the BBC, for whom I tried to obtain the best access and as many interviews as possible. One of my favourite achievements was an interview that I set up for Medvedev with the BBC's Andrew Marr in March 2009. First, I wrote a briefing note for the president, with the questions I expected Marr to ask. This was hardly difficult: as a BBC journalist, I could safely predict not only the questions but also the rough order in which they would be asked. I also made a video of highlights from Marr's shows, to help the president prepare. That was, of course, part of my job. But I also briefed Marr's producer (and Marr himself) on what Medvedev would be likely to say, and might wish to say. In other words, I effectively wrote the script for the entire interview. It took place in a baronial-style hunting lodge outside Moscow, where Medvedev first went for a stroll with Marr in the snowy gardens. Then we settled down for the interview, and I chuckled as Marr began asking exactly the questions I had predicted, and Medvedev gave the expected answers. I was sitting next to Natalia Timakova, Medvedev's spokeswoman. After a few minutes she started looking round at me with an incredulous look. I just shrugged modestly.

* * *

It was becoming painfully clear to me that GPlus and Ketchum were having no influence at all on how the Kremlin presented itself to the outside world, and that the Kremlin itself appeared to be genuinely unaware that it was its actions – not their presentation – that bothered the West. There were good reasons why the 'stereotypes' that irked Putin persisted. Since I appeared to be destined to work with his advisers for some time, I decided to try and enlighten them on this. I didn't entertain huge hopes of influencing Kremlin policy, but there was certainly no reason not to try, even if it strayed beyond my brief as a 'media' consultant. Some of this I did by inserting my thoughts into the memos and roadmaps and 'global team recommendations' that we sent; some of it I did in personal conversations and emails to Dmitry; and occasionally I was able to speak to decision-makers at the very heart of the Kremlin.

One day in the spring of 2009 I had a meeting with Putin's closest adviser, Alexei Gromov, the only person, according to Dmitry, who could walk into Putin's office without an appointment. Now he was Medvedev's deputy chief of staff. Walking to his office it struck me how different the Kremlin was from the American White House – or certainly from the frantic walk-and-talk world portrayed in *The West Wing*. Instead of open-plan offices, with transparent partitions, where you could just hail a colleague for a quick discussion, here the corridors were heavy with secrecy: offices were behind double sets of doors, usually upholstered for maximum privacy. You didn't just wander into a colleague's room for a chat: here, lowly officials sat in anterooms waiting for a secretary to usher them in. Nothing here was conducive to dynamic decision-making.

Gromov sat like a pasha in his grand office, chain-smoking Marlboros from a long cigarette-holder, occasionally swatting ash from his mauve and turquoise-patterned cardigan. The carpet was the colours of a forest floor in autumn; there were potted plants all around, and black leather sofas for the guests. Gromov had the squishy, creased face of a pugilist, and reminded me just a little of Richard Nixon. It didn't take him long to launch into Russia's grievances, primarily America's decision to install a missile defence system in eastern Europe. 'If this goes ahead, we will have no option but to deploy Iskander missiles [to take out the system if necessary], and our relations will quickly sink into the swamp.' But, he added in a more conciliatory tone, 'we take it step by step and send a response to every positive signal we receive from the Americans.' At one point, Oleg Dobrodeyev, the head of Russian television, walked in, and Gromov waved him through to a back room and told him to pour himself a drink while he was waiting. The two were clearly on such intimate terms that you immediately understood how the Kremlin's control of the media worked: this was not the Soviet era, where scripts were censored and formal instructions issued by the Party's propaganda department; now, it was all done in comfy armchairs over whisky and soda.

After listening to Gromov blaming the West for the worsening relations, I took the chance to put an alternative view to him. The thrust of my argument was that the reason the West distrusted Russia was because it had failed to distance itself fully from communism, and was still regarded as a barely changed continuation of the Soviet Union. Every demonstration that was broken up by riot police, every further move to monopolise the media, reinforced this impression. Having witnessed Gromov's closeness to Dobrodeyev, I urged him to commission television documentaries about Stalinism, to help the Russian people go through the process of *Vergangenheitsbewältigung* ('overcoming the past') that the Germans had needed in order to accept and move on from their Nazi past. Gromov replied that they could not yet denounce the Soviet past because they did not want to leave people with a sense of shame or guilt, or wasted lives. I pointed out that under Gorbachev and Yeltsin a start had been made to this process, and that if people were not forced to face up to the truth, the country would forever be tainted with the stain of communism. If the Kremlin did not draw a line between today's Russia and the Stalinist past, its enemies in the West would continue to conflate the two, leaving a sour smell of anti-Russianism lingering in the air. Gromov said the time would come for this, but it was too early. 'We must think about domestic public opinion, which is generally positive about the Soviet Union. Political stability within the country is paramount for us. We have to think about that above all else . . .'

Putin's reputation in the West continued to plummet, and it was perfectly clear to me that no amount of tinkering with the 'message', as opposed to the reality of his policies, would change anything. I composed a long memo that went way beyond our brief as 'media consultants', in the vain hope that I might finally manage to do something to improve Russia's relations with the West. Putin, I said, had to 'do a Gorby'! In the modern world, I wrote, domestic politics and foreign policies were fundamentally linked. The Kremlin's crackdown on human rights, democracy and the media fatally affected how the West viewed Russia's foreign policy initiatives. And there was a historical precedent that showed how perceptions could be changed.

'When Mikhail Gorbachev came to power in 1985,' I wrote, 'he was faced with an extremely hostile, anti-Soviet West (led by Reagan and Thatcher) and an unbridled arms race, including threats of a "Star Wars" missile shield. By the end of 1988 Gorbachev was able to travel to the United Nations to make a momentous speech which captivated the world's leaders and brought the Soviet Union "in from the cold". His motorcade caused gridlock in New York as hundreds of thousands came out to welcome him. Two years earlier in Reykjavik he actually persuaded Reagan to agree in principle to the abolition of all nuclear weapons. Gorbachev was able to do this *only* because the initiatives were preceded or accompanied by a series of radical, liberalising reforms at home: he had personally invited the dissident Andrei Sakharov to return from exile to take part in political life, he had freed the press and allowed open discussion of Soviet history, and at the 19th Communist Party Conference in June 1988 he had announced political reforms that convinced the West he was serious about change. His foreign policy success would have been impossible without the domestic political reforms, which inspired confidence and respect.'

Well, it was a good try! I don't imagine this advice went any further than Dmitry's own inbox. Even if he agreed, it was above his pay grade to suggest to Putin that he perform an about-face on human rights and democracy.

So – I thought, as my increasing enjoyment of red wine turned me into a better and better consultant – how about at least improving your bloody speeches? In January 2009 Putin went to the annual Rich Bastards' Knees-Up (aka World Economic Forum) at Davos, Switzerland, and delivered the kind of speech that surgeons might one day consider as a cheap alternative to anaesthesia. The Kremlin was now considering sending President Medvedev to the London School of Economics to repeat the therapy. I was furious, unconcerned now by what anyone thought of me, and in February penned a marvellous wine-soaked (non-GPlus) memo in the middle of the night. In it I slagged off the halfwits who wrote Putin's homilies, and explained some of the rhetorical devices that made brilliant speeches brilliant. 'Do you know,' I asked, 'that Putin's speech did not contain a single metaphor, or figure of speech, or any other rhetorical device? That's why he got just 15 seconds of applause at the end.' I ranted on for several pages, explaining exactly why Putin's speech had been such a disaster, and warning them not to send Medvedev out to 'pour another bucketful of cold rain over the public'. I thought – and perhaps secretly hoped – that I would get sacked. But instead Dmitry was delighted: 'Thank you very much for this note. It's much more valuable than sometimes tens and hundreds of recommendations!' Nothing came of it, of course. But it gave me the taste for being more straightforward with them.

In August I made one final attempt to influence Russian policy. Putin was due to visit Gdansk to commemorate the outbreak of the Second World War, on 1 September 2009 – an event bedevilled by memories of the Molotov-Ribbentrop Pact and the Soviet occupation that resulted from the war. I thought that this could be a perfect occasion to try to heal wounds with Poland and the other countries that were occupied by the Soviet Union, and suggested language that Putin could use that might manage to reach out to the Poles while at the same time not offending the Russian soldiers who had bravely fought in the war and sincerely believed they had 'liberated', not occupied, eastern Europe.

I don't suppose my note had anything at all to do with it, but Putin did in fact finally do something sensible: he condemned the Molotov-Ribbentrop Pact as 'morally unacceptable', and won plaudits in all the Western newspapers. Later, Russian television showed the film *Katyn*, by the Polish director, Andrzej Wajda – a powerful statement to the effect that the Kremlin now fully acknowledged one of the most brutal episodes of the war, the massacre of 22,000 Polish officers by NKVD firing squads.

I was now going mad with frustration. Advising the Kremlin was the last thing that interested me. I began a new round of letter-writing to see if any newspapers might finally be taking on staff – which of course they were not. To stave off a fresh bout of depression I recorded an album of my songs with Stephane Wertz, a brilliant guitarist and music producer in Brussels. One of them was called 'Head above Water', based on a famous photograph by Steve McCurry, which showed an old tailor wading through neck-high floodwaters in Gujarat, holding his sewing machine on his shoulder – and smiling, even though everything else was lost. It was supposed to be an inspiration to myself. But in fact, my head was way below water.

Then, suddenly, my flurry of activity produced the exit visa I longed for – an escape from GPlus, PR and the Kremlin's clutches. Approaching

Norma Percy, with whom I had worked nineteen years earlier on the *Second Russian Revolution* television series, was a last throw of the dice: I really did not expect anything to come of it. But by the great gift of synchronicity it turned out that she was just embarking on a new project – a four-part BBC series about Putin and his relationship with the West. Like the earlier documentary, its success would depend on persuading senior politicians to open up and tell the inside story of their discussions and relations with Western leaders – and no journalist at that moment had better access to the Kremlin's inner sanctum than I did. It took a while to tie up contracts, and work out notice at GPlus . . . but finally I was able to move to London, and return to journalism, film-making and normality. Or so I thought.

36

'Foreign agent'

I MIGHT HAVE wandered into a Russian fairy tale. We crunched through deep snow along the bank of the half-frozen Moskva River. Then we followed a beaten path to a gingerbread house with a twirl of smoke climbing from the chimney. The garden was surrounded by a low fence, and within it there were outhouses and a *banya*, a stable with a horse inside, and animals everywhere – turkeys and geese and ducks, two cats . . . and thirteen dogs, including four silky Afghan hounds. Inside the cabin a dog squatted on every chair and couch. As we sat eating (one of the turkeys), little dog-heads came poking up under your elbows or snuffling around your knees. It was like a scene from *101 Dalmatians*. But our hostess was not Cruella De Vil – it was the doyenne of Moscow's post-*perestroika* journalists' corps, Masha Slonim.

I had known Masha off and on for years. We had worked together in the BBC Russian Service in the 1980s, and on *The Second Russian Revolution*. At that time she lived in a country house in southern England, also with stables and horses, inherited from her late husband, Lord Robin Phillimore. Her passport still described her as Lady Maria Phillimore. Her picaresque life had begun in the famous House on the Embankment near the Kremlin: her grandfather was Maxim Litvinov, Stalin's foreign minister, whose wife, Ivy, was English. Under Brezhnev she became a dissident, and emigrated in 1974, first to America, then to Britain, where her purring, nicotine-stained voice became one of the best-known on the BBC's Russian Service. Her London apartment became a lodging house for passing Soviet dissidents and émigrés. One of her best friends was Vladimir Bukovsky, who had spent 12 years in jail for his exposure of Soviet psychiatric abuse. Masha's first car was a second-hand London black cab, in which she and Bukovsky used to tear around London after the pubs closed, searching for West Indian corner shops that would sell them vodka from under the counter. After her husband, Lord Phillimore, died in 1990, she returned to Moscow, where her apartment on Tverskaya Street became home to a political club, frequented by all the top politicians and journalists. Her connections were awesome, and after 16 years abroad she now enjoyed a special cachet, as a quasi-émigrée – a Lady, no less – whose cigarettes-and-vodka 'soirées' were the place to be seen in the early Yeltsin era. Not that this gave her any pretensions: I never saw her wearing anything other than ancient sweaters and worn-out trousers. According to her friend, Yelena Tregubova, Masha once turned up for an interview with a top politician carrying a carrier bag which she clattered down on the table, and feck-lessly explained: 'Oh, sorry – that's my bones . . . I mean, my dog's bones . . . well, obviously not the dog's bones, but cow's bones – I mean, to give to my dogs . . .' With Masha, you got exactly what you saw – and there was no better person to persuade politicians to open up.

Masha was now the Russian producer on the new BBC series, which eventually gained the title *Putin, Russia & the West*. Her fairy-tale cottage in the village of Ubory, where she lived with her menagerie and her husband, Zhenya, became one of our favourite retreats during research and filming trips to Moscow. Directly across the river, hidden in the woods, was President Medvedev's dacha – a tiny, tiny little house with three-feet-high doors and dwarfs in constant attendance.

The bulk of the work on the series was done by a small group of people – Norma Percy, the chief producer; Paul Mitchell, a Russian-speaking director and producer; Masha; and myself. Paul and I did most of the research and planning; Masha and I persuaded more than forty Russian officials to give interviews; all three of us carried out the inter-views; and Norma fussed around like one of Masha's clucking hens. Norma loved the little stories that politicians would tell us, and was happy to spend hours piecing together the precise sequence of events, which she then storyboarded into the 'humanised history' that her programmes did so well. But nothing mattered more to her than scalable fonts and margins. She spent days and days obsessing over the format-ting of written documents that would never be seen by anyone outside the production team. She also had a formidable temper. If I was abrasive (as a BBC producer once described me), Norma was a cheese-grater. Apart from in cartoon films I had never seen anyone actually stamping their foot up and down in fury, repeating, 'I am very, very angry!' She screamed blue murder at me for daring to send an email in Russian that she hadn't approved, and also at a poor Russian assistant who generously went out to buy Coca Cola for her and came back with bottles instead of cans. It was a very happy office. And an intimate one, too: since there was not enough money to stay in hotels during our long trips to Moscow, we rented cheap apartments and got under each other's feet. Norma taught the boys her 'special method' of drying shirts to avoid having to iron them – which left us with extra time for document-formatting late into the night.

It was a sign of the rollback in democracy since Gorbachev's days that it was now harder to persuade Kremlin politicians to open up, or even speak to us, than it had been on *The Second Russian Revolution* two decades earlier. Most of our requests for Kremlin interviews went through Dmitry Peskov, so my relationship with him was key, but he was never totally convinced by the project, which he suspected would end up as another hatchet job on Putin. Still, we got most of the politicians we needed – even if we sometimes had to wait, and plead, and beg, for the best part of two years.

Having such a long time to make four hour-long films was a luxury in the television business – but the process was very thorough, and I had no doubt that we were digging down to the real issues that came to bedevil east-west relations during the Putin/Bush and Medvedev/Obama period (from 2000 to 2011). Every story, or claim, was cross-checked with other politicians and eyewitnesses – not just in Russia but in the United States, the UK, Germany, France, Georgia and Ukraine.

The interesting thing about this method of making documentary films is that it forces politicians to tell the truth. Every interviewee knows that we will put his or her stories to the other side for corroboration, so there is no point in their making things up. By the time you have spoken to three or four people who personally witnessed a discussion, you know you have got it right.

We began with dozens of lower-level officials (and experts) on both sides of the Atlantic, piecing together the key moments from a decade of diplomacy to arm ourselves with the stories we hoped would stand up when we finally clawed our way towards the real players – the diplomats, politicians and military men who actually negotiated behind closed doors. Serving politicians were the hardest to get – in every country. Igor Shuvalov, now Prime Minister Putin's senior deputy in charge of the economy, was no longer the socialite who loved to wow audiences at the Valdai Club. He did give us a preliminary interview, off the record, in which he revealed all sorts of details that no one in the world had ever heard before – about private conversations between Putin and George W. Bush, for example. But he kept saying: 'I don't know if I can say this on camera. I'll need to check with Putin.' And in the end, despite hours of meetings and telephone calls with his assistant – and pincer-movements via Dmitry Peskov and others – Shuvalov refused to repeat his stories on camera.

Some of the participants were excellent. Sergei Ivanov, the gregarious deputy prime minister whom Putin had overlooked in his search for a successor, loved being on camera and regaled us with unexpected stories – such as the night he and the American National Security Advisor, Condoleezza Rice, sneaked out of a tedious performance of *The Nutcracker* to visit an avant-garde ballet performance instead. We took this to Rice, and she confirmed it. Similarly, on a much more important story, the vexed issue of Bush's plans to build a missile shield in eastern Europe, which the Kremlin saw as a threat to its security, we were able to confirm – from both sides – that Rice and Robert Gates, the US defence secretary, came up with a compromise in 2007 that delighted the Russians, but for which they were unable to secure support from the military and political hawks back in Washington. For me, that was a real scoop – a moment of diplomacy that nobody knew about, a moment that could have changed history and perhaps prevented the great freeze-over in US-Russian relations that followed. Dozens of interviews, with Americans and Russians, convinced me that no other issue was as important to Putin. He didn't like NATO's expansion either, but accepted it so long as it went no further. But the only way he would accept that the missile shield was aimed against Iran (as the Americans claimed), not Russia, was if they allowed Russia to take part in it too. This was what Rice and Gates proposed – and when the offer fell apart, Putin came to the only logical conclusion – that the shield was indeed directed against Russia. It is the one issue, I am convinced, that even today the West could exploit to win back Putin's friendship, or at least cooperation.

We tried everything to persuade Peskov to arrange an interview with Putin himself, but he was wary to say yes unless we could prove that his opposite numbers – Bush, Blair, Merkel, Chirac – would also be in the films. We even offered a paltry bribe – a box set of David Attenborough's latest wildlife series, which we thought Dmitry would enjoy. But he took one look at it and cried: 'Fantastic! I'll give it to Putin. He loves these things!' Putin may have loved it, but we didn't get the interview. I think the main reason was that in late 2011, when we made our last bid for him, he and Medvedev were still arguing about which of them would stand for president in 2012, and decision-making in the Kremlin was virtually paralysed again for several months.

By early 2012 the four films were ready for broadcast – and my book, *The Strongman*, which was based on the same research and interviews, was published. But none of us foresaw what would cause the biggest sensation – the trailer for the television series, which used a snippet from our interview with Tony Blair's former chief of staff, Jonathan Powell. In our interview with Powell (which was conducted more than a year earlier), we had asked him to comment on an incident that happened in 2006, when Russian television had shown what they said were British spies using a fake rock, planted in a Moscow park, to exchange information electronically with a Russian agent. The claim had been derided at the time – it looked like clumsy propaganda – but to our surprise Powell confirmed it: 'The spy rock was embarrassing,' he said, 'I mean, they had us bang to rights.'

Suddenly, conspiracy-obsessed opposition figures with no knowledge whatsoever of the processes involved in the making of a documentary started speculating about 'why' the BBC had chosen 'this moment' (shortly before the presidential election) to reveal the truth about the infamous spy rock. Vladimir Bukovsky, the former Soviet dissident, now based in Cambridge, England, wrote a preposterous blog for Echo of Moscow, saying he had no doubt that this was 'an FSB operation' designed to influence the election in Putin's favour. Bukovsky claimed that officials like Ivanov must have received guarantees from us that the film would not criticise the regime, and that the documentary 'could not have been released without their *approval*'.

The sad thing was that by jumping to such absurd conclusions, Bukovsky was showing himself, despite 25 years of living in England, to be a true *sovok* – saddled with a Soviet mindset, susceptible to silly conspiracy theories, and incapable of understanding that the Western media actually operate differently from media in the Soviet Union or Russia. His language about British journalists 'taking instructions' from the FSB was exactly the same as the language used by Russian propagandists about dissidents taking instructions from the CIA. His old friend, Masha Slonim, wrote a reply, in which she pointed out that interviewees in BBC programmes are *never* given guarantees about how their words will be used, or about what 'line' the film night take.

Bukovsky wouldn't give up: he said he 'knew' the BBC must have given guarantees to the Kremlin because . . . well, 'that's what Soviet television used to do!' He then launched into a personal attack on me, based on the fact that I had worked as a consultant to the Kremlin for three years – again, without knowing anything about what I actually did there. It was no fun to be vilified by a titan of the Soviet dissident movement, whom I had listened to late at night in Yasenevo, and worshipped as a student. It was also shocking to realise that the man whom I had admired for his exposure of the Soviet system of psychiatric abuse was in fact devoid of common sense. Bukovsky, incidentally, was such a BBC-hater that he refused to pay for a TV licence, and yet presumed to know all about how it 'worked'.

The criticism then snowballed. Despite the fact that the vast majority of viewers, judging from social media, thought that Putin emerged from the series as an out-and-out villain, several critics sought to portray the documentary as 'pro-Kremlin' simply because I had been involved in its production. I was stunned by this. The thrust of the documentary, and of my book, after all, was that relations deteriorated between America and Russia during the Putin/Bush period because of two separate factors: on the one hand, Western mistrust of Putin, due to his crackdown on human rights and democracy; and on the other, Russia's resentment of NATO enlargement and Bush's insistence on building a missile shield that the Kremlin viewed as a threat. This conclusion was supported by dozens of interviews with politicians on every side of the argument, and struck me as neither 'pro' nor 'anti' one side or the other. Both sides were to blame – mainly by failing to understand the other's concerns. My book was tougher than the films on Putin himself: I described him as a ruthless narcissist, a boorish control-freak, a man who instilled fear and trampled on human rights. But I also criticised Western policies towards Russia, and in the minds of some commentators, it seems, anyone who does that is guilty of 'following the Kremlin narrative'.

Towards the end of 2011 two things went badly wrong for the regime. First, Prime Minister Putin and President Medvedev announced they were going to swap jobs again, and huge swathes of the Russian public went: Excuse me, do *our* views matter? Then elections were held to the Russian parliament or Duma, in which moronic election officials went about ballot-stuffing on a grand scale, forgetting the fact that their fraud was being captured on closed-circuit cameras. The public had had enough, and tens of thousands took to the streets of Moscow for the first serious protests of the Putin era. Putin then committed his third error – by sneering at the protestors as nothing more than chattering monkeys, manipulated by the West. The American secretary of state, Hillary Clinton, herself had 'given the signal' for opposition activists to take to the streets. It didn't seem to occur to him that the Russian people might be less docile than he thought, and might object, even without Western prompting, to a return to communist-style fixing of elections.

I went back to Moscow in the New Year and found my old friends more excited than they had been since the days of *perestroika*. People-power was back. And it was precisely the *perestroika* generation that was demanding their revolution back: the demonstrators were mainly intellectuals, appalled by the diminishing freedoms they enjoyed under Putin, and the new middle classes – the men and women who were doing well in the new capitalist era but objected to the lack of reform and the corruption of the elite. Even the little whiff of change they had smelled during the Medvedev interregnum had been snuffed out. The opposition's new leader, the hero of the protests, was Alexei Navalny, whose website exposed gross corruption among Putin's cronies. Without the help of any PR agency he had brilliantly rebranded Putin's 'United Russia' party as the 'Party of Crooks and Thieves'.

Putin was duly re-elected president on 4 March 2012, and the following Saturday I went to another rally on Novy Arbat. It was the kind of affair that made you scream with frustration. How would Russia's opposition ever defeat the Putin clique when it was hopelessly divided and leaderless? A succession of morose speakers trooped to the stage and elicited faint applause from the crowd with lacklustre speeches. To this day, the opposition has failed to come up with a united platform. The only thing they can agree upon is that Putin should go. But half a dozen opposition figures all want to be leader – and until they can put their differences behind them it is hard to see how they will ever succeed.

The new Putin presidency proceeded in predictable fashion. A large rally on Bolotnaya Square on 6 May, the eve of his inauguration, was violently broken up by police, and several protesters were jailed. A female punk band called Pussy Riot staged an anti-Putin stunt in the Cathedral of Christ the Saviour, and were sent to prison camps. Navalny was found guilty of fraud. New laws brought restrictions to the internet, imposed massive fines for organising public protests, and forced any organisations that received funds from the West to register themselves as 'foreign agents'. This meant that many polling organisations, human rights groups and historical societies like Memorial, dedicated to preventing any attempt to cover up Stalin's Terror, had to put up a sign on their doors that effectively identified them as untrustworthy tools of Western governments.

As a born-again journalist, I penned a few articles, mainly for the *Guardian* and the *New Statesman*, about all of these events – and later about the invasion of Ukraine in 2014, the annexation of Crimea, and the downing of a Malaysian passenger jet, probably by Russian separatists in eastern Ukraine. But there was a catch. The newspapers insisted on identifying me, not just as a former BBC Moscow correspondent, but as 'a former adviser to the Kremlin'. For a while I put up with this – and even pointed out that my consultancy work might have given me a little extra insight into Putin's mind. But the comments my articles attracted almost all denigrated me as a Kremlin stooge or 'useful idiot' – a phrase that Russophobes love to bandy around to stigmatise anyone who fails to sign up 100 per cent to the Western line. Their ultimate term of abuse is *Putinversteher* – as though understanding (*verstehen*) your enemy was a bad thing. Never mind the fact that my articles were relentlessly critical of Putin; people saw what they wanted to see. What the hawks really hated, I think, was my belief that they themselves were Putin's best friend, because everything they said and did (the endless demonisation, sanctions, military confrontation) was a gift to him, making him more ruthless and more popular at home, helping him to stay in power.

I began to realise that the little descriptor that the papers insisted on using was tantamount to branding me as a foreign agent. Now I knew exactly how Memorial felt. It was a nasty, underhand way to gag your opponents. The Russophobes, it seemed, had learned a good lesson from the man they detested in the Kremlin.

In the summer of 2016 I went back to Moscow for a month, curious to see how the country was coping with the economic sanctions imposed by Western countries in 2014 following Russia's actions in Crimea and Ukraine. In conjunction with a sharp fall in the price of oil, these were said to be having a major impact on the Russian economy – though they showed no sign of persuading Putin to reverse his policies. To make things worse, Putin had responded with a typically counterintuitive measure of his own – banning the *import* of many Western foodstuffs.

This was intended to harm European and American food producers – but meant that Russians could no longer buy fresh produce from Europe. No more Camembert for the Russian middle classes.

Officials had implemented Putin's countersanctions with the kind of bureaucratic zeal that only Russians can exhibit, by staging an *auto-da-fé* for illegal shipments of foreign food. I split my sides laughing at one report that showed police officers raiding a shop and seizing three poly-thene-wrapped, frozen geese (solemnly reading out a detailed 'protocol' to explain their actions), in the presence of three witnesses (who also earnestly gave their names and addresses on camera). The police officers and witnesses then drove with the three geese to a 'destruction facility', where they were solemnly laid on open ground, like offerings in a pagan ritual, and a bulldozer with gigantic caterpillar tracks drove over them, back and forth, until they were flattened into submission. At first I thought this was a comedy sketch, but no, it was just Russia. Between the West's idiocy, in imagining sanctions would make Putin change his policies towards Ukraine, and Russia's, in sending out police squads to fight deep-frozen poultry, there was really no end to the amusement caused by this new cold war.

The *Economist* declared that sanctions were 'one of the most powerful tools' the West had in its dealings with Russia. Governments repeatedly extended them because they had helped to worsen Russia's economy – apparently forgetting that the original aim was not to impose more hardship on the Russian people but to force Putin to get out of Ukraine. Perhaps they hoped the ruination of the economy would bring with it a popular revolt against Putin.

I'm not sure why I believed any of this, but like most people I did. Arriving in Moscow in May, having absorbed the overhyped coverage of the recession in Russia, I expected to see shops almost as bare as they had been in Soviet times. I searched for the crisis everywhere. It is no exaggeration to say that in forty years I had never seen the city looking better. It was, quite simply, booming. Maybe some banks and businesses were experiencing difficulties, since the economy had officially contracted. But statistics don't always reflect what you find in real life. And maybe the rest of the country was not faring so well, of course . . . but Moscow was what mattered, because if a crisis was going to spark a revolution anywhere it would be in the capital.

The food shops were anything but empty. It was true that *fresh* produce from the EU was missing, but everything else was still there – British jams, Spanish olive oil, German beer and Italian wine, French mineral water, Coca-Cola, crisps, sauces, fruit juice, ketchup, ice cream, biscuits, frozen pizzas, pasta, coffee . . . And the dairy counters were full too, not with French cheese, but with imports from non-EU countries (including Switzerland), plus all the usual brands of yoghurt and cream – produced by Western companies *inside* Russia. Home-produced butters and cheeses were there in abundance, beautifully packaged. Fish? Meat? Caviar and smoked salmon? No problem. Fruit and veg? The shelves were groaning. The reality was that the sanctions had actually stimulated domestic production. True, Russian attempts to copy Brie and Roquefort were not terribly successful, but apart from that, life was getting better, comrades.

One Saturday I drove with my friend Seryozha to his dacha, three hours away from Moscow. It took the first hour just to reach the outskirts of the city, because the roads were clogged with cars – including hundreds of Mercedes and BMWs and SUVs – heading for the megastores and garden centres around the city limits. We stopped at one too, to buy provisions. Western companies were earning fortunes here, supplying everything from Perrier water and wine to garden compost and swim-ming pools. Near the dacha, in a small town some 80 kilometres from Moscow, we stopped at an ordinary food shop. I wanted to see how badly stocked it was. You could buy everything. And at the outdoor marketplace sellers were doing a brisk trade in fresh fruit and vegetables flown up from the south.

Back in Moscow, the main shopping street, Tverskaya, was under-going major refurbishment. Buildings were being cleaned, the pavements widened. In the outskirts major construction work was in progress – new roads, flyovers, tunnels, apartment blocks. The financial district had sprouted a copse of beautiful skyscrapers. Moscow had never been a place for cyclists – but now the centre was full of them, tinkling their bells as they cruised along new cycle-lanes in the sunshine. There were new gastropubs and cafés full of hipsters, sitting with their MacBooks and trendy salads. These poor benighted youngsters even vaped. Surely that should have been covered by the sanctions! Did Muscovites appear to be lagging behind in fashions? Not a bit of it. Did they look glum? Poor? Rebellious? Nope. Things were not just stylish, but ultra-stylish: if you had a Mini Cooper, then let it be the very latest, and customised with orange wing mirrors and hubcaps – and play *Russian* music as you drive by with the windows down. In the metro, young people, as everywhere, sat glued to their smartphones, logged on to the free wifi provided by the city government. I logged on too, and found no restrictions – I could read as many anti-Putin websites as I cared to. But most of the youngsters were on Facebook or WhatsApp, smiling at conversations with their friends. It really was outrageous how they acted as if everything was fine!

Were Western diplomats really still pretending to their governments that the sanctions were working? And why was the press giving such a misleading impression?

The first week of my trip came courtesy of a company called Political Tours, which offers groups of current affairs enthusiasts visits to exotic or newsworthy places such as North Korea, Iran, Cuba, Lebanon . . . and Russia. These are holidays for news junkies: no sun and sand – not even opera or ballet unless you make the effort – but full immersion in the country's politics. My job, as the group's resident 'expert', was to provide a drip-feed of anecdote and analysis. Our whirlwind tour of Moscow and St Petersburg included meetings with politicians, journalists and experts, and also visits to a farm and a factory. We experienced the whole gamut of political views, from Sergei Markov, an ultra-Putinist public figure and former member of the Duma, who regaled us for an hour with justification of every Russian action, from the annexation of Crimea to the bombing of Syria, to Dmitry Gudkov, a young opposition politician who was already campaigning in a Moscow constituency for the Duma elections that were due in September. He was confident that his door-to-door canvassing would defeat the state machine. (He was wrong – the new Duma ended up as bereft of opposition as the previous one. Putin's United Russia party, which experienced a boost after the invasion of Ukraine in 2014, became more dominant than ever.) Another prominent anti-Putin politician we spoke to, Vladimir Milov, spent most of the time rubbishing the leader of his own grouping, Mikhail Kasyanov, who he said was completely out of touch with ordinary voters and had just waltzed off to St Moritz on holiday. Once again I was left scratching my head over the inability of Putin's opponents to get their act together. Russian opposition politics was like the groove at the end of a vinyl LP. Empty, repetitive, and going nowhere.

We did, however, meet these politicians in some very fine eating places, about which I would like to enthuse for a paragraph or two. I suppose it may be because Moscow was once food hell that it now seemed like food heaven. In just two years since my previous visit, eating out in Moscow had undergone a transformation. We had now vaulted several light years from the cabbage-and-buckwheat Soviet period, through the vulgar faux-aristocratic eating-parlours of the Yeltsin years, and the deluge of McDonalds, Starbucks and Russian fast-food outlets, to 21st-century state-of-the-art culinary hipsterdom. We met Gudkov in a 'farmers' restaurant' called LavkaLavka, right in the centre of the city. This was a place that would satisfy the most fastidious and pretentious diner in any Western capital. It wasn't just the ambience, the distressed-brick walls and heavy timber tables – that was old hat; it wasn't just that it used only local, seasonal produce – that you could find anywhere; at LavkaLavka the menu actually named the individual farmers who produced every item on your plate! So if you went for the goose liver paté profiteroles, you were informed that the liver came from the Yudakov farm in Uryupinsk, the apple jam was made by Valery Zhomer, and the parsnips were grown by Natalia Pashkevich – and you could read their stories and see their pictures. In the current political climate, the 'all-Russian' menu had a nice little patriotic bite too: the mullet caviar was from Crimea, as were some of the delicious wines. The restaurant's philosophy, as stated in the menu, was that eating good food 'can make the world a better place' – beat that for pretentiousness – and that in creating their dishes the chefs had decided to 'ignore 20th-century trends of gastronomic degradation in Russia'. I'll drink to that! Even with Crimean red.

Our lunch with Vladimir Milov was at a stylish brasserie called Smart People, located in an old wine warehouse with domed brick ceilings, in the newly fashionable Vinzavod (Wine factory) district, just behind the seedy Kursk train station. Forget Shoreditch or Kreuzberg or the Meatpacking District. Moscow too has given its derelict industrial jungles a bohemian makeover. Nearby was 'Artplay', and the sprawling Arma gasworks, a set of beautiful red-brick buildings which had lit and heated Moscow since the nineteenth century. Down the river was the old Red October chocolate factory. Now they were the city's trendiest neighbourhoods, landscaped and gentrified, housing art galleries, exhibition spaces, cafés, fashion ateliers, design studios and music clubs, all entwined with bicycle lanes and flowerbeds. This was a real discovery for me – even if I can feign little interest in sculpted beards and tattoos. Free wifi everywhere. USB charging points for iPhones. Coffee with silly names. Moscow had just become *cool*. And creative. And tasty.

On our last evening with the Political Tours group, we sat at another fashionable outdoor café, in the Hermitage gardens, just inside the Garden Ring, wondering how all this trendiness squared with the world of Putin, state control, and unfreedom. We had just come from an appointment at TV Rain, the last surviving fully independent television channel (and even it had lost its spot on cable networks and was now restricted to internet streaming). The staff there, all enthusiastic young journalists who produced fearless reporting for extremely low pay, were in a panic. They had just heard that the editors of RBC, a critical newspaper, had been sacked, apparently because of their investigations into the alleged fortunes of President Putin's family and cronies. Maria Makeyeva, head of news at TV Rain, was close to tears: 'We just wait for them to come for us . . .'

We were surrounded in the garden café by young people, drinking beer and chilled wine in the warm late evening light. They looked reasonably well off – certainly not rich, but able to afford a nice night out. They looked like the kind of people who might watch TV Rain, who worked in business or the media or banks or IT. 'What do people like these think about Putin?' one of the group asked. 'They hate him, of course!' answered a Russian journalist who was with us, and that seemed to make sense: how could enlightened young professionals possibly approve of Putin's corrupt and undemocratic rule? But a member of the group went off to do some sociology. When he came back after chatting to a few English-speaking Russians at neighbouring tables, he reported: 'All of them like Putin. They're going to vote for him.'

This was the mystery of Russia today. Putin had achieved something remarkable: he had encouraged a new sense of patriotism; provided growing wealth (notwithstanding Western efforts to undermine it); he ensured all *personal* freedoms – from ubiquitous internet to package holidays abroad; and through this he bought the silence, or even approval, of the vast majority of the people. Most simply switched off from the Soviet-style news broadcasts on TV; they just didn't care too much, so long as they were left alone to enjoy their lives. When most people told opinion pollsters they 'approved' of Putin, I think what most of them meant was: he lets me get on with my life, which is slowly getting better, and that's all I really care about. No more upheavals, please.

Epilogue

*Each of our lives is a Shakespearean drama raised to
the thousandth degree ... the mute separations, the mute,
black, bloody events in every family, the invisible mourning
worn by mothers and wives.* – Anna Akhmatova

*Two Russians are drinking with a foreigner. They tell
him everything in Russia is shit. Finally the foreigner
agrees, and they beat him up.* – Russian joke

MY PURPOSE THAT summer was simple: I just wanted to let Russia swirl
around me like a wheat field in the wind, to delve into my memories and
see if anything still made sense. I felt battered by recent experiences,
exiled from the Russia I loved. I had seen too many threadbare carpet
runners, spent too many hours in Kremlin anterooms. Now I wanted to
return to the Russia whose voice had called to me as a student. I wanted
to hear that music again, the inflections of her language that had first
ensnared me – before I got dragged down into those dark, echoing
tunnels of politics and argument; that was where idiots lived, with no
melody in their souls – why the hell was I there too? *Dai mne naglyadet-
sya, radost, na tebya!* – *Stop and let me have a good look at you, my joy!*[1]
Russia was supposed to sing to me, not pull me down ...

On Sivtsev Vrazhek, the lane where Garik's studio used to be, the street
literally sang to me again as I passed the tenement where the poet Marina
Tsvetayeva briefly lived, now marked by a commemorative plaque. I am
not one of those people who can recite reams of Russian verse, but there
is one Tsvetayeva poem that almost every Russian knows by heart because

---

1 Russian folk song.

it became famous as a song in a Soviet-era movie. It's about unrequited love – and feigned indifference. (This is my part-translation, which doesn't begin to convey the sheer beauty of the sounds.)

> I like the fact that you're not crazy about me.
> I like it that I'm not crazy about you either,
> And that our feet are firmly planted on the heavy Earth.
> I like the fact that we can laugh, and relax,
> And not play with words,
> And that no suffocating blush rolls over me
> If our sleeves accidentally touch . . .
>
> I thank you, hand on heart
> For loving me so much
> (Though you don't realise you do!)
> For my unperturbed nights,
> For the rarity of our twilight encounters,
> For the moonlight walks we never have,
> For the sun that doesn't shine above our heads . . .
> For the fact that you, alas, are not crazy about me,
> And I, alas, am not crazy about you either.

I laughed to myself as I recalled it now. Didn't it just sum up my own 'romance' with Russia? She wooed me, kicked me out, took me back, but went off the rails and wouldn't listen to reason! And did I care? Not a jot . . . !

I stomped around Moscow on foot for days on end, as though I could kick some new truth out of the flagstones. Ghosts of the violent past lurked everywhere in these lanes – revolutionaries and counter-revolutionaries, orphaned children, secret policemen, executioners, and the executioners' fearful accomplices . . . and their victims. In 1941 Tsvetayeva's husband was shot by the NKVD, and she hanged herself. In 2007 they put up a statue of her in the Arbat. As I crossed town, I passed new monuments to other writers and musicians who were maimed or silenced by communism: Vysotsky, Okudzhava, Rostropovich, Joseph Brodsky . . . all honoured now.

I came to what I used to know as Art Theatre Lane, named after Chekhov's and Stanislavsky's famous theatre. Now it had its old name back: Kamergersky Lane. I sat with a cappuccino outside the Akademiya café, watching passers-by strolling in the intense early-summer heat. The art nouveau theatre itself looked great, all spruced up in fresh pastel shades. But the name 'Kamergersky' dredged up another memory . . . those awful lines from the end of Pasternak's *Doctor Zhivago*: 'Lara spent several days on Kamergersky . . . One day she stepped out of the house and never returned. She must have been arrested in the street and died or vanished somewhere, forgotten as a nameless number on a list which was later mislaid, in one of the innumerable concentration camps in the north.'

The people walking on these cobbles knew what seventy years of communism meant not from a textbook, as Westerners do, but from real life – 'on their own skins', as they say. And we, the pampered and superficial experts of the West, presumed to tell them how to deal with its legacy.

I set off to visit a new museum that opened recently, dedicated to the Gulag. Partly, I wanted to find out more about that strangely named camp, Alzhir,[1] where they incarcerated 'wives of traitors of the mother-land', and where Garik was born. I also wanted to see how the museum dealt with this most sensitive part of recent history. I kept hearing about the 'rehabilitation of Stalin' under Putin, with schoolbooks restoring his image as a 'great war leader'. On the other hand, a dramatisation of Solzhenitsyn's great labour camp story, *A Day in the Life of Ivan Denisovich*, was playing in a central Moscow theatre, and his novel *The First Circle* was serialised on national TV for weeks on end, as was Rybakov's *Children of the Arbat*, with its brutal depiction of the NKVD.

As I approached the Museum of the History of the Gulag, I saw the end wall of a tall block of flats, covered from top to bottom with a mural. But not Brezhnev's face. This was anti-Soviet agitprop. It was a portrait of Varlam Shalamov, the famous Gulag survivor who wrote about the camps in his *Kolyma Tales*. His stencilled face was imprinted with his own words, as though typed like a samizdat sheet onto the yellow brick wall.

The museum itself was another big abandoned building that had been put to good use. It presented the Gulag in a brutal light, as equivalent to Nazi death camps. It was eerily lit, with spotlights on manacles and torture

---

1 The word means 'Algeria', but the letters are an acronym for 'Akmolinsk Camp for Wives of Traitors of the Motherland'.

implements. You could stand in a tiny cell with an iron bedstead. You could read long lists of 'traitors' condemned to death, with Stalin's signature. There were photographs, letters, sound effects, and convicts' clothes; genuine prison-cell doors brought from Magadan. The opening exhibit stated plainly that Stalin 'instigated the Great Terror . . . to destroy every possibility of political opposition'. A guide told me school groups visited every day – so the message should slowly be getting through. I stood for a moment watching a newsreel film that praised a Young Pioneer for denouncing his own father, who had stolen 'socialist property'.

Nobody in the museum's research centre specialised in Alzhir, but they knew a woman who, like Garik, was born there, and they put me in touch with her. I met Tatyana Nikolskaya in a park near her home. We sat on a bench squinting into the sun, me the intrusive foreigner again. 'My mother's husband was a chemist, quite high up in a state research institute. He was arrested and shot in the Lubyanka. Then they took my mother in, stripped her, interrogated her, and sent her to Alzhir.' I said I wanted to ask a delicate question, about how the women could get pregnant in the camp. Her creased face broke into a laugh: 'It's not delicate! It's normal! There were male workers in the camp – tradesmen, guards, camp officers, and women could have relationships with them. I was born there. My twin died. I survived.' She was happy to share the few memories she had of her first five years. 'We got 140 grams of bread each day – for the whole family!' She laughed: 'I used to steal crusts from the mouths of other children when we were lined up on our potties!' Her mother had a little room in the camp, and there was a crèche and a kindergarten. Maybe she played there with Garik.

We talked about the present day too. Tatyana thanked Gorbachev for rehabilitating her family in the Eighties. But she condemned Putin for not doing enough to preserve the memory of camp victims. The Gulag Museum, she said, was planning finally to open a memorial on the corner of Sakharov Avenue in 2017, but she didn't like the design they had chosen – a 'wall of tears'.

Tatyana insisted on meeting me the next day on the platform of a metro station in the city centre, 'at the front of the northbound train'. She handed me a present – a little book of poetry written by women who survived Alzhir. Inside, she had written: 'A little memento, from someone who was born in the Gulag and lived there from 1941 to 1946. M. I. Nikolskaya.'

*   *   *

I wandered into the big Moskva book store on Tverskaya. It was full of all the works we used to dream of buying in the days when you could only find novels about tractors, or if you were lucky, excavators. Now they stocked all the classics, popular Russian contemporary writers, and the bestselling Western authors in translation, everything from Kate Atkinson to Solzhenitsyn. There were rows of books about current Russian politics too, including translations of critical Western biographies of Putin. Who was this 'Angus Roksboro' fellow? Another foreigner telling Russians what to think about themselves!

A large section was dedicated to the country's national sport – the search for the Russian soul. A hundred and sixty years ago much of the Russian intelligentsia fell into two camps – the so-called 'Westernisers', who favoured a European future, and the 'Slavophiles', who believed Russia had its own unique character and destiny. The same argument went on today, as some Russians – including Putin – proclaimed a new Russian exceptionalism, with traditions and values deemed superior to the West's. I leafed through some books by Alexander Dugin, renowned as the guru of Russian ultra-patriotism. I had met him back in Yeltsin's days, when we both took part in that television discussion about Russia's 'destiny', where I stood out because I was a stupid Westerner with no beard. I wrote down one of Dugin's statements at the time: 'Without a great idea or dream, it'll be pointless living, it'll be a waste of time.' He certainly had an idea now: it was sometimes given a fancy name – Eurasianism – though Dugin himself was not averse to calling it fascism. Not that nasty German fascism, of course, but a superior brand of Russian fascism. He praised Putin for starting (but only starting, alas) the journey towards 'full-blooded patriotism' and the establishment of 'Russia as a unique civilisation, independent of the West'.

During my month in Moscow I was interviewed one day by Kommersant FM, a generally liberal radio station. The station's editor, Anatoly Kuzichev, asked me whether, when mixing with Russians, I felt they were 'Europeans'. I found the very question laughable. 'Of course,' I replied. 'Russia has its own specificity, it's quite "exotic", but it's a European country.' 'Hm,' Kuzichev smirked, 'That's a shame!' He had designer stubble, was wearing American jeans, a leather (if I recall correctly) Italian-looking jacket and stylish European shoes. I was pretty sure he would feel very much at home in the coffee-shops of the cool Vinzavod district nearby. His disdain for 'Europe' seemed like an affectation. As if you couldn't be both Russian and European.

Fifteen years ago, most young Russians clamoured to be accepted as European, and to shake off the nasty image inherited from communist days. Now, perhaps as a reaction to the West's rejection of Russia's attempt to 'join' the West, some of them had turned to 21st-century Slavophilism, almost as a fashion statement.

I visited my friend Varya and her family at their dacha. In Soviet days foreigners couldn't go there because it was near an air defence installation. It still is, but no one cared now.

Dacha life is one of the delights of Russia – maybe half of all Muscovites can escape from their urban concrete blocks for the weekend, or all summer. We barbecued chicken and pork *shashlyk* in the unkempt garden, cursed the mosquitoes, and drank wine in the drowsy sunshine. Politics only came up when I asked about it: they all deplored the way that Putin had seized Crimea illegally . . . but was it right that Crimea should belong to Russia? 'Of course! Who asked the people of Crimea in 1954 whether they wished to be transferred to Ukraine?' Apart from that, the conversation revolved around the traditional Russian theme – the meaning of life as an intangible longing . . . and the more you drank, the more clearly you understood. There was a guitar, so I played and we sang a few Okudzhava songs together.

I remembered this moment a few months later, when Leonard Cohen died, and the former British MP Louise Mensch ranted on Twitter, evidently unaware of singer-poets like Okudzhava or Vysotsky: 'There are no Leonard Cohens in Russia, they have no rock'n'roll, no fun, no "hallelujah", and they are poor in everything, including spirit.'

Russia has always suffered from this lugubrious image. But I blamed Putin for making it worse. He had turned the Western world (which briefly had tried to like the Russians) into a snarl of Russophobes. I had grown tired of even arguing about it. Putin wasn't Russia! There was a deeper, eternal Russia that was much more important.

One of my walks took me to Zamoskvorechye, another of my favourite old parts of the city, which still had the bustling feel of the merchant quarter it once was. Nobly avoiding the temptation to try all the new cafés around here, I went to the Tretyakov Gallery, where Russian art from its beginnings up to the early twentieth century is displayed. I walked through the halls quite quickly – it was like stepping in a river of Russian life and history. And then I walked round them again. It was easy to pick out the commonest themes: hardship, creativity, intellectual achievement, and the great immovable, endlessly self-renewing Russian landscape. I had translated books about Russian art thirty-five years ago, and despaired at the bureaucratic twaddle of Soviet scholars. Now I looked afresh and saw scenes from Gorky and Tolstoy splashed onto canvas: barge-haulers, ragged children dragging a huge drum of water through a frozen street, mowing peasants, tsars, aristocrats, merchants, and the intense intellectual force of men like Dostoevsky and Mussorgsky. And what a strange fascination with springtime – so many paintings of melting snow in March, the first weak sunshine, the arrival of migratory birds for the brief northern summer.

The next day I set off to splash through the rapids of the twentieth century, at the Tretyakov's modern annex, which is housed in a brutalist concrete building on the Moskva river along from Gorky Park. There was a new bike-hire place nearby, run by dudes with stylish beards and shades. Their sign said (in English): 'YOU + BIKE = HAPPY!' Was this Moscow or Amsterdam? Who said Russians weren't European?

The modern Tretyakov thrilled me even more than the old one. I spent the entire day here, popping out from the exhibition halls every now and then for a coffee. Malevich, Kandinsky, Chagall, Tatlin, Popova, Lissitzky . . . this was when Russian art led the world. It's easy to assume that the Revolution gave birth to revolutionary art. But it was the opposite way around. The art came first! The Russian avant-garde predated, predicted, and straddled the Revolution. There was nothing either socialist or realist about the first works of revolutionary Russia – just a giddy experiment in colour and form! These rooms in the gallery buzzed with energy and hope. Even when the spark was largely snuffed out in the Thirties by the culture commissars, works sometimes appeared that were only thinly disguised as socialist realism. I stood for ages in front of a picture by Yuri Pimenov, painted in 1937, the year of the great purge. It is superficially 'on message' in that it shows an emancipated young woman behind the wheel of an open-top car, driving through the centre of Moscow. But the style is impressionist – Moscow shimmers like a Pissarro Paris street scene – and the woman is certainly not a house-builder in dungarees, or a collectivised peasant in a kerchief: with her light summer dress and fashionably cut hair she's more like *The Great Gatsby*'s Daisy Buchanan, or Isherwood's Sally Bowles, out on the razzle in Thirties Moscow.

It was hard even to think of anyone having fun in that era of fear and suspicion. Those were days of miraculous survival, in life and in art.

Imagine a country where ideas were so dangerous, where artists were so feared, where an ironic word, a misplaced brushstroke or a false musical sequence could cost its creator his or her life.

Down to the cafeteria again to check something on the internet, a half-submerged memory from student days: M . . . Meyerhold . . . Vsevolod Meyerhold . . . the great avant-garde theatre director (and one-time champion of the Revolution). He had staged *La Dame aux Camélias* with his beautiful wife, Zinaida Raikh, in the main role. Stalin came, and hated it. The press slammed it for 'aestheticism' or 'art for art's sake'. Zinaida, the reckless free spirit, wrote to the Great Teacher and told him he didn't understand anything about art. The theatre was closed down. Meyerhold was arrested. Zinaida was murdered in their apartment, stabbed through the heart and eyes and left to bleed to death. Then they tortured Meyerhold in prison, and dragged him before a firing squad.

This nation, with no hallelujahs . . .

Thousands of intellectuals, the brain and conscience of the nation, disappeared into the furnace of Stalin's Terror – tortured, shot, imprisoned. Some committed suicide. Many others went abroad, and ended their days dreaming of their homeland. I thought of the folk-singer Alexander Galich, who was forced into exile from the Soviet Union and wrote of his longing in a song:

> When I return, the nightingales will whistle in February
> That ancient tune, that hackneyed old forgotten song,
> And I'll fall down, defeated by my victory,
> And bury my head in your knees, like a harbour . . .
> When I return . . . when I return . . .

But Galich never did return. He died in Paris in 1977.

I went back up to the exhibition halls, turned into a room marked 'Graphic Art', and on the wall before me saw three of my friend Garik Basyrov's works! I looked at them with tears welling in my eyes. Two shapeless figures stand in dialogue, with leaves and twigs swirling round them; a man, hands covering eyes, floats over the city; lonely, alienated people contemplate the cosmos, listening to the mystery of life even in the empty suburbs of present-day Moscow . . .

I stumbled out into the late afternoon, and walked to a riverside café for something to eat. Families were relaxing, children playing, on the lawns by the embankment. Further along the river was a recreation area where fountains of water squirted up from the paving stones at random. Teenagers dashed in and out, squealing with delight, intentionally getting wet. A photographer was taking pictures of a model, posing in different dresses, against the background of the fountains.

I suddenly realised the madness of what I was doing – pounding the streets in search of something that wasn't there. I was acting like a Russian, crazily searching for meaning when there was no need to; trying to 'understand' Russia, instead of just accepting her. I remembered the famous lines written in the 1860s by the poet Fyodor Tyutchev: 'You can't understand Russia with the mind alone . . . In Russia you just have to believe.'

Yes, it was that simple. Russia was what she was, hewn from a thousand different stones – her history, her climate, her ethnic roots, her music and art, her language, her individuals and communities, her experiences and fears . . . But what experiences! This was a nation with collective PTSD. In the West, these days, all of that great diversity and complexity was so often reduced to a banal, one-dimensional, politicised image.

I passed back along the riverbank, under the Crimea bridge into Gorky Park, and stared up at the monumental columned gateway, still emblazoned with its Soviet emblem and official name: Order of Lenin Park of Culture and Rest named after A.M. Gorky. As the maudlin hours of twilight descended, I stopped and listened to Russians chatting as they strolled around the pathways and flowerbeds. Young women, arm in arm, heads bent together in confidence. A group of high-school students wearing graduation sashes, larking about by a pond. I still felt the same tingle as I did when those voices rang, at first without meaning, from my wooden radio set almost fifty years ago. I was not the only foreigner to have the same love-hate affair with Russia: most people who made the effort to learn her language found themselves drawn deep into her prickly embrace. Whatever sweet curse it was that drew me towards those Russian textbooks in the school library all those years ago, I could not complain. It led me into a place of extraordinary intensity, a world of beauty and dignity that in the last century alone has survived wave after wave of barely imaginable horrors.

I strolled numbly around the park as the sun dissolved into vapour over the city, and the lilac bushes fanned the air with perfume. Hidden in the crowns of the trees, some birds set up an evening chorus. The trees, I knew, were sycamores and limes, but what kind of birds were calling, I wondered. Nightingales? I still could not tell.

Acknowledgements

I WOULD LIKE to thank my agent, Judy Moir, who heard me merely muse about possibly writing a memoir and encouraged me to follow it through to completion, and also my editor at Birlinn, Tom Johnstone, for his meticulous work.

Over the years in Russia I enjoyed the friendship (and companionship in some dodgy situations) of many fine colleagues and would like to name here some of the great BBC cameramen and picture editors I worked with (because they are the real hidden talent behind the reports people see, yet rarely receive any acknowledgement): John Boon, Tony Fallshaw, Duncan Herbert, John Holden, Duncan Knowles, Tim Platt, Bob Prabhu, Dave Skerry, Allan Smith, Chris Wood.

I want to mention specially my ex-wife Neilian, and my children Ewan, Duncan and Katie, for making our years in Moscow such fun.

Several friends took the time to read a draft of this book and offer useful comments: I would like to thank James Thomson in Bratislava, and David Gow and Tony O'Donnell in Edinburgh. Above all, heartfelt thanks to my partner Olinka, the first guinea-pig for my ideas and drafts, for her constant encouragement and sensible advice.

Finally, I thank the *Sunday Times*, the *Guardian* and the BBC for giving their permission to re-use in the book elements from some of the reports I did while working for them. I'm very grateful to Phil Goodwin for his help in tracking down some of the BBC images used in the plate section; they are reproduced here with permission of BBC News.

I dedicate the book to my friends in Moscow, who entertained and educated me over so many years. In a few cases I have changed their names and some other details. It is thanks to them, in the end, that Russia came to mean so much to me.

Index